"God is graciously condescen[illegible] ives all around Latin America and the Arab world. It addre[illegible] atter of spirituality—the quality, source, and vitality of your life under God which overflows into all your relationships and responsibilities. I encourage you to read it in order to 'change the way you change.'"

Dr. Ramesh Richard

Director of RREACH International and professor at Dallas Theological Seminary, USA

"We have used this book at Dallas Theological Seminary and SETECA, and I can bear witness to its profound impact on the students. If you want to see deep changes in your life and in the life of your church, I highly recommend it!"

Dr. James Adams

Adjunct professor for Doctor of Ministry Studies, Dallas Theological Seminary, and professor at SETECA, in the USA and Guatemala

"Writing from the reality of his own personal spiritual struggle, Nicolás helps us turn from mere superficial change to join the work of the Holy Spirit in search of true transformation and humility."

Henry Clay

The Navigators

"Nicolás Tranchini is a man who loves the Word of God and who's deeply committed to communicating it in a clear, simple, and relevant way. Get ready to be challenged by this book!"

Greg Travis

Board member of Ante Su Palabra, Soldados de Jesucristo and The Gospel Coalition in Spanish

"Deep Changes is a book about genuine spiritual transformation. It's a practical and personal read that will give you a healthy sense of discomfort."

Dr. Daniel Wicher

Former President of Camino Global

"Nicolás Tranchini's book takes us on a journey to the world inside the human soul, its nature, its identity, its motives and its failings. At the end of each chapter, the reader will find a section on the addressed topics for personal reflection or discussion in small groups. Therefore, it's quite a practical tool both for 'ruminating' on the values set forth and to start a discussion group. I recommend the calm and peaceful reading of this book to all believers, whether they are church leaders or not."

Dr. Pedro Sanjaime

President of IBSTE Bible College in Barcelona, Spain

Nicolás Emilio
Tranchini

DEEP
CHANGES

When the gospel
transforms
what the heart desires

Translated by Gabriela V. Brunetto
Translation Revised by Elena Bradley
Desktop Publishing by David González Jara

English First Edition 2021
ISBN: 978-8-40932295-4

Published and distributed by
DEEP CHANGES
MINISTRIES
Málaga (SPAIN)
E-mail: contact@cambiosprofundos.com
https://www.cambiosprofundos.com/en/

Dr. Nicolás Emilio Tranchini

Author, speaker, and pastor at Christian Community Church of El Cónsul in Malaga, Spain.

Nicolás is the founder and director of *Cambios Profundos* (Deep changes), a global ministry that provides resources on Christian growth. He's also the Director of SERVE International in Spain. Nicolás earned a Bachelor's in Theology and Biblical Studies from the Baptist International Theological Seminary in Buenos Aires, Argentina, where he later obtained his Doctorate in Ministry. He also holds a Master of Arts in Cross-Cultural Ministry from Dallas Theological Seminary, and he's a TESOL graduate from the same institution.

Nicolás had a personal encounter with the Lord through The Navigators when he was thirteen. In 2003, he was ordained as pastor by Denton Bible Church in Denton, Texas. Since then, he's been a teacher of subjects such as Christian Life, Leadership, Discipleship, Hermeneutics, New Testament Studies around the world.

Nicolás is happily married to Annie, and they have three children: Micaela, Tomás, and Manuel.

To my beloved wife,
for being a reflection of God's steadfast love,
despite my immense need for change.

ACKNOWLEDGMENTS

There are six people who've have made for you to read this book. The first of these is my wife, Annie. Her patience, support, and help were the three great pillars that sustained me during all these months. My love, I will never forget what you've done. I have no words. Thank you.

The second person is my best friend David González Jara. You didn't just read every single word in this book, but you also encouraged me through something priceless: your loyal and close friendship. Even though you already know this, I still want to put it in writing: You are a brother to me.

The third person is David Pérez García. Thank you for giving so many hours and putting so much selfless effort into this project. You have been extraordinarily dedicated and meticulous. The Lord has seen your quiet service.

I also want to give special thanks to Gabriela Brunetto and Elena Bradley. You both worked incredibly hard for this book to be available to speakers of English around the world! ¡Muchas gracias!

Finally, there's "Someone" who deserves a paragraph of his own. It's "Someone" who, in his grace, has decided to use me, who's strengthened me when I didn't deserve it, and who's given me words and creativity that are rare in me. This "Someone" was faithful in my unfaithfulness, loved me when I went astray, and filled me with his Spirit when I deserved to be empty. To him and only him, "*to the only wise God, through Jesus Christ, be the glory forever. Amen.*"

TABLE OF CONTENTS

IMPORTANT: It's possible that you don't usually pay much attention to the Table of Contents of a book, but I encourage you to make an exception here. It's your travel guide to change. It provides an overview of where we're going, and it will also help you keep track of key concepts as you complete each chapter. Finally, when you finish the book, and you have had a more in-depth look into each of the truths it captures, I challenge you to read it yet again. Your appreciation and interaction with this travel guide will be entirely different.

Appendices

BIBLE VERSIONS USED IN THIS BOOK

INTRODUCTION

Changing the Way You Change

What does it mean to change? If you had to answer this question, what would you say? What would it look like for you to experience real and deep change? Let me share with you some of the most common responses I've heard:

"Change for me would mean not watching online porn anymore. I honestly think I'm an addict."

"For me, change would mean not compulsively shopping for clothes. I'm constantly checking my weight against other girls' weights, and the only thing that helps is hiding behind baggy clothes."

"In my case, change would mean not yelling when I'm angry. It'd be not arguing with my spouse. We really hurt each other when we don't see eye to eye."

"For me, change would mean sharing my faith with others. I want to do it, but I'm scared."

"Change, in my case, would be watching less TV and getting up early to read the Bible and to pray."

"What would it look like for me to change? To begin tithing. That would seriously mean I've changed!"

Have you noticed that all these responses have something in common? They all view change as transformed behavior. All these people see change as no longer doing something bad and starting to do something good. Change for them means "ceasing to fail." But what if real and deep change is more than that?

What if what I actually need to change is how I understand change? What if what needs to change is my way of changing?

You may be thinking, "You don't get it. The thing I'm struggling with is wrecking my spiritual life. Every time I fail, it tears me apart; I feel empty, separated from God, and defeated." I understand these emotions all too well. I've had them myself, and I still have them every so often. But what if that isn't the issue? What if the underlying problem isn't sex, money, anger, or reaching your ideal weight? Think about this for a minute: Does it take being a Christian in order to change any of the things mentioned above? Think it through. Can a Jehovah's Witness, a Muslim, or even an atheist undergo the changes I've pointed out so far? The obvious answer is: "Of course they can!" You don't need the Holy Spirit to experience that kind of change. Many nonbelievers treat their spouses with kindness and refrain from yelling at them. Mormons are experts at sharing their faith; in fact, they send more missionaries out into the world than Christians do! Jehovah's Witnesses regularly read the Bible, and it's entirely possible that, when it comes to sexual struggles, they may live amazingly pure lives. Muslims pray five times a day. Agnostics give money to a number of charities. If each one of them can make these kinds of "changes" without Jesus, could it be that my understanding of change is wrong? Could it be that what needs to change is my way of changing?

What is real change? How does it happen? What role does the Holy Spirit play? And what's my part? Walk with me through the upcoming pages, and we'll work together to answer these and many other questions.

PART I

What Is Superficial Change?

CHAPTER 1

How Does Superficial Obedience Work?

What Are my Deepest Desires?

"Why?" This is possibly the most important question every human being needs to ask themselves to advance their spiritual life. Why do I read the Bible? Why don't I read it? Why do I try to talk to my friends about Jesus? Why don't I try? Why do I serve others? Why do I find it hard to serve?

I would like you to take a moment to think about a woman who is driving her car to church. Imagine that, for whatever reason, she has decided that she won't contribute anything when they collect the offering that Sunday. The woman arrives at church, the service begins, and she delights in taking part in the gathering. However, when the offering plate starts going around, someone announces that they're having a special fundraiser for the needy and that, on this particular occasion, church leaders will be collecting the offering. She quickly dismisses the announcement. She's already thought this through, and she's decided that she has good reasons to pass on the opportunity to give. Nonetheless, she suddenly realizes that the person passing the offering plate is one of the leaders she greatly respects and admires. In fact, this man leads the small group she regularly attends. To make matters worse, the topic they were discussing that week was "generosity." Therefore, she desperately gets some loose change out of her purse and places it on the plate with great relief.

The woman in our story is doing something good, right? After all, giving money for the needy is a good action. However, why is she doing it?

What does she love deep in her heart? Her group leader's opinion! In other words, she loves herself! She doesn't want to look bad in front of her leader, and for that reason, she gives money.

Taking a close look at our motives, our deepest desires, helps us realize that sometimes what seems good often isn't, and what appears terrible may not be, either! Take a moment to think about what it would look like for this woman to love God, and not herself, in a situation like this. The answer sounds unchristian. Maybe it would have been best for her to not have given any money for the needy! Not giving might place her in a position where her leader or other people might think she lacked generosity, commitment to the needy, or love of God. However, for her, in this particular situation, *that* would be loving God with all her heart, with all her soul, and with all her strength. Why? Because she'd be willing to "look bad" out of love for God. Because, in her heart, she'd be saying, "God, you love me, and your love is enough for me. If others think I'm not generous, their opinion is less valuable to me than yours is. I rest in the fact that you fill my heart and not in the opinion of my leader."

Let me give you another example. Picture a young man, a collegiate who parties on weekends, whose goal is to "conquer" a new girl each night. What's his motivation? For him, it goes beyond lust. He does it because he wants to be the most popular and successful guy in his group, and that's the way he thinks he'll get there. He wants to have a "collection" of romantic conquests under his belt so that he can boast about how well he's doing.

Now imagine that this young man gets to know Jesus and becomes a Christian. Little by little, his life undergoes significant "changes." He forsakes his promiscuous adventures, begins attending church, volunteers for several ministries, and begins serving with enthusiasm. A few years later, that same young man becomes a devoted and successful missionary. Many people come to Jesus through him. He's even invited to speak at conferences, and he travels around the world sharing the testimony of how God has used him. No one doubts his change. Everyone believes that he's a different person.

But has he changed? The most typical response seems obvious. Of course he's changed! However, the only way to know if he's really changed where it matters is to ask "why?" Why has this young man given it all up (including sex and his weekly adventures) to serve God?

As we will see over the course of this book, the Bible challenges us to go beyond superficial, perceived changes and to focus on changes of the heart.

"*God sees not as man sees, for man looks at the outward appearance, but the Lord looks at the heart*" (1 Samuel 16:7; Luke 16:15). A simple way to "look" at our hearts is to ask ourselves, "why?" Why did this young man want to be a missionary? There are, of course, countless possible answers to this question, but let us consider one of them. Before turning to Jesus, this young man's goal was to "conquer" girls Why?

As we said earlier, he wanted to be ***popular***; he wanted to be ***successful*** among his friends. After this young man came to Christ, his goal became telling the whole world about Jesus. He wanted to become a ***popular*** and ***successful*** missionary. Can you see it? In the past, this young man wanted to be popular by "conquering" girls; now, he wants to be popular by "conquering" souls and converting people. His behavior changed, but did his desires change? Did his heart change?

An illustration I like using to explain this dynamic of change is that of an iceberg. An iceberg has two parts: a visible, external one, representing our actions, and an internal one, which is below the surface and out of sight, representing our motives, our deepest desires. As the passage in 1 Samuel shows us, when God looks at human beings, he doesn't focus so much on what they do, but rather on *why* they do it.

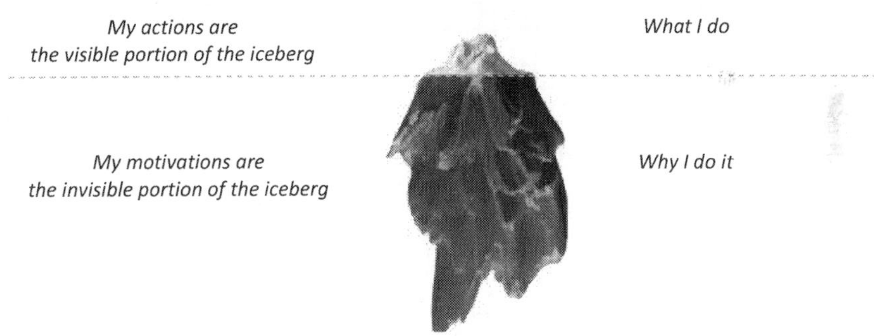

"Why?" That's the key question. Why do I give money? Why do I read the Bible? Why do I serve in the church? Why do I get mad at my spouse? Why do I want to have a better job? Why do I want to change? In the Sermon on the Mount, Jesus challenges his disciples—or rather commands them—to contemplate this reality.

If you take a close look at Matthew 6:1-18, which we'll do together at the end of this chapter, you'll conclude that the main focus of this section of the Bible is neither giving (as 6:2-4 seems to indicate) nor praying (as

6:5-15 seems to show) nor fasting (as 6:15-18 seems to point at). The main focus of this passage is defined and summed up in the first verse of the chapter: "*Beware of practicing your righteousness before men to be noticed by them; otherwise you have no reward with your Father who is in heaven.*"

In this passage, Jesus isn't talking about the need to give. Jesus is calling his listeners to ***reflect on what motivates them to give***. Jesus isn't focused on challenging them to pray. Jesus is focused on whether his followers ***seek to uncover what motivates them to pray***. Jesus isn't concerned here with whether or not people fast. Jesus is trying to lead his disciples to ask themselves, "***Why do I fast?***" If you carefully read the passage, you'll see that this is the case.[a]

"Why?" is the great question that leads us to unmask our inner reality, and it's precisely the main theme Jesus develops in this section of Matthew. Through this passage, we discover that a person may be doing "spiritual" things without actually being spiritual—just like the woman giving the offering or the successful missionary in the examples above. According to our Lord, the Father doesn't so much see and evaluate what we do on the outside, but rather *why* we do it—that is to say, what on the inside is motivating us to do the good things. As Martyn Lloyd Jones once wrote:

> Nothing is quite so fallacious as to think of sin only in terms of actions; and as long as we think of sin only in terms of things ally done, we fail to understand it. The essence of the biblical teaching on sin is that it is essentially a disposition of the heart....
>
> We tend to think of sin as we see it in its rags and in the gutters of life. We look at a drunkard, and we say: There is sin; that is sin. But that is not the essence of sin....
>
> In order to get an accurate image of its essence and to really understand it, we must picture a great saint, an unusually devout and devoted person, and we must look at them there on their knees, in the very presence of God. [As Jesus puts it in Matthew 6:5] Even there, the "self" is already laying siege to the saint, and the temptation is for them to think pleasantry and pleasurably about themselves and to worship themselves rather than Go.
>
> This, and not the other, is the true picture of sin...[1]

[a] At the end of this chapter, you'll find a chart that will help you do an in-depth study of the passage in Matthew 6:1-18.

Examining our motivations is essential because, in doing so, we'll uncover that which our inner self ***really loves***. If you think about it for a minute, in this passage in Matthew, we learn that we can obey the commandments (such as giving, praying, and fasting) without actually following the Great Commandment (to love God with all your heart). If we fast so that others may see us, what we really love is the glory of men and, thereby, we love ourselves, for we're the beneficiaries of such action. On the other hand, if we fast in order to set aside a special and unique time to be alone with God, what we really love is God and the joy of his presence. Thus, an alternative or additional question we could ask besides "why?" would be: ***Who or what am I loving with what I'm doing?***

It's very interesting, as we'll see further on, that, in the context of Matthew 6, to do something in a truly spiritual way is to do it *by enjoying* the Father. By contrast, to do it in an improper or sinful way is to do it *by enjoying being seen by others*. In this way, through this passage, Jesus allows us to venture into one of the greatest predicaments of the human condition: the search of identity through the approval of others. In Paul Tripp's words:

> Human beings are always assigning to themselves some kind of identity. There are only two places to look. Either you will be getting your identity vertically, from who you are in Christ, or you will be shopping for it horizontally in the situations, experiences, and relationships of your daily life. This is true of everyone, but I am convinced that getting one's identity horizontally is a particular temptation for those in ministry.[2]

Remember the young missionary at the beginning of the chapter? Do you think that I'm exaggerating or that he's just an illustration? Consider, then, eleven of the most dedicated people who have ever set foot on this planet: Jesus' disciples. They must be different! There must be something different about them! But, is this how the gospels portray them? From the moment of their calling until the final hours of Jesus' life, the Bible shows us that even the apostles themselves weren't exempt from this tendency.

On the contrary! After Jesus announces to them his imminent death, they begin to fight over who is the greatest (Luke 22:24-27; Mark 10:35-45). Take a moment to meditate on what this incident shows. Their argument (something external), reveals what ***their hearts actually love and desire*** (something internal); namely, recognition, power, glory, status, and thus finding in those things their meaning, worth, or identity. "I have value because I've managed to come out on top." This is their underlying reasoning.

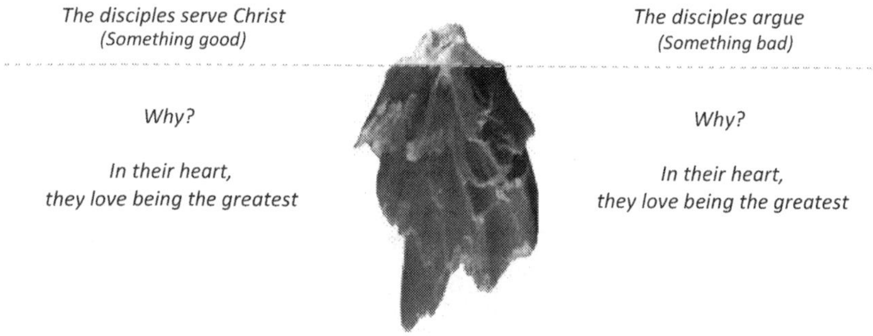

When I examine my heart, I can see that I am not that different from the disciples. Since my "job" is ministry, I can identify with their struggle. As Tim Keller so fittingly wrote:

> Why do people go into a life of ministry? Noble motivations, right? Some years ago, I read this line in a book for ministry students by Charles Spurgeon: "Don't preach the gospel in order to save your soul." I was in my twenties at the time, and I remember thinking, "What kind of idiot would try to save his soul by preaching the gospel?" But after a few years in the ministry, you start to realize that if your church does well and grows and people like you, you feel disproportionately good—and if your church doesn't do well and people don't really like you, you feel disproportionately devastated. You're working outside in. You had assumed: "If people like me and say, 'Oh, how much you help me,' then God will like me and I will like myself, and then that sense of inconsequentiality, that sense of uncleanness, will go away." But it doesn't...[3]

In Need of the Light

Blindness. Perhaps that's a fitting word to describe how well we know ourselves (Matthew 15:14; Ephesians 4:18). We believe that it isn't so. Like the disciples, we think that we understand ourselves, that we know why we behave the way we do, that we know our own heart, and that we do what we do out of love, but the Bible constantly confronts us with just the opposite. ***Living in a deceived state is the norm*** (see Jeremiah 17:9; 1 John 1:8-10).

That's why the primary ministry of the Holy Spirit is to bring light into our lives! (John 16:7-14; Ephesians 1:18-19)

No one, not even the most dedicated man or woman, is exempt from this. Consider, for instance, the Prophet Isaiah. The most terrifying moment in the prophet's life came when he was able to internalize the distance between the reality of his broken inner self and the amazing holiness of the person of God. That's when he pronounced his famous words: "*Woe is me, for I am ruined!*" (Isaiah 6:5).

In Luke 5:8, the same thing happens to Peter *when he declares*, "*Go away from me Lord, for I am a sinful man!*" Or with Paul in Romans 7:24 when he says, "*Wretched man that I am! Who will set me free from the body of this death?*" The experience they all have is like that of the person Jesus calls "*poor in spirit*" (Matthew 5:3). This is a person who can see themselves for what they are. This is someone who, upon examining themselves, succeeds in seeing deep within, and finds nothing that could hold any moral or spiritual value before God. Not even their good works! Paraphrasing Matthew 6, this is someone who realizes that not even in their moments of greatest dedication (fasting), of greatest closeness to God (praying), or of greatest generosity (giving), are they exempt from that inner inclination to live for themselves.

Examining our deepest motivations and desires is essential because it allows us to gradually overturn an idea that, either consciously or unconsciously, many of us Christians hold: "We're good, and people who aren't Christians are bad. They sin greatly, such as by committing adultery or stealing, but we don't. They need the gospel; not us." Taking a close look at our motivations allows us to see that outward behavior may vary, but the essence, the inner motivation that leads us to steal (a "great" sin) or to exaggerate (a "lesser" sin), is the same: ***self-love***.

What, then, is superficial change? Simply put, ***superficial change is where my external behavior changes without a change in the deepest desires of my heart***. It's a type of change where I stop doing bad things, and I start doing good things; however, either consciously or unconsciously, I'm still loving myself. Just like the woman who gives money, or the young missionary who tells others about Jesus, or even like the disciples, who leave everything to follow him.

Paul brilliantly sums it up in Ephesians 2:3: "*Among them we too all formerly lived in the lusts of our flesh, indulging the desires of the flesh and of the mind, and were by nature children of wrath, even as the rest…*" Can you see it? For the apostle, true conversion is ***a change of desires***. It's a matter of evaluating whether or not the deepest passions and affections of our hearts have changed.

Why Looking "Below the Surface" Matters

Before ending this chapter, I would like to give you two reasons why it is absolutely essential that we examine our hearts. First, ***there's the genuine possibility that we have not experienced a true conversion.*** Towards the end of his second letter to the Corinthians, Paul exhorts believers, saying, "*Examine yourselves to see if your faith is genuine. Test yourselves*" (2 Corinthians 13:5, NLT). I'm aware that it's neither a commonly taught truth nor a popular one, but if our eternity with Christ is at stake, it's worth pausing and reflecting on it.

Prophesying about the End of the Age, Jesus highlights a very sad reality. Matthew 7:22-23 says: "*Many [notice that he doesn't say a few, but many] will say to Me on that day, 'Lord, Lord, did we not prophesy in Your name, and in Your name cast out demons, and in Your name perform many miracles?' And then I will declare to them, 'I never knew you; depart from Me, you who practice lawlessness* [emphasis added].'"

It's important to note that the context of this passage is Jesus talking about itinerant prophets, i.e., the equivalent of modern-day, well-known leaders, renowned pastors, or celebrated keynote speakers that we often hear at large conferences. In this imaginary dialogue, Jesus tells these men that only those who do the will of the Father will enter the Kingdom of Heaven. It's striking to see that these leaders respond exactly the way we predicted. ***They claim to have done the Father's will citing the ministry they carried out in his name***. They say that they have prophesied, cast out demons, etc. However, Jesus' answer is categorical: "*I never knew you.*" In fact, that isn't the only thing he tells them. Instead, he further calls these deeds done in his name "*lawlessness.*"

Read the passage again because what you're about to read may shock you. Jesus says that they were practicing lawlessness by serving God! He doesn't say that they were doing something wrong on the side, rather that they were practicing lawlessness by performing their ministry! There was something, *not in what they did*, but in the ***way*** they did it (in their hearts) that made Jesus dismiss them and label them as non-Christians. Something like what happened to the young missionary at the beginning of the chapter happened to them, too. What was that something? The passage is clear: they didn't know Jesus! They had convinced themselves that they were believers, but in reality, they weren't.

Jesus clearly said that "*many*" will have this problem. This word "*many*" breaks my heart, and it lays a tremendous burden on me—especially since he isn't talking about atheists or followers of a different religion. Jesus is referring here to people who claim to be Christians and who are convinced they're true believers, but that, in reality, are not. These are people dedicated to full-time ministry! We must heed the weight of the warning: ***Even I could be one of those people!*** If you examine the atmosphere that surrounds the passage, you'll notice that there's a sense of *great surprise*. The response of these men is something like this: "Lord, we thought we were doing your will. How come you're leaving us out now?" Who are these "*many*"?

In the Lord's own words, they are people who are "*in sheep's clothing, but inwardly are ravenous wolves.*" (Matthew 7:15) Let's remember the context of the passage. Jesus isn't talking about false prophets whose main problem is with their doctrine (as is the case, for instance, when Paul writes in Galatians 1:6-9). Jesus is talking here about false prophets in the sense that, *on the outside,* they appear to be very good and have a highly respected ministry, but *on the inside* they aren't living out the Sermon on the Mount—that is, they're not aware of their spiritual poverty and their need of Christ in order to be able to live out the Sermon. The "*many*" Jesus is referring to are respected Christian leaders, successful in their ministry, yet ***oblivious*** to the fact that they have no real knowledge of Jesus. Naturally, they know who he is, they're well-versed in theology, they've taught others, and they've worked miracles in his name. It isn't a matter of doctrine. They don't know him in the deepest sense of the word. They do not ***delight*** in him, if you will; their delight is in the benefits of the ministry. There's no living, true and close communion between them and Christ. That's why he says: "*I never knew you.*"[b] As Henri

---

[b] In John 2:23-25, we find an enlightening example that emphasizes the truth we've just examined. As you read the passage, I encourage you to pay attention to one significant detail. For John, "believing" isn't synonymous with being "regenerated." In other words, just because a person claims to "believe" in Jesus, it doesn't mean that this person has experienced a true conversion. The passage reads, "*Now when He [Jesus] was in Jerusalem at the Passover, during the feast, many believed in His name, observing His signs which He was doing. But Jesus, on His part, was not entrusting Himself to them, for He knew all men, and because He did not need anyone to testify concerning man, for He Himself knew what was in man* [emphasis added]." Can you see it? Many claim to believe in him; many even begin to follow him. However, John brings a truth to our attention that's "hidden" from all the people who're witnessing this event. Jesus isn't looking at what they *say*, nor focusing on what they *do*; Jesus is looking at the *heart*! The passage clearly tells us that "*he knew what was in man*"; that is, he knew their hearts; he looked at the invisible portion of the iceberg and was able to recognize their true motivations in following him. (In this context, they followed him because of the signs and miracles he performed. You could say they followed him "for the loaves and fishes." Here there is no real love for Jesus; there's a fascination with what he does and,

Nouwen puts it: "The basis of all ministry rests not in the moral life but in the mystical life. The issue is not to live as well as we can, but to let ***our life be one that finds its source in the Divine Life*** [namely, in the person of Christ; emphasis added]." [4]

As we'll see over the course of this book, a true believer isn't someone who stops sinning and strives to obey (although a true believer does obey); in fact, we could almost say that it's precisely the opposite! A true believer is someone who's increasingly aware of the depth of their sin, but who's also more and more aware of the incredible goodness of Jesus Christ, who loves them ***despite*** their sin. A true believer is someone who looks at the desires of their heart and feels like the disciples did: filled with mixed motives, but at the same time fascinated with the fact that Jesus was willing to die for them. A true believer is someone who, in contrast with the lack of self-knowledge shown by the false prophets in Matthew 7, is well aware of their own hidden desires, but who's also aware that when "*sin abounds, grace abounds*," too. A true believer is a person who doesn't lean on their works (or their ministry) to be accepted by God; instead, they lean on the incredible love of Christ, who accepts them in spite of their wrongdoings (and poor ministry). This two-fold reality, on the one hand, makes the true believer a humble person; on the other hand, it enables them to appreciate and treasure Jesus Christ and his work with ever greater intensity.

Finally, the motivations or desires of the heart are extremely important because the Bible says that ***all Christians will be judged according to them!*** In 1 Corinthians 3:10-15, Paul states that each of us must be careful as to ***how*** we build the church; that is, how we serve God. Notice here, too, that he isn't referring to the service itself, but rather to ***how*** we perform the service. In verse 13, the apostle points out that what determines whether a deed will be approved on the Day of Judgment is "*the quality of the deed*," not the deed in and of itself. (Naturally, in the context of the passage, he's talking about the final judgment to determine a person's ***reward***, not their salvation, which he states in the same passage is only through Christ). That is, God won't judge our deeds, but rather our ***motivation*** for doing them. The passage reads, "*each man's work will become evident*." That's to say, ***the nature of their work will be revealed***. Whether it belongs with deeds made of "*gold, silver, and precious stones*" (that is, if they were performed with the right motivation at heart); or if it belongs with those made of "*wood, hay, and straw*," which, upon being

most certainly, a self-centered interest in how those miracles might yield some sort of personal benefit.)

put through the fire, vanish and become evident as having no real consistency (in other words, their motivation was self-centered, much like the young missionary in our example).

Why do I read the passage this way? Because that's what Paul himself does! A few verses down in 1 Corinthians 4:5, the apostle himself clarifies the meaning for us, "*Therefore, do not go on passing judgment before the time, but wait until the Lord comes who will both bring to light the things hidden in the darkness and disclose **the motives of men's hearts**, and then each man's praise will come to him from God.*" Can you see it? At the End of the Age, the Lord will do the same thing that he's been doing since the beginning of time; he won't look at the outward appearances but at the deep changes of the heart. "*For God sees not as man sees, for man looks at the outward appearance, but the Lord looks at the heart*" (1 Samuel 16:7).

BRIEF SUMMARY

The key to change: *In order to avoid superficial change, I need to consider: What are the deepest desires of my heart? (Matthew 6:1).*

- *One question that might help me: Why do I do what I do?*
- *Another question that might help me: What is it that I really love in doing this?*

Superficial Obedience: *Superficial change takes place when I, consciously or unconsciously, change my behavior as an act of self-love; that is, my actions change, but the deepest desires of my heart remain unchanged (Matthew 15:8).*

Genuine conversion: *A true believer is someone who recognizes the depth of their sin, but who also recognizes the incredible goodness of Jesus Christ, who loves and forgives them in spite of their sin. For them, this truth (the gospel) isn't just mere belief but a reality that captivates them and gradually transforms them (1 John 4:10).*

FOR PERSONAL REFLECTION OR DISCUSSION IN SMALL GROUPS

It's very tempting to skip over this last section of the chapter. Don't do it; stop. Don't ignore what the Holy Spirit may be teaching you through this chapter; don't rush. Take time to meditate on these questions and/or discuss them with others.

1. *In what way has this chapter either changed or confirmed your understanding of how changes take place?*
2. *Sum up in one or two sentences the concepts that had the greatest impact on you in this chapter.*
3. *Carefully read Matthew 6:1–18. In doing so, you'll notice that verse 1 is a summary of the entire section and that the passage develops in a clear pattern that we could summarize as follows:*

Action	*"When you [fast, pray, or give]..."*	*verses 2,5,16*
Illustration	*"Don't [do]... as the hypocrites who..."*	*verses 2,5,16*
Motivation	*"In order to be seen..."*	*verses 2,5,16*
Reward	*"They already have their reward..."*	*verses 2,5,16*
Contrast	*"But you..."*	*verses 3,5,17*
Action	*"When you [fast, pray, or give]..."*	*verses 3,7,17*
Illustration	*"Do this..."*	*verses 3,7,17*
Motivation	*"The Father who sees what is done in secret..."*	*verses 4,6,18*
Reward	*"The Father will reward you..."*	*verses 4,6,18*

After reading Matthew 6:1–18 in detail, answer the following questions: What is important for God according to this passage? Why?

4. *In your own words, how would you explain a superficial change? And a deep change?*
5. *In studying Matthew 7, we saw that there are people who think they're believers but, in reality, are not. Why does this happen? What does being a true believer mean to you?*

CHAPTER 2

How Does the Heart Work?

What Is the Heart?

Why do people act the way they act? Why does a man lie on his tax return? Why does a woman choose to wear a notoriously provocative dress to work, knowing that she has no intention of cheating on her husband? Why does a teenager start drinking alcohol or smoking when they don't really enjoy it? Why does a person mislead their boss by providing distorted information about their teammates' performance? Why do people act the way they act? The answer to all of these questions is the same. Our inner ***desires*** determine our outward behavior. ***That "place" where our deepest desires dwell is what we call the heart***.

In order to fully understand what the heart is, we must study how the Bible describes human beings. The Bible divides man into two: the outside, our body; and the inside, our hearts (Ephesians 3:16). While the Bible describes the "*inner man*" in many different ways (it calls it "*soul*," "*spirit*," "*inner self*," "*mind*," "*bowels*," etc.), the term the Scriptures most often use to describe it is "*heart*." For this reason, from now on, when you read the word "*heart*" in this book (or in the Bible), you shouldn't exclusively associate it with your emotions. Biblically speaking, this association isn't accurate.

The Bible uses the word heart in a much more comprehensive sense. The heart doesn't merely feel and experience emotions (Acts 2:37). The heart thinks (Matthew 9:4; Mark 2:8; Romans 1:21). The heart is that portion of our being that has the potential to see and appreciate spiritual truths (Matthew 13:15; Ephesians 1:18-19). The heart stores within itself "treasures," things that it loves and appreciates (Matthew 12:35). The heart is the source of all our words (Matthew 12:34); it's capable of committing adultery (Matthew 5:28), making decisions (Proverbs 16:1), and even putting its trust in God or in its own ability to discern what's best for us (Proverbs 3:5; Matthew 24:48). Jesus said that "*out of the heart come evil thoughts, murders, adulteries, fornications, thefts, false witness, and slanders.*"

Can you see that the heart is much more than the "place" where our feelings lie? According to the Bible, our hearts house not only emotions but also our thoughts and the decisions we make. The heart is the command center of our entire being. It is there where our goals and priorities are established (I'll give money when they pass the offering plate because, if I don't, they'll think I'm not spiritual enough). It is there where our targets are fixed (I'll share the gospel because, if I do, people will see me as a successful missionary).

The heart is the place where we complete the phrase: **"I DESIRE..."** I desire a good reputation (and that's why I give money and spread the gospel). I desire to feel loved (and that's why I'm willing to look for a non-Christian partner). I desire rest (and that is why I get angry with the kids if they disturb me when I'm watching TV). I desire meaning in life (and that's why I work long hours). I desire pleasure (and that's why I argue with my spouse if they don't want to have intercourse). I desire freedom (and that's why I fail to make a commitment). I desire a quiet life (and that's why I don't get more involved in church). I desire financial security (and that's why I save money and I struggle to be generous). I desire people's respect and admiration (and that's why I go shopping for and wear designer clothes). I desire to achieve success (and that's why I am controlling and a perfectionist). I desire intimacy (and that's why I get depressed if you don't listen to me).

Deep within our hearts lies the answer to the question: What is it that I actually want?

In short, ***the heart is the "place" where the thing I actually love can be found.*** Think about the following example. Picture a man who passionately loves soccer. Let's say that by the time the World Cup begins, this man is employed as a laborer with a company and his shift starts really early on Monday morning. However, since the World Cup is taking place on a different continent, his team will be playing at midnight on Sunday. Not only is the man determined to watch the soccer match, but he also experiences great anticipation and anxiety in the days leading up to the big game. Although he never goes to bed late on a Sunday, he wouldn't dream of missing the match, even when it means going to bed after two o'clock in the morning. He reads all the sports magazines that cover his team, he looks at the stats, he talks about it with his friends, he daydreams about the final score, and he puts off all other activities for several hours just to sit in front of the highly expensive flat-screen TV he has bought for the sole purpose of enjoying watching his national team play.

At the beginning of the book, I said that the most important question you should ask yourself if you want to experience growth in your spiritual life is "Why?" Let's ask this question about him now. Why does this man do what he does? The answer is pretty obvious: because he ***enjoys*** soccer. Because ***he likes*** watching his team play. Because doing so ***gives him pleasure***. Now, let's say this man is a Christian. Moreover, let's imagine that, contrary to good judgment, his church pastor decides to hold an all-night prayer meeting that same Sunday night, precisely at the time when the national team is playing. Someone invites him to attend the event, but he makes excuses saying that he has to work the next day. What does this experience reveal to us? What this man ***doesn't love***! It's not a question of being able to attend; it's a question of not wanting to attend—of loving something else over prayer. Let's now imagine the pastor approaches this man after making the announcement and tells him in a tone of camaraderie, "I'm counting on you tonight. You're my man! I know others will be watching the game, but I'm positive you'll be joining me." This time, because of his pastor's words, the man decides to attend. What does this story reveal to us? Does the man love prayer? Well, on the outside, it looks like he does. After all, hasn't he sacrificed his night's sleep and his chance to watch the soccer game in order to attend the meeting? However, ***what is it that this man actually loves?*** Looking at this question is critical because, what may on the outside appear to be sacrificial, in reality, is not. If we take a moment to analyze it, we'll realize that ***before, this man loved himself by not attending the prayer meeting, and now, he continues to love himself by attending the prayer meeting*** (wanting his pastor to think well of him). His outward behavior has changed, but his heart is still intact. He's still loving himself! This is what Jesus is constantly warning us about: "*This people honors Me with their lips, but their heart is far away from Me*" (Matthew 15:8).

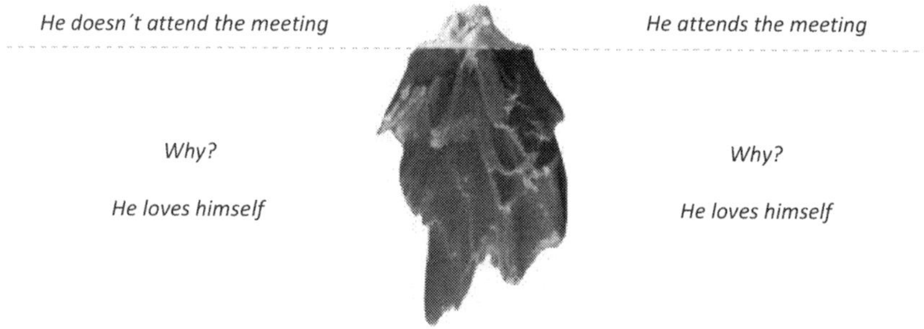

In Matthew 6:21, Jesus said: "*For where your treasure is, there your heart will be also.*" What does Jesus mean by this statement? Let me paraphrase it: "The thing I find the greatest delight in (my treasure) will drive all my decisions, fantasies, passions, emotions, commitments, and acts of surrender (i.e., it's the thing I'll give my heart to, the thing I'll love)." It's in our hearts that we find what we long for most, our treasures. In other words, the heart is the invisible portion of the iceberg.

Changing the imagery, the heart is like a safe deposit box. When you open a deposit box, you find a person's most valuable items—gold, jewelry, money, etc. The same thing happens when you examine the heart. That's where what I truly value lies! What I genuinely love. Just as Jesus encourages us in Matthew 6:1, by "*taking a look*" inside we find what we truly treasure. In our story, we see that the man treasures soccer. However, after he talks to his pastor, we see that an even greater treasure is the desire to please others. In this man's case, his pride, which he derives from his pastor seeing him as spiritual, is greater than his desire to enjoy a soccer game. Nevertheless, don't overlook a key element here. Notice that, either consciously or unconsciously, it's his pride that moves him to "be" a spiritual person and attend the meeting; that is, to do something good! His ego drives his good deed, not a genuine desire to be with Jesus.

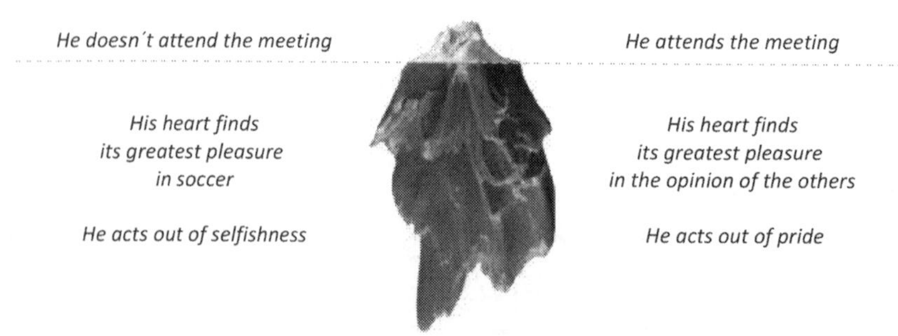

Why Does God Care So Much about the Heart?

As you can clearly see from the example you've just read, according to the Bible, ***the heart determines what we love, what we enjoy, what gives us real joy and pleasure.*** In it dwell the genuine motives and desires that guide us and move us. All things are born of it, and everything springs from it. Proverbs 4:23 declares, "*Watch over your heart with all diligence, for from it flow the springs of life.*" According to this passage, our most important job in life is to ***watch for what our hearts desire.*** The reason for making such a warning is very clear, ***what our hearts truly long for will drive everything*** that happens in all other areas of our lives. The passage is crystal clear: From the heart "flow," "spring," "originate" all the decisions and actions in my life.

If my heart is the source of my problem, then ***a real, lasting change must always journey through the highways of the heart.*** Adjusting my behavior or changing my life situation and circumstances isn't enough. Jesus Christ transforms people through a radical transformation of the heart. If the heart remains unchanged, the person's words and behavior may change temporarily due to external pressure or incentive. However, once that pressure or incentive is no longer present, those changes will vanish.

This is the case with the man who attends the prayer meeting. The Holy Spirit isn't changing and transforming him into someone with a passion for spending time with God and interceding for others. He did attend the prayer meeting; however, is he a "man of prayer" now? Has his heart changed in such a way that he no longer just attends prayer meetings, but he has developed a new conviction of how beautiful it is to intercede for others? Will he keep doing it throughout the week? The following month? When no one sees him? This truth is what the Pharisees failed to see and what Christ pointed out in Matthew 23:25-26: "*Woe to you, scribes and Pharisees, hypocrites! For you clean the outside of the cup and of the dish, but inside they are full of robbery and self-indulgence. You blind Pharisee, first clean the inside of the cup and of the dish, so that the outside of it may become clean also* [emphasis added]."

Just as Paul warns us in 1 Corinthians 13:1-3, I may "*speak with the tongues of men and of angels*" and have no genuine love. I may "*prophesy*" motivated by self-love. I may "*know all mysteries and all knowledge, and have faith so as to remove mountains,*" but I may do all that out of the wrong motivation. I can even "*give money*" without being generous. I can go so far as to "*give my life*" and die for my faith, and be loving myself in the process. As we have seen in Matthew 6:1, even when I perform my most charitable acts (such as giving, praying, and fasting), I tend to fall into this pattern. That's why, for Jesus, our focusing on the heart is so essential. It determines whether we've really come to experience his love or whether we're simply unredeemed, religious people.

In Luke 18:18-30, Jesus has quite a remarkable encounter with a rich young man. This young man is extremely interested in and attracted to who Jesus Christ is, so much so that Mark 10:17 says that he "*knelt before Him.*" As he approaches Jesus, the rich young man asks him what he must do to inherit eternal life. Jesus' response seems puzzling. "You must obey the commandments." (His response seems to contradict everything the Bible teaches if we fail to grasp Jesus' real intent). This young man's response is also quite striking. According to his own words, he has obeyed all of God's commandments since childhood. (Interestingly, none of the people present stands up to say: "That's a lie!" In fact, the opposite is true. At the end of the story, everyone concludes: "If he couldn't be saved, who could?") When Jesus hears this young man's response, we reach the climax that reveals Jesus' true motive: "*One thing you lack: go and sell all you possess and give to the poor, and you will have treasure in heaven; and come, follow Me.*"

The young man's response is extremely revealing. He's deeply saddened (because he can't do it), and he leaves Jesus behind. What happened? ***Jesus has just shown him what he really loves!*** Jesus has just penetrated his heart. He's exposed this man's true treasure, his love of money. What is Jesus' great teaching to us here? ***The heart has enough room to love multiple things all at once; however, it only has enough room to love one thing as its greatest treasure***. True, this young man was interested in Jesus, but once Jesus competes against money, what this young man's greatest love really is reveals itself. In the Lord's own words: "*No one can serve two masters; for either he will hate the one and love the other, or he will be devoted to one and despise the other*" (Matthew 6:24).

Something similar to what happens to this rich young man happens to the man who loves soccer. His heart has room to love many things at once (buying a flat-screen TV, talking to his friends about the World Cup, preparing his house for the big event, even going to the prayer meeting if it were at a different hour of the day), but something happens that replaces his love for soccer and confirms that he can't have two "masters" as his greatest treasure. Through the conversation with his pastor, it becomes clear that he loves his reputation more than soccer. ***He can't love both at the same time,*** and so ***he chooses what he loves most: his own ego***.

What Is the Underlying Problem?

As we study our own lives and look at what we need to change, it's easy to stay at surface level: I struggle with anger; I find it hard to forgive; I do not give my offering regularly; I find it hard to go to church; I am considering starting a relationship with someone who isn't a Christian. Yes, it's true; all these things are of real importance. However, in our efforts to obey God and "avoid sin," we run the risk of "obeying too quickly" and not scrutinizing our hearts enough to see what's driving us to desire these things.

What do I mean by "obeying too quickly"? I mean, we strive to do what we don't want to do, and we don't stop to reflect on the big question that could help us experience a deep and lasting transformation. Why? Why do I want this? Why am I tempted to do these things? What is it that my heart enjoys that moves me to act the way I do?

Natalie and Rob have been married for several years. Since early on in their marriage, they've had intense arguments and disagreements about how to spend their money. Natalie loves shopping for clothes. She never misses a sale. Her favorite pastime is shopping. She has even lost track of how many pairs of shoes she has in her closet. Rob is Natalie's exact opposite. Not that he doesn't like clothes, but he doesn't want to waste money. As far as he's concerned, making investments is what matters. Rob's passionate about trading in the stock market. He sets aside every last dime he owns to buy stocks. Rob struggles to understand how Natalie could be so wasteful. Natalie struggles to understand how Rob could be so stingy. She says she likes to look nice for him. He claims he's looking out for the family's future. What's the surface solution? For her to spend less money and for him to make fewer investments. Everybody's happy. Problem solved. If they do this, no one will have changed!

If Jesus were the marriage counselor for this couple, he'd do what he did with the rich young man. He wouldn't stay at the surface level; he'd aim straight for the heart. Interestingly, unlike the rich young man, Natalie and Rob's problem isn't money. Money is a symptom of something deeper. Natalie flips through all the fashion magazines. Rob's constantly following the stock market. Natalie buys anti-aging creams for her hands. Rob hires a new financial adviser. Natalie splurges at the salon. Rob spends a handsome figure on life insurance. Can you see it? Consciously or unconsciously, all of Natalie's decisions come from a single place. She desires to look pretty. The same goes for Rob, but his desire is to save up. They both need to ask the same question: why? Why do you so desperately desire to be pretty? Why do you so desperately desire to have savings?

If they examine their hearts, Natalie and Rob will be able to uncover their deepest desires. It's these deep desires that move Natalie and Rob to use money the way they do. One's moved by spending too much. The other is moved by saving unreasonably. If we only consider the surface level, we may conclude that the problem is "buying" versus "saving." If we look underneath the surface, we'll realize that they both love money. Yes, both of them! Natalie loves it by spending it, and Rob loves it by saving it. However, if we are patient and dig even deeper, we will find the real problem. Why does Natalie love money? Because she wants others to see her as pretty. In other words, she loves the opinion of others. Why does Rob love money? Because he wants to have enough resources in case something happens in the future. In other words, what he really loves and seeks is security. Can you see what's going on here? Natalie's fantasies, thoughts, and emotions are captivated by seeking the approval of others, which she thinks she'll find if she looks good. Rob's fantasies, thoughts, and emotions are captivated by seeking security, which he believes he'll find if he saves money. Just as we've clearly seen from Proverbs 4:23, ***what your heart loves dictates the course of your life***. It determines your decisions, your goals, and your desires. It determines the way you spend your money, make use of your time, and invest your efforts. It even determines what thing a married couple fights over!

In light of the example we have just studied, you may have realized that "getting below the surface" is crucial and ***examining the underlying cause,***

the "why" beneath the "why." In order to do this, it may be quite helpful to differentiate between two types of desires.[a]

I'll call the first set of desires ***superficial desires.*** Superficial desires drive our actions but, in reality, ***are means*** to reach something we long for at a deeper level. They may appear to be our greatest treasure, but they aren't! In Natalie and Rob's case, a cursory analysis of their motives would seem to indicate that they both have a problem with the love of money, and they actually do! However, the point is that there's a problem beneath their problem. Money is a means to get something else.[b] She uses money as a means to feel accepted. He uses money as a means of obtaining security. As you can see, superficial desires are only skin-deep. They're visible and easily recognizable, but in reality, they serve as tools to achieve a different goal.

In fact, superficial desires are fairly easy to modify. I would dare say that it doesn't take the Holy Spirit to change them. Do you remember the young missionary in Chapter 1? Do you remember the woman with the offering? They both undergo partial changes. They change their outward behavior. They even change their superficial desires (he traded sex for doing ministry; she changed her lack of generosity for apparent generosity). However, if you think about it for a moment, you don't need to be a Christian to make this kind of change. An atheist gives by supporting UNICEF. A Jehovah's Witness remains sexually pure. A Mormon may dedicate his life to his ministry. Examples of this kind of desire are money, sex, leisure and distraction, physical beauty, a partner, family, friends, ministry, the pursuit of knowledge, comfort, personal goals or objectives, etc. The list could go on almost endlessly.

We could refer to the second set of desires as ***deep desires***. Our deep desires ***are what we long for the most***. They're the hidden treasure of our hearts, what we actually live for. They're the very engine of our behavior. They're the cause beneath the cause. As we've seen with Natalie and Rob, our deepest desires determine our fantasies and dreams, define our mood, and account

[a] It goes without saying that this classification is merely illustrative. I don't intend to come up with a taxonomy of how the Bible breaks down desires; rather, as I tried doing through Natalie and Rob's example, my goal is to show you how our desires interact with one another. Given that the Bible declares that our hearts are deceitful (Jeremiah 17:9) and that we have a tendency to "deceive ourselves" (Hebrews 3:13), my goal in making this distinction is only to present you with an illustration helpful for easily unmasking your motivations.

[b] It's true. The Bible says that "*the love of money is a root of all sorts of evil*"; however, it isn't about loving a piece of paper. It's about the love of what that piece of paper can provide for you: it can give you security and power, it can satisfy your pleasures, etc. Think about it. If you were alone on a deserted island, what would you rather find floating on the coast by the ocean: a chest full of money, or a chest with an inflatable boat? Either way, you can still include money under the category of deep desires. As I said before, it isn't a fixed and indisputable taxonomy.

for the reasons behind our fantasies and dreams. Our deepest desires have a characteristic that sets them apart: they are unchanging. If you take a close look at your heart, you'll recognize them as repeated patterns in your life. You'll notice that they're recurrent, that they show up in different relationships, that they're present in the various contexts in which you move. Whether at work, at home, or in ministry, in your relationship with your spouse, your boss or your children, you'll notice that they subtly drive your responses and decisions. Moreover, these kinds of desires are frequently present even in the "changes" we make. In the case of the young missionary in Chapter 1, his desire to be successful is persistent despite his conversion, despite having abandoned sexual sin, and despite having radically changed his lifestyle. Some examples of this type of desire are getting the approval of others, security, the search for meaning, the need to feel accepted, yearning for deep relationships, a sense of intimacy, success, pleasure, power, rest, control, a longing to feel loved, etc. As we'll see in detail further on, another basic characteristic of our deepest desires is that they are impossible to change, or rather, to eradicate [c]. We all long for these things, and, ***by divine design, we can't (and we shouldn't) cease to desire them***. I know this is a pretty bold statement. I realize that it deserves to be backed up through Scripture and explained in detail. Be patient with me; we'll return to this idea in the chapters to follow. For now, let me just give

[c] **IMPORTANT NOTE**: What do I mean when I say that deep desires can neither be changed nor eradicated? Simply that you can't stop desiring to be accepted, that you can't eradicate the desire to feel loved, and that it's impossible to stop desiring to feel safe. You and I will always long for these things, whether we are unbelievers or fully committed Christians. The point, as we'll explore over the course of this book, is that these desires can only be fully satisfied in Christ. Did they change? In a sense they did, because you no longer rely on money, but on Christ; however, they "remain unchanged" in that the desire for security lingers.
In this sense, it's important to make a distinction that we'll further emphasize over the rest of this book. While at first we all come to God out of need (to be loved, to be forgiven, to go to heaven, etc.), there is a point in our spiritual life when we ***grow to appreciate Jesus for who he is and not for what he gives us***. When this happens, our deepest desires are "forgotten" or "surpassed" by our appreciation of Christ and they take on a completely secondary role; as a result of appreciating the glory of God in Christ, we stop thinking about them. Let me give you an example. One of the things I enjoy the most in creation are trees. Their height, the fact that their trunks are so sturdy, the different shades of green they come in are extremely attractive to me. I could spend hours on end staring at them. Take a moment to picture me in a cabin in the middle of a lush forest where I go out for a walk after having had a delicious meal of roast beef and potatoes for lunch. The setting is idyllic. My stomach is full, the temperature is perfect, the place is fabulous. Then, I find a beautiful apple tree in the middle of the forest. How do I enjoy this tree? By admiring it! I look at it and I go, "WOW! It's amazing!" Its shape, its color, its glossy fruit. In short, ***I enjoy and love it for what it is***. Now let's change the scenario. Imagine I'm lost in the woods. I haven't eaten in three days, and I stumble upon the apple tree. How will I enjoy that exact same tree? By destroying it! I'll eat its fruit all the way to the very last apple. I no longer appreciate the tree for what is, ***I appreciate it for what it gives me***. According to Bernard of Clairvaux, there are four degrees of love. The first degree of love is ***loving myself for my own sake***. This means that everything I do (buying a car, going on vacation, serving in church), I do out of self-love. The second degree of love is ***loving God for my sake***. In other words, I love God for what he gives me. It's like finding an apple tree right in the middle of the woods. I'm hungry; I have a need (for love, forgiveness, etc.) and God met that need. The third degree of love is ***loving***

you a sneak peek. What does it mean to change? As we learn from Jeremiah 2:13, ***changing isn't eradicating these desires, but rather satisfying them in God.*** To change is to stop trying to get these things on my own (thus becoming my own savior), and to start appreciating the love of a God who wants to give me the things I'm so desperately seeking apart from him. "*For My people have committed two evils: They have forsaken me, fountain of living waters, to hew for themselves cisterns. Broken cisterns that can hold no water*" (Jeremiah 2:13; emphasis added).

Superficial desires	***Deep desires***
They are a means to obtain something else	*They are what our hearts really long for*
They can be seen more easily	*They are far less visible*
They vary with age, context, our situation in life, our role, etc.	*They remain consistent*
They may be modified fairly easily.	*We cannot avoid longing for them, and they can only be satisfied by God*
Money, sex, leisure, ministry, physical beauty, a spouse, a family, knowledge, comfort, fun, goals, etc.	*Approval, security, meaning, acceptance, deep relationships, intimacy, success, pleasure, power, rest, control, a need to feel loved, etc.*

Before looking at one final detail, I would like you to pause and consider a key point. If you skim through the list of desires that I've included in the chart, both superficial and deep, you'll notice that ***none of these desires are either bad or sinful.*** On the contrary! Each of these desires represents good things, gifts from God, even promises from him to us.

Does this mean that all our hearts' desires are good? Of course not! The Bible also mentions sinful desires. Some of these are envy, hatred, jealousy,

God for God's sake. In other words, I love God for who he is. I meditate on what he's done and I'm ecstatic. I reflect on the fact that he was hung on a "tree" and he was "bitten," ripped apart and torn to pieces for my sin, and I can do nothing but be admired but him. At that moment, my hunger (my needs, my superficial and deep desires) ceases to be important and it vanishes before the cross. I love him for who he is. I love his precious glory. Finally, Bernard says, the fourth level of love is ***loving myself for the love of God***. This means that my whole life now begins to revolve around a God who has done three things. He has freed me from selfishness (first level), has satisfied my deepest desires (second level), and has shown me his beauty and love in full (third level). In this way, I can now access God's creation to "love myself" (buying a car, going on vacation, serving in the church, etc.), but these created things aren't a means to love myself, rather they are tools that I use to love God and others. Not only that, but his blessings (the car, the vacation, the service) are a means through which I continue to appreciate the unbelievable love he has for me; that is, ***I love the God who blesses and not his blessings***. If you are confused, don't worry. Keep reading the book all the way through and you will see that this is the direction we are going.

lust, etc. However, I've decided not to deal with them in this chapter for two reasons. First, because they're easy to identify. A sinful desire (envy) produces sinful behavior (speaking ill of someone). You don't need too much knowledge to identify and recognize them as bad. Our conscience almost certainly tells us they are. Second, because sinful desires are also prompted by our deepest desires. We're jealous (a sinful desire) because we're seeking acceptance (a deep desire). We hate (a sinful desire) because we don't feel loved (a deep desire). We're anxious (a sinful desire) because something compromises our security (a deep desire). We're envious (a sinful desire) because we see our need for success (a deep desire) jeopardized. We struggle with lust (a superficial desire) because we crave pleasure (a deep desire). Can you see it? Even sinful desires, which we could also include under the category of superficial desires, are rooted in a deep desire we're trying to satisfy on our own.

This prompts us to consider one last concept. Think about Rob and Natalie one more time. If you study it carefully, on an even deeper level than we've looked so far, they both share the same problem. ***Both are trying to take God's place. Both want to provide for themselves what only God can provide.*** They both perform an "***invisible action***" whereby they decide to take control of their lives and satisfy their deepest desires. She uses money as a means to feel accepted—acceptance that ***God <u>wants to</u> and <u>can</u> give her***. He uses money as a means to obtain security—security that ***God <u>longs to</u> and <u>is able</u> to give him***.

Have you noticed? We're back in the Garden of Eden! For Rob and Natalie, the snake's temptation is as real today as it was for Adam and Eve back then. Satan's words in Genesis 3:5 were, "*Do this and you will be like God.*" This is the fundamental problem with which we all struggle: trying to save ourselves They tried to save themselves and improve their lives by eating of the fruit; we try to do it through beauty treatments or strategic investments. So, the challenge we find in Isaiah 55:1-3 is to consider ***<u>who will quench my thirst</u>?*** (My thirst to feel safe, loved, successful, accepted, etc.) "*You there! Everyone who thirsts, come to the waters; and you who have no money come, buy and eat. Come, buy wine and milk without money and without cost. Why do you spend money for what is not bread, and your wages for what doesn't satisfy? Listen carefully to Me, and eat what is good, and delight yourself in abundance. Incline your ear and come to Me. Listen, that you may live; and I will make an everlasting covenant with you, according to the faithful mercies shown to David* [emphasis added]." Can you see it? God isn't opposed to me seeking to satisfy my deepest desires. God is opposed to me trying to satisfy them on my own, apart from him. He's against me becoming my own god and rejecting his amazing offer—that is, for him to be Lord of my life!

Let's review Rob's case. If you carefully think about it, it wouldn't be too difficult for him to stop saving compulsively. All he'd have to do is buy an insurance policy that, in case of an accident, would abundantly cover his and his family's financial needs for life. If he did that, he very well may have felt free to spend his money. Why? Because his deepest desire (for his family to be financially secure) would have been met. Can you see what would have happened here though? Rob has placed himself in God's place. He would have replaced God with an insurance policy and become his own savior.[d] Who will Rob love: God or money? Who has given him what he was seeking? Money is the "god" that allows him to get what he most desires; therefore, it makes sense that he loves it!

The key to the transformation of the heart is to repent of the "sin beneath the sin." It's to realize that we have tried to be "lords" of our own life, "masters" of our own decisions, and "owners" of our own salvation by using God's gifts (money, beauty, sex, etc.) as means to obtain what our hearts so desperately desire (security, approval, acceptance, etc.). Paraphrasing John Calvin, David Powlison said, "***The evil in our desires often lies not in what we want but in the fact that we want it too much.***"[5] This is what James 4:1 calls to "over-desire," an inordinate desire, an unrestrained desire, a passion, something we want so desperately that we're willing to set God aside and sin to get it. What's wrong is transforming a legitimate desire into a demand, into something that I must have no matter what it takes. This is what the Bible calls idolatry: taking something good, a gift from God (anything from physical beauty, to money, sex, ministry, or my goals and objectives), and transforming it into something that could save us and give us life. As Tim Keller puts it: "Our idols are those things we count on to give our lives meaning. They are the things of which we say, 'I need this to make me happy,' or 'If I don't have this, my life is worthless and meaningless.'"[6] Why do we do this? As we've seen, the reason is that we're trying to satisfy a deeper kind of desire: feeling loved, safe, important, etc.

Let me give you a personal example so you can see how this dynamic works in everyday situations. One of the things I most enjoy doing when I get up in

---

[d] Does this mean that getting an insurance policy is a sin? Of course not! I have one myself. What matters is what drives me to get one. I may be moved by a healthy desire to provide for those God has entrusted to me (1 Timothy 5:8), or I may be moved by an unhealthy insecurity to assume God's role and to try to save myself and my loved ones. The heart's desire "turns" something neutral into a "pseudo-savior." Remember, God sees the heart.

the morning is reading the news on my cell phone while I'm eating breakfast. To me, these first fifteen minutes of the day are almost sacred. They're my patch of heaven on earth, my me-time. The kids are asleep. The house is quiet. There are no interruptions. I love finding out what's going on around the world, and I'm especially fond of reading the sports section. Some time ago, my wife sat down next to me while I was having breakfast, and, with openness and a noticeable burden, she began to pour her heart out and tell me about some of her most profound struggles. While she was talking to me, I was torn between looking at my phone, eating my toast, and trying to listen to her (I guess it must have been a tragicomic scene). I tried my best to listen to her, but when the time came for me to say something, I was straightforward and insensitive. Naturally, I wanted to end the conversation as soon as possible and get back to my own business. (After all, couldn't she see that I was busy?)

In response to my words, she said, "Honey, you haven't shown any compassion toward me. You talked to me without empathy and in a condemning way." Honestly, I didn't want to do that, but it didn't take much insight to realize that I had. I apologized to her, I hugged her, and I told her that she was right and that I hadn't been sensitive to her. However, the moment of greatest clarity for me came a few minutes later. During my quiet time, I felt God asking me: "Why do you treat her like that? This isn't the first time you've done it. With other people, you're sensitive and patient. Why aren't you like that with her?" Answering that question was rather painful. "I'm not sensitive and patient with her ***because she bothers me***." Yes. As hard as it may be to accept, it's true. My wife bothers me. ***She bothers me because <u>she interrupts something I love</u>.*** I love those fifteen minutes of me-time. I love the distraction. I love my own peace and quiet. I love my personal time to find pleasure in the world. I hate being bothered when I'm focused, when I'm enjoying myself, when I'm having a good time and doing something that I love. Seeing this reality produced in me a deep, heartfelt conviction of sin. However, in his grace, God granted me an even greater level of clarity. He allowed me to see the "sin beneath my sin." As I continued to talk to God in prayer, I felt that he was asking me, "So, why do you love reading the news so much?" Then, clarity "hit" me again. "***Lord, I do it <u>because I love to rest</u>. But it's even worse than that. Lord, I do it <u>BECAUSE I DON'T FIND MY REST IN YOU</u>!***"

This realization was even more "painful." Can you see the problem beneath the problem? I was seeking something in my phone that God wants to give me. Not in vain does Jeremiah 2:13 say that ***every time we sin we commit two evils***: *"For My people have committed two evils: they have forsaken Me [the first evil], the fountain of living waters, to hew for themselves cisterns, [the second evil], broken cisterns that can hold no water."* Our problem is twofold. There's a problem beneath the problem. Before committing any sinful action (such as speaking in a condemning manner to my wife), internally, I've already committed "two evils." I have abandoned God as my "fountain of water," and I've sought something else to satisfy my thirst (for leisure and rest): in my case, reading the news on my cell phone. Is there something wrong with reading the news every morning? Of course not! What's wrong is that I've taken control of my heart (becoming my own god) and, (setting God aside) I've made my cell phone the source of my rest and leisure for fifteen minutes, my reason for living, my "broken cistern" that can't give me true life.

If you think about it for a moment, there are two ways to deal with this problem: dealing with my sin in a superficial way or dealing with the root cause of my sin. I could pray saying, "Lord, help me quit staring at my phone every morning. Help me be more patient and empathetic. Help me treat my wife with love. Help me avoid using simplistic and condemning words." However, neither my phone nor my words are my real problem; they're a symptom of an underlying problem. ***The real problem is that during those fifteen minutes, I don't find my rest in Jesus!*** I've set Christ aside, I've suppressed the Spirit, and I've crowned myself king.

The problem is that I love being distracted by my phone so much that I seek peace, joy, and rest in it. The problem is that I'm deceived into thinking that my phone can give me what Jesus wants to give me. The problem is that every morning I'm trying to "save myself," I'm seeking life in the news; paraphrasing Pascal, I'm trying to fill my heart with created things when it can only be filled with the Creator. What's the solution? Throwing my phone away? Keeping it turned off until I get to the office? Of course not! ***That won't give my soul "rest." That would just leave me empty, and it would only be a matter of time until I find something else to replace my phone.***

The solution, according to Jeremiah, is to go back to drinking from "the fountain of living water." The solution is for me to return to treasuring Jesus Christ. It's for me to appreciate once more the fact that he came to give me a much richer and fuller life than I can get from reading the news on my cell phone (John 10:10). The solution is both simple and profound. ***Christ must again become my resting place,*** my security, my source of acceptance; in other words, the one who satisfies my deepest desires. Only when this happens—when he becomes my greatest pleasure and delight—will I be able to hold the phone with "open hands." That is, I'll be able to be interrupted and not get frustrated, and I'll be able to give my wife the attention and love she needs. "Why?" Because only then will my heart be filled with "living water" that truly satisfies.

One Final Challenge

As you walk through your day and face countless situations that trigger within you different kinds of actions (good and bad), try to develop a habit of asking yourself these two questions:

- Why did I do that? (Or why did I respond that way?)
- What is it that I'm seeking that I should be seeking in God?[7]

BRIEF SUMMARY

What is the heart? *The heart is the "place" where my desires dwell; that is, what I really love, enjoy, and treasure.*

Why is the heart so important? *Because what my heart loves drives why I act the way I act. If I really want to change, what my heart holds most dear must change.*

What is the problem of the heart? *We have deep desires that we try to satisfy by turning God's good gifts into idols. Only when Jesus becomes our greatest treasure again will there be real change in our hearts and, consequently, a genuine change in our behavior.*

FOR PERSONAL REFLECTION OR DISCUSSION IN SMALL GROUPS

It's very tempting to skip over this last section of the chapter. Don't do it; stop. Don't ignore what the Holy Spirit may be teaching you through this chapter; don't rush. Take time to meditate on these questions and/or discuss them with others.

1. *In what way has this chapter either changed or confirmed your understanding of how changes take place?*

2. *Sum up in one or two sentences the concepts that had the greatest impact on you in this chapter.*
3. *In your own words, how would you define the heart? (In order to answer this question, you can read the passages from the Bible that I quoted at the beginning of this chapter).*
4. *Why do you think that we Christians should focus more on the heart than on outward behavior?*
5. *Deep desires determine not only my actions, but also my more superficial desires. In fact,* ***they work together with them to generate a hierarchy of values within my heart of what is and is not important to me****. How is this hierarchy determined? As you can see in the box below, it depends on how it fits together to satisfy my deepest desires. Let me give you two examples for the sake of clarity.*

<u>Case #1</u>*: Let's assume that my deepest desire is <u>to be accepted</u> by others. Will external beauty be important to me? Yes, if I conclude that it helps me be accepted by others. If this is the case, I'll go on a diet, I'll go to the gym, and I'll spend long hours in front of the mirror. How will I use, for instance, money? I'll probably spend it on clothes and beauty products.*

<u>Case #2</u>*: Let's assume again that my deepest desire is <u>to be accepted</u> by others. However, let's just say I'm not a particularly attractive person. Will external beauty be important in my value set? Probably not. But I still long to be accepted! Then, what could I do? It's likely that, without even realizing it, I'll come up with a new set of values. Given that I'm quite smart, I'll use my intelligence to get what someone attractive achieves through their beauty. Will I go on a diet? Will I go to the gym? No, but I'll have a deep desire to increase my knowledge. I'll be a straight A student, I'll strive to attend an Ivy League school, and I'll do my best to earn multiple diplomas. How will I use money? I'll probably spend it on books and training courses.*

<u>ME</u>*: Now it's your turn. Fill in the blank boxes, trying to be as honest as you possibly can. What would you say is/are your deepest desire(s)? Where do you seek to satisfy it/them? Finally, what observable things do you do to get them?*

	Deep Desire	*Superficial Desire*	*Outward Behavior*
	What am I looking for?	*Through what means do I seek it?*	*What do I do to get it?*
Case 1	*To be accepted*	*My image*	*I go on a diet* *I go to the gym* *I eat very little* *I hide my physical defects* *I sing in the worship team*
Case 2	*To be accepted*	*My intelligence*	*I study a lot* *I choose an elite university* *I take multiple classes* *I read the Bible and theology books* *I teach Sunday school*
Me			

6. *If you had to advise these two people, what would you do to help them change? (I know we haven't discussed this much yet but trying to answer this question may be good brainstorming for what's coming next.)*

CHAPTER 3

How Does Love Work?

The Nature of Love

What does it mean to "love"? What does loving something imply? I'm not referring to what Christian love looks like, but rather to the things that must take place inside the human heart for any individual (Christian or not) to be able to say, "I love this woman," "I love to travel," or "I love my job." I'm well aware that defining the essence of love isn't an easy task. The Bible doesn't give us a dictionary definition to settle the matter, but it does leave us clear clues for identifying what loving something implies.[a] Since loving God is the first and greatest commandment, it's critical that we have a correct, biblical understanding of what it means to love something.

As we saw in the previous chapter, Jesus tells us in Matthew 6:21 that ***the heart loves when it finds something valuable***. "*For where your treasure is, there your heart will be also.*" In other words, ***love is the heart's response to what is perceived as attractive.*** The reason I use the word "response" is that it more

[a] I imagine some of you may be thinking: "Wait a minute. The Bible does give us a definition of love; 1 Corinthians 13:4 says, "*Love is patient, love is kind. It does not envy, it does not boast, it is not proud...*" Isn't that the definition of the essence of love?" I don't think it is. I believe these are *manifestations* of love or, if you will, *the ways I live* when I really love someone or something. In fact, they're the characteristics of Christian love, which would certainly be different from the ones atheistic or non-Christian love would put forward, where "serving," for instance, is failing to love oneself, where "suffering" is rejected, where "enduring" is perceived as unhealthy and as an act of cowardice, where "rejoicing in the truth" is not an option because there is no truth, but rather subjective ideas of it, etc. Can you see it? Paul is offering the characteristics of Christian love; he isn't defining what loving someone or something implies.

closely communicates the idea Jesus teaches in Matthew 6:21. According to Jesus, the heart ***responds, pursues, chases after*** the thing that has become its greatest treasure. In other words, for Jesus, love is the ***consequence*** of having found something precious. It's the ***outcome*** of having found a treasure. It's a ***reaction of appreciation*** towards something that, as we will see later on, goes far beyond a decision or a feeling. According to Jesus, when the heart finds something precious, it can't help but treasure it. It's inevitable. Therefore, we could complete our definition by saying that ***love is the response (unforced, yet uncontrollable) that involves appreciating with all my heart (my intellect, emotions, and will) the "beauty" of an object or person.***

I know the definition I've just provided is somewhat philosophical and far-fetched, so allow me to break it down and explain its various parts bit by bit.

1. *Love is a response that involves appreciating the "beauty" of something.*
2. *Love is a response that can't be forced.*
3. *Love is a response that involves my whole heart (my intellect, my feelings, and my will).*
4. *Love is a response that carries with it a degree of surrender.*

1. Love is a response that involves appreciating the "beauty" of something

As we have seen, Jesus says that our heart is always chasing after a "treasure." A treasure is something valuable; it's something appealing, precious; something priceless. But not all of us consider the same things "beautiful" or "appealing." What may be a treasure for one person may be something of little value to another. For instance, I personally don't enjoy shopping, I don't take pleasure in it, and I don't get excited doing it. Going to a mall isn't something I consider "beautiful" or appealing. However, other people find great pleasure in it. For them, it really is like a "treasure." They find it "beautiful," appealing, precious. On the other hand, I love putting together and designing photo albums of our family. (Notice that, by using the word "love," I'm already attributing "beauty" to the process of designing these albums.) This is perfectly natural.

We don't all find pleasure in the same things, but we ALL find pleasure in something. We all "treasure" something. We all love. Jonathan Edwards explains this dynamic as follows:

> God has endued the human soul with two central faculties. The first of these is called ***understanding***, by which we discern and judge of things. The other faculty is that by which we behold things, not merely as an indifferent unaffected spectator, but as one who, liking or disliking, pleased or displeased, approves of or rejects these things. We sometimes call the latter ***inclination [or attraction]***.[8]

When human beings see something they consider appealing, they can't help but admire it. A young man sees a pretty girl walking down the street, and he turns around to appreciate her figure. A grown man who enjoys vintage cars goes to an exhibition and he can't stop enthusiastically admiring each and every car. A teenage girl walks around the mall and can't stop picturing what she'd look like in the dress she sees at a clothing store. To love something is to be able to appreciate its value. Of course, there are degrees of love. The appreciation one may have for a car isn't the same as the appreciation one may have for a loved one. Since we'll look into this later, the point I want to emphasize here is that ***loving something is a consequence of finding that thing valuable and appealing***. Paraphrasing the Apostle Paul, it's the outcome of having the "eyes of my heart" opened to the "beauty," for example, of a vintage car or God.

Naturally, the opposite effect works the same way. If I don't appreciate the "beauty" in something, I won't find pleasure in it, and therefore, I won't love it. I personally experience this kind of indifference towards paintings. I see Leonardo da Vinci's works, and they don't move me, they don't stir up any kind of appreciation within me. Everyone talks about the beauty of Mona Lisa's smile, and I honestly don't even see her smile. The problem is with me, not with the painting! I haven't been able to see its appeal, to recognize its value, to discover its charm. I look at it, but I don't see it. I observe it, but I don't appreciate it. I perceive it, but I don't treasure it. Consider once again the words of Jonathan Edwards, but this time, focus on how this concept applies to God:

> There is a twofold understanding or knowledge of good, that God has made the mind of man capable of. The first, that which is merely speculative or notional.... The other is that which consists in the sense of the heart: as when there is a sense of the beauty, amiableness, or sweetness of a thing.... Thus there is a difference between having an

> opinion that God is holy and gracious, and having a sense of the loveliness and beauty of that holiness and grace. There is a difference between having a rational judgment that honey is sweet, and ***having a sense of its sweetness***.... When the heart is ***sensible of the beauty*** and amiableness of a thing, it necessarily ***feels pleasure in the apprehension*** [in perceiving it]... which is a far different thing from having a rational opinion that it is excellent...[emphasis added][9]

As we'll see over the course of this book, coming to appreciate, treasure, and love the 'beauty' of the person of God and what he has done is what truly produces deep changes. As Paul said: "*I pray that* ***the eyes of your heart*** *may be enlightened, so that you will know [the extraordinary things God has done for us in Christ]*" (Ephesians 1:18-19). However, as we have said, ***grasping*** this concept and ***enjoying*** God (i.e., loving him) are two very different things.

2. Love is a response that can't be forced

I can't force myself or others to love. Do you remember the man who stays up to watch his national team's soccer game? No one has to put a gun to his head for him to find pleasure in watching his team. On the contrary! Because he finds pleasure in soccer, he loves it. And, because he loves it, he behaves in ways that reflect his love (he stays up on a Sunday night, buys an expensive flat-screen TV, etc.). You can't force love; it's a response! No one forces me to love; I love because I perceive the object of my affection to be a "treasure," in this case, the soccer game.

One of my favorite books is *Tortured for Christ*. In this work, its author, Pastor Richard Wurmbrand, describes the terrible tortures that he and other Christians had to endure in the communist concentration camps during the war. "They broke four vertebrae in my back, and many other bones. They carved me in a dozen places. They burned and cut eighteen holes in my body."[10] As Richard Wurmbrand himself once said, in a concentration camp the guards can force you to do anything they want, except for one thing. They can force you to eat your own feces, they can force you to dig your own grave, they can force you to kill your own child (by giving you a gun with a single bullet and threatening to kill all your children and your wife if you don't do it or if you commit suicide), they can force you to do this and a whole lot more. But there's one thing they can't do. ***They can't force you to love them...*** Why? Because love is a response. It can't be forced.

Grasping this concept is absolutely essential in order to understand how deep changes take place. I can't force anyone to love something; I can't even force myself! Love is a response that ***involves an unforced decision, yet one that even I myself can't control!*** As we mentioned, and we'll continue to study, I love when, for any number of reasons, I enjoy and treasure something. [b]

Some time ago, we held a fundraiser in our church to send money to a Sudanese missionary who was about to get married. This young man and I are friends. I know how committed he is. I've trained him both in Bible studies and theology. I've seen his love for Jesus firsthand, and I'm also well aware of his extreme poverty. In Sudan, the groom has to pay a dowry to the bride's father before he can marry her. Needless to say, when we announced in church that he needed help funding his wedding, I felt very happy and privileged to be able to participate. A fair number of people in our church community were also moved to help him. Now, think about this. We gave money. We were happy to do so. It was a beautiful moment. But what if you were say to me, "Nico. In your heart you must feel the same way you'd feel if your daughter Micaela were getting married. You must love this man just as much as you love your daughter." Clearly, I would answer, "I can't do that!" I can't love this missionary with as much love as I love my own daughter. I can't have as much passion, devotion, and commitment as I would if my own daughter were getting married—and if you're honest, you probably couldn't either. If my daughter were marrying, I would save for months to help her pay for the wedding. I would go with her to pick out her wedding dress. I would do the impossible to make sure she went on a honeymoon to whatever place she wanted. Day and night, I would be thinking of ways to give her everything she needed so that she'd have the best day of her life—you'd probably do the same for your own child.

You can ask me, you can demand of me, or even force me to give more money toward the missionary's dowry, and perhaps I might even do it (a behavior); but you can't ask me, demand of me, or force me to love my missionary friend the way I love my little girl (a heart change). There's nothing you can do that

---

[b] If you think about it for a moment, hatred, which is the opposite of love, is also a response. In this case, a response of rejection and non-appreciation towards something we find reprehensible and despicable. For instance, no one can force me to find pleasure in having one of my children tortured or killed. You can restrain me so I won't do anything about it. You can force me to watch you while you do it. However, even if you threaten to kill me, you can't force me to find pleasure in it. No one, not even I, has the capacity to force me to love that action. Why? Because just as with love, hatred is a response that takes place (in a way that can't be controlled) as the result of rejecting something.

will get me there. Even I don't have the power to force myself to love him that way. True love can't be forced, controlled, or manipulated.

Understanding this concept is critical because, among many other things, it shows us that ***what we do externally is determined by what we enjoy internally***. Think again about the man who enjoys watching his national soccer team play in the World Cup. You can force him to miss the game (by bribing him or putting a gun to his head), but you can't force him to stop loving the game and, for example, start loving figure skating. Something ***radical*** must change inside him for this to happen. If this is so, it begs the question: How could we ever get this man to change so drastically? The only way this man will stop loving soccer is ***if his heart finds something that gives him more pleasure*** than soccer itself. Something that seizes him at the very core of his being. Something that alters his affections. This way, ***in response to this new passion***, he'll willingly stop watching the soccer game.

If, for instance, while he's in front of the TV, someone calls to say that his daughter has been in a terrible car accident, ***inevitably*** the news will seize his whole being, and he'll stop watching the game. Surely he will leap out of his couch—not thinking for an instant about how much he paid for his flat-screen TV nor bothering to watch his team kick a penalty—and, in despair, leave for the scene of the accident. What has happened? How was his love for soccer overcome? By a greater love. By a new passion. As we'll see later, ***we can only overcome our addiction to a specific pleasure with a new addiction to a greater pleasure***. Why? Because the heart makes decisions ***in response*** to what it loves. As Thomas Chalmers so fittingly puts it:

> There are two ways in which a practical moralist may attempt to displace from the human heart its love of the world, either by a demonstration of the world's vanity, so as that the heart shall be prevailed upon simply to withdraw its regards from an object that isn't worthy of it; or, by setting forth another object, even God, as more worthy of its attachment, so as that the heart shall be prevailed upon not to resign an old affection, which shall have nothing to succeed it, but to exchange an old affection for a new one. My purpose is to show, that from the constitution of our nature, the former method is altogether incompetent and ineffectual and that the latter method will alone suffice for the rescue and recovery of the heart from the wrong affection that domineers over it.[11]

Let me show you an illustration that clarifies the quote you've just read. Picture a little boy who's addicted to lollipops. I don't mean a child who has a lollipop now and then, but one who has lots of them on a daily basis. If you were his parent, how could you help him break the addiction? You could give him a command saying: "Don't eat lollipops!" However, I doubt he'd listen to you. You could tell him about all the benefits of eating healthy food, but I don't think that would work, either. You could yell at him or threaten him. You could beg him and explain how bad it makes you feel as a parent that he has those many lollipops. You could ultimately discipline him by saying that you'll never buy lollipops for him again and, after getting rid of all the lollipops left around the house, you could lock the boy in his room until he decides to change. Will he stop having lollipops? Of course he will. After all, he no longer has access to them. However, what will he be thinking about when he goes to sleep? (Just think about what's on your mind when you go to sleep, and you'll have discovered what you're addicted to.) How do we typically go about changing? How do we help others change? We use commands, guilt, manipulation, threats, discipline, etc. Does the child stop having lollipops? Yes. But the deeper question is this: ***Does he stop loving lollipops? Does he stop finding pleasure in them? Will he stop fantasizing about them?*** In order to help a child who's addicted to lollipops, there's something very simple you can do: offer him chocolate! Once the boy tastes chocolate, he'll give up his addiction to lollipops and become addicted to chocolate. He'll have a new treasure, a new passion.

How do deep changes take place? Change takes place in the heart when my eyes are opened to the reality that ***Jesus Christ is more precious than any other thing the world could possibly offer*** (Ephesians 1:18-19). When, as it says in Revelation, I remember "*my first love*" for him.

3. Love is a response that involves my intellect, my feelings, and my will

Love involves my ***whole*** heart—my entire inner being—not just a part of it. There are typically two opposite ways of defining love. Some people say, "Oh! Love is a feeling! Love is feeling passion!" Others say, "No! Love is a decision. It's an act of the will that I choose to give or not give." While more liberal cultures tend to define it by the first approach, more traditional ones tend to define it by the second. In Christian circles, churches with a more progressive inclination tend to align themselves with the first definition (and they often identify loving God with what they ***feel*** during worship). More conservative churches tend to lean towards the latter (and they often identify love for God with what they ***know*** about God when the Word is preached). I believe that, from a biblical standpoint, neither description is complete.

When we love something, we don't set a portion of the heart aside; we use all of it! We don't stop using our brains, nor do we rely exclusively on what we feel. In loving something, your whole being is "at work." You study, consider, weigh, evaluate, but you also feel, experience, judge, and even taste—just as someone does when they taste a chocolate cake. In doing so, you use all your senses. You look at it, you smell it, you touch it, you get a taste of it, and then you give your verdict as to whether or not you liked it. Your whole being is at work.

From a biblical point of view, when I love something, three things happen inside my heart:

- My mind thinks, "This is beautiful"
- My feelings confirm, "This is beautiful"
- My will decides, "This is beautiful"

As we'll see in detail in the next chapter, according to James 1:12-18, all temptation follows this same process. By definition, temptation is something appealing, something precious, something "beautiful." Chocolate cake when I'm on a diet; a glass of whiskey when I'm committed to sobriety; a vacation in paradise when I'm stressed out from work. No temptation is ever unpleasant. If it were, I wouldn't be tempted! In our hearts, you and I are continually judging what things are "beautiful" and what things are "unappealing." We are always deciding what is or isn't worthy of our love. It's impossible not to. It's part of God's design. Sometimes this internal process is more conscious than at other times, but it's something we carry with us wherever we go.

Before moving on to the last point, I would like you to analyze the following statement carefully: ***I always do what I <u>most</u> desire to do.*** Please reread the statement. It has tremendous implications. What do you think? Is it true? Someone might object and say: "Wait a minute. There are thousands of situations where I do things I don't want to do. For instance, at work. My boss always makes me do things I don't want to do." If you reflect on that in depth, you'll realize it isn't true. You do what your boss asks because, whether you are aware of it or not, ***you're seeking what you <u>most</u> desire***. If your boss asks you to lie about the details in a document, you have two options: you can choose to do what he asks of you and lie, or you can choose not to. You always have a choice. If you decide to lie, you'll be doing what you most desired to do in that moment—even if you didn't get any pleasure out of it. Why? ***Because what you desired most, what you loved most, what you treasured most, was to keep your job.*** (Maybe because you love money, maybe because you didn't want to displease your boss, perhaps because of the uncertainty that would come out of being out of work, etc.) It's possible that you "didn't want" to do it, but if you do it, ***you have done what you most desired to do.*** Jonathan Edwards puts it this way: "The will always chooses according to its strongest inclination at the moment."

We looked at this truth when we analyzed the case of the rich young man and his encounter with Jesus. He chose his wealth over Jesus. Not necessarily because he hates Jesus, but because of what choosing him demands. How did he make his decision? Based on what he ***most*** loved. In terms of what he perceived most appealing in that moment: his wealth. ***Always, in every situation, and at all times, whether consciously or unconsciously, I choose what I (either rightly or wrongly) believe will bring me the greatest possible good.***

What does it mean to change? It means for God to become what I desire most. It means coming to see, to realize, to appreciate that ***God is my greatest possible good.*** It means that my heart (intellect, feelings, and will) can appreciate God's value. It means that my eyes have been opened by the Holy Spirit and, upon seeing the incredible glory of Jesus Christ, I choose him above all other things this world has to offer. It means that he has become what I desire most. After all, isn't that what Jesus is asking from us? That we love him "*with all our heart, with all our soul, and with all our mind*" (Mt 22:37, Mk 12:30, Lk 10:27). How do you do it? You'll have to keep reading.

4. Love is a response that involves different degrees of surrender

There's a well-known saying that goes: "Love is an action." Although this quote is incomplete if the points we discussed above aren't considered, it does hold a significant amount of truth. Love always involves some kind of action or surrender. Every morning, as soon as we open our eyes, we begin to evaluate, consider, or judge each person, idea, object, or situation we come across. Consciously or unconsciously, we begin to assign a measure of appreciation and love toward everything. Most likely, the first thing you do when you get up every morning is brush your teeth. Why? Well, for a number of reasons. You don't want to get cavities; you don't want your teeth to turn yellow; you don't want them to fall out, and so on. In other words, you have a measure of love for your teeth. If you analyze your deep desires, it's possible that you brush your teeth because you value the way you look, because you don't want to suffer (by having to go to the dentist), etc. The point is that your love for your teeth moves you to action. Not brushing them is not loving them. Loving them brings about a certain degree of surrender. In this case, you surrender five minutes of your time every morning to brushing them with dedication.

The measure of surrender, of sacrifice, of devotion that we're willing to give toward something (whether it's to brushing our teeth, watching a soccer game, shopping at the mall, or even to God himself) ***is determined by the level of appreciation we have for that object***. That is, the more we value it, the more we'll surrender ourselves to it. The more "beautiful" we find it, the greater our devotion, the greater our willingness to give ourselves to it, the greater the level of response in our heart. Watching a neighborhood soccer game doesn't produce the same level of response in the heart as watching the World Cup Final does. Waiting for your spouse to come out of an operating room isn't the same as waiting in line at the bank.

In this sense, it's helpful to differentiate between two levels or degrees of love. Of course, each of them brings forth a different degree of devotion or a different kind of response in us. On the one hand, we find ***emotions***. On the other, we find what Jonathan Edwards has called the ***affections*** of the heart. Emotions have a superficial degree of love for something. Affections show appreciation for the fullness of the beauty of an object—whether it is soccer, art, God, etc.—and, for this reason, they carry a much deeper degree of love or surrender. Crying over the loss of a child isn't the same as crying because I lost my car keys. Although I love both of them and both of them engage my emotions (in both cases, I am sad), the degree of affection I have for my car will never come close to the degree of affection I have for my own child.

In this sense, it's important to avoid confusing affections with extreme emotional reactions. Although they may look similar, in reality, they're not. Let's say you're reading an online newspaper. While you're browsing through the headlines, you come across a story that reads, "Child Massacre in Africa." Upon reading the story, you notice that they've posted a video showing what's happened. The video is extremely graphic and explicit. What's the result? It moves you. In fact, you may have even cried when you saw it. The story has tapped into your emotions. But, has it actually tapped into your affections? If you're like me, chances are that in the blink of an eye you'll go back to reading the newspaper and then you'll go on to watch a sports video or check your Facebook. On the other hand, if you're really sensitive, you might be so moved that you even share the video with others. However, unless you take a plane and travel to Africa, unless you start preparing for a career as a humanitarian, or unless you join a charity and devote your life to doing something about it, that story has only tapped into your emotions; it hasn't reached your affections. It hasn't reached a level where it has influenced and it has changed what you treasure most. When I really love something, I respond, I commit myself, I submit myself, I surrender. I can't help it!

Emotions	***Affections***
They imply a superficial love	*They imply a deep love*
There's little appreciation for the "beauty" of the object	*There is full appreciation for the "beauty" of the object*
They perceive the object as having moderate value	*They perceive the object as having ultimate value*
They're fleeting	*They remain constant*
They easily change	*They don't change easily*
Losing an object you have surrendered your emotions to results in a certain degree of sadness	*Losing an object you have surrendered your affections to destabilizes your whole life*

One of the most relevant characteristics of our affections is that they are constant. That is to say, they don't change easily. The opposite happens with our emotions. As can happen when reading a compelling news story or listening to a song you love, emotions vary all the time. One minute you may hear a lively song and feel like dancing; moments later you start listening to a sentimental ballad and you feel like crying (which should lead us to seriously consider whether our times for worship are merely an emotional moment or whether they truly are an expression of our deepest affections).

Let me give you another example. Do you remember Rob and Natalie, the couple who were arguing about how to spend their money? Rob used the money for investments. Natalie used the money to buy clothes. How does Natalie feel when she buys new clothes? Exhilarated! Happy! What emotions did she experience? Happiness! Joy! Why? Because, through clothing, she can satisfy one of her deepest affections: to be accepted by others through her image. How does Natalie feel when she can't buy new clothes? Sad, disheartened. She might even get depressed. Can you see it? She experiences the opposite emotions from the ones she feels when she has new clothes. However, despite feeling down, have her affections changed? Of course not! What she loves most (her image) is still there! In fact, her feeling disheartened confirms her love for looking pretty and pleasing others. Loving isn't exclusively associated with emotions; it definitely involves them, but it's something much deeper. Loving something deeply involves the experience of intense affection for something that promises to give me life.

Understanding this is essential to comprehending what deep change is. Loving God isn't about having an emotional moment with him (although it obviously could, and it often should, involve moments like that). Nor is it obeying God even if you don't feel like doing it (although, naturally, there will be times when you must). Experiencing deep change involves transforming the core, the center, of what I treasure—changing my affections!

In Matthew 13:44, Jesus tells the story of a man who walks through a field and finds a hidden treasure. With evident joy, he renounces his possessions and sells everything he owns to purchase that field. Think how ridiculous this situation appears to be. In fact, picture yourself in a situation like this. Imagine yourself selling your house, your car, and all your possessions to buy a piece of land of no apparent value. If you did, your family, your friends, and your neighbors would think, "What's wrong with this nutcase? How can he give up everything for that worthless, worn-out piece of land?" The point of this short parable is obvious. There is a treasure hidden from the naked eye! There is something exceedingly precious!

What the man buying the field thinks is: ***"I've found something worth losing everything for."*** Jesus Christ is that treasure! In other words, I'm willing to set aside my kingdom, my money, and my interests, ***only*** after I find Jesus more appealing than them. This is what change looks like. It's for the deepest part of my heart to find Christ more valuable than any other thing placed before me, including security, success, power, the esteem of others, etc. This is precisely what Paul says in Philippians 3:7-8 (NLT): "*I once thought these things were valuable, but now I consider them worthless because of what Christ has done. Yes, everything else is worthless when compared with the infinite value* *of knowing Christ Jesus my Lord. For his sake I have discarded everything else, counting it all as garbage, so that I could gain Christ* [emphasis added]."

Can you see it? Changing isn't ceasing to do bad things and beginning to do good things. Changing isn't ceasing to disobey and beginning to obey. Even though the outcome of changing involves these things, changing is something much deeper than that. Changing is finding something in Christ that's more precious than anything you have ever tasted. Changing is when the affections of your heart come to see Christ as the hidden treasure. Changing is when he becomes your pearl of great value.

In the book "*God is the Gospel*," John Piper asks a revealing question: ***Would you be happy in Heaven if Christ weren't there?***

> If you could have heaven, with no sickness, and with all the friends you ever had on earth, and all the food you ever liked, and all the leisure activities you ever enjoyed, and all the natural beauties you ever saw, all the physical pleasures you ever tasted, and no human conflict or any natural disasters, could you be satisfied with heaven, if Christ were not there?[12]

I could ask myself the same question today: ***Would I be happy if I had everything and not Christ?*** Think about it for a moment. Imagine having everything you desire most. Everything from the apologies and forgiveness of those who have hurt you to the influence in ministry you've always dreamed of, even the level of education, the title, the job, the spouse, the car, the vacations, or the ideal weight for which you've so longed. ***Would you be happy having whatever you want without having him?***

In 2 Corinthians 4:4, Paul makes an accurate diagnosis of the problem of our heart. In this passage, Paul states that "*the god of this world* ***has blinded the minds*** *of the unbelieving* ***so that they might not see*** *the light of the gospel of the glory of Christ, who is the image of God.*" Can you see what our greatest problem is? Failing to see, appreciate, and treasure the beauty of the gospel. Being blind to the glory of his nature in such a way that we can't respond to it. How do we change? We change when the Holy Spirit opens our eyes, and God's sacrifice on the cross becomes the deepest affection of our heart. In other words, we change when we love him. Or, as we will gradually discover along the way, it might be more accurate to say that ***we change when we love (when we appreciate) the love that he has for us.***

Food for Thought

I wouldn't want to end this chapter without clarifying a concept that I'll elaborate on in the chapters to follow. In defining love as a response, I have emphasized the idea that no one can force you to love. Despite the truth of this statement, I think an important disclaimer is in order. ***Love can't be forced; however, love can be learned.*** In fact, every one of us learns what to love. What do I mean? I mean that, at a certain point in life, I might be indifferent towards something, and as time goes by, I may start to feel a deep appreciation for that same thing. Personally, I had that experience with beer. I never liked it when I was young. I always found it bitter and unpleasant. Even as a teenager, I would drink beer with my unbelieving friends, but I didn't really enjoy it; I did it because I wanted to fit in. For years, even as an adult, I only drank water or Coke. However, something happened when I moved from Argentina to Spain. When I got here, I tried beer again and something changed. I found it delicious! Suddenly, the same drink that I used to find disgusting I now found absolutely delicious. Nowadays, nobody has to force me to have a beer with olives and cheese. I don't do it to fit in with my unbelieving friends. I enjoy it! (In moderation, of course.)

What happened? I've developed a new taste. My appreciation and regard for it have changed. I've learned to love something I used to hate. Love can't be forced; however, love can be learned.[c] We all learn to love new things. In fact, if you think about it, ***we are all taught what to love.*** That's what marketing is all about! It's about teaching you to love and consume things that you hadn't before seen as "beautiful." It's about exposing you to the "virtues" and the "excellencies" of the product. It's about you and I learning to appreciate and value an object. The Holy Spirit is the one who does this work in you and me. The work of the Spirit is to show us the "virtues" and the "excellencies" of Christ. His ministry is to work in us so that we can see him as precious and appealing and appreciate Christ for what he truly is: someone far better than anything this world has to offer. After all, as Matthew 13:45-46 says: "*the kingdom of heaven is like a merchant seeking fine pearls, and upon finding one pearl of great value, he went and sold all that he had and bought it.*"

[c] As we'll see in detail in Chapter 12, since love can be learned, God has given us the responsibility to expose our hearts to those things that influence us to desire him and teach us to love him. Prayer, reading the Bible, fasting: these are some of the means we can and should use to "teach" our hearts to find pleasure in him.

BRIEF SUMMARY

What does it mean to love?
Love is my heart's response to something that is perceived as appealing.

What does loving involve?

1. *Loving something involves seeing the "beauty" in it.*
2. *Loving something involves a response that can't be forced.*
3. *Loving something involves my entire heart (not just my feelings).*
4. *Loving something involves an act of surrender:*
   - *I may respond with a low level of attraction and surrender through my emotions only.*
   - *I may respond with a high level of attraction and surrender through my affections.*

How does what I love change?
My heart will always choose what it perceives as its greatest treasure. That is why my heart will change what it loves only after it finds something more valuable than the thing it already possesses. This is why I need to appreciate the "beauty" of the gospel in order to change.

FOR PERSONAL REFLECTION OR DISCUSSION IN SMALL GROUPS

It's very tempting to skip over this last section of the chapter. Don't do it; stop. Don't ignore what the Holy Spirit may be teaching you through this chapter; don't rush. Take time to meditate on these questions and/or discuss them with others.

1. *In what way has this chapter either changed or confirmed your understanding of how changes take place?*
2. *Sum up in one or two sentences the concepts that had the greatest impact on you in this chapter.*
3. *Do you agree with the statement: "Love is my heart's response to something that is perceived as appealing"? Why? What are its implications?*
4. *Try to meditate on what you truly love. Be as honest as you can. Remember that Jesus loves you so much that his cross has already cleansed you of you most "unclean" desires, so there's no need to hide them. Here is a list of questions that may help you: What discourages you? What makes you angry? What things*

frustrate you? What things worry you? When are you afraid? What things make you happy? What do you fantasize about? What's your greatest dream?

5. *Jonathan Edwards said that to love is to see the "excellence" in something. To appreciate its "beauty." To be able to see its value. Look at the following chart listing desires and try to analyze which of these things you perceive as "excellent." Which of these desires would you say have become the affections of your heart? Why do you think they're so precious to you?*

Superficial desires	***Deep desires***
Money, sex, leisure, ministry, physical beauty, a spouse, a family, knowledge, comfort, fun, goals.	*Approval, security, meaning, acceptance, deep relationships, intimacy, success, pleasure, power, rest, control, a need to feel loved.*

6. *What is the means or the tool that God uses the most in your life to captivate you and make you fall in love with him all over again?*

CHAPTER 4

How Does Temptation Work?

Just as in the medical field, correctly diagnosing the disease is the only way to eradicate the real problem. You can try various treatments; however, they'll all fail if you don't tackle what's really causing the issue. To understand what's at the core of the predicament of the heart, we need to briefly focus on the creation of human beings. Despite being a well-known passage in the Bible, Genesis 1 through 3 has much to contribute in our attempt to diagnose the underlying problem men and women face. Let's meditate on two great teachings that this story leaves us.

My Heart's Design

There are two clear and paradoxical, yet not opposing, teachings that the first verses of the Bible leave us. On the one hand, after creating the man and the woman, God is pleased with his creation and he declares that it's "*very good*" (Genesis 1:31). In other words, there's no defect in his creation. They aren't flawed, mistaken, or damaged people. Yet, on the other hand, they have needs. We see they have a *physiological* need for food, air, water, sunlight, etc. And we also see they have needs that we could call relational or, even better, *spiritual*. God openly declares, "*It is not good for the man to be alone*" (Genesis 2:18). This shows us his need for companionship, for "*a helper suitable for him*." The passage also describes a continuous communion and dialogue between God and his creatures, emphasizing their need for an intimate relationship with their Creator. In other words, correctly understanding the original design of the heart implies understanding that the ***human being was created without defect, but with needs***. Just as Paul Tripp claims:

> Our culture tends to think that we need help because of something we did or something that was done to us—the result of either bad biology or bad personal chemistry. But Genesis 1 confronts us with the fact that ***our need for help preceded sin***. We were created to be dependent.
>
> Trying to live without God's help is to assign myself a sub-human existence.... Personal ministry must begin with a humble recognition of the inescapable nature of our need. If there had been no Fall, if we had never sinned, we would still need help because we are human. A proper understanding of yourself and the work God has called you to starts here.[13]

This need, this dependence, isn't a design flaw. It doesn't result from any error on God's part in creating us. On the contrary. It's part of a plan and design that was like that before the Fall, that is like that today, and that's going to be like that for all eternity. Just as Revelation 21:22-24 shows us, we'll never cease to depend on God: "*I saw no temple in it, for the Lord God the Almighty and the Lamb are its temple. And the city has no need of the sun or of the moon to shine on it, for the glory of God has illumined it, and its lamp is the Lamb. The nations will walk by its light...*" Even in eternity, we will need the light of his glory to survive.[a]

To grasp this concept more vividly, take a moment to imagine you walk into a toy store to buy an RC car for your son. The little car is fiery red. It's in perfect condition: it's brand new and gleaming, and there are no defects in it. However, in order to work, it has to have batteries. Without them, it will never function the way it should. Yes, your son could push it; he could also tie a rope around it and drag it, but for that car to function properly, it needs

---

[a] I'd like to point out that, when I talk about "needs," I don't mean to say that God created and designed *every one* of our desires or needs and that, therefore, they aren't sinful and should be satisfied. Certainly, there are countless inner desires that have their origin in our selfishness and don't fit within God's original plan and design. What, then, do I mean when I speak of "spiritual needs of the heart"? Paraphrasing Pascal, I'm talking about a God-shaped "hole" in our hearts. I'm referring to a state of the heart that's incomplete without a life-giving bond to "the Creator" and that, as a result of the Fall, we're constantly trying to fill with "created things" (a holiday trip, a better job, a new car, a girlfriend or boyfriend, success, or an infinite number of other alternatives). In other words, when I talk about needs, I'm referring to those "deep desires" that we discussed in Chapter 2.

batteries. That's not a defect; it's how the car is designed. It's created that way on purpose. Without batteries, it's incomplete. It needs them.

You and I both need God. You and I both need everything he is in order to be complete. You and I were both designed with a need that can only be satisfied when we're filled with him. As discussed in Chapter 2, we have needs, deep desires that, far from being sinful, are part of God's design for us to depend on him. Let's examine four highly relevant implications resulting from this teaching.

1. *The deep desires of my heart aren't sinful.*
2. *The deep desires of my heart can only be satisfied by God.*
3. *The deep desires of my heart were designed by God so that, by enjoying him, by loving him, I would glorify him.*
4. *The deep desires of my heart aren't the problem; the problem is how and where I satisfy them.*

1. The deep desires of my heart aren't sinful

At the risk of being misunderstood, I would like to challenge you to consider that neither longing for happiness nor trying to fill your heart are in themselves sinful. They are something God created and designed; therefore, we shouldn't condemn ourselves over them. All our needs, both physiological and spiritual, were designed by God to be, either directly or indirectly, filled by him. Seeking our joy and well-being isn't just something we're able to do; it's something ***we can't avoid doing***. It's intrinsic to our nature, and it isn't bad in and of itself.

Blaise Pascal said, "All men seek happiness. This is without exception. Whatever different means they employ, they all tend to this in the end... The will never takes the least step but to this object. This is the motive of every action of every man, even those who hang themselves."[14] C. S. Lewis got it right when he wrote to a friend: "It's a Christian duty, as you know, for everyone to be as happy as he can."[15] As the puritan Thomas Watson stated, "He has no design upon us, but to make us happy."[16] Similarly John Piper says, "The pursuit of pleasure is an essential motive for every good deed. If you aim to abandon the pursuit of full and lasting pleasure, you cannot love people or please God."[17] Of course, as we'll see next, since the Fall, pursuing our greatest good has the potential for turning into something bad. However, we need to state, with confidence and conviction, that there's nothing intrinsically wrong with desiring that our deepest spiritual needs be met. It's part of God's design. We're little RC cars. We need him in order to properly function. In fact, if you think about it for a moment, you'll realize that God is the only being who has no needs, who is entirely self-sufficient, and who doesn't depend on others (except for himself) to be happy and complete. To think about humans as beings who have no needs would amount to falling into the snake's trap and seeking to become like God![b]

Take a moment to consider the following statement Jesus made, "*For whoever wishes to save his life will lose it; but whoever loses his life for My sake will find it*" (Matthew 16:25). What is Jesus saying in this verse? In one of his books, Tim Keller interprets the passage as follows: "If you seek happiness more than you seek me, you will have neither; if you seek to serve me more than serve happiness, you will have both."[18] I believe I understand what Keller means by this statement, and there's some truth to it. Nonetheless, despite the fact that he is one of the authors I most admire and that, in fact, he's the author I quote the most throughout this book, in this particular instance, I differ with him. I believe that the idea that Jesus is trying to share with us could be more accurately paraphrased like this: "***If you try to seek happiness in the world, you won't find it; but if you stop seeking happiness in the world and seek it in me, you will find it.***" How is it different? Read both paraphrases again slowly; the distinction is significant! Keller's interpretation presupposes that I could seek Jesus without seeking happiness, without seeking my greatest good, without "seeking life." This is impossible. As Pascal says, we don't take a single step without seeking this end. On the contrary. *In seeking* Jesus, we're seeking happiness! (We do it the same way that we seek happiness in anything this world has to offer.) *We seek Jesus as the outcome of his becoming more attractive than the world; of our eyes being opened; all of a sudden, we see Jesus as more valuable than money, sex, prestige, or anything else this world has to offer.* I first see that in him there's life and that, contrary to what sin promises, I find that life. Understanding this difference is essential

[b] As we'll see further on, pursuing happiness isn't only not sinful, but rather it's man's greatest duty, because the glory of God is at stake. As Piper claims, "If it is true, that God is most glorified in us when we are most satisfied in Him, then look at what is at stake in our pursuit of joy. The glory of God is at stake! If I say that pursuing joy is not essential, I am saying that glorifying God is not essential. But if glorifying God is what ultimately matters, then pursuing the satisfaction that displays his glory is ultimately important. Christian Hedonism is not a game. It is what the whole universe is about. The radical implication is that pursuing pleasure in God is our highest calling." John Piper, *The Dangerous Duty of Delight*, (Colorado: Multnomah Books, 2011), iTunes, 35.

to being able to understand how the heart works. In seeking Jesus, I'm already pursuing my happiness. Otherwise, I wouldn't seek him! As we learned in the previous chapter, my heart always pursues the thing I've turned into my treasure, whether it's Christ or the world.

2. The deep desires of my heart can only be satisfied by God

Isaiah 55:1-2 offers us one of the most powerful invitations in the whole Bible: "*You there! Everyone who thirsts, come to the waters; and you who have no money come, buy and eat. Come, buy wine and milk without money and without cost. Why do you spend money for what is not bread, and your wages for what doesn't satisfy? Listen carefully to Me, and eat what is good, and delight yourself in abundance.*" The passage is very clear. God not only ***doesn't condemn the thirst in our soul, but he invites us to fill it*** through him. As St. Augustine said, "You have made us for yourself, O Lord, and our heart is restless until it rests in you." The Book of Psalms echoes these words: "*In Your presence is fullness of joy; in Your right hand there are pleasures forever*" (Psalm 16:11). "*For a day in Your courts is better than a thousand outside. I would rather stand at the threshold of the house of my God than dwell in the tents of wickedness*" (Psalm 84:10). Christ himself declared that the reason he came to save us was so that we would have life "*abundantly*" (John 10:10). Moreover, a few chapters later in the Gospel of John, Christ went so far as to say, "*These things I have spoken to you, so that My joy may be in you, and that your joy may be made full*" (John 15:11). The Bible leaves no room for doubt. It invites us to find our greatest pleasure in him. He's what we need the most. As John Piper fittingly declares:

> When I saw the truth that God is most glorified in us when we are most satisfied in him, I was freed from the unbiblical bondage of fear that it was wrong to pursue joy. What once had seemed like an inevitable but defective quest for the satisfaction of my soul now became not just permitted but required. The glory of God was at stake.[19]

What does the phrase "the glory of God was at stake" mean? I would like to ask you to meditate on this very revealing question for a moment: What's my greatest duty as a Christian? Take a few moments to consider the question. Don't rush; meditate on it. What's your greatest duty as a Christian? Someone could answer, "My greatest duty as a Christian is to serve God." Someone else could claim, "No. My greatest duty as a believer is to evangelize;

to carry out the Great Commission." Another person could say, "My greatest duty is to obey him or perhaps read the Bible and pray." Finally, someone could claim, "Our greatest duty as Christians is to carry out God's will and to try not to sin." None of these (nor many other alternative answers we may receive) is the right one. Our greatest duty as Christians is ***to enjoy God.*** Why? Because, as we've seen in previous chapters, ***we enjoy what we love, and the greatest commandment God has given us is to love him!*** (Matthew 22:37-38). In the words of the well-known Westminster Catechism, "Man's chief end is to glorify God, and to enjoy him forever."

Accepting and living this truth is absolutely essential for three reasons. First, because only God can fill the deepest needs of our soul. Just as Psalm 16:11 says, "*In Your presence is fullness of joy; In Your right hand there are pleasures forever.*" Notice the word "fullness." The great takeaway for us as human beings is that when God isn't enough, nothing this world has to offer will be, but when God is enough, we will need nothing this world has to offer. The second reason is that we could do any of the things we mentioned above (evangelizing, serving, reading the Bible, praying, even doing his will) ***without*** loving God. Jesus had already warned us about this in Matthew 6:1. Paul reiterates this in 1 Corinthians 13:1-3. The apostle is very clear in this passage. I could give all my money to the needy and have no love for them! This is the reason why God is much more interested in our motivations than our actions, more in a transformation of our desires than in a mere change of our behavior. And last, because, as we'll look at together in the next section, it's by enjoying God that we value him, treasure him, and cherish him; in other words, we glorify him. As Jonathan Edwards rightly wrote, "God is glorified not only by His glory's being seen, but by its being ***rejoiced*** in."[20]

3. The deep desires of my heart were designed by God so that, by enjoying him, by loving him, I would glorify him.

In other words, God's purpose in creating us with needs was to reveal his glory and goodness by meeting those needs. Their design is meant to reveal his wonderful love towards us in such a way that we ***enjoy, appreciate, value, and love that love***. As Paul declares in Ephesians 1:3-6, his plan is centered on *sharing* his glorious grace with us: "*Blessed be the God and Father of our Lord Jesus Christ, who has blessed us with every spiritual blessing… to the praise of the glory of His grace, which He freely bestowed on us in the Beloved.*"

> God's goal at every stage of creation and salvation is to magnify His glory. You can magnify with a microscope or with a telescope. A microscope magnifies by making tiny things look bigger than they are. A telescope magnifies by making gigantic things (like stars), which look tiny, appear more as they really are. God created the universe to magnify his glory as a telescope magnifies the stars. Everything He does in our salvation is designed to magnify the glory of His grace like this... He (God) created you so that you might spend eternity glorifying Him by enjoying Him forever.[21]

4. The deep desires of my heart aren't the problem; the problem is how and where I satisfy them

The problem isn't our dependence. The problem isn't the inner "hole" we feel. The problem isn't longing for happiness or trying to fill our hearts. The problem is how we meet our deepest needs, our emptiness, and our lack of identity, purpose, meaning, and value. As Paul Tripp puts it: "You cannot understand the world of personal ministry without Genesis 1. It explains that our need for help is part of our design. It isn't the result of the Fall. Human beings need truth from outside themselves to make sense out of life."[22]

Jeremiah 2:13 depicts this dynamic in a clear way. The passage reads, "*For My people have committed <u>two evils</u>: they have forsaken Me [the first evil], the fountain of living waters, to hew for themselves cisterns, [the second evil], broken cisterns that can hold no water.*" Does God blame the people for their *thirst*? Does he condemn them for their *need*? Does God accuse Israel because of the problem they have? Of course not! The two evils Israel commits have nothing to do with their need; rather these evils have to do with how Israel meets that need. The problem the people have, as we'll see below, is that they've abandoned God and they've sought a solution outside of him. As John Piper so masterfully points out, "Nothing makes God more supreme and more central than when people are utterly persuaded that nothing—not money or prestige or leisure or family or job or health or sports or toys or friends—is going to bring satisfaction to their aching hearts besides God... The essence of satisfaction is delight in God."[23]

In another book, and referring to the passage from Jeremiah 2, Piper also states:

> God pictures himself as a mountain spring of clean, cool, life-giving water. The way to glorify a fountain like this is to enjoy the water, and praise the water, and keep coming back to the water, and point other people to the water... And ***never, never, never prefer any drink in the world over this water***. That makes the spring look valuable. That is how we glorify God, the fountain of living water.
>
> But in Jeremiah's day, people tasted the fountain of God's grace and did not like it. So they gave their energies to finding better water, more satisfying water. Not only did God call this effort futile ("*broken cisterns that can hold no water*"), but he called it evil: "*My people have committed two evils.*" They put God's perfections to the tongue of their souls and disliked what they tasted; then they turned and craved the suicidal cisterns of the world. That double insult to God is the essence of what evil is.
>
> So preferring the pleasures of money or power or fame or sex over the "*pleasures...at [God's] right hand*" (Psalms 16:11) is not like preferring caramel to hot fudge [a simple matter of taste].... ***Esteeming God less than anything is the essence of evil.***[24]

If you carefully consider the passage in Jeremiah 2:13 you'll reach a conclusion that is absolutely necessary in order to understand the way changes take place. ***<u>BEFORE</u> I begin seeking pleasure in the world, I've <u>ALREADY</u> stopped finding pleasure in God***. In other words, the reason I try to satisfy my deep desires with the things creation has to offer is that God has ***<u>already</u>*** ceased to be my greatest pleasure. That is to say, ***<u>before</u>*** watching pornography, two things happen. First, I cease to find pleasure in God (the first evil), and then I begin devising an alternative source of pleasure outside God (the second evil) through a superficial desire (sex) that I turn into an idol. Then, I engage in a sinful external action (watching pornography) to try to satisfy my need. Let me give you another example. Before I compulsively begin saving money, several things happen. First, I cease to find security in God (the first evil), and then I begin devising an alternative source of security outside of God (the second evil) through a superficial desire (money) that I turn into an idol. Then, I engage in a sinful external action (compulsively saving money) to try to satisfy my need. That's why enjoying God is so essential! Because ***<u>when</u> we stop enjoying him, we begin pursuing alternative sources of joy elsewhere***. This, as we will see next, is the essence of sin. It's to leave him behind in search of something else. That's where our idolatry begins: in the moment we replace God with something else, with another "god," in order to fill our emptiness.

The First Evil		*The Second Evil*	
I first abandon God	*I'm at my own mercy*	*I make myself into my own god*	*I seek to satisfy my thirst with created things*
The source of living water	*I'm thirsty*	*I come up with an alternative*	*I build a cistern*
I stop appreciating and enjoying him	*I have a deep desire that needs to be fulfilled*	*I begin to appreciate and enjoy creation in an unhealthy way*	*I turn a superficial desire into an idol*

The Problem with My Heart

The second major concept the first chapters of Genesis leave us is that human beings choose to sin because they believe the lie that what they are choosing (something other than God—an idol) will meet their needs and give them more happiness than they have. Understanding this concept has absolutely crucial implications.

Implication #1: I sin by believing a lie

I would like to challenge you to closely consider the statement you'll read next. ***Our heart only chooses what our mind perceives as good or beneficial.***[25] This is such an important statement that I'll type it again so that you don't overlook it. Our heart only chooses what our mind perceives as good or beneficial. In other words, ***we always choose what we are convinced is in our best interest***. No one sins thinking that sin will destroy them. According to Genesis 3:6, Eve decided to sin because "*she saw that the tree was good for food, and that it was a delight to the eyes, and that the tree was desirable to make one wise...*" We may, like Eve, be deceived in making our choice, but we'll always make it based on what we've come to believe will do us good and give us the highest level of happiness. Something similar happens with a fish that is swimming in a pond and, upon seeing a worm floating around, decides to eat it.

Why does he do it? The reason is obvious, he's been deceived. He's seen the worm. This worm looks desirable and appealing. This convinces the fish of a great lie (namely, that the squirmy little creature will meet its need), and so, he decides to respond by (mistakenly) believing that eating the worm will be in his best interest. Naturally, the fish has failed to see the hook, and what once promised to bring him life, ends up causing his death. James 1:14-15 sums up the same process of enticement, "*Everyone is tempted by his own desires as they lure him away and trap him. Then desire becomes pregnant and gives birth to sin. When sin grows up, it gives birth to death*" (GW). Just as John Owen says, "Sin's deception of the mind consists in presenting things unto it in such a way that their nature, causes, effects, or present conditions remain hidden to the soul."[26] Sin's great deception is to make us believe that we're choosing life—something better than our present situation: "a worm"—, when in fact, we're choosing our own misfortune (Proverbs 8:36). As the renowned early modern theologian Richard Baxter said, "the will never desires evil, as evil, but as... seeming good."[27]

It's fascinating to notice that it's in Eden where, for the first time, humans are faced with this predicament that something other than God could met their needs. This leads us to engage our faith in the decision-making processes. Who should we believe? God or the serpent? As we already know, rather than trusting God, our ancestors decide to trust Satan. Instead of believing in the Lord's goodness, in his desire to protect them and in his sovereign love, they believe the lie that there's something better away from God. And so it's clear that any temptation is an offer of life. A means of meeting a need. The key is to decide who we're going to trust.

Let's bring this idea closer to our own lives and reflect on it again: Is the need the problem? Of course not! ***The problem is that we don't believe that God <u>wants to</u> and <u>can</u> satisfy our genuine needs***, and, turning ourselves into our own masters, we run after alternatives that promise to give us what God has committed to provide. As St. Augustine said, "Thus does the soul commit fornication, when she turns from You, seeking without You, what she finds not pure and untainted, till she returns to You."[28]

> Sin not only makes us helpless rebels and idolaters, it also reduces us fools. We tend to love lies, to be self-deluded, to be the most strongest believer of our empty arguments. We are susceptible to the Enemy's tricks and temptations. We live for what is already in a state of decay and ignore what will remain forever. We tend to hide, ignore or be blind to our own sin, while we are obsessively focused on the sins of

> others… If grace addresses the moral results of the Fall (our rebellion and inability) then the truth addresses the noetic effects of the Fall, [i.e.,] sin's impact on how we think about life and interpret it.[29]

This truth is masterfully expressed in *Ephesians 4:17-24, "So I tell you this, and insist on it in the Lord, that you must no longer live as the Gentiles do, in* ***the futility of their mind, being darkened in their understanding****, excluded from the life of God because of* ***the ignorance*** *that is in them,* ***because of the hardness of their heart****, and they, having become* ***callous****, have given themselves over to sensuality for the practice of every kind of impurity with greediness. But you did not learn Christ in this way,* ***if indeed you have heard Him and have been taught in Him****, just as* ***truth*** *is in Jesus, that, in reference to your former manner of life, you lay aside the old self, which* ***is being corrupted in accordance with the lusts of deceit****, and* ***that you be renewed in the spirit of your mind****, and put on the new self, which in the likeness of God has been created in righteousness and holiness of the truth."*

Implication #2: I sin by replacing God with something else

Just as was the case in the Garden of Eden and as we saw in Jeremiah 2:13, the essence of human sin is rejecting God and subsequently replacing him with an alternative. This attitude is a rejection, a repudiation of God's love and goodness. It's an act of rebellion against him. It's a declaration of independence. This attitude eventually brings about two unavoidable effects.

In the first place, it turns me into my own savior. Having rejected God, it's now up to us to see to it that our needs are met and sustained. What was once God's job is now ours. What was once a healthy need of our heart has now shifted into a sinful obsession. This new order in life has profound consequences. Whoever sets themselves up as their own savior, consciously or unconsciously, rejects God's ***sovereignty***, ***goodness***, ***wisdom***, and ***grace***. Naturally, the ultimate consequence of this rejection is the dishonor of the glory of God.

In other words, every time we sin, we say to the Lord, "I choose to control my own destiny (becoming my own master, thus rejecting your *sovereignty*). I choose to accept my own truth as trustworthy and not yours (becoming wiser than you are, thus rejecting your *wisdom*). I choose to love myself better than you love me (becoming better than you, thus rejecting your *goodness* over my life).

I choose to use my power and influence and not yours (becoming greater than you, thus rejecting your <u>*grace*</u> to intervene in my life)."

The essence of sin is independence from God. It's becoming our own god by trying to control what, according to our own judgment, will bring us true happiness. It's hard to find anything that would bring God greater dishonor and denigrate his glory more than this. Just as dependence exalts his person and his goodness, independence robs God of all glory. When we depend on him, we cry out, "You're good! You're wise! You're sovereign!" And, in enjoying his undeserved favor, we're enraptured with his glory; that is, we worship him, we glorify him. However, the opposite is also true. When we sin and try to satisfy our emptiness ourselves, we cry out the exact opposite. "You're not worthy. You're not good." As Donald Carson points out, and as we'll see next,

> "The heart of all evil is... the de-godding of God. It is the creature swinging his puny fist in the face of his Maker and saying, in effect, 'If you do not see things my way, I'll make my own gods! I'll be my own god!' Small wonder that the sin most frequently said to arouse God's wrath is not murder, say, or pillage, or any other 'horizontal' barbarism, but idolatry—that which dethrones God. That is also why, even in every sin, it is God who is the most offended party, as David himself understood: "Against You, only, I have sinned, and done what is evil in Your sight... (Psalm 51:4).[30]

Second, it makes us fall into a state of constant idolatry. The Bible defines idolatry as replacing God. This indeed is the great problem of the human heart.

> What is an idol? It is anything more important to you than God, anything that absorbs your heart and imagination more than God, anything you seek to give you what only God can give... An idol has such a controlling position in your heart that you can spend most of your passion and energy, your emotional and financial resources, on it without a second thought... An idol is whatever you look at and say, in your heart of hearts, 'If I have that, then I'll feel my life has meaning, then I'll know I have value, then I'll feel significant and secure.'"[31]

God has created us for him. God has designed us to find joy in him. God has shaped us to find pleasure in him. To sin is a replacement, a negation of

God. To reject everything he is and wants to be and do in us, and to choose something else, anything else, as a substitute for him. It's exchanging the satisfaction that God offers for the alternative joys that creation does. In John Piper's words:

> Lust is turning away from God to *find satisfaction* in sex... Covetousness is turning away from God to *find satisfaction* in things... Impatience is turning away from God to *find satisfaction* in your own plan of action... Bitterness is turning away from God to *find satisfaction* in revenge... Anxiety is turning away from God to *find satisfaction* in being in control of our lives... Pride is turning away from God to *find satisfaction* in self. Unbelief is a turning away from God and his Son in order to *seek satisfaction* in other things.[32]

Idolatry is when we are persuaded that we must have something other than God to be happy. That's what tempted Adam and Eve; and that's what tempts us, too. It's key, therefore, for us to realize that idolatry is always the *reason* we sin and act in ways that are wrong.

Idolatry is turning a deep desire or a legitimate need into a god. Idolatry is, as we said in previous chapters, the answer to our "whys." Why does the man in our story decide to spend a considerable amount of money on a flat-screen TV? Because he *enjoys* soccer, and in buying the TV, he's loving himself. Why does that same man decide to stay at the prayer meeting when it's time for the game? Because he *loves* his pastor's opinion (above the soccer game and above God), and in staying, he's loving himself. Not going to the prayer meeting seems to be an act of the flesh, while going to the prayer meeting seems to be a spiritual act. Nothing could be further from the truth! That is why it's so important to examine the motivations and desires of the heart. When we only examine outward behavior and leave what we really love unchecked, we'll never get to see progress in our spiritual life.

To sum up, it isn't enough to examine whether our behavior is good or bad; what we really need to examine is what we love, enjoy, or give value to through our behavior, be it good or bad. Our goal should be to *uproot* sin, not merely lop off its visible fruit. Understanding this is crucial and decisive for us to be able to find an effective solution to our real problem.

I would like to end this chapter by reflecting on one last key concept that anticipates what we'll look at in the next chapter. If the problem of the heart was replacing God with an idol, the solution to the problem is to dethrone the idol of the heart and to give back to God his rightful place. As Tim Chester wrote,

> Sin arises because we desire something more than God. Overcoming sin begins by reversing this process: desiring God more than other things. The Bible calls this "repentance." That word means "turning": we turn away from our idolatrous desires and turn in faith toward God.[33]

This is where the gospel fits in! We were, and still are, *deceived* by our flesh, by the world, and by Satan, to live according to what they have to offer and to fill our hearts in the wrong place. This, because of the *lie* we have believed, is why what we need most is the *truth* in the gospel: Christ. He's the only one who can truly set us free (John 8:32). Through his Spirit, he alone has the power to *enlighten* our darkened hearts (Ephesians 1:18-19), to allow us to *see* our idolatry and not become so discouraged at the sight of it that it destroys us (1 Corinthians 7:10). He's the only one who has the means *to help us understand* that what we really need is to run to the Savior and Sustainer of our soul, who's eager and pleased ***to forgive us*** for our idolatry and to give us the ***power*** both to dethrone it and to change.

The table below sums up key concepts related to the needs of the heart, and it anticipates some ideas that we'll further develop over the course of this book.

The Creation ⇨	*We have deep needs and desires*	*We have a dependent heart*	*The pursuit of happiness is not the problem*	*It's a natural thing designed by God*	*It's neither sinful nor a flaw*
The Fall ⇨	*We have an inclination to satisfy our needs through created things*	*We have a blind, rebellious heart that seeks to be its own savior*	*Pursuing happiness in creation is the problem*	*It's a consequence of the Fall and gives rise to idolatry*	*It causes addiction and death*
The Cross ⇨	*The gospel is an open offer to have our needs met*	*We have a heart in need of constant redemption*	*To seek joy in the "beauty" of Jesus Christ is indeed the solution to our problem*	*It's the only thing that glorifies God*	*It transforms the heart and produces life*

As I've tried to stress in this chapter, what motivates our heart sin is "finding pleasure in something" that promises to meet our deepest needs. Understanding this truth will help us deal with the thing with which our hearts really struggle. It will help us accurately diagnose our underlying problem. It will free us from offering behavioral solutions that can't really change what we love. Last but not least, it will lead us to turn to Jesus once again as the solution to our problem. As we'll look at in the chapters to follow, he alone is capable of *redeeming* and *transforming* both non-Christians and those who have been Christians for a long time.

BRIEF SUMMARY

My heart's design

1. *The deep desires of my heart aren't sinful.*
2. *The deep desires of my heart can only be satisfied by God.*
3. *The deep desires of my heart were designed by God so that, by enjoying him, by loving him, I would glorify him.*
4. *The deep desires of my heart aren't the problem; the problem is how and where I satisfy them.*

The problem with my heart

1. *I sin by believing a lie.*
    - *I choose something I perceive as good for me.*
    - *I choose something that promises to satisfy me, but it fails to do so.*
2. *I sin by replacing God with something else.*
    - *This turns me into my own savior.*
    - *This makes me fall into idolatry.*

FOR PERSONAL REFLECTION OR DISCUSSION IN SMALL GROUPS

1. *In what way has this chapter either changed or confirmed your understanding of how changes take place?*
2. *Sum up in one or two sentences the concepts that had the greatest impact on you in this chapter.*
3. *Do you agree with the idea that "seeking joy in God" isn't sinful? Why?*
4. *Read Acts 5:1–11 and answer: Why do you think Ananias and Sapphira lied? Why do you think they gave part of the money? (Remember that it wasn't*

mandatory for them to give, and that they kept part of the money. Could it be that they had more than one goal in their hearts?) What was the lie that Ananias and Sapphira believed? In what situations have you found yourself struggling with the same thing they did?

5. *In your own words, how would you define idolatry?*
6. *Think about your struggles against a particular idol. What lies does this idol promise you that you tend to believe? What do you think is the most biblical way to battle against it?*

CHAPTER 5

What Is the Wrong Way to Change?

What Moves Me to Change?

In the preface of his book *Sex and Money*, Paul Tripp writes:

> It's the afternoon following the morning that I finished the book that you're now reading. The best description of my mood right now is that I am a sad celebrant. ***I am devastated by what this book has exposed in me.*** I am ***grieved by the lust*** that still resides in my heart, and I am saddened by the evidence that I still ***throw away money*** on things that simply don't matter.[34]

Did you notice it? An author who writes about sex and money, acknowledging that he still has deep struggles with sex and money. I'll be honest with you. I sometimes feel like Tripp. I'm writing about how to change, yet I often wonder if I myself am changing.

What's the most common response when a Christian discovers the reality of their heart? What does a pastor do when he realizes that he's struggling with the same imperfections and sin he's just told the members of his church they should abandon? What happens deep down in our hearts when we discover our idolatry and sinfulness?

Without us being quite aware of it, when we're confronted with our shortcomings and blunders, ***our identity inevitably comes under attack***. Our ego gets hurt. Our sense of worth diminishes. Our inner self perceives itself to be impoverished. When this happens, what we do at that moment will be crucial. ***What we believe*** in that fleeting moment (i.e., our theology) will determine the subsequent development of our identity and, consequently, it will shape our internal motivations, and therefore, define our outward behavior.

If our theology says, "***You're accepted and worthy based on that which you do or fail to do***"—i.e., sanctification by works—our motivations, either conscious or unconscious, will lead us to one of four extremes. One possible response would be ***to try to silence***, hide, or purge the evil we've done; that is to say, we'll start acting the right way out of guilt. A polar opposite response would be ***to try to show, prove, or argue that we're not as bad*** as it seems; that is to say, we'll start acting out of pride. Third, there's a chance I might do the right thing to ***avoid the likely consequences*** of my poor behavior; that is to say, I'll act the right way out of fear. And finally, I could change because, in doing so, ***there will be some kind of beneficial outcome for me***; that is to say, I change out of selfish reasons.

Conversely, if we base our theology on the gospel, then our heart will remember: ***"You're accepted despite what you do or fail to do, and you're worthy because of what Christ has done for you."*** Then, after failing and being confronted with our spiritual poverty, our faith will lead us to ***repentance*** and to a renewed ***sense of wonder*** at the beauty of God's unconditional love towards us. This experience, as we'll examine in detail later in the book, will bring about a renewal of our "*first love*" (Revelation 2:4), and that renewed love for Christ will motivate us to act, moved by the glorious grace of a God no words can fully describe. As Richard Lovelace rightly states:

> We all automatically gravitate toward the assumption that we are justified by our level of sanctification, and when this posture is adopted, it inevitably ***focuses our attention not on Christ but on the adequacy of our own obedience***. We start each day with our personal security not resting on the accepting love of God and the sacrifice of Christ but on our present feelings or recent achievements in the Christian life. Since these arguments will not quiet the human conscience, we are inevitably moved either to discouragement and apathy or to a self-righteousness [some form of idolatry] which falsifies the record to achieve a sense of peace.[35]

Motivation	*What I Really Want to Change*	*Unconscious Thoughts*	*How I See God*	*The Outcome*
Guilt	*I change because I want to eradicate a feeling that upsets me*	*I perceive myself as bad, and I want to numb that feeling*	*God is someone I must appease*	*I do things I don't want to do to make it up to someone I don't love*
Pride	*I change because I want to prove my worth*	*I'll prove that I'm good*	*God is someone I should please*	*I do things I don't want to do for someone I think I love*
Fear	*I change because I want to avoid likely consequences of my actions*	*I'll be good so that things don't go wrong for me*	*God is someone I should fear*	*I do things I don't want to do for someone I don't love*
Selfishness	*I change because I want to get something out of it*	*I'll be good so that things go well for me*	*God is someone I must win over*	*I do what I don't want to do in order to get something I don't have*
Love[a]	*I change because I'm loved, and I find pleasure in loving him*	*I'm not good, yet I'm loved by Christ*	*God is someone who loves me unconditionally*	*I do the things I've grown to desire for someone I love*

When Guilt Drives Change

Let's go into detail with what happens when guilt drives us. Let's picture a situation where a husband spends an excessive amount of time watching television. This man is a Christian, and he knows that he's neglecting his family because the minute he gets home from work, he ignores his wife and kids, and he turns on the TV. There's obviously nothing wrong with watching TV, but he desires, loves, and enjoys doing it above all else. One day, this husband goes to a marriage conference, and he finds himself confronted with his own sin when the preacher for the day talks about the importance of spending quality time with our partners. He knows he that he hasn't been doing it and that he needs to change. When the husband returns home, he has a decision to make. Is he going to slouch in front of the TV or is he going sit down and engage in conversation with his wife? Let's say the husband

[a] Although in this chapter we won't do an in-depth analysis of the right way to change, please don't worry. We'll discuss it throughout the rest of the book. I encourage you to come back to this chart after you've finished reading the entire book. You'll see how the truths you find in it will spring to life.

chooses to sit down and talk to his wife. Has he changed? Has he overcome his selfishness? Has he carried out God's will?

If you've read this far, you already know the answer. We must first ask the key question: Why? Why does the husband choose to engage in conversation with his wife? What is it that's driving him to make outward changes? A more careful and honest look will lead us to uncover the fact that he actually did it because he ***"felt bad"*** when the preacher accurately pointed out his sinfulness. This sense of having done something wrong moved him to ***try to purge (by doing something good) a feeling that made him uncomfortable and that he so desperately wanted to eradicate.*** After being confronted with his sin, the husband noticed the condition of his heart; he was disappointed with what he saw and, not wanting to be that kind of person (i.e., not wanting to have a negative image of himself), he decided to make up for his shortcomings through an "act of love" towards the thing that confronted him with his reality.

At this point, we need to raise the following questions: Who is the husband thinking of? His wife? Jesus? The husband is still thinking of himself! It's the discomfort of feeling bad about himself that drives him to do something that looks good on the outside. However, on the inside, he remains as self-centered as ever. Has he engaged with his wife in conversation because something changed in his heart, and does he now *enjoy* and take *pleasure* in talking to her? The answer is obvious: He doesn't.

Let's think about it. Has the husband changed? On the outside, he seems to have changed; he's done something good! However, when we look at his heart (his motivations, his deepest desires), he's still thinking of himself. It pains him to be the way he is. The sense of guilt upsets him. He wants to get rid of it. He found a way of doing that by listening to his wife. But what he loves remains unchanged. Deep down, he continues to desire, love, and enjoy the TV above his wife. Guilt can't bring about deep changes; guilt can't change what we love.

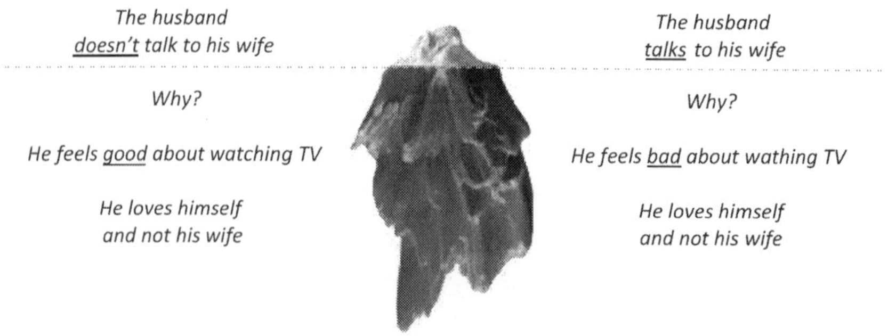

José de Segovia writes in *The Wonder of Forgiveness*:

> In his book *The Trial*, the Czech writer Franz Kafka raises the same question [about guilt]: When the book opens, Josef K leads a relatively normal life. But suddenly, he is arrested. No one tells him what he's being charged with. Everyone is unpleasant and unkind towards him. And so, he begins mulling over his life; maybe he has been arrested for this reason or for that. At the end of the book, a guard executes him.
>
> In one of his journals, Kafka discusses what he meant by this story: [it points to] the state of guilt we find ourselves in. Just like this agnostic Jew, one may not believe in heaven or hell, or the idea of sin, but reckons there is something wrong with us. ***It is as if we were under the impression that we must take an exam that we cannot possibly pass. That is why we constantly need to prove to others that we are worthy.***[36]

We, pastors, preachers, and leaders in general, are not only not immune to this reality, but we're far more prone to fall prey to it than we're willing to admit.

For those of us who regularly engage in public speaking (whether in the pulpit, at Bible school classrooms, or in a small group) it's a predicament we have to deal with almost daily. How? Let's say that we ***value*** (though it would be more accurate to say ***we idolize***) our ability to teach the Bible and communicate clear, relevant ideas to an audience. Let's say that on a given Sunday morning after delivering our message, we didn't quite get there. What will happen? Most likely, when we get home, we'll experience a deep sense of guilt for not having reached an "adequate" level of teaching. It's quite possible that, in our blindness, we'll even attempt to justify our sense of guilt by convincing ourselves that we feel that way because it pains us that the members of our church were unable to grow or to know God better through our teaching.

While it could be so, we must acknowledge the fact that many times our ego pains us much more than the edification of the church—Matthew 6:1 will never cease to be relevant. Sadly, this feeling of guilt will push us to prepare our next message better, and this feeling will only be mitigated, silenced, and "redeemed" by a good public exposition the next time we preach. This, as we'll stress further on, is pride moving us to action and, as this example clearly shows, the person who holds a moralistic theology (i.e., an attitude towards change based on his works) would irrationally shift from one extreme (guilt) to the other (pride) in a matter of seconds. Just as it happened with the disciples at the Last Supper. ***They first argue amongst themselves to determine who is the worst of them, and in the verse right after that, they argue over who is the best. Such amazingly polar behavior within a single verse!*** "*And they began to discuss among themselves which one of them it might be the one who was going to do this thing [to be the one to betray Jesus]. And there arose also a dispute among them as to which one of them was regarded to be greatest*" (Luke 22:23-24; emphasis added).

> No sin can be crucified either in heart or life unless it first be pardoned in conscience, because there will be want of faith to receive the strength of Jesus, by whom alone it can be crucified. If it be not mortified in its guilt, it cannot be subdued in its power.[37]

It's impossible for me to change until my guilt is removed (Hebrews 9:14). I can modify my behavior, I can change what I do, I can make tremendous efforts to be a better person, but ***I can't change what I love***. That being said, there's good news yet. ***I don't need to change to get close to Jesus. I need to come to him unclean and thirsty so that he can change me***.

> Only when we turn away from looking at our sin to ***look at the face of God***, to find his pardoning grace, do we begin to repent. Only by seeing that there is grace and forgiveness with him would we ever dare to repent and thus return to the fellowship and presence of the Father.... Only when grace appears on the horizon offering forgiveness will the sunshine of the love of God melt our hearts and draw us back to him.[38]

When Pride Drives Change

Let's take a few moments to look at what happens when we're driven by pride. A few years ago, a missionary friend and I were chatting, and we came to the following conclusion. She was struggling with serving Christ so that others would praise her for her service—she wanted others to see her worth. I was struggling with serving Christ to feel good about myself—I was out to prove my worth to myself. She was struggling with idolizing acceptance. I was struggling with idolizing success. She was overly concerned with people's opinions. I was overly concerned with my own opinion. Can you see it? Even though she and I have different idols, we both share a single problem: our ego.

Tim Chester has identified three possible wrong reasons for the change: ***to prove myself to God,*** and thus earn his forgiveness or his favor, ***to prove myself to other people,*** and thus earn their acceptance and love, and ***to prove myself to myself,*** and thus feel good about who I am, regardless of whether others recognize it or not.[39]

Let's work through some examples. At one point when I was young, I was going over the biography of Dawson Trotman, founder of a missionary agency called *The Navigators*, and I read something that amazed me. Trotman would share the gospel once a day. Can you imagine that? He would never go to bed without having talked to someone about Jesus! In fact, one evening, he went to bed without having shared the gospel, and upon realizing it, he got up at two o'clock in the morning to do so! The example he set captivated me. I felt compelled to do the same, and the saddest thing was that I did it! I grabbed a calendar and, for months on end, I used different colors to log what I was doing each day. A blue circle meant that I had shared the gospel, a red circle meant that the person had come to Christ, a black circle meant that I had been spending time with an unbelieving friend, etc. I think you get the idea.

I didn't intend to share the calendar with anyone. I did it for myself! I did it so I could say to myself, "Look how much you're growing. Look how well you're doing. Look at your level of commitment. God ought to be satisfied with you." Can you see it? I was sharing the gospel, but I wasn't enjoying Christ! Why? Because ***I enjoyed my works, not his!*** This is what pride does; it mistakes commitment for true love. ***A prideful individual doesn't love Jesus; they use him to their own end.***

Let me share with you yet another rather embarrassing personal experience. A few years ago, I had agreed to meet for coffee with a fellow pastor I was mentoring. As I was leaving my house, I noticed that I was running late (which I frequently am). What did I do to fix it? I started driving with complete disregard for the speed limit. Need I say why? The reason is obvious. I didn't want to be late! But why didn't I want to be late? Because I didn't want my friend to think I was irresponsible. (After all, I was supposed to be going there to "help" him!) In other words, I broke traffic laws out of pride. However, the story doesn't exactly end there.

When I arrived at a roundabout close by the restaurant where we were going to meet, I found myself stuck behind a car whose driver wouldn't dare move forward because of the amount of traffic coming in every time he attempted to go. I waited a few seconds that seemed like forever. Eventually, in a fit of frustration, I pulled half my car up on the sidewalk and drove past the vehicle in front of me. Seconds later, I began having an internal conversation with God. "Lord, you know I was in a hurry. There's this pastor who's waiting for me. The thing is that this man wasn't ever going to move. Besides, this is a very important meeting. You get me, right?"

As I went on trying to reason through my self-justification, I casually looked through the rearview mirror just to realize that the person who didn't dare move was actually the pastor I was on my way to meet. A rush of emotions immediately overwhelmed me: despair, remorse, a desire to turn back time. Then, glancing at the rearview mirror several times over, I earnestly pleaded with God, "Oh, Lord! Please let it not be the pastor! Please, let it not be him! Please let it be someone else!" Then, out of that unspeakable tangle of emotions, I asked God to forgive me for what I had done. Despite all this, moments later, God had mercy on me and used his Spirit to bring light to my mind about what had actually happened. Suddenly, I began asking myself: Why did I pray for God's help? Why did I ask him to forgive me? What was it that pained me? Was it failing to be as patient as Jesus? Was it not having observed the speed limit? Was it my selfishness in climbing onto the sidewalk? Was it the fact that I could have accidentally injured the other driver? Was it the risk of running over a pedestrian? Did having failed to glorify God even hurt at all?

Naturally, the answer to all these questions was the same: Of course not! What did hurt was my ego. What moved me to pray was the fact that the person I was going to minister to had witnessed my sin, and now I'd been exposed. I experienced shame, anguish, remorse, and guilt, but each of these emotions was entirely self-centered; they were born out of love for myself, out of wanting to look good, out of pride.[b] All these feelings are born out of an identity that has been wounded and that unconsciously brings out "good" actions (such as praying or asking for forgiveness) when in reality,

---

[b] An example from the Bible that is very similar to the one I'm presenting here is the case of Saul in 1 Samuel 15. Samuel confronts the king about his disobedience. After offering excuses and blaming others, the king finally admits to his sin, but he doesn't stop loving what had led him to sin in the first place. What had motivated Saul not to kill Agag and the best of his animals was receiving honor before the people (verses 8, 9 and 12); similarly, receiving honor before the people is what drove him to "repent" and to accept that he'd sinned. As we clearly read in verse 30, "Then he said, 'I have sinned; but please honor me now before the elders of my people and before Israel, and go back with me, that I may worship the Lord your God.'" Saul's words openly give away the true motivation of his heart. Yes, he asks for forgiveness, but what motivates him to do so is the possibility of attaining what he truly loves: the glory of men.

there has been no genuine repentance but rather a pseudo-sense of grief or mere remorse.

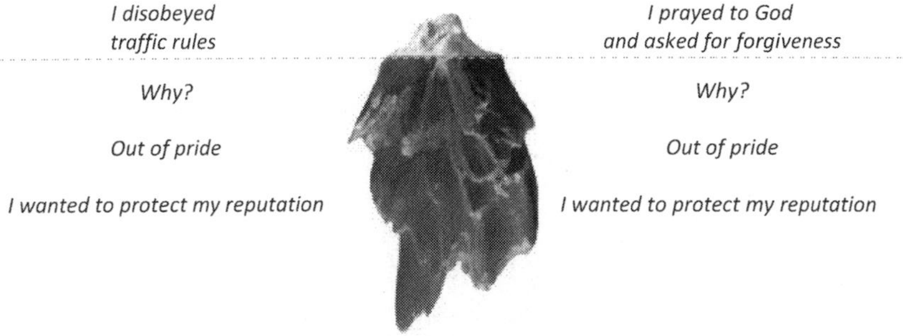

As Tim Chester wrote, "Ongoing guilt makes your opinion the one that matters most; shame makes people's opinions what matters most. Repentance makes God central and accepts his declaration that you're righteous in Christ."[40] In the chart below, you can see a contrast between how a good action (like praying and asking for forgiveness) can be brought about internally by two diametrically opposed motivations:

Remorse	*Repentance*
The consequences of sin hurt me	*The pain my sin causes hurts me*
It's self-centered	*It centers on God and others*
It arises from my emotions	*It's inspired by the Holy Spirit*
It fails to bring about real change	*It produces deep changes*
If I change my behavior, it's because it's in my best interest	*I change because I've been loved and forgiven*
My desires remain unchanged	*Jesus becomes my greatest desire*
I continue to live for myself	*I derive pleasure from living for him*

An Example from the Bible. Did Jonah change?

Let's take a few moments to consider the story of the prophet Jonah. In the first chapter of the book, God asks Jonah to go and preach to the city of Nineveh. Jonah doesn't do it; he openly disobeys God. Let's ask ourselves the question that leads us to uncover his motivation. Why? Why does he disobey God (something external)? The passage gives us a clear answer to the question: Because in his heart (internally), he hates the Assyrians. Jonah doesn't want God to exercise mercy and forgive his enemies (Jonah 4:1-2). He wants them dead.

Chapter 2 is tragicomic, as it's Jonah who is about to die now. The prophet is out in the ocean in the middle of a storm, and God sends a big fish to swallow him and take him back to Nineveh. What does Jonah do? The same thing I did in the car. He prays. He asks God for help because he's thinking of himself. He doesn't want to die inside this fish, and so he asks for help. Jonah 2:1-2 reads, "*Then Jonah prayed to the Lord his God from the stomach of the fish, and he said, 'I called out of my distress to the Lord, and He answered me. I cried for help from the depth of Sheol; You heard my voice.'*" In contrast to Jonah's attitude toward the people of Nineveh, God decides to preserve his life by showing him mercy and bringing him safely to land.

The beginning of Chapter 3 is almost a verbatim copy of Chapter 1. God asks Jonah for the second time to go and preach to Nineveh. This time Jonah obeys; he does exactly what God asks of him. It begs the question, then: If God were only interested in our outward obedience, would we even have a fourth chapter?

Jonah obeyed God, but did he change? On the outside, he did what God had asked him to do, but on the inside, ***did he undergo a deep change, or did he continue to desire the same thing he did in the first place?*** At the beginning of the book, Jonah *hates* the Ninevites. By end of the book his heart remains unchanged! This passage clearly shows us that ***it's possible to obey God without really having changed.*** It's possible to make external changes without actually having made any internal changes. It's possible to do things that are very "spiritual," such as preaching (just like Jonah) or praying (like me in the car), with a heart that isn't actually driven by spiritual motivations. Matthew 6:1 becomes relevant again. We must "beware," examine, and ask ourselves: "Why am I doing this righteous act?" God is after our hearts, not our superficial obedience. That's what Chapter 4 shows us. The question that closes the book confirms this: "Jonah, do you realize you're still incapable of showing mercy? Can you see that you don't feel what I feel? That you don't love the way I love. That you have obeyed my command, but you have not changed."

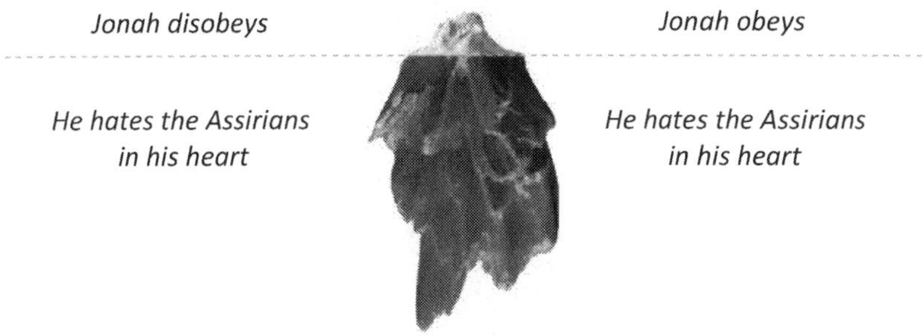

When Fear Drives Change

Let's briefly look at what happens when fear moves us to change. Every one of us, to a greater or lesser extent, has an *inclination* and a moral *education*. From an early age, we learn the law of cause and effect. We quickly learn that if we plug our fingers into an outlet, we will be electrocuted (or disciplined by our parents). If we misbehave, we won't get to watch TV. If we don't study for an exam, we'll flunk it. It doesn't take long before we realize that our behavior has consequences. We find these consequences distasteful, and they keep us in check.

As adults, we're no different from children. Just go for a drive on any highway and watch what happens to our right foot when we approach a speed trap. Just like "magic," we take our foot off the gas before reaching the speed trap, and we put it back where it was only seconds after we drive past it. Why? Because we love traffic laws? Because we're distracted? Because we're trying to prevent an accident? A brief, but honest, inward look will reveal what we genuinely desire. We don't want to suffer the consequences of our infraction; we don't want to get a ticket! The sad and awful truth about this type of motivation is that, just as the example shows, ***we only obey when we believe we might get caught, surprised, or exposed***.

What fuels this type of behavior is entirely self-centered. There's no love of God (or of his laws); there's just love for oneself. There's love for avoiding suffering. There's a love for ***controlling our behavior so that we avoid suffering***. There's love for doing "what's good" so that we don't suffer. Another fairly common example of this kind of "goodness" is our reluctance to confront the sin of others. We see someone do something wrong, whether against us or others, and out of fear of their reaction (fear that they'll yell at us, humiliate us, ridicule us, deprive us of their friendship, etc.), we smile and overlook their offense. Is this love? No. It's fear of the consequences.[c]

When Selfishness Drives Change

Finally, let's look at the way selfishness motivates us. To consider this, all you have to do is think of a young man trying to conquer a girl. What does he do? He invites her to dinner, he brings her flowers, he buys her candies, he talks to her using kind words. Why? Is it out of the generosity and kindness of his heart? Of course not! It's because he's trying to win her over! The key to understanding his selfish motivation is to look at the way he treats that same girl ten years into their marriage. Does he still buy her candies? Does he still use kind words with her? Not likely. In fact, if you take a moment to think about it, and you're honest with yourself, you have to admit that we all got married out of selfishness. None of us chooses the most horrible, selfish, and evil individual we could possibly find to spend the rest of our lives with. No one is that selfless. We all choose the one person who appears to have all the finest qualities. What do we do to win them over? We change! We show the best version of ourselves. We behave the "right" way to get what we so desperately want. Whose best interest do we have in mind? What moves us to "love"? Can you see it? The "flowers" ***aren't the <u>outcome</u> of our love; they're a <u>means</u> to gain their love and to be accepted***. We treat God the same way. We keep trying to win him over. We bring him "flowers" (good works) so that he'll accept us and bless us. Here's my question: How could such works be "good" if they are aimed at my own blessing?

Let me give you another example. Think of a non-Christian woman who really struggles with criticizing others. Her whole family and all her friends, at one time or another, have had to endure her nasty comments. Let's say this woman becomes a Christian. As one might expect, soon after she starts attending church, the members of the congregation begin experiencing the effects of her tongue, and several people get hurt. This leads her pastor to approach her privately and explain the situation, exposing her sin tactfully and lovingly, yet in an assertive manner. Right after their meeting, she drastically changes her behavior. A few months go by, and all the church members can tell the difference. They all arrive at the same conclusion: Praised be the Lord! Jesus Christ has changed her!

---

[c] We'll look at this type of response in detail in Chapter 13 when we discuss how to change through conflict.

She's stopped criticizing others; however, has she really changed? The only way to know if her heart has been transformed is to ask why. Why has she stopped criticizing people? It turns out that she was so embarrassed when her pastor confronted her—no one had ever spoken to her in such a loving, but assertive way before—that she said to herself, "I'll never be this humiliated ever again." And she never spoke negatively of anyone after that. Why did she change? Out of self-love! ***Before, she was selfish by criticizing others; now, she's selfish by avoiding criticism!***

> Moralistic behavior change simply manipulates and leverages radical selfishness without challenging it. It tries to use that selfishness against itself by appealing to fear and pride. But, while this may have some success in ***restraining*** the heart's self-centeredness, it does absolutely nothing to ***change it***. Indeed, it only confirms its power...
>
> Think for a moment of all the ways you can say no to ungodly behavior. You can say:
>
> *No* — because I'll look bad.
>
> *No* — because I'll be excluded from the social circles I want to belong to.
>
> *No* — because then God will not give me health, wealth, and happiness.
>
> *No* — because God will send me to hell.
>
> *No* — because I'll hate myself in the morning and lose my self-respect.
>
> Virtually all of these incentives use self-centered impulses of the heart to force compliance to external rules, but they do very little to ***change*** the heart itself. The motive behind them is not love for God. It is a way of using God to get beneficial things: self-esteem, prosperity, or social approval.[41]

Why Do I Try to Change by My Strength?

I would like to offer four reasons why we choose these wrong paths in order to change. ***In the first place, we try to change ourselves because, consciously or unconsciously, we think that our obedience is what makes God accept us***. The best news in the gospel—not just for non-Christians, but especially for Christians—is that we're sinners, and we'll never live up to the standards of holiness that God expects of us. Through the gospel, this truth, far from discouraging us, turns out to be ***our greatest source of security and acceptance before God***. Since we have never done anything to please him—nor will we ever be able to do anything to please him—for this reason, for this very reason (because we're accepted through Christ) ***we can never do anything to displease him***! The fact that he accepts us is based on what his Son has done, not on the way we may live. Romans 8:33-39 clearly illustrates this truth. ***"Nothing can separate us from His love because there's nothing we have done to buy His love."*** As Romans 5:8 says, what's *amazing*, what's *inconceivable*, what's *unexpected* about God's love is that he loved us "*when we were yet sinners, [and when we were in that condition] Christ died for us.*"

Moralism denies this truth, and it tries to live a kind of sanctification where pleasing God is something we do and not something ***he does for and in us.*** This is the typical Pharisaic mentality: "I've lived well, I have kept the law, God must be happy with me." Throughout the Gospels, it's hard to find a mode of thought that Jesus would stand against more frequently than this. Yet, in our daily Christian lives, it's just as hard to find a mode of thought we trip over more frequently than this.

Second, we try to change ourselves because, consciously or unconsciously, we think that our obedience can meet the standards of holiness that God expects of us. Romans 3:20 and Romans 5:20 let us see one of the most neglected and least preached Christian truths. ***The primary purpose of the law is to show us that we cannot fulfill the law*** and, by showing us that we can't fulfill it, it helps us see how much we need grace! Paul develops the same concept in his famous passage in Romans 7. The more someone tries to fulfill the law, the more they realize they can't live up to it. Who can say that they pray without ceasing? Or that they love God with all their heart, soul, and mind? Who loves their neighbor as themselves? If we were to stop and try to live either of these commandments (or any other) to its fullness, we would realize that we'll never be able to do it. The harder we try, the more we'll join Paul in saying, "*I can't do what's right. Wretched man that I am! Who will set me free from the body of this death?*"

As the story of the rich young man shows us (Luke 18:18-30), even when we think we've done everything right, Jesus confronts us with our hidden selfishness, from which we're unable to escape. That's why the moral line of the story is: "*The things that are impossible with people are possible with God.*" Paul makes the same argument in Galatians 3:24, where he says that "*the Law has become our tutor to lead us to Christ, so that we may be justified by faith.*"

Thus, ***just as we've been faced with our inability to <u>save ourselves</u>, we need to be confronted with our inability to <u>change ourselves</u>.*** God hasn't called us to live a *<u>good</u>* life. God has called us to a lifestyle *<u>that we can't sustain</u>* (Matthew 5:48), and that only Christ *in us* can live (John 15:5). As we'll stress several times throughout this book, the Christian life isn't a hard life to live; ***the Christian life is an impossible life to live.*** Until we fully grasp this truth, we'll continue to try to change by our strength. In Paul Tripp's words: "The law cannot do what only grace can do. The law can *reveal* sin. The law can, to an extent, *restrict* sin. But the law cannot *free us* from sin."[42]

Third, we try to change ourselves because, consciously or unconsciously, we think that our sanctification is our work and not God's work. Closely connected to the fact that we believe we can fulfill the commandments lies intertwined the thought that the work of sanctification within the believer is the work of the believer. Given that we think that we're capable of living God's commandments, we deceive ourselves, thinking that what truly changes us is our work and not his. It's as if someone told us that we have to throw a stone, and we think that our task is to pick it up and toss it. The problem is that we didn't realize we were actually asked to lob the stone all the way up to the moon. It's not in our power to do it, nor is it our efforts that will get us there. Jesus didn't just buy our justification; he also bought our sanctification and our glorification. What we long to be and what we'll become is his work (Philippians 1:6). He's our sanctification (1 Corinthians 1:30). He's the one who changes us (John 15:5). He produces fruit in us (Galatians 5:22). He works in us "*both the will and the doing by His good pleasure*" (Philippians 2:13). We are what we are due to his work in our lives, his efforts, his intervention in our affairs, in our circumstances, and especially in our hearts. As we'll explain further on, this doesn't bring about a passive attitude—on the contrary. God's work in our lives brings forth an enormous amount of new energy, new motivation, and a new power that transforms us into tremendously active people for his glory.

Finally, we try to change ourselves because, consciously or unconsciously, we think that our obedience deserves God's favor in return. Moralism is a way of controlling God through obedience. The underlying thought is: "Since I've obeyed, you now owe me your blessing." As explained by José de Segovia:

> If, like the older brother [in the Parable of the Prodigal Son], you want to control God through your obedience, then your morality is just a way

of using God to get the things you want. In Peter Shaffer's *Amadeus*, taken to the big screen by Milos Forman in 1984, Salieri believes that in his young years he had entered a covenant with God:

"I would offer secretly the proudest prayer a boy could imagine: 'Lord make me a great composer! Let me celebrate your glory through music—and be celebrated myself! Make me famous through the world, dear God! Make me immortal! After I die, let people speak my name forever with love for what I wrote! In return, I vow I will give my chastity—my industry, my deepest humility, every hour of my life. And I will help my fellow man all I can! Amen and amen!'"

With this vow to God, Salieri keeps away from women, he works diligently on his music, he trains many musicians for free, and he works tirelessly for the poor. His career is going well, and he thinks God is going to keep his end of the deal.

Then, Mozart shows up with a musical genius that overshadows Salieri. He has the gift of his middle name, *Amadeus*, 'beloved by God,' yet he is vulgar and capricious, a 'little brother.'

"It was incomprehensible!" Shaffer writes. "Here I was, denying all my natural lust in order to deserve God's gift, and here was Mozart indulging his in all directions—even though engaged to be married—and no rebuke at all!"

So, Salieri tells God, "From now on, we are enemies—You and I!" And all his efforts are aimed at destroying Mozart.

God and the needy were nothing but handy tools for Salieri, who proved himself to be a true "older brother." He has told himself that he is sacrificing his time and money for God and the poor, but in reality, he isn't making any sacrifices. He did it for himself, to become famous, to have success and self-esteem. "I liked myself," he says, "until he came. Mozart." Soon, the moral and respectable Salieri shows greater wickedness and immorality than that of the vulgar Mozart.[43]

What Is the Outcome of Trying to Change by My Strength?

First, the changes are temporary. Imagine a man who's on vacation in a small wooden cabin on the side of a mountain surrounded by a lush forest. This man works for a major company in the middle of a crowded city, and he's been dreaming for months about the peace and quiet he's currently enjoying. One day, he gets up early and goes for a hike in the mountains in what seems to him an almost mystical experience. However, as he looks around, he sees a creek overflowing with trash. He's surprised and angry at first, but then he decides to grab a bag and start picking it up. A couple of hours later, he's done with it. He's tired—quite tired, actually—but he's pleased with himself, and he decides to resume his hike and continue enjoying his vacation. The following day, he gets up at the break of dawn, and he decides to go on the same walk. To his surprise, when he arrives at the creek, he finds the same amount of garbage he had seen the day before. This time, he decides to investigate where all that trash is coming from, and he begins to follow the creek upstream. The further up he goes, the more garbage he finds. Finally, he arrives at the spring of the creek, and with unbelieving eyes, he witnesses two large garbage trucks dumping waste into the stream. A few yards ahead of them, he notices a big sign that reads: City Dump."[44]

One of our biggest problems as Christians is our moralistic tendency to "pick up the trash." When a couple has difficulties in their marriage, we advise them to go for a romantic dinner. When someone is in debt, we offer help in organizing their budget. When someone has weight issues, we tell them to go to the gym. When someone is addicted to gambling, we recommend that they cancel their credit cards. When a person tells us they have anger management issues, we encourage them to count to ten. All of this is picking up trash. What's the result? Eventually, they go back—or rather, we go back—to doing the same thing, just as when I find a speed trap on the highway. No deep change has taken place. There's been no real change. Why? Because we're working in the wrong place. What needs to be transformed is our hearts, not our behavior. Once the heart changes, so will our behavior. As we saw earlier in Proverbs 4:23, the command is to work on our hearts: "*Watch over your heart with all diligence, for from it flow the springs of life.*" The heart is the driving force behind everything we do. This is where all our decisions have their *origin*. That's where all our thoughts, our words, and our actions are born. Therefore, that's where change must take place. For good reason Jesus said, "*The good man out of the good treasure of his heart <u>brings forth</u> what is good; and the evil man out of the evil treasure <u>brings forth</u> what is evil*" (Luke 6:45).

Second, changing by my own strength only brings about a change of behavior, but there's no real change of the heart. In other words, my actions change, but my desires remain the same. I really like the image of a wolf in a cage staring at a sheep. Does the wolf eat the sheep? Of course not! It "behaves." After all, it's caged. It can't do it. However, a deeper question would be: Does the wolf want to eat the sheep?[45] The question isn't whether we, out of fear of man or in order to make a great name for ourselves, do great things for God or avoid committing certain kinds of sin. The question is whether our heart has ceased to find pleasure in the world and it's beginning to find real pleasure in Christ.

Let me use one last example to reflect on the outcome of the moralistic lifestyle. Let us think of a pastor who loves Jesus deeply and who, because of that love, is extremely committed to the work of the Lord. Early in his ministry, this man has been faithful, self-sacrificing, upright, and highly devoted to both his ministry and Jesus. Let's say that, for reasons beyond his control, there's division in the congregation, and he loses half the church membership. After this incident, the pastor is dejected. He's aware of his own feelings, and he knows that, on the one hand, it's only natural and reasonable that he should feel this way; but on the other hand, he's also begun to notice that, even though it's been months since the church split, he's still unable to find some alone time with God. What does he do? He continues to pastor his church out of "faithfulness." He continues pastoring them because he knows it's his responsibility, out of a sense of duty; after all, "we have been called to persevere, even when our feelings don't follow." And so, little by little, the pastor leaves behind his love for Jesus, and he ends up ministering out of obligation, "because he doesn't want to abandon the brothers and sisters who have stayed." The pastor's heart has changed. ***His focus isn't on the joy of what Jesus has done for him anymore, but on what he must strive to do for Jesus.***

Why do we persist in our ministry when, consciously or unconsciously, we've lost our passion for Jesus? Naturally the list of reasons may be unlimited, and these vary from one case to the next and from one individual to the other. Maybe we do it out of the pride that comes from not wanting to fail, out of the fear of being unemployed, out of the love that we receive from others, out of the love of money, or maybe out of the prestige and status that go hand in hand with being a pastor or a leader. The salient though sad thing I want to emphasize here is that we continue to do ministry! Externally nothing has changed, we're still doing the same old thing, but internally, we've lost the one and only source of power we need in our ministry: our joy in Jesus Christ! The pastor in our example continues to preach every Sunday; he continues visiting and counseling his congregation; he keeps meeting with the church elders; nothing seems to have changed. However, in his heart, everything is different. The image below illustrates the concept.

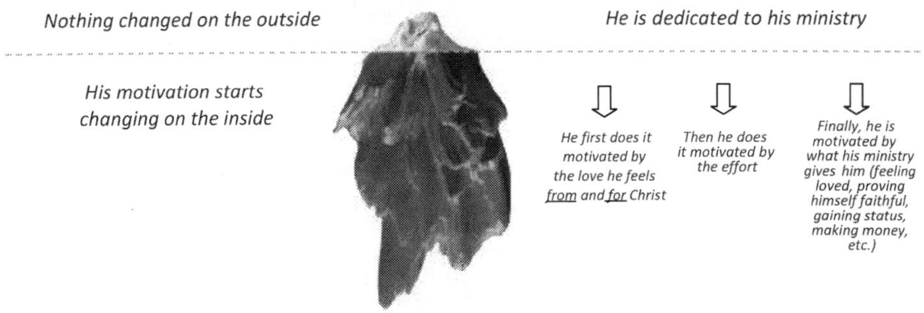

Realizing that the problem of the heart doesn't start when the person reaches the third stage is key. The problem begins at the second stage. When the individual begins to live under a pattern or lifestyle where either duty or effort *motivate* their actions. Take notice that here we're looking at what *motivates* their actions (what's inside), which is not to say that those actions shouldn't demand a physical effort (what's outside). Naturally, an individual who *is motivated* by Jesus' love will strive and give their best, even to the point of exhaustion. However, as Paul says in Colossians 1:29, Christ will produce the labor and the effort, not him. "*For this purpose also I labor, striving according to His power, which mightily works within me.*"

Why, then, does the problem begin at the second stage and not at the third? Because the pastor has lost the source of power in his ministry (John 15:5). Because now it's his strength and not Christ's that drives him. The problem is that, for some reason, Jesus has stopped being his source of pleasure. What should a pastor who realizes he's at the second stage do? He should remember the gospel. What does that mean in this context? Well, it just means he should ask himself: "Why? Why don't I feel love and passion for Christ when I minister to others anymore? What do I genuinely love *today*? What has led me to this lukewarm state inside?"

Answering these questions will allow him to identify his idol, that thing that, possibly without even realizing it, has become his reason for getting up in the morning, his deepest motivation, his breath of life and his source of happiness. In the case of the pastor in our example, self-pity, which is pride in disguise, could easily have been the cause. If you think about it, does God have an obligation to bless our ministry? Is it unfair that someone who has served him faithfully wouldn't have a large church membership? Isn't it God's church, and can't God do whatever he pleases with it?

> It is so easy to confuse your kingdom with the Lord's. It is so easy to tell yourself that you are fighting for the gospel when what you're really fighting for is your place. It is so easy to tell yourself that you're simply trying to be a good leader when what you really want is control. It is so easy to tell yourself that you want to build healthy ministry relationships when what you really want is for people to like you. It is so easy to tell yourself that you're trying to help people understand the details of their theology when what you're actually working to do is impress them with how much you know. It is so easy to tell yourself that you're fighting for what is right when what is really going on is that you're threatened by someone's rising influence. It is so easy to tell yourself that you just want what is best when what you want is a comfortable and predictable ministry life. It is so easy to tell yourself that you want God to get glory when really you enjoy ministry celebrity more than you are willing to admit. It is hard to be in a position of ministry prominence and influence and to know your place... It is here that I need to be rescued from myself. I can change ministry positions and locations, but I cannot escape the thoughts and desires of my own heart. So again, this morning I cry out for the rescue of my Redeemer. I pray that he would fight on my behalf, that his grace would cause me to love Him more than I love myself. I pray that He would give me such a profound satisfaction in his glory that I will have no interest in seeking my own. And as I pray, I know that I will need to pray this prayer again tomorrow, because tomorrow I will once again be tempted to lose my place and to make my ministry be the one thing it should never be—all about me.[46]

Just as the last words in the quote point out, once the pastor realizes this—or whatever it is that he was idolizing and has led him to drift away from Jesus—he should remember the second most significant aspect of the gospel. That is, he should remember the forgiveness and unconditional acceptance of a God who became human to die on a cross for someone who, like this pastor, ***internally*** doesn't love him! For someone who, perhaps inadvertently, loves himself through service.

Seeing the idolatry of our hearts and our inability to do anything about it will lead us to an intense and renewed sense of spiritual poverty (Matthew 5:3). It's in this new state of awareness, of new enlightenment, that we realize once again that the Christian life isn't just a ***hard*** life to live—we've already had our go at it and we've failed—the Christian life is an ***impossible*** life to live. When we come face to face with this reality, ***we see Jesus Christ and what he did all over again, not merely as appealing, but rather as absolutely essential, desirable, and precious***. Once again, as a result of what we received from him (the gospel), we love him the way we should.[d]

This is the reason why we can only overcome an addiction (our idolatry) with a more powerful addiction (Jesus Christ). This is why seeing the beauty of "all of what God is in Christ for us" is the only thing that can truly change our hearts.

> Now [that I realized that living the Christian life is impossible] there was only one hope, the sovereign grace of God. ***God would have to transform my heart to do what a heart cannot make itself do, namely, want what it ought to want.*** Only God can make the depraved heart desire God. Once when Jesus' disciples wondered about the salvation of a man who desired money more than God, he said to them, "*With man it is impossible, but not with God. For all things are possible with God*" (Mark 10:27).[47]

That rediscovery of the beauty of—and our need for—Christ, as we'll show in the next chapter, is the only thing that can help the pastor, or anyone else, stop seeing themselves as a victim and genuinely change. As Tim Keller observes:

> The great pastor and hymn-writer John Newton once wrote about this continuous struggle: "If I may speak my own experience, I find that to keep my eye simply on Christ, as my peace and my life, is by far the hardest part of my calling.... It seems easier to deny self in a thousand

[d] In Revelation 2:2-5, Jesus writes a letter to the "angel" (i.e., *the pastor of the church* in Ephesus) and tells him: "*I know your deeds, and your toil and perseverance, that you cannot tolerate evil men, and you put to the test those who call themselves apostles, and they are not, and you found them to be false; and you have perseverance and have endured for My name's sake, and have not grown weary. But I have this against you, that you have left your first love. Therefore, remember from where you have fallen, and repent and do the deeds you did at first* [emphasis added]." What does Jesus mean when he says that the pastor—and the church in Ephesus—must do "*the deeds they did at first*"? Don't rush your answer! Read the passage carefully. Do you know what Jesus is saying? Jesus isn't saying that he has to change what he's doing—the passage clearly states "*you have perseverance and have endured.*" What Jesus is saying is that he has to *go back to doing those same things the way he was doing them in the beginning: out of love for Jesus*, instead of out of duty and responsibility.

instances of outward conduct, than in its ceaseless endeavors to act as a principle of righteousness and power."

The man or woman who knows the difference that Newton refers to—the difference between obeying rules of outward conduct rather than setting your heart on Christ as your peace and your life—is on the road to freedom from the counterfeit gods that control us.[48]

Three Ways to Live				
As a non-Christian	*Being deceived, they think they'll get pleasure from created things*	*They fail to see the beauty of Jesus Christ, and they think they don't need him*	*Creation doesn't satisfy their emptiness*	*They feel empty, whether they get what they want or not*
As a moralist	*Being deceived, they think they'll get pleasure from striving to do the right thing*	*They fail to see the beauty of Jesus Christ, and they don't realize how much they need him*	*Obedience doesn't satisfy their emptiness*	*They're torn between guilt (when they fail to obey) and pride (when they do)*
As a Christian	*They've been enlightened to see that neither can created things satisfy them, nor can they change their hearts through their efforts*	*They see the beauty of Jesus Christ and their constant need for him*	*Because Christ satisfies them, they can enjoy creation without idolatry*	*Their identity derives from Christ, not from their accomplishments or failures*

BRIEF SUMMARY

What moves me to change?

Guilt	*I want to silence a feeling that bothers me*
Pride	*I want to prove my worth*
Fear	*I want to avoid probable consequences*
Selfishness	*I want to get something out of it*

Why do I try to change by my strength?

- *Because I think my obedience makes God accept me.*
- *Because I think my obedience can meet the requirements of holiness that God expects of me.*
- *Because I think my sanctification is something I do and not God's work.*
- *Because I think my obedience deserves God's subsequent favor.*

What is the outcome of trying to change by my strength?

- *Changes are temporary.*
- *Changes are on the outside alone, and they have no effect on the heart.*

FOR PERSONAL REFLECTION OR DISCUSSION IN SMALL GROUPS

1. *In what way has this chapter either changed or confirmed your understanding of how changes take place?*
2. *Sum up in one or two sentences the concepts that had the greatest impact on you in this chapter.*
3. *Read Luke 18:9–14 and answer: What's the central teaching in this parable? What does that teach us about God's heart? Who do you identify with, the Pharisee or the tax collector? (The aim of the parable is for me to identify with the Pharisee!) If I identify with the tax collector, it's precisely because I've failed to understand the parable! I, too, need to repent of my "goodness" every day, and of my attempts to "buy" God's love through my own righteousness, a righteousness that he freely offers through the righteousness of his Son.*
4. *Look at the chart showing the four wrong motivations for changing and answer: Which of the four wrong motivations do you most identify with? Why do you think you are struggling with it? When do you feel most tempted to fall into this life pattern? What do you think is the solution?*
5. *What does it mean "to change by my strength"? What does it mean to "change in Christ"? How would you explain the difference to a person who doesn't know Jesus?*

PART II:

What Is Deep Change?

CHAPTER 6

Discovering the True Desires of My Heart

John Owen wrote,

> Be acquainted, then, with your own heart: though it be deep, search it; though it be dark, inquire into it; though it deceives by giving its disease a different name, don't trust it. If people did not remain blind to their own selves, they wouldn't stay in the paralyzed state in which they are. However, they try to assign different names to their own frail state. They strive to justify, palliate, or excuse the evils of their hearts, instead of uprooting them and ruthlessly destroying them. They never have a clear and realistic view of themselves. A useless and scandalous life stems from this unawareness of one's own self. How few are those who seek to know themselves truly or have the courage to do so![49]

Our Real Problem: The Desires of Our Hearts and Our Inability to Change Them

Living in the light of the gospel confronts us. The gospel tells us the problem isn't outside of us, rather it's in our own hearts. Our sinful responses aren't a product of our circumstances, our past, other people, or our genes. Our sinful responses are a product of the selfishness in our hearts. However, do we live our lives in this way? Is this the way we practice our Christianity on a daily basis? When, for example, we come into conflict at home with our spouse, at work with our boss, or at church with a leader or another church member, who do we blame for our response? Do we blame our heart's blindness and stubbornness or theirs? Do we remember that the problem is inside us and not outside? That we are responsible for our anger, our bitterness, our criticism and our hurtful words? That the way we respond doesn't come from fighting injustice or abuse, something on the outside, but from our own heart (which means the problem is on the inside) (Luke 6:45)?

Let's think of an everyday life situation that illustrates this truth. It's Friday afternoon, and a wife decides to show her love for her husband by preparing a very special meal for him. It's been a tough week for her. In addition to working in a clothing store, this woman has three young children, and her mother, who lives with the family, is showing the first signs of Alzheimer's. Despite feeling exhausted, she decides to go to great lengths to cook for her husband, while she daydreams about spending some relaxed, quality time with him.

However, when her husband arrives home, worn out from the day's work, he sees his favorite meal on the table and says, "Oh, honey, thank you for being so loving. That's my favorite meal right there.... Today especially, when I'm so tired...today especially, when the game that I've been waiting for is on." A second later, he sits at the table, turns the TV on, and starts watching the game to his heart's content. The wife gets frustrated and disappears to bed early, without even saying goodnight to her husband. When he walks into the room, he asks her, "Honey, what's up with you?" Giving him the cold shoulder, she says, "Nothing!"

Let's analyze the situation from a biblical perspective. On the outside, the wife appears to have done something good. She's gone the extra mile for her husband by cooking his favorite meal. However, let's take a look at her motivation. Why did she do it? Did she do it, as it seemed at first, because she loves her husband and she wanted him to enjoy himself? If that were her true motivation, why wasn't she happy with her husband's happiness? Her frustration, her anger, and the silent treatment give away her true desires. She was unable to find pleasure in her husband's delight. Why? Because in reality (at least by the end of the evening) she wasn't loving him, she was loving herself through him. Are the wife's anger and bitterness her husband's fault? Of course not! The anger and bitterness that she feels are born out of a heart that hasn't received what it wanted: a quiet, romantic dinner.

Paul Tripp provides us with an explanation for the way in which this wife's desire shapes how she responds to her husband:

> If my heart is ruled by a certain desire, there are only two ways I can respond to you. If you are helping me get what I want, I will be happy with you [in other words, ***you will be a vehicle for my happiness***]. But if you stand in my way, I will be angry, frustrated, and discouraged when I am with you [in other words, ***you will be an obstacle to my happiness***].... My problem is not you or the situation we are in together. My problem is that a legitimate desire has taken over my heart and is now in control. This desire has so much power that it is no longer legitimate. It has become an inordinate, sinful desire, because it has grown to a position of authority over my heart. This authority belongs to God alone, who sent his Son to set up his kingdom there. The focus of James's discussion [in James 4:1] is not evil desires (desires for the wrong thing), but inordinate desires (desires that may be right in and of themselves, but must never rule my heart). It is not wrong to desire relaxation at the end of a long day. It is wrong to be ruled by relaxation in such a way that I am irritated with anyone who gets in the way.[50]

Of course, there's nothing wrong with the wife ***wanting*** to have a romantic dinner with her husband. The problem lies in the moment when that desire becomes a ***demand*** (something I must have no matter what). In other words, **it isn't a matter of *having no desires* but of *having no demands*.** The former is a legitimate need; the latter is idolatry.

Outward Behavior	*The wife prepares a meal (something good)*	*The wife gets angry (something bad)*
Superficial Desire	*Why does she do it? She wants to spend quality time with her husband*	*Why does she do it? She wants to spend quality time with her husband*
Deep Desire	*She seeks love and intimacy*	*She seeks love and intimacy*
Inner Motivations	*She has taken God's place by idolizing a desire and turning it into a demand*	

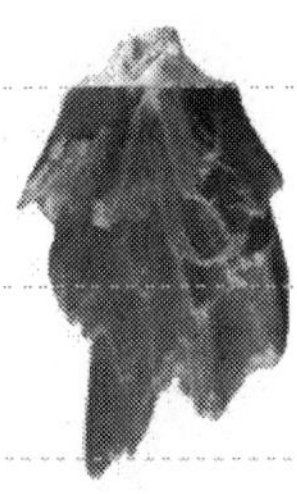

As James 4:1 declares, "*What is the source of quarrels and conflicts among you? Is not the source your* ***pleasures*** *[the inordinate desires] that wage war in your members?*" Lane and Tripp pose the following question:

> What tends to produce conflict in your life? Is it comfort, pleasure, recognition, power, control, or acceptance? Here's how those good

> things can become "selfish desires" [as ***passions***] that lead to conflict.... These things are not sinful in and of themselves until they turn selfish. Comfort, pleasure, recognition, power, control, or acceptance can be blessings to be enjoyed. But ***they become sinful when we allow them to move from blessings to things that replace the One who blesses***.
>
> Comfort drives me to fear hard work.
> Pleasure drives me to fear pain.
> Recognition drives me to fear being overlooked.
> Power drives me to fear being told what to do.
> Control drives me to fear unpredictability.
> Acceptance drives me to fear rejection.
>
> [If you think about it for a moment, ***each of them is the exact opposite of what we desire***.][51]

Where do the wars and conflicts among us come from? ***From that which our hearts love and from that which our hearts fear; from those desires we tend to turn into idols.*** It is likely that the wife in our story started cooking for her husband out of a good place, where her original intent was to show him her love. However, by the end of the evening, ***that desire changed***. Her heart was no longer ruled by the love of her husband but by the love of herself. In this way, her motivation was no longer to love him and to find pleasure in that experience, but rather it turned into something very different. Without much consideration or self-examination, that (rightful) desire turned into a demand (a wrongful thing). At that point, the desire to get what she wanted (a quiet, romantic dinner) ***replaced God as the sovereign giver of happiness of her heart***. The Bible calls this an idol. An idol comes into existence out of a legitimate need that is elevated to the place of a ***saving demand***. It's leaving God behind (who has promised to meet all our needs) for a substitute (in this case a special dinner) that promises to give us the same thing or an even better one than God does. This process of elevating (or idolizing) our desires, of turning them into an urgent need or a demand, is much more commonplace and subtle than we would like to admit. According to Paul Tripp,

> This happens to us more than we would tend to think. The desire for success at work becomes a demand for appreciation from the boss. The desire to have enough money to pay the bills morphs into a lust for affluence. The desire to be a good parent becomes a desire to have children who enhance my reputation. The desire for friendship

> becomes a demand to be accepted and anger when I'm not. What was once a healthy desire *takes control*, and when this happens, the desire that originally motivated me changes into something very different. Rather than being motivated by a love for God and my neighbor, I am motivated by a pursuit of what will bring me pleasure, and I am angry at anyone who stands in the way.[52]

Let's consider the major "exchange" that took place in this wife's case. The same person who had been the object of her love suddenly becomes the object of her anger! Was the husband to blame for the wife's anger? Of course not! The wife's anger originated from idolizing a desire of her heart. From replacing God with her husband. From believing the lie that something created can give her what, in reality, only the Creator can. In doing so, the desires of her heart ended up ruling over her by replacing God as the ruler of her heart.

Can you see it? We fall into idolatry when we do two things, or rather when we "deify" two things: creation and ourselves. On the one hand, we take something good that God has given us (sex, money, a romantic dinner, etc.) and elevate it to the status of a god. How? By internally concluding: "If I have this, it will give me true life. This is the source of my well-being." In other words, we make something created into our god and savior.

On the other hand, we reject the sovereignty and goodness of God, and we take control of our future and good fortune. How? By internally concluding: "This is better than what God has to offer. I know the source of my well-being better than God does." In other words, we make ourselves our own god and savior.

Do you remember Jeremiah 2:13? The problem is twofold: to have abandoned God and to have sought a new source of life-giving water. Paul Tripp describes this abandonment of God and elevation of our desires as "spiritual adultery":

> It is hard for us to hold our desires loosely. Instead, they tend to take hold of us. Our desires tend to get elevated to a position where they should never be. Here is what happens: A ***desire*** battles for control until it becomes a ***demand***. The ***demand*** is then expressed (and usually experienced) as a ***need***. ("I need sex." "I need respect.") My sense of ***need*** sets up my *expectation*. ***Expectation*** when unfulfilled leads to

> ***disappointment*. *Disappointment*** leads to some kind of ***punishment***. "You want something, but you cannot get it. You quarrel and fight." So when James says, "You adulterous people," he is not changing the subject. He is saying something very significant. Adultery takes place when I give the love I have promised one person to someone else. Spiritual adultery occurs when I give the love that belongs to God alone to something or someone else. James is saying that ***human conflict is rooted in spiritual adultery***![53]

The key question we should ask ourselves in every situation is: ***Who am I loving through this action?*** Or, if you'd rather, who or what's ruling in my heart right now? Yes, we've done a "good" thing. We've made sacrifices for our spouse, the church, or a coworker, yet who were we loving in doing so? Them? Christ? Ourselves? What motivated us to do what we did?

To overlook the motivations of the heart is to ignore the most significant aspect of the Christian life. They're the ***reason*** we live the way we do. They're what ***causes*** us to act the way we do. They're what ***produce passion for God or idolatry***. As Tim Keller says,

> The Bible does not consider idolatry to be one sin among many.... Rather, idolatry is always the reason we ever do anything wrong. Why do we ever fail to love or keep promises or live unselfishly? Of course, the general answer is "because we are weak and sinful." The specific answer is always that ***there is something besides Jesus Christ that you feel you <u>must</u> have to be happy***, that is more important to your heart than God, and that is enslaving the heart through ***inordinate desires***. For example, we would not lie unless first we had made something—human approval, "face," reputation, power over others, financial advantage—more important and valuable to our hearts than the grace of God. So ***the secret to change is to identify and dismantle the basic idols of the heart*** [emphasis added].[54]

Focusing on the motivations and desires of the heart helps us see that the main human problem isn't our behavior, but rather our idolatry. Our behavior is a consequence of the thing that is the "god" of our heart; of the thing that is our greatest treasure. As Jesus pointed out several times, our actions (something on the outside) are the outcome of what we love and treasure (something on the inside). "*And He was saying, 'That which proceeds out of the man, that is what defiles the man. For from within, out of the heart of men, proceed the evil thoughts, fornications, thefts, murders, adulteries, deeds of coveting and wickedness, as well as deceit, sensuality, envy, slander, pride, and foolishness. All these evil things proceed from within and defile the man*" (Mark 7:20-23; emphasis added).

Meditating on this reality confronts us with an even more significant problem. If it's true that idolatry is related to our desires (desires we love to such an extent as to turn them into demands), we're now facing a new and much deeper predicament. As we've seen in detail in Chapter 3, we can't change what we desire. We can't force ourselves to change what we love, treasure, and value because love is a response. It's an uncontrollable response towards something that is perceived as attractive; towards something that shows itself to be the greatest good for our soul; towards something that claims to be able to satisfy our needs and to give us absolute happiness—in the case of the wife, a dinner.

If we want to properly understand how deep changes take place, ***it's essential that we grasp how important it is that we can't change what we love. Love is a response that we can't force!*** Think about it for a moment. When two of our kids are arguing heatedly, we can force them to stop arguing (i.e., change their behavior) but we can't force them to feel conviction of sin (i.e., to recognize their idolatry). We can force them to be quiet and listen to one another (appealing to guilt, threats, pride, fear, or physical discipline) but we can't force them to understand each other and put the other's interests first. We can ask them to say word for word how they've wronged their young sibling, but we can't force them to feel pain in the face of their own sin. We can demand that they ask for forgiveness, but we can't force them to not be bitter or to feel at peace with each other. ***We can't change what really needs to be changed.*** Not in our children, not in our spouse, not in ourselves! We can't change what we *desire.*

This leads us to rediscover a precious truth. Since we can't change what our hearts love, ***sanctification has to be a gift!*** God's work and not ours! A divine transformation! A supernatural achievement! We can force others (and even ourselves) to make superficial changes. We can ask people to go to church on Sundays, to give their offering, to read their Bible, to pray, but we can't ask them to change what they love.

Conversion is a change in our desire; it's to no longer desire sin and to begin to desire Christ. ***So is sanctification!*** We were incapable of bringing about the first one by ourselves, nor are we capable of producing the second one. That's right; ***justification is a gift***, and ***so is sanctification***. Think about it for a moment; ***our fundamental problem isn't a matter of ignorance;*** we know perfectly well what we have to do (in the case of the woman, it's not getting angry with her husband). ***Our fundamental problem is a matter of capabilities:*** we lack the *desire*—that is, the *power* to do it. Knowing what we have to do, we're *unable to* do it (Romans 7:18-19). And we can't do it because we can't change what we love.[a]

When we see this, when we're confronted with the true state of our hearts, we have two choices. As we saw in Chapter 5, we can keep trying to change by our strength, or we can humbly accept our condition and allow the gospel to change us. ***What do we have to do to change?*** The same thing we did the day we converted. ***We must stop trying. We must come before Christ, as we did on the day of our conversion, with empty hands.*** With nothing to offer. We must stop blaming the world for our sinful responses and our discontent, and we must accept the fact that we are the spiritual adulterers who constantly exchange the Kingdom of God for our own kingdom.

When we view this reality with a new, deep intensity (that is, with conviction of sin and contrition—experiences that are a gift and that only the Holy Spirit can bring about), we then realize that we need both of these "gifts" (or treasures) that the gospel has to offer: ***forgiveness*** (not just for our *wrongdoings*, but for *loving something that puts distance between God and us*) and ***power*** (not just for *doing good*, but in order *to love God by doing so*). When, as the title of this chapter says, we discover the true desires of our hearts, we'll then realize that we need the gospel today just as we did the first day.

[a] Tim Chester says, "Sometime people say conversion is all God's work, but sanctification is a cooperation between us and God. Neither statement is entirely true. Conversion is all God's work, but we have a responsibility *to respond with faith and repentance*. But it turns out that faith and repentance are also God's work in us, his gift to us. God opens blind eyes. God grants repentance (Mark 8:18–30; 2 Corinthians 4:4–6; 2 Timothy 2:25). That's why conversion is entirely an act of God's grace. But, at God's initiative and with God's help, we're involved. And it's the same with sanctification. Sanctification is God's work. But we're not passive. We have to *respond with faith and repentance*. And again it turns out that faith and repentance are God's work in us." Tim Chester, *You Can Change*, p 60. As Paul puts it in 1 Corinthians 15:10, *"But by the grace of God I am what I am, and His grace toward me did not prove vain; but I labored even more than all of them, yet not I, but the grace of God with me* [emphasis added]." Our part in growing is to appropriate for ourselves—through faith and repentance—the grace that God wants to impart to us. In other words, to change, not by our strength, but by his Spirit.

What Can We Do to Change Our Hearts?

What can we do to bear fruit? Let's meditate on Jesus' response without rushing. "***Nothing***."[b] Please, don't get frustrated with me if this shocks you; these are not my words, but Jesus' words. ***Without him***, we can do ***nothing***. "*I am the true vine, and My Father is the vinedresser. Every branch in Me that does not bear fruit, He takes away; and every branch that bears fruit, He prunes it so that it may bear more fruit. You are already clean because of the word which I have spoken to you. Abide in Me, and I in you. As the branch cannot bear fruit of itself unless it abides in the vine, so neither can you unless you abide in Me. I am the vine, you are the branches; he who abides in Me and I in him, he bears much fruit, for apart from Me you can do nothing*" (John 15:1-5; emphasis added).

What does Jesus mean when he says that "*we cannot bear fruit on our own*"? What does the phrase "*you can do nothing*" mean? To accurately understand what Jesus is saying, we need to correctly understand the immediate context of the passage. In the first place, we have to begin by noticing that Jesus is addressing Christians; he's addressing believers, converted people. Not only that, but Jesus is also teaching on how to change. He's describing how a Christian can produce "fruit."

What does the word "fruit" mean in this context? Some scholars believe he's talking about "the fruits of the ministry"; in other words, fruit in the form of people or new believers. Others claim that Jesus is talking about the "fruit of the Spirit"; that is to say, changes in our character (Galatians 5:22-23: love, joy, peace, patience, etc.). Which of the two interpretations is the correct one? In my opinion, both of them are! Jesus is talking about a person can be capable of living both the "Great Commandment" and the "Great

[b] As we will return to in Chapter 12, the claim that humans are incapable of doing anything to change their own hearts shouldn't be misconstrued as God having failed to provide the necessary means for the Spirit to bring about our transformation. These means that we call "means of grace," (for instance, the spiritual disciplines, the church, confrontation, the presentation of His Word, our trials, etc.) are precisely that: means. Just as preaching is the means by which the unbeliever hears the gospel (Romans 11:14) and, without it, it would be "impossible" (or at least unusual) for a person to come to Jesus, the means of grace are instruments for the believer to be exposed to the gospel all over again. They can do nothing for us in and of themselves, but they can draw us closer to the One who can. Thus, the fact that God enlightens humans to see his beauty and glory doesn't mean that the natural faculties (such as the mind, reason, imagination, etc.), and the various external means (such as those mentioned above) are not used by God to achieve his goal. As Jonathan Edwards says, "The mind cannot see the excellency of any doctrine, unless that doctrine be first in the mind; but the ***seeing of the excellency*** of the doctrine may be immediately from the Spirit of God; though the conveying of the doctrine or proposition itself may be by the Word [or any other means that God may find fit to use]." José Moreno Berrocal, Jonathan Edwards, Pasión por la gloria de Dios (*Passion for the Glory of God*), Barcelona: Andamio Publications, 2008, p 71. (Although it would be ideal for you to gradually discover the way this dynamic works, if you'd like, you can take a look at the iceberg figure in Chapter 10 which clearly explains what you are and are not capable of doing.)

Commission"! If I had to sum it up in one sentence, I would say that ***fruit is everything that Christ wants to produce in an individual and everything that only he is capable of producing in them***— that is why it involves both. That is what the passage shows us. That is why, in the parable, he is the vine!

If Matthew were writing this passage, he'd say that ***our acts of justice done with a pure heart are the fruit.*** Do you remember Matthew 6:1? "*Beware of practicing your righteousness before men to be noticed by them; otherwise you have no reward with your Father who is in heaven.*" Matthew would say that "bearing fruit is offering, praying and fasting with the right motivation." Bearing fruit is doing what you do without a hidden agenda, without self-love, without trying to satisfy a selfish desire, without falling into idolatry. Bearing fruit is doing what you do, enjoying the Father, thinking of him. (Bearing fruit is the wife in our story fixing dinner with selfless love for her husband.) If it were Paul writing John 15, he'd say that "bearing fruit is doing whatever you do, whether it is speaking in angelic tongues, giving money, prophesying, etc., with a genuine love for others" (See 1 Corinthians 13:1-3). Although I'll further elaborate on this idea later on, I would put it this way: ***fruit is something good done with a good motivation***. It is showing true love in everything I do (1 Timothy 1:5).

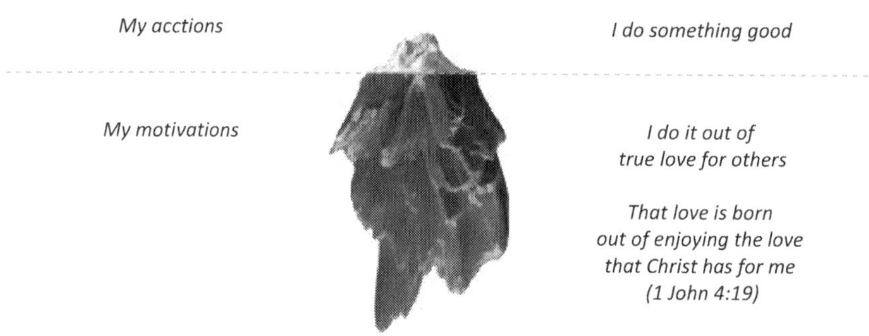

What does Jesus say about ***this kind*** of fruit? Jesus says that I can ***only bear this kind of fruit if I remain in him; if he's the vine, if I'm connected to him.*** Look carefully at the passage. What does the vine represent as an image? What does John mean when he says that Jesus has to be a "vine" and I a simple "branch"? That it is ***he who must give me the power to bear fruit***. In other words, he must provide me with the ability to live in a way that I can't. John 15 is very clear: fruit is something that ***only*** Jesus can produce in me. He must be involved in order for it to happen! I can't do this on my own power.

The reason this is so hard for us to understand is that we still think we're capable of living the way God expects us to live. But it isn't just difficult to live the Christian life; it's impossible! Christianity isn't a self-help program. Christianity is a process of continually rediscovering that, ***without Christ, I can't grow***.

Let me ask you a question. What would be your worst nightmare? Take a moment to think about it before you read on. What's the worst that could happen to you? If we're true Christians, the answer to that question should be the same for each one of us. It will surely surprise you but consider it carefully. "My worst nightmare would be for God to take the Holy Spirit away from me." (Yes, I know. For a true believer this is impossible; I'm just asking you to use your imagination.) Think about it this way: If tomorrow you woke up without the Holy Spirit, would you notice it? Would your family notice it? Would your friends notice that you've "lost" God? Would they ask you at work what happened to you and why you're such a different person?

Consider yet another hypothetical scenario. Let's say God becomes human again, and you meet him. After introducing himself and amazing you with miracles that confirm beyond a shadow of doubt that it is him, God moves in with you to live in your house. This way, you have the privilege of having breakfast and lunch with him by day and dinner at night. During the day, he teaches you beautiful things, and as months go by, you build up an amazing friendship. Your spiritual life has never had such a level of depth. However, after three years, he tells you, "*It is to your advantage that I go away*" (John 16:7; emphasis added).

Surely, at that moment, you (like the disciples did) will think, "To my advantage? How is it *to my advantage* for you to leave? What could be better than God himself becoming human and living with me every day, teaching me, praying with me, and helping me grow? That's impossible! There's nothing better than that." The answer is fascinating. There is something better! The presence of the Holy Spirit inside our hearts. That's what John 15 is about. It's about ***having God INSIDE us***! Living "connected" to the vine is what Paul would call "living filled with the Spirit." What John is saying is that you can't live the Christian life. ***You need Christ to live like Christ***. The only way to bear fruit and change is through the Spirit of Christ. Yes, it's true; the Spirit will never be taken away from us. However, the Spirit can be "grieved," "suppressed," "diminished." How? Simple. It can be summed up in one statement: ***by trying to live life without the Spirit.***

Jesus said, "*Apart from Me, you can do nothing.*" According to Jesus, there's not a single commandment that I can live without him. There isn't a single change I could make without his help. Yet we keep trying. Imagine God asking me to play basketball like LeBron James. Not to just dribble and score once in a while, but to have his ability and play basketball the way he does. The outcome is foreseeable. I could quit my job, spend my whole life training, hire the best coaches in the world to teach me all the best techniques, and I would still never play like him! I just don't have what it takes! The only way I could play like LeBron is if LeBron, in some supernatural way, gets inside my body and "it's no longer I who play, but LeBron plays in me." (This is my paraphrase of Galatians 2:20.) That's precisely what the image of the vine represents. I can't live the way Christ lives, but he can do it for me. How does he do that? Through his Spirit.

So what does "you can do nothing" mean? If you think about it for a moment, the statement sounds somewhat illogical and contradictory. There are an endless number of things we can do without Christ! We can get out of bed every morning without Christ. We can brush our teeth, do our hair, have breakfast. We can drive to work, talk to our coworkers, and work in the office without being bothered. We can watch TV, play chess, and go shopping. Do we need to have Christ within us to do these things? Of course not! Can't a Muslim or an atheist do any of them?

In fact, if we dig deeper, we can do a number of really good and "spiritual" things without him. Matthew 6:1 reminds us that we can give our offering, we can pray, and we can fast without him. When Jesus says, ***"apart from Me you can do nothing," he doesn't mean that I can't do good things; he means that I can't do anything out of pure love, out of true love, with good motivations.*** According to John's reasoning, it means that I can't bear the kind of "fruit" that glorifies God (John 15:8).

In other words, I can't do something that God looks at and says, "This thing Nico has done is amazing! It's worthy of my approval! He's full of selflessness and love! He makes me look good. He glorifies me." Why? "*God sees not as man sees, for man looks at the outward appearance, but the Lord looks at the heart*" (1 Samuel 16:7; emphasis added). And what's the state of my heart? Dirty! Like the wife's heart in our story, even when cooking a meal for someone I love, I love myself! One of the most devoted pastors who ever lived wrote:

> I do not know what you may think, but I can say that I cannot pray but I sin. I cannot preach to you or any others but I sin. I can do nothing without sin; and, as one says, my repentance needs to be repented of, and my tears to be washed in the precious blood of my dear Redeemer. Our most accomplished deeds are no different from our extraordinary sins. Before there is peace in your heart, you must first be made sick of your past and current sin, confessing the uselessness of your righteousness and the lack of valor in your accomplishments. You must be filled with deep conviction of your own inability. That is the last idol taken out of our heart. The pride of our hearts will not let us surrender to the righteousness of Jesus Christ. But unless we feel this deficiency we would never draw near to Jesus Christ. There are many who say, "Well, we believe all this," but there is a great difference between what one says and what one feels. Have you ever felt the need of a Redeemer? Have you felt at some point that you are missing Jesus because of the inadequacy of your own righteousness? And can you now say from your heart, "Lord, you may justly damn me for the inadequacy of my good works?" If you have not felt at any point this great truth, you can speak of personal peace, but it won't be true peace.[55]

John 15:4 says that ***you cannot bear fruit on your own; do you truly believe this?*** Do you genuinely live your Christian life consciously aware of the fact that you can't change? Are you aware that the fruit that God expects of you is **<u>IMPOSSIBLE</u>**? Jesus says plainly that you can't do anything (without him). The situation in which you and I find ourselves is as if we were disabled and couldn't walk, and someone told us, "Get up!" What would your response be? Mine would be, "Are you out of your mind? Can't you see the wheelchair? Don't you see my condition? ***I can't do what you're asking of me!***" That should be our response every time we think of changing or read any command in the Bible! Can you see it? Every time you read a commandment or teaching in the Bible, your reaction should be similar to that of a paralyzed person. "I can't do it!"

However, what is our response? We do just the opposite! We say, "I'll give it a try. I'll do my best to deliver. I'll give it my best shot. And then, when we fail, we are disappointed, even though Jesus had already told us, "**YOU CAN'T LIVE IT**." Why does this happen? Because we're putting our trust in the wrong person. I am putting my trust in me instead of seeking the power of Jesus, as John 15 says. ***Fruit, real change, is an <u>OUTCOME</u>. Deep change is the <u>result</u> of what he accomplishes in us, not what we do for him.***[c]

What the Gospel Says

Isn't it remarkable that to be a Christian, I have to stop being a good person? Have you carefully read what I wrote? To be a Christian, I have to stop trying to be good! Isn't that what we tell people we are trying to evangelize? After all, isn't that the reason Jesus died in the first place? Didn't Jesus say multiple times, "*It is not those who are healthy who need a physician, but those who are sick; <u>I did not come to call the righteous</u>, but sinners*"? As Paul says, if one could become righteous by obeying God, his death would be unnecessary (Galatians 2:21)! ***For Jesus, your sin isn't your biggest problem. For Jesus, your <u>goodness</u> is your biggest problem.*** Your attempts to change without his help. John 3:16 says I can't save myself. John 15:5 says I can't change myself. For either of them, what I need is Christ!

Let me shake you up and test your convictions. Think about what Jesus would say in a hypothetical situation where a pastor watches pornography on a Saturday night, just one day before preaching his message! Here's my question to you: What should this pastor do? Should he resign his position as a pastor? Should he publicly confess what he has done? Should he stop preaching?

Let me answer this question with yet another question: What would you tell a non-Christian friend who says they can't believe Jesus forgives them for having watched pornography the night before? Maybe you'd say something like, "*It is not those who are healthy who need a physician, but those who are sick; <u>I did not come to call the righteous</u>, but sinners*" (Mark 2:17; emphasis added). How does an unbeliever typically respond when we tell them this (i.e., when

[c] Consider the following question, what does the famous phrase "living in the flesh" mean? It's possible that the first thing that comes to your mind when you think of an answer is someone whose sin is obvious or someone who is doing something they shouldn't. While it's true that Galatians 5:19 speaks to what the "works of the flesh" are (and in this respect it does make reference to improper behavior), from a biblical standpoint, "living in the flesh" is something else. ***<u>A person living in the flesh is one who is trying to change themselves by their own strength</u>.*** They're someone who lives their Christian life disconnected from the Spirit. Galatians 3:2-3 reads, "*This is the only thing I want to find out from you: did you receive the Spirit by the works of the Law, or by hearing with faith? Are you so foolish? <u>Having begun by the Spirit, are you now being perfected by the flesh</u>?*" (emphasis added). Can you see it? The phrase "living in the flesh" describes a person who has started to live the Christian life through the Spirit of God, and who is now trying to live it by their own strength. ***They are obedient!*** They're someone who is trying to advance their spiritual life without the Holy Spirit! They're someone who is doing what they "must do," but they're doing it independently from God. What is "living in the flesh"? ***<u>It's everything I do without depending on him</u>.*** I really like responding to this question through an equation. ***Living in the flesh = Me, minus the work of the Holy Spirit.***

we first share the gospel with them)? "Are you telling me I don't have to do ***anything*** to be saved? Are you telling me that God will forgive me for ***everything*** I've done simply by believing in what Jesus did *without doing anything else*?" Can you see it? To be saved, and to change, we have to "do" the same thing. We have to accept who we are: deeply selfish, proud, and self-centered people, and we have to appropriate for ourselves by faith what Christ has done for us. We have to experience the gospel all over again!

At least with our mouths, most Christians in the world affirm that both justification and sanctification are achieved by grace alone.[d] That is, they are a gift from God that we receive through repentance and faith. However, is that what our *praxis* shows? Think about it for a moment. What does a person have to do to be justified? They have to *accept* their sinful condition, *recognize* the reality that their works can't save them, *put their trust* in the cross of Jesus Christ and *receive* by faith the gift of what he has done for them. What does a person have to do to be sanctified? Exactly the same thing! They have to *accept* their sinful condition, *recognize* the reality that their labors can't change them, *put their trust* in the cross of Jesus Christ and *receive* by faith the gift of what he has done *for* them and of what he wants to do *in* them through his Spirit.

Justification is a gift, and so is sanctification! ***It is accepting what the Spirit of God wants to do in us***. We were recipients where justification is concerned, and we're also recipients when it comes to sanctification. Of course, this grace has such an effect on us that it works. Yet it isn't we who work, but Christ in us. It isn't our power but the power of the Spirit. It isn't our strength but God's strength. As Paul says in Galatians 2:20, "*it is no longer I who live, but Christ lives in me.*"

Think back to the example of the pastor who watches pornography on a Saturday night. What do people tend to think about a situation like that? Most likely, something like this, "After what I just did, I'm not worthy of preaching tomorrow. I'll find someone to take my place." What is the implicit rationale? "***Before*** I did this, I was worthy!" What's going on here? The pastor is leaning on his works (good or bad). His authority derives from the way he behaves. He's relying on his own abilities. Why doesn't the pastor have the same sense of guilt and unworthiness ***every time*** he has to preach? Why instead does he

[d] As theologian James Garrett rightly points out, "That sanctification is God's work is made clear by the recurring use of the passive voice of *hagiazein* [sanctify] in the New Testament. In the Old Testament one often finds the words, "Sanctify yourselves," but the New Testament pattern is "Be ye sanctified." As the work of God sanctification, to be sure, is not something that occurs contrary to the human person's consent, but ***God is the Sanctifier***." James Leo Garrett, *Systematic Theology*, Vol. II, Second Edition (Eugene, Oregon: Wipf & Stock Publishers, 1990), 399.

only feel this way ***that*** particular Sunday? The answer is obvious. He thinks ***this time*** he's done something wrong enough to be unworthy, but ***all other Sundays, he hasn't***![e]

This kind of reasoning is entirely moralistic; it relies on our good works, and it's similar to the Pharisees' attitude. "God, I thank You that I am not like other people... an adulterer" (Luke 18:11). If we were to examine our hearts correctly, the way Jesus masterfully does in the Sermon on the Mount, we would realize that we may have never looked at pornography, yet ***would feel a deep conviction about how scandalous is the lust hidden within us*** (Matthew 5:28). Not only that, but we would also be afflicted and moved because we ***constantly*** (not just on Saturday evening) break that and every other commandment God demands of us. Is our hunger and thirst for justice greater than our hunger and thirst for recognition? Do we passionately intercede for our church leaders who criticize us? Would our spouses say that we bless them when they mistreat us? To correctly understand the Sermon on the Mount (and the Christian life in general) is to realize that ***the beginning of true spirituality is a recognition of our lack of it*** (Matthew 5:3).

Of course we should be hurt and horrified by the condition of our heart, yet not only if we watch pornography, but every time we examine ourselves in the light of the Word and realize how far we are from where we should be (Hebrews 4:12; James 1:23-24). ***The problem with this pastor's reasoning isn't that he feels unworthy after watching pornography. This pastor's problem, and our problem too, is not feeling unworthy every day.*** The problem, for him and for us, is that we don't live in a state of constant dismay over who we are.[f] The problem is that our hearts are not enlightened enough to say along with Paul, "*It is a trustworthy statement, deserving full acceptance, that Christ Jesus came into the world to save sinners, among whom I am foremost of all*" (1 Timothy 1:15; emphasis added). (Notice that it says "I am" and not "I was." For Paul, this is a present reality, not a distant memory.)

[e] Even though at first glance it may seem otherwise, this reasoning has a very low view of God's holiness. Only sin of the "greatest" kind separates me from him and puts me in a position where I need his grace, but not the "little" ones. This is entirely unbiblical. God is much holier than that, and his demands for holiness are much higher than simply keeping from falling into "great" sin! That is why his grace and sacrifice are so important. His demand is so high that no one can meet it! At all times, at any given moment, even when we serve him, we're entirely dependent on his grace. As we will see in detail in Chapter 12, what the pastor in our story should do is talk to someone he trusts and tell him about his struggle so that, as Galatians 6:2 says, someone close to him can help him carry his "burden." And so, with the help of the body of Christ, he will be able to overcome this and any other struggles he may have.

[f] As David Powlison puts it, "Repentance is not only how we start the Christian life; it *is* the Christian life." Heart of the Matter, (New Growth Press, Greensboro, NC, 2012), 17

Together with the apostle, we have to admit that we are much worse than we thought. That is why we need the good news of the gospel, which reminds us that, ***because of what Christ has done, we are forgiven and accepted in spite of what we are***. *That* is what gives us the authority to be able to preach the message on Sunday (or to do anything at all for God). Not our own merits (of not having fallen into "great sins") or our faults (of having fallen into "great sins"), but the merits of Christ (who never fell into any sin and who gave himself so that we might have authority). ***Only when we see our continuing spiritual poverty will we be aware of our continuous need for Christ's forgiveness*** (2 Corinthians 8:9). And only by seeing how he fills our need will we be freed from looking at pornography (or from any other kind of idolatry).[g]

The gospel is the good news that we don't have to do anything to be ***saved***; Christ did everything for us. In the same way, the gospel is the good news that we can't do anything to be ***holy***; Christ must also do that for us. For this reason, just as it was at the moment of our conversion, understanding and accepting that we are sinners is the best news. For this reason, if we really want to change, we have to be firmly grounded in our inability to do so, in order that we can be firmly grounded in God's grace.

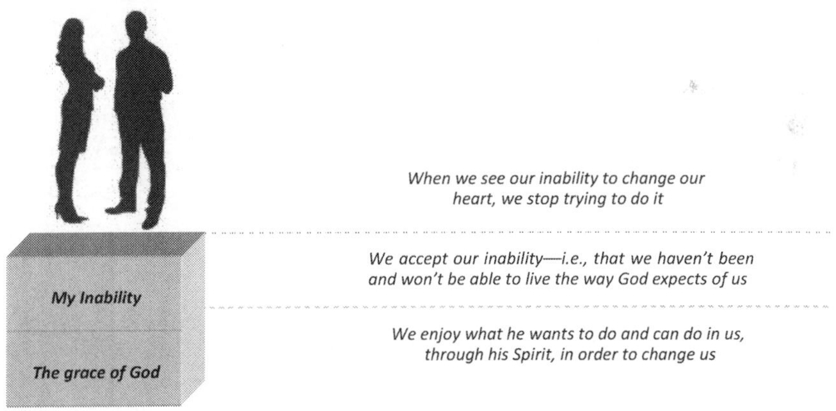

[g] The gospel, when correctly understood, may cause confusion. Not a few people arrive at the following conclusion: "If God forgives *all* our sins (even the pastor's sin or your worst struggle) then it doesn't matter so much how I live. After all, it can't be *that* serious if repenting and trusting him is all it takes." On the contrary! It's such a serious, dramatic, holy matter that it ***requires that God become human and be killed on account of it***! What is free for you and me, cost him everything. On the other hand, far from lowering God's standards of holiness, the gospel raises them to a level which NOBODY but God himself dying on a cross could ever meet. Nothing! Nothing but God's own death can pay the price (for watching pornography, for getting angry with your spouse, or for any other sin "big" or "small").

The gospel tells us, "You do not need to change yourself." The gospel tells us, "You can't do it." The gospel tells us, "His commandments are too high. You'll never be able to live up to them." The gospel says, "There is none who understands, there is none who seeks for God" (Romans 3:11-12). But it also says, "*What is impossible for you is possible with God*" (Matthew 19:26). It also reminds us that Jesus "*did not come to call the righteous, but sinners*" (Mark 2:17). It also reveals that "*he who abides in Me [Jesus] and I [Jesus] in him, he bears much fruit*" (John 15:5). When we understand this truth, when we remember all our failed attempts at self-improvement, when we come to see the true reasons for our "good works," then Christ, the gospel, will cease to be just an old and beautiful memory (a message for non-Christians), and he will transform into our greatest desire, our greatest longing, and our greatest need once again.

Picture the following scenario. If you're walking along the beach and a friend introduces you to the lifeguard, you'll surely smile at them, greet them with respect, and after exchanging a few superficial words, you'll continue your walk on the sand without giving the matter a second thought. But, if you're out in the middle of the rough sea and you're drowning, the lifeguard will no longer be someone you'll casually greet; they'll suddenly become the most important person in your life, your greatest treasure.

As Ephesians 1:18 says, God is in the process of ***opening the eyes*** of our hearts to see that we weren't just rescued on the day of our conversion and now it's up to us to swim on our own. God is in the process of showing us that we cannot swim (change) on our own, and that he rescues us every day because every day, of our own will, we throw ourselves into the sea of our idolatrous desires. Only when we see how great our inability is will we see how much we still need him. Only when we cease to rely on our ability will we be affirmed in His grace. Only then will we return to the One who has what all of us (not just the pastor who watches pornography) need: ***forgiveness*** and the ***power*** to change.

God didn't tell us: "There's the finish line, right across the ocean. Now, swim!" No. God told us: "There's the goal. I know you can't get there. Hop on. I'll carry you." "*For I am confident of this very thing, that He who began a good work in you [God!], will perfect it until the day of Christ Jesus*" (Philippians 1:6; emphasis added). [h]

[h] The renowned theologian J. I. Packer wrote, "Knowing God ***is a matter of grace.*** It is a relationship in which ***the initiative throughout is with God***—as it must be, since God is so completely above us and we have so completely forfeited all claim on his favor by our sins. *We* do not make friends with God; *God* makes friends

> John Bunyan describes it in this way: One day as I was passing into the field... this sentence fell upon my soul. ***Thy righteousness is in heaven.*** And... I saw with the eyes of my soul Jesus Christ at God's right hand; there, I say, was my righteousness; so that wherever I was, or whatever I was doing, God could not say of me, he [lacks] my righteousness, for that was just before him. ***I also saw, moreover, that it was not my good frame of heart that made my righteousness better, nor yet my bad frame that made my righteousness worse, for my righteousness was Jesus Christ himself***, "The same yesterday, today, and forever." Heb. 13:8. Now did my chains fall off my legs indeed. I was loosed from my afflictions and irons; my temptations also fled away... now went I also home rejoicing for the grace and love of God.[56]

When this truth takes hold of your heart, when it becomes your greatest treasure, when it seizes your affections, then you will have experienced deep change. Then, what is "*impossible with men, but possible with God*" will have happened: ***you will have changed what you love***, you will have returned to your "*first love.*"

BRIEF SUMMARY

For deep change to take place, I need to see the idolatry in my own heart.

- *Idolatry results from desiring something (good or bad) more than I desire God. In other words, **I make something created my god and savior**. Something other than God (sex, money, a romantic dinner, etc.) is now what will give me true life.*
- *Idolatry develops when I turn a desire into a demand. In other words, I make **myself my god and savior**. I will now use my wisdom, my strategies, my decisions, and my power to find true life.*

For deep change to take place, I need to realize that the fruit is a result.

- *"Fruit" is all those good things I do out of a love that is pure because I enjoy Jesus' love. "We love, because He first loved us" (1 John 4:19).*

with us, bringing us to know him by making his love known to us." J. I. Packer, *Knowing God* (Dowers Grove, IL: Inter Varsity Press, 1993), chap. 3.

- *"Fruit" is something I can't yield, but rather is the consequence of Jesus' work in me (John 15:5).*

For deep change to take place, I need to accept the fact that I can't change my desires.

As I realize that I fall over and over again into making idols out of my heart's desire, two things become clear:

- *First, I still need as much **forgiveness** as I did on the day of my conversion. (Not just for my actions but also for my motivations and my selfish desires.)*
- *Second, I need the **power** of the Holy Spirit to live in a way that I could never live without it (John 15:5).*

When I realize that both these things are offered to me freely and through no merit of my own, but rather as a result of Christ's sacrifice, I fall in love with him again. What I love changes! Christ is again my great need, my greatest treasure and my first love.

FOR PERSONAL REFLECTION OR DISCUSSION IN SMALL GROUPS

1. *In what way has this chapter changed or confirmed your understanding of how changes take place?*
2. *Sum up in one or two sentences the concepts that had the greatest impact on you in this chapter.*
3. *In your case, what are some personal examples of how you tend to elevate a desire to the status of an idol? What do you think drives you to do that? What is it that you are chasing after through this desire?*
4. *What do you typically do after falling into sin that is "great" for you? (By "great," I mean a kind of sin that "greatly" discourages you when you fall. Obviously, what one person may view as a "great" sin may not be so for another. For one person, it may be something of a sexual nature; for someone else, it may be yelling; for another person, it may be not having the courage to share the gospel; for yet another, it may be comparing their body against others', feeling jealousy, etc.) In light of what you have read in this chapter, what do you think God expects from you at that point?*

5. *Read John 15:1-5 carefully. In your own words, how would you explain the meaning of the phrase "apart from Me you can do nothing"? How would you define the term "fruit"? What must one do to "abide" in Christ?*
6. *Your two greatest needs are **forgiveness** and **power**. In what way is God working in your life to convince you of this?*
7. *Try to be as honest as you can. What "level" of appreciation do you have for the gospel today? Not the level of appreciation you had yesterday or the one you should have, or you wish you had, but the one you are experiencing today. Why do you think that is?*

CHAPTER 7

Discovering the Beauty of the Cross of Christ

Amazement Produces Change

Picture a church where both believers and nonbelievers attend the morning service on Sunday. How can you tell the difference between a non-Christian, a carnal Christian, and a spiritual Christian? All three of them are listening to the same message. All three of them hear the same truth. All three of them receive the same teaching. However, it only has an impact on one of them. What is it about the last one of them that the other two don't have? The answer can be summed up in a single word: awe. Wonder, the ability to appreciate and value what they have heard. Something has happened inside the spiritual Christian's heart so that the most precious thing in the world to them is something of little or no value to the other two.[a]

From a spiritual standpoint, ***seeing*** is the most valuable experience a human being can have because when we see, and only when we see, we ***enjoy*** things. Just as happens when a person goes on vacation to the idyllic place they've always dreamed about: their desire doesn't lie in *arriving* at their destination; rather, their enthusiasm lies in *seeing* the place they've been hoping with such great anticipation to visit. Seeing it, *enjoying* all its beauty, appreciating all its virtues, contemplating the clear waters, the white sand, the corals, the

[a] The Parable of the Sower in Matthew 13:1 and following is an example related to this idea. Verse 23 uses the idea of the person who genuinely bears fruit because they "understand" the word; that is, they have grasped its full reality or "beauty."

colorful fish, the palm trees, the blue sky; seeing all these things gives way to a joyful experience. Seeing has an impact on the individual. (Imagine what it would be like to arrive at the place of your dreams but to be temporarily blind and unable to see.) Seeing brings joy; it gives us pleasure; it makes us happy. Seeing ***brings about transformation***.

Seeing is the single most valuable experience a human being can have because only when we see Christ, ***only when we see his glory, do we change what we treasure and enjoy***. Seeing his love, seeing his loveliness, seeing his beauty (manifest at its greatest fullness on the cross) is what makes an impact on us and changes us. Seeing his value is what gives us pleasure and transforms our hearts by giving us true peace, joy, and happiness.

In his book *Seeing and Savoring Jesus Christ*, John Piper beautifully illustrates this point:

When we see Jesus for who he really is, we savor him. That is, we delight in him as true and beautiful and satisfying. That is my goal, because two things flow from such an experience of Jesus Christ: He is honored, and we are freed by joy to walk the narrow way of love. Christ is most glorified in us when we are most satisfied in him. And when we are satisfied in him, we are crucified to the world.... As the Apostle Paul said: "*We all, with unveiled face,* ***beholding*** *the glory of the Lord, are* ***being transformed*** *into the same image from one degree of glory to another. For this comes from the Lord who is the Spirit*" (2 Corinthians 3:18). ***Beholding is becoming. Seeing Christ saves and sanctifies***[emphasis added].[57]

The beauty of Christ transforms the heart.[b] ***The beauty of Christ sanctifies. The beauty of Christ changes the affections of our hearts.*** Seeing him and enjoying what he has done for us is what ***motivates us***; it is the ***engine***; it is the ***fire*** that burns away our selfishness and captivates the deepest part of our being, so that ***after*** seeing him, our greatest joy is to live for him. Matthew 13:45-46 expresses this truth in a really vivid way: "*Again, the kingdom of heaven is like a merchant seeking fine pearls [that is, he was looking for something that could really fill his heart, and he couldn't find it], and upon finding one pearl of great value [that is, when he saw that Jesus is better than any "pearl" this world has to offer], he went and sold all that he had and bought it [that is, he exchanged the world for Jesus Christ].*"

As Galatians 6:14 says, "*But may it never be that I would boast, except in the cross of our Lord Jesus Christ,* ***through*** *which the world has been crucified to me,*

[b] When I use the expression "the beauty of Christ," I use it as a synonym for "the glory of Christ."

and I to the world." Paul is very clear. The gospel, the cross of our Lord Jesus Christ, ***only the work and person of Jesus have the power to do what no one can do on their own: to stop desiring to live for themselves and to stop desiring all the things the idols of this world can give.***

I would like to share with you a true story that a missionary friend told me so that you can grasp the transforming power of the gospel.[c] A Christian woman from Kenya lives with an abusive husband. He routinely mistreats her, showing her enormous contempt and humiliating her. Even though my missionary friend tells this woman that she can leave her husband (at least temporarily until he stops hurting her), the woman chooses to stay with him, and she continues to serve him and love him despite the continued beatings and the bruises. One night, her husband gets drunk like never before. This time, he decides to bring a few of his friends home with him. When he arrives, he strips his wife naked in front of his friends, and he abuses her while they drink and laugh.

Once her husband is done with her, something both remarkable and "divine" happens. The woman rearranges her clothes, fixes her hair, walks into the kitchen, and without uttering a single word, she prepares a meal for her husband and his friends. When she returns to the dining room, she lays the tray on the table, and she lovingly tells them, "I've prepared this for you." At that moment, the husband breaks down. With tears in his eyes, he asks her, "Why are you doing this? How can you treat me like this after everything I've done to you? How can you still love me?" With an angelic voice, his wife answers, "If I have to suffer all this so that you can see how much God loves you, I'll gladly endure it." At that moment, her husband falls to his knees broken, and he accepts Christ. On ***seeing*** his wife's love, grace, and steadfastness, the husband changes.

Pay attention to what you read next. ***Christ is the Kenyan wife; you and I are the husband*** (1 Peter 3:18)! Even though we are Christians, we reject him, hurt him, and exchange him for our idols. Even as Christians, we turn our backs on him, abuse his love, and commit adultery (James 4:4). Even though we're Christians, we get drunk with selfish desires and, according to the Bible, we live the way the prophet describes, *"At every street corner you built your lofty*

[c] **Important note**: The purpose of the story isn't to advocate for how a woman should respond to abuse. My intention is simply to present an analogy of the gospel, without passing judgment on the ethical aspects of this woman's decision. In other words, I'm not advocating that a woman who is abused should stay with her husband. I'm just describing an event that actually happened. In fact, I strongly believe that the most appropriate thing to do in a case of abuse is to report the abuser and to immediately get out of the dangerous situation.

shrines and degraded your beauty, spreading your legs with increasing promiscuity to anyone who passed by" (Ezekiel 16:25 NIV). However, ***he was literally <u>stripped naked</u> and <u>abused</u> by us!*** (Matthew 27:27-30). You and I abused him! He was publicly beaten and wounded, while being mocked and laughed at! "*He was despised and forsaken… A man of sorrows and acquainted with grief… Surely our griefs He Himself bore, and our sorrows He carried… [He was] smitten… and afflicted… He was pierced through for our transgressions. He was crushed for our iniquities… He was oppressed…yet He did not open His mouth… [although] he had done no violence, nor was there any deceit in His mouth*" (Isaiah 53:3-9). However, "Jesus was saying, '***Father, forgive them; for they do not know what they are doing***.' *And they cast lots, <u>dividing up His garments amongs themselves</u>*" (Luke 23:34; emphasis added).

Until you realize you hate God, you can never love him. And until you realize that he accepts you in spite of this, you can never see the extent of his love (Romans 5:10). We do not commit "tiny" sins that deserve a "tiny" Savior and that demand a "tiny" sacrifice. On the contrary! We're like the husband of the Kenyan woman in that we abuse a God who allows us to shame him over and over again out of love for us, and who tells us over and over again, "If I have to suffer all this so that you can see how much I love you, I'll gladly endure it." The Kenyan woman's words are Jesus' words. That is the gospel. And seeing it, appreciating it, being amazed by it, will change you. Yes, the cross is the best news for nonbelievers, but it's also the best and most needed news for those who have believed for years.

Here's the key: ***The same God who enticed us and drew us to himself with his cross in order to <u>save us</u> is the God who entices us and draws us today to be <u>holy</u>.*** How do we change? By seeing. By seeing unimpeded the depth of our wickedness and the inexplicable greatness of his love. ***By seeing what we are like and remembering what he is like***. By seeing how our idols still dominate us and by being amazed that he still loves us and wants to free us. By seeing how today, after being a Christian for years, we are still in need of a Savior. As St. Augustine cried out, "Yes, Lord, do it: stir us up and awaken us; humble us; kindle us and draw us closer so that we, inflamed by your sweetness, would love you and run in search of you!"[58]

The gospel reveals two very simple yet very deep truths. ***We are wicked,*** which is precisely what we are unwilling to accept and what we tend to deny by making excuses or blaming others. ***Jesus Christ is good***. He is and will be the greatest need of our life. When we *see*, *feel*, and *experience* these realities, two other extraordinary things happen. ***Jesus Christ is valued***. Because we now enjoy his beauty, because we now appreciate him for his true worth; that is, we glorify him. ***We are valued***. Accepting the condition of our hearts doesn't denigrate us or destroy our self-esteem; on the contrary, it dignifies us. It creates in us ***an identity based not on what we do but on what he has done for us***. Our worth doesn't come from doing good things or denying our wickedness, but from the immense price that he paid for us *in spite* of it.

Paraphrasing Tim Keller, *by examining our motivations*, and not just our behavior, we realize that we are much more sinful than we ever dared believe. But *when we look at the cross of Jesus*, we realize that we are much more loved than we ever dared to imagine.[59] As John Newton said, "My memory is nearly gone. But I remember two things: that I am a great sinner, and that Christ is a great Savior."[60] Tim Keller puts it this way:

> If we are deeply moved by the sight of his love for us, it detaches our hearts from other would-be saviors. We stop trying to redeem ourselves through our pursuits and relationships, because we are already redeemed. We stop trying to make others into saviors, because we have a Savior. The only way to dispossess the heart of an old affection is by the expulsive power of a new one.[61]

In other words, only when we rediscover how amazing God's love in Christ is for us will we feel loved in such a way that we'll no longer need other lovers, and we'll be freed from our idolatry. When God fills our hearts again as he did on the day of our conversion, only then will we be "converted" again; only then will we change.

Jonathan Edwards describes that rediscovery like this:

> All Gracious affections [emotions or desires] arise from a spiritual understanding, in which the soul ***has*** [sees] the excellency and glory of divine things revealed to it. ***All spiritual discoveries are transforming***.... "*But we all with open face, beholding as in a mirror the glory of the Lord, are changed into the same image, from glory to Glory, even as by the Spirit of the Lord*" (2 Corinthians 3:18). ***Such power as this is properly divine power, and is peculiar to the Spirit of the Lord***.[62]

The more we see the glory of our Lord, the more we'll change. The more we enjoy him, the less we'll enjoy the world. The more amazed we are at his work, the less obsessed we'll be with our own. When we see all that he is and all that he's done, we'll change. That is the work of his Spirit: to open our eyes so that, when we see, our idols are dethroned, and we put Christ in his rightful place. Not only in our outward behavior, but also in the depths of our hearts. Only by living this experience can we truly love him as he expects us to: with all our heart, with all our soul, and with all our mind.

The key to change is awe
1. *We need to examine our motivations (our idolatry), not just our actions. In doing so...* 2. *We'll see that we can't change ourselves and that we still need a Savior all over again. In doing so...* 3. *We'll see the beauty and value of what Christ has done all over again. In doing so...* 4. *We'll delight in and fall in love with Jesus all over again. In doing so...* 5. *We'll give him the glory he deserves all over again. In doing so...* 6. *Our motivations will begin to change, and our identity will be built, not on what we do, but on what he's done for us. In doing so...* 7. *Our behavior will begin to change, driven by a renewed love for him.*
The only way for us to be awed is for God to open our eyes, through his Spirit, so that we can see our poverty and so that we can see His beauty.

What Happens When Deep Change Takes Place?

I've tried to say it in many ways and in many forms since the beginning of this book, but I'll try one more time: ***I change when what I love changes.*** How does what I love change? It doesn't happen when I make an effort to love Jesus, but when I realize that he loves me. When I see, appreciate, and treasure Christ's amazing love for me. 1 John 4:19 says it plainly: "*We love, because He first loved us.*" That is to say, ***my ability to love*** either God or others, ***is born, it originates, it becomes possible, when I marvel once more at the fact that he loves me.***

I would like to ask you to do something. Please, open your Bible to John 15:9. I know you would expect me to quote this passage, and I will, but I would like to ask you, just this once, that you set the book aside and look it up in your own Bible. I believe that John 15:9 is possibly the most remarkable verse in the entire Bible. Highlight it, underline it, memorize it. Meditate on its meaning as you work, study, or drive your car. If you do that, you'll notice something. This verse teaches such an amazing truth that you'll find nearly heretical. This verse contains such a fascinating and compelling truth that even if you read it, understood it, and believed it, it would take you a lifetime to enjoy it to the fullest.

John 15:9 reads, "*Just as the Father has loved Me, I have also loved you; abide in My love.*" What is this passage saying? Are you ready to be amazed? Carefully read the following sentence. This passage says that God loves you with as much love as he loves himself. Jesus loves you with as much love as the Father loves him. May I rephrase it? ***God loves you with as much love as he loves his Son, Jesus Christ.*** Read this carefully. "Just as," that is, with as much love as the Father has loved me (in other words, with the same "intra-Trinitarian" love that has existed since before the foundation of the world and that God the Father has for God the Son), I have **ALSO** loved you." Is it too good to be true? It is! It is! It is! Do you feel it? Do you enjoy it? Do you live it? Does it fill you?

Let me show you how this is possible. Throughout my career in ministry, I've had to deal with many people saying some pretty ugly things about me. Some of them may have been right; others may not have been. By the grace of God, for the most part, even in the worst moments, I've kept my cool, and I've tried to respond appropriately. I don't think I deserve any credit for it. It wasn't me; I clearly understand that it was Christ in me. However, I'm also well aware that there's a kind of situation where it would be very difficult for me not to "lose it." If anyone ever wanted to see me respond badly, they would have to mistreat one of my kids. If someone hurt one of them, I'm pretty sure I wouldn't have the temper to respond the way I would if it were me getting hurt. Why? Because I love them! ***I love them just as much or even more than I love myself.***

One of the things my daughter Micaela enjoys the most is hearing me tell her bedtime stories. One of the things I enjoy the most after doing it is saying this to her: "You know, sweetheart. If a bad man ever came into the house and tried to hurt you, Daddy would always stand up for you. ***I'm ready to die for you.***" (The three or four times I've told her this, she's hugged me tightly, telling me that she loves me with tears in her eyes.) So, I tell her, "Sweetheart, Daddy is ready to give his life for you. But you know what? God has done that already! He's given his life for you. He loves you so much that he died on a cross to save you. Sweetheart, God's love is greater than Daddy's love." (At that point, she usually gives me another hug, and tears start flowing again.)

Can you see it? ***I have as much love for my kids as I have for myself. I would give my life for them!*** (I'm sure that if you have children, you would too.) What you and I feel for our kids is an extremely tiny image of the love God has for you. Do you get it now? ***God loves you with as much love as he loves his Son, Jesus Christ.*** As Jesus said in Matthew 7:11, "*If you, then, though you are evil, know how to give good gifts to your children, how much more will your Father in heaven give good gifts to those who ask Him!*"

What is the commandment in the second part of John 15:9? "*abide in My love.*" In other words, live your life in light of this reality. ***Live as if you feel you are the most loved person in the universe—because you are!*** That is Jesus' commandment! Do you now understand Matthew 6:1? Do you now understand why my greatest duty as a Christian isn't to obey the commandments but to enjoy God? Can you now see why what you need the most is to enjoy the love he has for you?

When you see this in its fullness, it changes you, and it transforms you; ***it sets you free*** (John 8:32)! It turns you into a person who doesn't need to roam the world with an empty cup in their hand, begging for love. Your cup is full now! You no longer need sex, power, a better job, or a good body to feel loved. You now feel loved! And that completely changes your whole life, your relationships, your behavior, and who you are. It changes what you do, how you relate to others; it even changes how you respond to rejection. You can now be plump or slim; it doesn't matter. You can now have hair or be bald; it doesn't matter. You can now lose an argument or win it; it isn't that important anymore. However, let me clarify something for you. Does *knowing* this change you? Of course not! What makes a difference is to experience it deep in your heart!

As we said at the beginning of the chapter, you need to see, feel, taste, and appreciate Christ's love, not just know that he loves you. That's why ***our greatest duty as a Christian is to enjoy God's love for us (on Christ's behalf). That's why our greatest duty as a Christian is to "abide in his love."*** As we read in 1 John 4:10, "*In this is love, not that we loved God, but that he loved us and sent his Son to be the propitiation for our sins.*" How do we change? ***We change when we love (that is, when we see or appreciate) the love he has for us.***

So, What Are the Commandments Good For?

If you keep reading John 15, you will notice a beautiful truth in verse 10: "*If you keep My commandments, you will abide in My love, just as I have kept*

My Father's commandments and abide in His love." What is Jesus saying in this passage? Pay close attention. This is what Jesus is saying: ***Keeping the commandments <u>isn't the reason</u> why we are loved. Keeping the commandments is <u>the means</u> by which we abide in his love.*** Jesus <u>doesn't</u> say, "Live by my commandments; then I'll love you." Jesus says, "Live by my commandments; then you'll experience my love." In other words: "Live as I command you, and you'll get to enjoy me! You'll be able to see how much I love you. You'll progressively be able to appropriate for yourself the reality of the love I have for you."

Allow me to paraphrase Jesus' words. Here's what he says: "If you sin, my love for you won't change, but you won't be able to feel my love, you won't be able to appropriate it, you won't be able to enjoy it." When you sin, what happens to you is like what happens to an ostrich that buries its head in the ground and can no longer see the light of the sun. Nothing has changed; the sun is still there, only she can't see it anymore.

Why does Jesus want you to know this? (Get ready for another verse that is among the most striking in the entire New Testament.) John 15:11 reads: "*These things I have spoken to you so that <u>My joy</u> may be in you, and that your joy may be made full [perfect].*" Have you paid close attention to Jesus' words? ***The happiest person to have ever walked on Earth wants me to experience as much happiness as he experienced.*** The God of the Universe wants me to be as happy as he is! This is absolutely fascinating. Jesus wants me to live in his commandments so that I can abide in his love and, in doing so, enjoy the joy that I have always been pursuing apart from him! How can someone be so completely amazing? My heart turns away from him, and I chase after my idols. He dies in my place to bring me back to him. And then he tells me that he wants to give me what my idols can't. "I want to love you and fill your cup. Live as I ask of you, and you will experience this."

How Can God Love Me Like That?

You might be thinking, "Are you saying God loves me with as much love as he loves his Son? How is that possible? Maybe ***<u>before</u>*** I converted Jesus was willing to die for me. After all, I didn't know him. I was apart from him, I didn't really know who God was, I didn't have the Holy Spirit; but ***<u>now</u>*** that I've been a Christian for a while, I'm not sure anymore. There are things I've done ***<u>after</u>*** I turned to Jesus; my intimate thoughts, the cycles of sin that I repeat. Honestly, I find it hard to accept, hard to believe, and hard to enjoy."

Why do we feel this way? I believe the answer can be summed up in a single sentence. We tend to be great students of what we have done, but very poor students of what Christ has done. We don't fully understand (nor enjoy) the gospel. Let me explain. When most of us think of the gospel, the first thing that comes to mind is that, in essence, the gospel is about Jesus forgiving our sins. Yes, that is true. It's about that, but it's much more than just that! That's only half of the gospel. There's another half that's missing there. Theologians call this other half "double imputation." Let me explain this to you.

2 Corinthians 5:21 reads, "*He made Him who knew no sin to be sin on our behalf, so that we might become the righteousness of God in Him.*" According to the passage, two things happen when we convert. In dying on the cross, Jesus doesn't just take your iniquity and carry it away (i.e., he forgives you); he takes his righteousness and ***transfers it to you*** (i.e., he blesses you in a new way). In financial terms, it's as if you had huge monetary debts; he wouldn't just clear your bank account of debt forever (that alone would be amazing); rather, he'd clear his own account and transfer all of his wealth into yours. In financial terms, he turns you into a billionaire. This has massive spiritual implications!

Let me break it down for you in a different way. Picture yourself moving your life into complete chaos—sex, alcohol, drugs, etc. Soon you run out of money. You start stealing. For many years, you get away with it and you don't get caught. You swindle many people, cheat on your tax returns, and make countless shady decisions that hurt your friends and family. However, the day comes when you finally get caught. You are guilty. You know that. The judge knows that. No plea could possibly get you off the hook.

Now, imagine the following situation. Let's say that Phillip VI, the King of Spain, walks into the courtroom and, to everyone's disbelief, he shouts for them to stop the trial because he's ready to exonerate you. Let's pretend, for a moment, that he does have the power to do something like that and that, after issuing a royal decree, he pardons you.

For many people, that is the gospel. We have sinned and the king has forgiven us. What happens next? Phillip VI goes back to his castle and you go back home. The end. That isn't the entire gospel! That's only "half" the gospel.

If you lived in Spain, you would most likely know who Princess Leonor is. She is Phillip VI's eldest daughter, the heir to the throne. The gospel doesn't *just* say the king forgives you; the gospel says that now you are Princess Leonor of Spain! The gospel says that you are now Phillip VI's child. ***You're now***

everything the Son is before God! His righteousness is yours! As a consequence, all of His benefits are yours; all of his privileges are yours; all of his inheritance is yours; even his free access to the throne is yours! You are now his child!

Think about what you just read. Before the throne of God in heaven, because Christ has granted you his righteousness, ***you are now treated as he would be***. In fact, ***you are now loved as if you were him!*** In our illustration, Phillip VI doesn't just forgive your wrongdoings; he loves you as if you were Princess Leonor! His own daughter! ***Because of what Christ has done, you are "like" him.***[d] God treats you and loves you as if you were him. As Hebrews 2:11 says, "*For both He who sanctifies and those who are sanctified are all from one Father; for which reason* ***He is not ashamed to call them brethren***."

Let me bring the illustration down a little bit to make it more concrete. Imagine I had a teenage son, and that he and one of his buddies took my brand-new car for a spin behind my back for a few hours while I was out of the house. (I'll be honest with you, I did this when I was young, so this example is close to home.) Let's say that after he convinces my son that he'll never be able to drive a car this nice because he's an orphan and doesn't have much money, my son's friend ends up behind the wheel. Let's say they crash. No one gets hurt, but the car gets totaled. Let's just say the insurance company doesn't cover the costs. Now, this young man owes me. He has a debt he can't pay. He has neither parents nor any money. Yet I choose to forgive him. Surely, when I tell this boy that I've forgiven him, he'll be extremely happy and grateful.

However, think about this. What if instead of telling him that, I tell him, "I don't just want to forgive you, I also want to adopt you. I want you to be part of my family. I want you to be my son." Now his debt isn't just cleared; our relationship is going to be completely different! Now, everything changes! My kids walk into the restroom while I'm shaving. My kids climb into my bed at night when they are frightened. My kids have a right to call me, day or night. My children will inherit my entire "fortune." My kids receive **ALL** my attention, love, and sacrifice. ***I love them just as much as or even more than I love myself.*** That boy who crashed my car will now have all the same privileges and all the same rights as my daughter Micaela and sons Tomás and Manuel! Now he too will be able to call out to me at night and tell me, "Dad, I can't sleep. Will you stay with me?"

---

[d] Of course, when I say that you are "like" Christ, I'm not saying that you are God or any heresy of that kind. What I mean is that you are "like" him in the sense that, since he "clothed" you with his righteousness, you are now a child of God in its full sense (Colossians 1:13; 22).

John 1:12 says that to those who believe in Christ, "*He gave the right to become children of God.*" Can you see how amazing this statement is? You have the same rights as Jesus! Why? Because you're a child of God! How can God treat you and love you like this? ***It's not because of you but because of Christ. It's not because your righteousness has increased but because Jesus has shared his with you.*** He is the hero, not you! ***And inasmuch as you didn't earn it, you can't lose it either.*** He was forsaken (Matthew 27:46) so that you'd be accepted (John 1:12). As 1 John 3:1 puts it, "***See how great a love the Father has bestowed on us, that we would be called children of God; and such we are....***"

Enjoy, experience, get a taste of this truth! Why? Because as John goes on to say a few verses after, appropriating this for yourself is what changes you: "*Beloved, now we are children of God... And everyone who has this hope fixed on Him purifies himself...*" (1 John 3:2-3). As the apostle says, seeing, appreciating, treasuring this reality can change you! It isn't about what you do (good or bad); it's about what Christ has done, which is simply insurmountable. It's all about the gospel.

What's Important Isn't What I Do; What's Important Is for Me to Learn to Appreciate What He's Done for Me

What do we have to learn to see? Everything that God, in Christ, has done for us. When writing to the Ephesians, Paul does something relatively strange and unexpected. The apostle leaves a luxuriously detailed record of three reasons for the prayer he passionately prays on behalf of other believers. Don't miss this. He doesn't pray this on behalf of people who don't know Jesus, but for believers! Ephesians 1:18-19 says, "*I pray that the eyes of your heart may be enlightened, so that you will know what is the hope of His calling, what are the riches of the glory of His inheritance in the saints, and what is the surpassing greatness of His power toward us who believe...*" (emphasis added).

Notice that, as he begins his prayer, Paul expresses the chief or core reason that encompasses his three other reasons. What he prays for is that believers would be able to ***see three things***! That their hearts (that is, their entire inner being: their intellect, emotions, and will) be able to appreciate the value of the three truths he mentions afterward. These three truths are part of the gospel. Or, if you will, they are three consequences of the gospel.

In other words, what Paul wants is for God to work supernaturally in them in such a way that the affections of their hearts (and yours) are captivated by these truths. That they may treasure them; that they may come to appreciate them to the point that they find pleasure and joy in them. Also notice the pronouns Paul uses in the passage. Paul wants to make it very clear that it's *Jesus'* calling, that it's *Jesus'* inheritance, and that it's *Jesus'* power. In other words, each of these benefits is God's work and not the believer's. Let's briefly go over each of them.

The first thing we need to see is that our hope for change increases significantly when we understand that the calling is something God has done. Take a good look at the passage. According to verse 18, Paul intercedes "*so that you will know what is the hope of His calling.*" That is, I want you to understand what kind of hope you can have because the calling came from God. In other words, it's ***because*** God has called you, it's ***as a result*** of God having called you, it's ***on account*** of God having called you, that you can have hope! In other words, this calling brings hope because it's based on a commitment that *God* (God himself!) has made to complete a transformation and change that he himself began in us on the day that he called us. This is what Paul himself writes in Philippians 1:6: "*For I am confident of this very thing, that He who began a good work in you [neither you nor I, but God] will perfect it until the day of Christ Jesus.*" Think about it for a moment. What is one of the most challenging struggles (perhaps the most challenging of all) for anyone who *really* wants to change? Let me answer that for you. The sense of discouragement that comes from feeling that you can't change. The hopelessness that comes from feeling you are addicted to certain recurring sins. Whoever you are, I know that, like me, you have a particular sin, something you struggle with, a tendency that you keep coming back to over and over again, which you feel is wrecking your spiritual life. Maybe it's something of a sexual nature; maybe it's a character flaw; maybe it's something else.

What is Paul saying in this passage? What do people need to see in a situation like this? He's saying God is the one who initiated your process of conversion, not you; and that God himself will bring that process to completion! As Romans 8:30 says, "*and these whom He predestined, He also called; and these whom He called, He also justified; and these whom He justified, He also glorified.*" ***One of the most important truths I have to remember in order to change (the first truth according to Paul's prayer!) is that God has made a commitment to change me.*** He's promised to do the impossible! He's able to do what I can't! He finishes what he starts! This is Paul's prayer. As a result of meditating on who it is that has called me, I can have hope for change. The sense of discouragement is born out of looking at yourself; hope is born out of looking at him. It's his work, not yours.

The second thing we need, according to Paul, is to see the kind of inheritance Christ has passed on to us. Think about it for a moment; the first thing that anyone who receives an inheritance does is to see how much money they have received; they assess the kind of inheritance they have received! This is what we have to do with our inheritance in Christ. How does Paul characterize the inheritance Jesus has passed on to us? Huge! Worth millions! Rich! Glorious! In verse 18, he clearly says that we should reflect on "*what the riches of the glory of His inheritance* are." Now, think about this. Why does the passage say "his" inheritance? Because an inheritance is something you get without having done anything at all.

For years, my father would get up every day at seven in the morning to go to work. Monday through Friday, without exception, he would leave our house at 7:30 in the morning and return home from his company at 7:00 in the evening after a one-hour commute to and from downtown Buenos Aires. I can honestly say I don't remember a single day when my father didn't go to work—not even when he got sick! In fact, before he retired, he held three different jobs: he ran his own foreign trade company, and he held two chairs as a professor in two different universities. On top of that, none of these jobs was in the same city. He really worked very hard. When my father died, my sister and I inherited the fruit of the "riches" he accumulated after years of hard work. One day, we sat down at a lawyer's office, signed some papers, and all his "riches" were passed on to us. Think about this. Who worked for years? Who worked hard? Who got exhausted giving their best? My sister and I did nothing to deserve what we received. We inherited it. We simply started enjoying the blessings my father earned for us.

The same thing happens through Christ. Paul's prayer is that we can see the dimension of the "*riches of the glory*" of the inheritance that Christ earned for us. What is the best of them? (Though it's definitely not the only one.) God loves you! (Do not miss this statement.) God loves you! Now, right this very moment, and forever! ***Because Jesus passes his righteousness on to you*** (the righteousness he earned through a lifetime of perfect obedience), ***God will never look at you as if you were what you actually are: unrighteous!***

Now, when he looks at you, he doesn't see your uncleanliness (he sees Christ's cleanliness); he doesn't see your pride (he sees his Son's humility); he doesn't see your selfishness (he sees Jesus' selflessness); he doesn't see the envy or the jealousy in you, or your constant state of dissatisfaction (he sees the perfect contentment of the one who said, "*not my will but yours be done*"). However, let me clarify something for you. When I say that God doesn't "see" your sin, I don't mean that he doesn't notice your sin or that he turns a blind eye when you do something wrong. What I mean is that ***he treats you as if you haven't sinned.*** He still loves you! He still accepts you! He still looks at you as if you were Jesus![e]

How is it possible for God to treat us this way? That's precisely Paul's prayer: for you to see that God can do this because ***it's part of your inheritance!*** What is free for you and me cost him everything. In Christ, God left heaven; he allowed a woman to change his diapers (meditating on this alone takes my breath away), his family to reject him, his friends to abandon him, people to call him Satan, spit in his face, strip him naked, beat him up for the fun of it, and nail him to a cross. What is free for you and me cost him everything. Paul says you need to stop and think about the riches of your inheritance. Are you aware of all of what you have inherited because of the cross? Do you use it? Do you enjoy it?[f]

John Owen used to say, "The greatest sorrow and burden you can lay on the Father, the greatest unkindness you can do to him, is..." Fill in the blank. Take some time before you answer. What do you think? What's the worst thing you can do to God? What would hurt him the most? For most of us, our minds would jump to some "major" sin; perhaps that very sin we are addicted to. "Yes. That has to be the worst thing I could do to him." John Owen, the Bible, and even God himself would tell you, "You're wrong." ***The greatest sorrow and burden you can lay on the Father, the greatest unkindness you can do to him, is not to believe that he loves you.*** Why? Because he has proved that it is so on the cross. Enjoy your inheritance!

Finally, Paul prays that we can see that his power brings about change (not my own effort). Even though I like running, I've never tried to run a whole marathon. I find it impossible to run 26.2 miles non-stop. I think of all the cities and towns that are 26.2 miles away from my place, and just thinking

---

[e] Can God discipline you if you continue to sin? Of course, he can. But not for the purpose of punishing you! Instead he does it to help you treasure his love again. As we read in John 15:11 he wants you to walk in his commandments so that you can "abide in his love," and in doing so, enjoy the joy that comes from being close to him!

[f] Other examples of our inheritance are: free access to the King's throne to ask for his favor (Hebrews 4:16), the steadfast love and forgiveness of the Father (Romans 8:38-39), the promise of his Spirit that lives in us (Acts 1:8), the promise of the Spirit that intercedes for us (Romans 8:26-27), the assurance that one day we will be glorified (Romans 8:30), and many other realities that would be impossible for me to list in this passage.

about it, I give up. But it's different when you go by car, isn't it? The distance is the same, but it is the car making the effort, not us. Yes, either you or I may drive, and in a way, we can say, "I went from Madrid to Barcelona." But in reality, we didn't do it; it was the car that got us from one destination to the other. It was *its* power, not ours.

This is the truth that Paul longs for us to see through his prayer, and what he clearly expresses in 1 Corinthians 15:10, "*But by the grace of God I am what I am, and His grace toward me did not prove vain; but <u>I labored</u> even more than all of them, <u>yet not I, but the grace of God with me</u>.*" Paul's prayer is clear: for us to change, our eyes must be opened to the reality that we have God's power (his own power!) at our disposal to do so. Only through that power will we come to experience deep change. Neither our resolutions, nor our commitment, nor our dedication cause us to change. It's *<u>his</u>* ability to do *in* and *for* us what we could never do (as we saw in LeBron James' example in the previous chapter or like when we drive from one city to another).

This power is so extraordinary and inexplicable that, for us to comprehend it, we must compare it to the resurrection of Jesus. What no human can do, God has done by *<u>his</u>* power. Paul prays precisely for us to be able to see that ***if God had the power to bring about what he did in Christ***—that is, "*He raised Him from the dead and seated Him at His right hand in the heavenly places, far above all rule and authority and power and dominion, and every name that is named, not only in this age but also in the one to come (Ephesians 1:20-21)*"—***he's certainly able to bring about real and lasting changes in our hearts.*** He can do what you and I could never do. As we will see in the following chapters, God (God himself!) now lives in your heart through his Spirit. What is Paul's prayer? That we will come to appreciate the amazing implications of this truth.

I'll end this chapter with a brief reflection. I have more than once received an email that reads something like this "Make $2,500 a week. Work from home. Click here." What do I do when I get this kind of email? I delete it. Why? Why wouldn't I want to make that kind of money? Is it because I'm not interested in working from home? Of course not! I delete it because I don't think it's true. I know it's spam. What it promises is too good to be true, and so I dismiss it. I would like to encourage you not to do this with the gospel. I know that if you've read this far, you wouldn't do this openly and consciously; however, it's possible to "delete" these truths from your heart by giving yourself fully to whatever it is that you have to do after you're done reading these words. Don't do it. Highlight this book. Underline it. Use markers on it. Make notes on it wherever you find space. Meditate on the gospel throughout your day. You're his child. You have his Spirit. The God of the Universe loves you. Embrace this reality. Live under its light.

BRIEF SUMMARY

For deep change to take place, ***I need to be in awe of the gospel again****. For this to happen, God must "bring light to the eyes of my heart" so that I can see two great realities:*

- ***I'm a great sinner****. I don't love God (I love myself), and I give myself to things life offers that enslave me and leave me empty.*
- ***God is a great Savior****. His grace is amazing. He still loves me even though I constantly give myself over to the idols I make for myself.*

When I'm awed by these two realities again, I fall in love with Christ, and I change. Why? Because I start enjoying the love that Christ has for me, and that moves me to love him and others.

*One of the keys to being awed is meditating on my "****inheritance****." God doesn't just forgive me; he makes me his son or daughter; this means that he ALWAYS loves me, and he ALWAYS treats me as if I were Jesus. His righteousness is mine! And so are his privileges.*

FOR PERSONAL REFLECTION OR DISCUSSION IN SMALL GROUPS

1. *In what way has this chapter either changed or confirmed your understanding of how changes take place?*
2. *Sum up in one or two sentences the concepts that had the greatest impact on you in this chapter.*
3. *In your own words, how would you describe what it means to "see the beauty of Christ"?*
4. *Carefully reread the chart that summarizes how deep change takes place. In your own words, how would you explain it? Feel free to try to improve, simplify, or personalize it so that you can easily share it with your group or other people. Although I've listed seven items, you may be able to do a better job than me and narrow it down to even fewer.*
5. *Do you agree with the claim that "God loves us as much as he loves his Son"? Why? What are the practical implications of this truth for your everyday life?*

6. *In your own words, how would you explain the statement: "We change when we love—that is, when we see or appreciate—the love he has for us"?*

PART III:

What Are the Outcomes of a Deep Change?

CHAPTER 8

A New Identity

What makes you worthy? What makes you special? What makes you different? My youngest son is four years old. Right now, in his own words, he's the "total pro," by which he means he's an "expert," "gifted," or "skillful." He's the "total pro" at playing soccer. He's the "total pro" at running. He's the "total pro" at swimming, biking, drawing, and even reading! (In a sense he might be, given that his ten-year-old sister is teaching him how to read, and he's actually doing quite well.) In no uncertain terms and no matter what activity we are doing, my son needs to proclaim to the whole world how good he is. Then, he looks at me, seeking approval, and asks: "Right, Dad? I'm a 'total pro,' aren't I?"

What's going on here? My son is beginning to develop his identity. He's beginning to discover who he is (he's someone who can run, draw, play soccer), and he wants to find out if he's worthy in light of who he is and what he can do. How does he know that he is special, worthy, and loved and accepted by his father and peers? He highlights his virtues—to the point of magnifying them a "little bit." My son proclaims to the whole world how great his skills are, and he longs for everyone around him to recognize them as such. You and I aren't all that different; we're simply more modest and inconspicuous about it. We know that it isn't exactly appropriate to proclaim to the world that we are the "total pro," and so we seek socially acceptable ways to fit in, to assert our worth, and to feel loved and accepted by others.

Not long ago, I read an article in an online newspaper about various real-life stories of people who ended up either dead or seriously injured while trying to take a selfie. At a safari park, a family almost died sitting inside their car while trying to take a selfie with a lion that was standing next to the vehicle when the feline pounced on them and tried to bite them through a partially open window. In India, a man tried to take a selfie with an elephant, but he got so close to it that the animal got scared and ended up trampling him to death. A famous YouTuber climbed a huge skyscraper, and he instantly dropped to his death while attempting to capture the event with his camera. As I read this article, I wondered: "What moves these people to do such crazy things?"

You don't really need a Ph.D. in psychology to figure out the answer to that. They're seeking the same thing my son is. They have a virtual audience through social media, and they want that audience to cheer them on, to be amazed at their accomplishments, and to say: "You are a 'total pro.'" They want to tell the whole world as loudly as they possibly can that they've done something special, something different, something that no one has ever done before. Like my son Manuel, they seek validation; they want to feel worthy and loved. (If this weren't the case, they wouldn't need to take the picture and post it. To live the experience without sharing it would be enough.)

As we've already seen, in Matthew 6:1, Jesus tells us that these examples aren't exceptions; they're vivid expressions of how the heart of every human being works, even in Christians! We have the same problem. The only difference is the way we try to find our worth. We use things like ministry, fasting, offering, and prayer as a means to feel accepted or special. (Have you ever thought about the reason why you sound so different when you pray in public than you do when you pray by yourself? Could it be that having an audience somehow influences what you say?)

If you think the most "devoted" people such as missionaries, evangelists, or pastors are somehow different, trust me, they are not. In fact, allow me to let you in on a secret. Do you know what is the first question leaders ask each other at pastors' meetings? I'll tell you what it is. "How many members does your church have?" Some of them openly ask this question; others "conceal" it in an attempt to be inconspicuous; others don't even ask the question in order to avoid being exposed—yet it's still on their minds!

The point is that, although James 2:1 warns us about the danger of loving people because of their social status, no one treats a celebrity pastor the same way they treat one whose church membership is less than a handful of people. The way they treat the former and the level of respect he receives is very different than with the latter. Why is that so? I'm extremely embarrassed to admit it, but deep in our hearts, one of them seems worthier than the other.

A Case from the Bible

In Acts Chapter 5, we find a compelling story. A couple named Ananias and Sapphira sell their house, and they give most of the money to the church. I know you know the story, but keep in mind that anyone doing something like this nowadays would be regarded as the most devoted person imaginable! Think about the following: what would have to happen in your heart for you to decide to sell your home and give most of the money to the church? A miracle! (That would be my case, too.) However, there's something in Ananias and Sapphira's heart that they love more than their home. That something moves them to make a decision that you and I would find almost impossible to make. What is that something? The praise of other believers!

Think it through. What they did wasn't wrong—after all, giving money to the church is a good thing. What was wrong was their motivation for doing it. Consider the power of seeking the approval of others. The need, the urge, the desire to feel accepted was so strong that they sold the most precious thing they had. Now, let me show you through the passage itself how Peter confronts Ananias' and Sapphira's sin, "*Why [notice that he uses the key question we've been stressing since Chapter 1] is it that you have conceived this deed in your heart [that is, the problem lies right in the heart]? You have not lied to men but to God*" (Acts 5:4). What does "lying to God" or "lying to the Holy Spirit" mean? (Both phrases are used as synonyms in verses 3 and 4.) "Lying to God" is living a counterfeit Christianity. It is to live as a Christian, but without the Holy Spirit. It is to do the right thing out of the wrong motivation. It is to use ministry, service, an offering, or practicing your "righteousness" (Matthew 6:1) as a means of gaining recognition and acceptance from a group of people. It is to build my identity around my own righteousness, rather than on the righteousness of Christ (think back to the previous chapter.)

	Ananias and Sapphira	***Barnabas and others***
Ourward Behavior	*They sell their homes and give the money away*	*They sell their homes and give the money away*
Superficial Desire	*They want to be seen as generous*	*They want to bless others by being generous*
Deep Desire	*They seek the approval of others*	*They enjoy God's approval*
Inner Motivations	*They build their own identity: They manipulate others in order to feel valued*	*They receive an identity: They are free because they feel worthy in Christ*

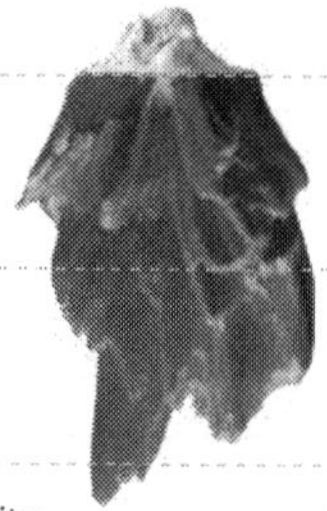

Now, consider this. Why did Ananias and Sapphira sell their home? At this point, I'm not referring to their motivation, but to the reason why they sold their house to earn the Christian community's appreciation instead of doing something else, like going out as missionaries or serving at church. Why would they sell their home at all? The answer to this question is at the end of Acts 4. The reason they did it was that Barnabas and many other believers were already doing that (Acts 4:32-37). Ananias and Sapphira didn't come up with some kind of master plan. They saw that several people in the early Christian church had done it and, on seeing them do it, they mistakenly assumed that if they did it too, it would result in acceptance, appreciation, and status.

What do we learn from this story? That ***our culture—and our Christian subculture—determines, to a large extent, what is regarded as acceptable and worthy*** in the eyes of the people who are part of the community. If you think about it for a moment, these values are entirely variable depending on the locale (for instance, burping after eating is considered polite in some countries and disrespectful in others), the times (what was fashionable in the 1920s may look ridiculous and tacky today), and many other cultural factors that aren't worth exploring right now. The point is that what for one group may be socially acceptable, valuable, and worthy of ultimate recognition, for another group may be worthy of outright rejection and disdain.

Let me give you an example. Imagine that a non-believing friend invites you to a wedding where none of the guests are Christians. I doubt that in a context like that, right in the middle of a beautiful reception, dressed in your finest clothes and holding a glass of champagne, you would be tempted—like

Ananias and Sapphira—to say: "Did you know that I give 10% of my income to the church? In fact, I've been reading the Book of Acts in the Bible, and after praying and fasting, I'm considering selling my home and giving the proceeds to my church's pastor." No one in the world would say that at a wedding full of unbelievers! If you did, they would surely check your champagne glass to make sure you weren't drinking something else! Why? Because no one in that context finds it worthwhile. Because within that group, in that place, and in that particular situation, engaging in that kind of "crazy" behavior isn't something to be admired or accepted (as it was in the context of the early church). At a bar, no one would have a problem saying that they had defrauded the IRS on their tax returns or that they had spent a heap of cash on their vacation, but they would if they were at church.

In the follow excerpt, Tim Keller analyzes how cultural context influences behaviour:

> Imagine an Anglo-Saxon warrior in Britain in AD 800. He has two very strong inner impulses and feelings. One is aggression. He loves to smash and kill people when they show him disrespect. Living in a shame-and-honor culture with its warrior ethic, he will identify with that feeling. He will say to himself, "That's me! That's who I am! I will express that."The other feeling he senses is same-sex attraction. To that he will say, "That's not me. I will control and suppress that impulse." Now imagine a young man walking around Manhattan today. He has the same two inward impulses, both equally strong, both difficult to control. What will he say? He will look at the aggression and think, "This is not who I want to be," and will seek deliverance in therapy and anger-management programs. He will look at his sexual desire, however, and conclude, "That is who I am."
>
> What does this thought experiment show us? Primarily it reveals that we do not get our identity simply from within. Rather, we receive some interpretive moral grid, lay it down over our various feelings and impulses, and sift them through it. This grid helps us decide which feelings are "me" and should be expressed—and which are not and should not be. So this grid of interpretive beliefs—not an innate, unadulterated expression of our feelings—is what shapes our identity. Despite protests to the contrary, we instinctively know our inner depths

are insufficient to guide us. We need some standard or rule from outside of us to help us sort out the warring impulses of our interior life.

And where do our Anglo-Saxon warrior and our modern Manhattan man get their grids? From their cultures, their communities, their heroic stories. They are actually not simply "choosing to be themselves"—they are filtering their feelings, jettisoning some and embracing others. They are choosing to be the selves their cultures tell them they may be. In the end, an identity based independently on your own inner feelings is impossible.[63]

We Are All Trying to Justify Our Worth—Through the Opinion of Others

Think about it for a moment. Why does a child collect baseball cards; an adult, stamps; and a millionaire, invaluable paintings? Why does a woman have ten, if not more, pairs of shoes in her closet? Why does a man brag to his friends about the size of the fish he caught? Why are two young men fighting over which is the best soccer team? (A team they've never been on and never will be.) Why do we feel the urge to replace our car (which, by the way, works perfectly well) with a newer model? Why are we so excited about shopping for sales and getting new clothes? Why are we so desperate for our home to be tidy when we're having guests over? Why do we like to know what our classmate scored on the exam? Why are we interested in finding out the size of a friend's paycheck?

The answer to each of these questions is the same: we seek to find worth in what we are, in what we have, or in what we have achieved, and to do this, we need positive feedback from those whose opinion we deem worthy. For this to happen, we need to compare, measure, evaluate ourselves against others, and still come out on top—or at least get close enough. By default, ***there's an inertia within all of us that drives us to build our identity based on who we are, what we do, or what we have.***

In the movie *Troy*, Brad Pitt plays the famous mythological hero Achilles. Before he leaves to fight in the famous Battle of Troy, Achilles has a very revealing conversation with his mother, who, in great sorrow, prophesies him: "If you stay here, you'll find peace. You'll find a wonderful woman, you'll have sons and daughters, and they'll have children, and they'll love you. When you're gone, they'll remember you. But when your children are dead, and their children after them, *your name will be lost*. If you go to Troy, *glory will be asked*. They'll write stories about your victories for thousands of years. The world will remember your name. But if you go to Troy, you'll never come home for your glory walks hand in hand with your doom."

What does Achilles decide to do? If you know the story, you know the answer, and if you don't, you can figure it out. He responds according to what gives him the greatest pleasure: being admired. Later in the movie, surprised by the power and energy Achilles shows in every battle, someone asks him, "Where do you get the strength to fight? What are you fighting for? What do you want?" His response is extremely revealing, "I want the same thing all mortals want: glory. I just want it more."

What does Achilles want? The same thing my youngest son wants, the same thing Ananias and Sapphira wanted, the same thing you and I want when we take a selfie, change cars or post pictures on Facebook. The same thing all human beings want. To have glory. To be famous. To stand out. To be special. To feel worthy. Achilles does the same thing we all try to do, he tries to justify his courage and, to do so, he needs the opinion of others.

As we saw in Chapter 2, our deepest desires are what we long for the most; they are the hidden treasure of our hearts; they are what we really live for. Although they aren't easy to recognize, they are the actual driving force behind our actions. They're the why beneath the why. On the other hand, our superficial desires are the means we use to satisfy those deeper desires. In Achilles' case, being a great warrior—his superficial desire—is the means through which he believes he'll satisfy his deepest desire: to be respected and admired for generations to come.

Of course, Achilles' inner struggle is relatively easy to identify; however, it's significantly more challenging to see how this is also a reality in my everyday life.

Although it may take some time to recognize this, if you carefully examine your heart's motivations, you'll realize that ***almost everything you do in life is aimed at proving your worth***. Your clothes, your body size, your credentials, the trips you take, your Facebook page, and even your efforts to serve God may have a much more self-centered origin than you may be willing to admit. To show you how deeply rooted this dynamic is in our hearts, let me give you a less obvious and much more commonplace example. A few days ago, I argued with my wife. The core issue in our argument was that she got frustrated with me because, in her own words, I "*didn't want*" to help her with the housework. I tried to explain to her that my *intention* was to help her, but for various reasons, I hadn't gotten around to it. She didn't see it that way, and she kept insisting that I "*had no desire*" to do so. Hearing these words made me very angry. I was offended, hurt, and above all, I felt unjustly accused. I want you to carefully read the exact words I said to my wife, "***You're making me out to be a bad person***. You don't know my heart. ***I am not the person*** you say I am (a lazy person). I wanted to help. I don't have a problem helping. ***It hurts me that you think that of me***."

What am I doing by saying these words? ***I'm justifying myself!*** I'm trying to defend my honor, my own righteousness, my goodness, and by extension, my worth as a human being in front of her. Can you see it? The argument I was having with my wife was rooted in my inability to appropriate the justification I already have before God. ***What she thought of me was more important than God's opinion.*** When this happens, my own worth starts carrying more weight in my heart than Christ's. What's the result? I have to protect my worth! I have to prove to her, or anyone else for that matter, that I'm good and that I'm not the kind of person they're making me out to be. My son Manuel, Ananias and Sapphira, Achilles, and I struggle with the same thing. ***We're trying to justify our worth***.

	My response without Christ	***My response in Christ***
Onward Behavior	*I argue with my wife*	*I yielded to my wife's accusation*
Superficial Desire	*I don't want to be seen as a selfish*	*There's no need to argue that I'm not selfish*
Deep Desire	*I seek my wife's approval*	*Whether I am or not, I'm approved by God in Christ*
Inner Motivations	*I build my identity: I get angry at her until she admits she's wrong*	*I receive an identity: I'm freed from my wife's opinion because I enjoy the opinion of Christ more than I do hers*

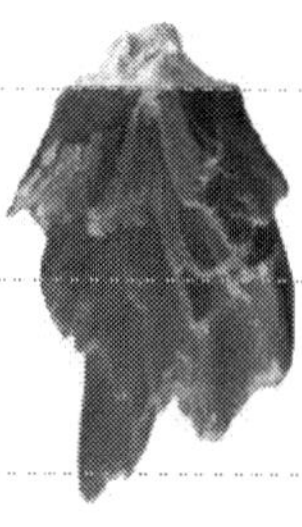

None of us is immune to this. We all seek our worth in the opinion of others. As I said before, our culture (and our Christian subculture) teaches us what is worthy, acceptable, and worthwhile. It's "the eyes of the world" who play the role of judge in deciding what "justifies" our worth and existence. For Achilles, it was to be a great warrior; for a girl, it could be to have a boyfriend (while not having one might be catastrophic); and for a businessman, it could be traveling first-class or achieving a long-awaited promotion at work. All of us are trying to justify our worth. We do it when we argue, at a gala dinner, and even in church. We are constantly "buying into" these offerings, and we live for them.

Seeking Recognition from Others Enslaves Us and Leaves Us Empty

Pay attention to the following passage: "*It happened as they were coming, when David returned from killing the Philistine [Goliath], that the women came out of all the cities of Israel, singing and dancing, to meet King Saul, with tambourines, with joy and with musical instruments. The women sang as they played, and said, 'Saul has slain his thousands, and David his ten thousands.' Then Saul became very angry, for this saying displeased him; and he said, 'They have ascribed to David ten thousands, but to me they have ascribed thousands. Now what more can he have but the kingdom?' Saul looked at David with suspicion from that day on*" (1 Samuel 18:6-9).

What has just happened? The most beloved, most blessed, and most respected man in the entire ancient world, King Saul, has just lost his sense of worth. A simple song was enough to show how short-lived, how fleeting, and how inadequate the opinion of others is to fully fill a man's heart. What happens next? His emptiness makes him sink into a spiral of addiction and wickedness. He begins a ruthless hunt to try to kill David, the very person who had saved his life! (Just think about it: if David hadn't killed Goliath, Israel would have been defeated, King Saul would have been taken prisoner, and he would have been executed.)

Paul Tripp masterfully describes the spiraling path from desire to addiction in this way:

> The dynamic of addiction is that if you look to something that God created, to give you what it wasn't intended to give you, either you get discouraged quickly, and wisely abandon those hopes, or you go back again and again, and in so doing, you begin to travel down addiction's road. That created thing will give you a short-term buzz of euphoria, it will offer you temporary pleasure, it will provide a momentary sense of well-being, it will briefly make you feel that you're something, and it may even make your problems seem not so bad for a bit. It's all very

> intoxicating. It all feels great. The problem is that the created thing that you're looking to has no capacity to satisfy your heart. It wasn't designed to do that. It cannot give you inner peace. It cannot give you the heart rest of contentment. It cannot quiet your cravings. In a word, it cannot be your savior. And if you look outside of the Savior for something to be your savior, that thing will end up not being your savior but your master.
>
> You'll love the short-term buzz, but you'll hate how short it is. So you'll have to go back again quickly to get another shot, and before long you've spent way too much time, energy, and money on something that can't satisfy; but because of what it has briefly done for you each time, you're convinced that you can't live without it. You're hooked and you may not know it. The thing you once *desired*, you're now persuaded that you need, and once you've named it a *need*, it has you....
>
> We are all propelled by a quest for identity, inner peace, and some kind of meaning and purpose. And we'll all look for it somewhere. Here's the bottom line: looking to creation to get what only the Creator can give you will always result in addiction of some kind. The thing that you hoped would serve you pulls you into its service. What seemed like freedom ends up being bondage. The thing is not the problem; what you've asked of it is.[64]

The opinion of others isn't enough. Even if we had, as Saul did, the whole world at our feet, we would still be empty if we based our sense of worth and security on what created things have to offer. When the famous billionaire John Rockefeller died in 1937, his fortune was the equivalent of $340 billion today. This is more than four times Bill Gates' fortune. When a reporter asked him, "How much money is enough money?" his response was, "Just a little bit more."

The reality of it is very obvious: it's never enough. None of what we so desperately seek in this world can satisfy our needs. What is the key to change? ***To identify how I'm doing it***. In what ways am I trying to prove my worth? From what achievements am I getting my sense of worth? In what way am I using a created thing to feel worthy and appreciated?

The Fullness of the Heart Comes When I Am Amazed by the Fact that I Am Justified before God

God wants to freely give me, in Christ, that thing that I'm so desperately seeking in the world; it is part of my "inheritance." It is for this reason (because ***it's something I receive*** by being justified) ***that having a healthy identity is an outcome.*** It is the outcome of appropriating for myself what Christ has already done. It is the consequence of feeling that I'm justified in the eyes of the Father. It is the product of treasuring God's opinion above that of men. It is appreciating the value of being justified before the One whose opinion really matters. It is finding pleasure in the reality that God looks at me and is completely satisfied.

How then could we define our identity? Like a double-sided coin, our identity as Christians has two inseparable and equally important faces. On the one hand, I'm a person who has great struggles and a need to change; yet on the other hand, I'm someone who is loved and accepted in Christ in spite of them.

Different Ways to Define a Christ-centered Identity
• *I'm a sinner who's been justified. Both.* • *I'm an addict who's been accepted. Both.* • *I'm an adulterer who's been forgiven. Both.* • *I'm someone disobedient, loved by grace. Both.* • *I'm a terribly flawed person, but I'm both loved and accepted despite that. Both.*
You can pin "and I'm undergoing changes" to the end of all these descriptions.

Last night, while I was writing, my wife approached me in heartfelt, humble sorrow, and she said, "I've realized that I don't love people." (To be completely honest and objective, it's unlikely you'll find a person as loving as my wife, Annie. Please don't think it's just my opinion or that I'm trying to make her look good. Anyone who knows her would agree with me. She's a sweetheart.) So, what happened? Why would she say that? Because God is helping her to own her identity in Christ—and to be free from having an identity based on how good she is. How does God do this? He reminds us of the gospel. He shows us our inner darkness in a new dimension (a tremendously loving woman realizes that she doesn't love others), yet at the same time, he shows us his love with a new intensity (an extremely kind Father who gives himself over for us to be what we ourselves are not).[a]

Having your identity grounded in the work of Christ sets you free. It enables you to fully accept who you are, to the point where you don't need to hide or cover up your struggles anymore; and, it also enables you to fully enjoy who you've become as a result of Christ's sacrifice. This dual dynamic, when appreciated and treasured with pleasure by the heart, unleashes an indescribable "power" of love towards both God and others. As Jesus said in John 8:32: "*You will know the truth [i.e., you will embrace the gospel], and the truth will make you free.*"

Allow me to illustrate this truth through a story. I would like you to picture for a moment that you are driving at night on a fairly remote highway. It's late, and visibility is rather limited. However, you know that very soon, either the soccer game you've been waiting for or your favorite TV show will soon start (choose whichever you most prefer). You constantly check the time on your cell phone because you want to be on time for it. You're anxious. You gradually start driving faster and faster. All of a sudden, and without giving you time to react, a small child runs across the road out of nowhere, and you run him over. You stop the car. You stare at the boy who's lying on the road all drenched in blood, and you can't believe what you've just done. As you weep inconsolably, you wish you could turn back time. After what you just did, the soccer game or the show you wanted to watch has completely left your mind. All you can do is look at the child lying lifeless in front of you. There's only one word that describes the current condition of your heart: broken. You can't believe how far your selfishness has come.

Yet, while you hold the child in your arms, you feel a warm hand on your back. A man kneels beside you and, contrary to what anyone would expect, he hugs you lovingly as he looks at the child. You can't believe anyone would show any empathy for you after what you've done. There's no anger or condemnation in this man's eyes. There's one word that describes his attitude: understanding. You're puzzled as he extends his hands over the child and says, "I make all things new." And suddenly, while you're still on your knees

[a] If you read Luke 7:1-10, you'll see it is striking to compare *the opinion people have* of the Roman centurion against *the opinion* he has of himself. When Jesus goes to heal the centurion's servant, everyone who knew him "*earnestly implored [Jesus], saying, He **is worthy** for You to grant this to him*" (Luke 7:4). However, when Jesus is approaching his home, the centurion (like my wife) claims the exact opposite about himself, "***I'm not worthy** for You to come under my roof*" (Luke 7:6). "*Now when Jesus heard this, He marveled at him, and turned and said to the crowd that was following Him, 'I say to you, not even in Israel have I found such great faith*'" (Luke 7:9). And Jesus healed his servant.

wondering what is going to happen, the child opens his eyes. All his wounds have been healed. Now you start weeping without being able to hold back your tears. But you're not crying because of the soccer game or because you aren't going to jail. No! You're crying for two very different reasons. You're crying because of what you've done and because of what this man has done for you. Unable to hold it in, you melt into a healing embrace that transforms you. "Thank you! Thank you! Thank you!" That's all you can say as you cry. Moments later, while you're still hugging each other, you feel the man lose all his strength and collapse on you. Then you understand. Your sin has been fully atoned, but it cost him his life.

Carefully read these words from the apostle Paul in Romans 8:15-17: "*For you have not received <u>a spirit of slavery</u> leading to <u>fear</u> again, but you have received <u>a spirit of adoption as sons</u> by which we cry out, 'Abba! Father!' The Spirit Himself testifies with our spirit that <u>we are children of God</u>, and if children, heirs also, <u>heirs of God and fellow heirs with Christ</u>*..." (emphasis added). What is the Holy Spirit's main work according to this passage? ***The ministry of the Holy Spirit is <u>to take away your fear</u>.*** Read the passage. You tend to engage God as if you were a slave! How do slaves engage with their masters? Through fear! Slaves try to do everything they possibly can to please their master. Why? Because they know that if they do something that displeases their master, there will be consequences. What's the result? Fear, insecurity, desperate attempts to cover up or justify any shortcomings or failures. (Just as I did when I was arguing with my wife; I was a slave to her opinion.)

Paul says: "That's not the way you should engage God! The Holy Spirit wants to show you something else. You are his child! There's no need to please Him." How does the Spirit show me that I am His child? He doesn't do it by hiding or covering up what I've done. He does the exact opposite! The Spirit shows me what I've done, but not in order to leave me stranded out there on the road, compulsively staring at my terrible failures. ***The Spirit shows me what I've done so that I can see the level of love and unconditional acceptance I have as a result of what Christ has done!*** He reminds me of the gospel! He makes me appreciate the work of the Son. He allows me to see the extent of my justification.

The Spirit doesn't convince you that you are evil and that you need to be good—that is the spirit of slavery. ***The Spirit convinces you that you can't be good; yet you're accepted, loved, and treated as God's child***—that's the spirit of adoption. What is the key to developing a healthy identity? It is to take possession of my inheritance. It is to appreciate the outcome of my justification. It is to enjoy God's steadfast love. It is to live as his child. My son Tomás doesn't ask me, "Dad, are you going to provide food for me today?" He doesn't say, "Dad, will you provide clothes for me to wear today? Will I be able to sit at the table with the rest of the family today? Will I be able to use my bed tonight?" He's my son, and he lives out of that identity! He knows he's home, and he enjoys that reality.[b]

You may think, "Well, that's great! Now, how do I apply this truth to my daily life? What are the implications?" I'll let Tim Keller take that question for me:

> The gospel, if it is truly believed, helps us out of the extreme neediness that is natural to the human heart. We have the *need* to be constantly respected, to be appreciated, and to be highly regarded. We *need* to control our lives—not trusting... anyone else with them. We *need* to have power over others in order to boost our self-esteem. The image of our glorious God delighting over us with all his being (Isa 62:4; Zeph 3:14; cf. Deut 23:5; 30:9)—if this is a mere concept to us, then our needs will overwhelm us and drive our behavior. Without the power of the Spirit, our hearts don't really believe in God's delight or grace, so they operate in their default mode. But the truths of the gospel, brought home by the Spirit, slowly but surely help us grasp in a new way how safe and secure, how loved and accepted, we are in Christ. Through the gospel, we come to base our identity not on what *we* have achieved but on what has been achieved for us in Christ.

---

[b] I really like the way Tim Keller defines justification. ***To be justified means that <u>I've been found acceptable</u> before Someone I want to please.*** What do a young man and a young woman who're about to go out on a date do? They groom themselves! They dress in their best clothes, wearing their best shoes and their best cologne or perfume. They use everything in their power to conceal their defects and highlight their strengths. Why? The answer is very obvious: they want to look good; they want to appear presentable; they want to be accepted in front of someone they want to please. That's why they put "makeup" on their imperfections and cast off anything that might be embarrassing to them. The same thing happens when you put together your *résumé*, you bring out your best qualities on it! (And you hide or omit anything that might embarrass you.) You want to be accepted by the interviewer, so you show the best in you. Our relationship with God shouldn't work this way. Why? Because justification changes this dynamic. Yes, we know that we must stand before a holy judge. We know that we aren't what we should be. However, we also know that the key isn't to cover up or hide our iniquity, but to appropriate the reality that Christ's justice is now ours. ***To be justified means that I am <u>viewed in a different way</u> before the One I long to please.*** As a result of what Christ has done, God sees me in a different way. His view of me changes. I'm still what I am (unjust), but in his eyes, I'm something I could never be (just). It's a reality that makes me acceptable, and it's a reality that has the power to transform me. I've taken and adapted this reflection from https://gospelinlife.com/downloads/justified-sinners-5896/.

> And when the gospel, brought home to our hearts (see Eph 3:16–19), eats away at this sin-born neediness, it destroys the inner engines that drive sinful behavior. We don't have to lie, because our reputation isn't so important to us. We don't have to respond in violent anger against opponents, because no one can touch our true treasure. The gospel destroys both the pride and the fearfulness that fuel moralistic behavior change. The gospel destroys ***pride***, because it tells us we are so lost that Jesus had to die for us. And it also destroys ***fearfulness***, because it tells us that nothing we can do will exhaust his love for us. When we deeply embrace these truths, our hearts are not merely restrained but changed. Their fundamental orientation is transformed.[65]

Many years ago, a great preacher is said to have said about himself, "I don't know about the rest of my brothers and sisters, but sometimes I wonder if I have the slightest love for the Savior."[66] Long before that, Paul said, "*But God demonstrates His own love toward us, in that while we were yet sinners, Christ died for us*" (Romans 5:8). When the Spirit shines light for us to see, two major things happen. On the one hand, he shows us who we really are (the way he did for Spurgeon and for my wife). Yet, on the other hand, he shows us who he is (and once again, he shows us that he loves us *in spite of* who we are). It's only through this dual reality that an identity grounded in Christ emerges, and not through our merits and shortcomings, our triumphs and failures, or our obedience and disobedience. *We're worthy* because of the love that Christ shows us on the cross. Henri Nouwen contrasts the effects of seeking our identity in the opinions of others with the joy of an identity rooted in God's love for us:

> The enormous propensity to seek recognition, admiration, popularity, and renown is rooted in the fear that, without all this, we are worthless. You could call it the "commercialization" of love. Nothing for nothing. Not even love.
>
> The result is a state of mind that makes us live as though our worth as human beings depended on the way others react to us. We allow other people to determine who we are. We think we're good if other people find us to be so; we think we're intelligent if others consider us intelligent; we think we're religious if others think so too....

> Thus, we sell our souls to the world. We're no longer master in our own house. Our friends and enemies decide who we are. We've become the playthings of their good or bad opinions....
>
> If we had a firm faith in God's unconditional love for us, it would no longer be necessary to be always on the lookout for ways of being admired by people, and we would need, even less, to obtain from people by force what God desires to give us so abundantly... For a very long time, I considered low self-esteem to be some kind of virtue. But now I realize that the real sin is to deny God's first love for me, to ignore my original goodness. Because without claiming that first love and that original goodness for myself, I lose touch with my true self and embark on the destructive search among the wrong people and in the wrong places for what can only be found in the house of my Father.[67]

In 1 Corinthians 4:3-4 (GNT), Paul states, "*Now, I am not at all concerned about being judged by you or by any human standard; I don't even pass judgment on myself... The Lord* is the one who passes judgment on me." In this passage, Paul makes an astonishing claim. He isn't troubled by the Corinthians' opinion of him. He isn't bothered by the view the rest of the world has of him. In fact, he doesn't even fall prey to self-evaluation in terms of his own opinion. (Am I good? Am I evil? Will God be pleased with me?) ***The only opinion he considers is that of the Lord.***

But what is that opinion? How does God judge him (and us)? In Christianity, the moment we believe what God says about us, "*There is no condemnation now for those who live in union with Christ Jesus*" (Romans 8:1 GNT). That's what he thinks of us! As Tim Keller points out, "Do you realize that it is only in the gospel of Jesus Christ that you get the verdict before the performance?"[68]

> In Christianity, the moment we believe, God imputes Christ's perfect performance to us as if it were our own, and adopts us into His family. In other words, God can say to us just as He once said to Christ, "You are My Son, whom I love; with you I am well pleased" (Mark 1:11).
>
> You see, the verdict is in. And now I perform on the basis of the verdict. Because He loves me and He accepts me, I do not have to do things just to build up my résumé. I do not have to do things to make me look good. I can do things for the joy of doing them. I can help

> people to help people, not so I can feel better about myself—not so I can fill up the emptiness. [69]

In Christ, we can (like Paul in Corinth) endure criticism without being torn apart. In him, we can accept the world's rejection without feeling inferior. Thanks to him, we can stop continually judging ourselves and checking to see if we meet the standards that the world, the church, our parents, our co-workers, ourselves, or, allegedly, God asks of us. Because Jesus Christ was judged in our place, and he was condemned and put to death for us, we can now step out of the defendant's seat and stop listening to the voices (those of others and our own) that try to judge us in light of our performance. We should respond to these daily trials against us as Paul did: "*The Lord is the one who passes judgment on me. There is no condemnation now for those who live in union with Christ Jesus.*" ***The key to developing a Christ-centered identity isn't thinking negatively about ourselves*** (feeling great guilt about our sin) or thinking highly of ourselves (feeling great complacency about our obedience); ***the key is to think little of ourselves and highly of what Christ has done for us.*** *Understanding* this truth, *enjoying* this truth, or in Jesus' words, *knowing* this truth, is what ***will make us truly free*** (John 8:32). As Paul Tripp puts it:

> Only when our confidence is in the Lord, that is, in his constant help and forgiveness, are we able to step out into the light, unafraid of what we may be asked to face. When we really do believe that his grace has already covered anything we may have to confess and given us power for every change to which we may need to commit, **we will not be afraid of living**… [70]

A Change of Approach, a New Opinion

A change of identity, true freedom, takes place when God's opinion is more important than the opinion of others. Your identity is either the result of striving to win over people's opinions or it is the outcome of delighting in God's opinion of you because of Christ. The former makes an addict of you and leaves you empty. The latter turns you into a confident person. Why? Because no one can snatch the love God has for you away from you.

One of the passages that I have quoted the most in this book is Matthew 6:1. This is no accident. I believe it to be a passage packed with meaning. Let me type it again here so that you can thoughtfully meditate on the way it ends. "*Beware of practicing your righteousness before men to be noticed by them; otherwise you have no reward with your Father who is in heaven.*" The passage is very clear. If I want to be rewarded by God, I have to live according to the truths we have discussed so far. God must be my audience, and the cross of Christ that in which I glory (Galatians 6:14). However, I want you to notice something: Jesus repeats the same phrase three times in this portion of Matthew 6. Give your offering in secret, and "*your Father who sees what is done in secret will reward you*" (Matthew 6:4). Pray in secret, and "*your Father who sees what is done in secret will reward you*" (Matthew 6:6). Fast in secret, and "*your Father who sees what is done in secret will reward you*" (Matthew 6:18).

What is this reward that Jesus promises? If you study Matthew 6 in detail, you'll notice that the passage doesn't seem to explicitly say what is that reward. Nor does it seem to mention whether it's something present or future. (Some versions incorrectly use the phrase "he will reward you in public," which isn't part of the original since it isn't found in the older manuscripts.) However, although the passage may seem vague about the reward, Jesus leaves a clue at the end of each example that helps us identify what he is referring to. Would you like to know what it is? Brace yourself because it's something magnificent, spectacular, amazing. It's something that, according to psychologists, everyone is looking for, and no one can find. ***The reward Jesus is talking about is to have a heart that's free from the slavery of pleasing others, and that finds its satisfaction and fulfillment in the reality that "the Father sees."***

Shall I put it in a nutshell? It's to be free from pleasing others! For the person Jesus describes in Matthew 6, God is enough! The Father's gaze suffices! God's eyes are all they need! What Jesus offers is a miracle. It's what no one can accomplish. (That's why it's a "reward"; it's something God gives us.) What Jesus is saying is that enjoying God—and enjoying the fact that he loves me in Christ in spite of who I am—brings about a new identity and such a profound and unparalleled sense of worth that I no longer need the approval of others! My intimate, personal, secret relationship with God is so satisfying that, as a "reward" (one that I get when I live my life *in* Christ), Jesus promises I'll get an internal reality like the one he offers in John 8:32, "*You will know the truth, and the truth* ***will make you free***."

Changing Our Identity; a Process Not an Event

Some time ago, my wife, the official household stylist, gave one of our boys a rather unusual haircut. He was thrilled with his new haircut until one of his friends made fun of him. What happened next? He felt so sorry for himself that he wore a hat to school. The problem didn't stop there; instead, when he came home from school, he didn't want to go to his weekly soccer practice, and he didn't want to go out and play with his neighborhood buddies either. My son loves playing with his friends, so it was very clear it was all about his new haircut. When I realized what was going on, we went into his room, I sat on his bed, and I asked him why he didn't want to go. He just came back saying he didn't feel like it. So, I tenderly asked him, "Buddy, are you worried they'll make fun of you because of your haircut?"

He nodded his head.

At that moment, I gave him the "little talk." I tried to explain to him that our heart is like a small cup that we are trying to fill with other people's love, but Jesus was able to fill it to the brim with his love. So, I asked him, "Buddy, what does Dad think about your haircut?"

He replied, "You like it, Dad."

Then I said to him, "Buddy, what does Jesus think about your haircut?"

He replied, "He likes it, Dad." I then said this to him: "Son, do you see that poster of Captain America hanging on the wall? What would happen if I tried to punch you real hard as you hide behind Captain America's shield?"

"Nothing."

"Would it hurt?"

"No, Dad."

"What if I tried to shoot a gun at you?"

"Nothing, Dad. The bullets would ricochet off from me."

"That's what Jesus wants to do in your heart, Buddy! He wants to be a shield around you. You're always going to meet people in life who will hurt you or say nasty things to you. But he wants you to enjoy his love in such a way that if other people don't love you, or say hurtful things about your hair, their 'bullets' will bounce off of you because you're shielded with his love for you! Does that make sense, Buddy?"

He nodded. Then, I hugged him tightly, and we prayed together for Jesus to fill his heart with his love.

When we finished praying, full of hope, I asked him, "Buddy, do you want to go play outside with your friends?" He answered that he didn't.

I'll be honest. A little disappointed, I debated whether to force him to go out with his friends. Eventually, I decided not to. Why? Because I began to remember my deepest struggles over my own identity. What would it be like for me to stand behind the pulpit and give the message wearing a haircut with which I felt very uncomfortable? Or maybe to walk around half-naked in front of the church members? Or to preach the same message two Sundays in a row? (Or my worst nightmare: to be irrelevant!)

Living in the light of who we are in Christ is a life-long process of growth, not a moment of light that changes you forever. Yes, it's true; everyone at some point in their Christian experience feels that they've been "touched" by God in a unique way. We all experience one or more instances when we feel his love seize us. Maybe you had this kind of experience when you converted, or maybe it was much later. Those moments are very special, and most of the time, we believe that their effect will last forever in our hearts. But our experience and the Bible show us that it doesn't work that way.

We live in a fallen world with a fallen heart. Our full appreciation of the work of Christ will only come on the day we are glorified. Until then, as Paul prays in Ephesians 1:18-19, we pray and seek to know him more, but we know that the "quest for joy," as John Piper defines the Christian life, is just that: a quest, a process, a race (1 Corinthians 9:24-29). This reality, far from discouraging us, is an immense source of hope. Neither you nor I will be able to live every moment of our lives in agreement with our identity, but both you and I are moving in that direction, and we are gradually appropriating our "inheritance." As someone once said, "I am not what I ought to be, I am not what I want to be, I am not what I hope to be in another world, but still I am not what I once used to be, and by the grace of God I am what I am."[71]

Peter, a Terribly Encouraging Bad Example

I would like to ask you one last question before I end this chapter. What is the sin that devastates your spiritual life the most? Please, stop to think about it for a moment. Perhaps you're thinking of a sin you've repeatedly fallen into or something obvious that is difficult for you to overcome. However, let me show you an alternative. ***The most terrible and devastating sin isn't so much the one we keep repeating, but the one we fail to see***. Do you remember the rich young man? "*I have kept all these things from my youth up*" (Mark 10:20). Jesus tells him, "Give away all your possessions and follow Me..." In other words, "Let me show you the selfishness that you are unable to see. This is your biggest problem, and what really keeps you from me."

In this sense, one of the most interesting cases is that of Peter the Apostle. After Jesus plainly told all his disciples that each one of them would struggle with the fear of man and that they would all turn away the moment he ends up in prison (Mark 14:27), here's Peter's response: "*But Peter said to Him, 'Even though all may fall away, yet I will not'*" (Mark 14:29). That is, "I'm Peter. I'm a rock. I'm nothing like other people. I'm one of a kind." In my youngest son's words, "I'm the 'total pro.'"

If you read the Gospels and analyze Peter's life in detail, you'll conclude that this man is a born leader: someone with a strong character, an energetic man who shows little regard for what others may think. After all, he was so irreverent and brazen (like my youngest son) as to openly and blatantly verbalize that he was different from all the others. (If you go over Mark 14:31, you'll notice that the rest of the disciples thought the same thing about themselves. What's different about Peter is that, impulsive as he was, he said it first.) We all know what happens next. Peter tells a servant girl, "*I do not know this man you are talking about!*" Neither you nor I could ever comprehend the magnitude of what just happened. Peter denies Jesus in front of a servant! Why should it matter that she was a servant? In their culture, women (and even more so female servants) were regarded pretty much as objects. Back then, they were so low on the social scale that they weren't even considered reliable and dependable witnesses in a court of law. Can you see the irony? Even if this woman had accused Peter of knowing Jesus, her testimony wouldn't have been valid. Yet Peter is terrified! He panics! His fear goes so far that he even insults Jesus (Mark 14:71)!

What happens next? The Bible says that Peter "*wept bitterly.*" In other words, for the first time, Peter is able to see what he fears. He now sees his own struggle. He can now see that he isn't unlike others, that he isn't any different, that he is not special. But what happens forty days later? Peter, empty of himself, became "*filled with the Holy Spirit and began to speak the word of God* ***with boldness***" (Acts 4:31). What an amazing transformation just a month and a half later! The Bible tells us that Peter was perfectly willing to be beaten, to be locked up in prison (Acts 4:3), to receive death threats (Acts 4:17; 18; 21), and even to contradict the very authorities who had had Jesus killed! ("*Annas, the high priest, was there, and Caiaphas,*" Acts 4:6.) As a result of experiencing the gospel, Peter is a different person. Now he truly is unlike others. But you and I know why. It isn't Peter; it's the Holy Spirit filling him and allowing him to live according to his new identity.

Is the struggle over? Is he done with the fear of man? Of course not! In Galatians 2:1-9, Paul says, "*Then after an interval of fourteen years* [that is, long after Peter confronted Annas and Caiaphas] *I went up again to Jerusalem with Barnabas,... and I submitted to them [to the apostles] the gospel which I preach among the Gentiles... seeing that I had been entrusted with the gospel to the uncircumcised, just as Peter had been to the circumcised (for* ***He who effectually worked for Peter*** *in his apostleship to the circumcised effectually worked for me also to the Gentiles), and recognizing the grace that had been given to me, James and* ***Cephas*** *[Peter] and John, who were* ***reputed to be pillars****, gave to me and Barnabas the right hand of fellowship, so that we might go to the Gentiles and they to the circumcised"* (emphasis added).

Notice something significant this passage points to. The passage says that the moment God worked in Peter, God worked "***effectually***" in him. The passage doesn't say he worked halfway or that his work was incomplete; it says he worked in an appropriate, proper, comprehensive, effective way. "*But, [Paul goes on to say in Galatians 2:11–12] when Cephas came to Antioch, I opposed him to his face, because he stood condemned. For prior to the coming of certain men from James, he used to eat with the Gentiles; but when they came, he began to withdraw and hold himself aloof,* ***fearing*** *the party of the circumcision.*"

Peter ***doesn't fear a group of people who could end his life, but he does fear a group of people who might have a poor view of him***. To work "effectually" doesn't mean to work "completely." Growth in the Christian life isn't an event; it's a process. Be filled with hope; you're far from being alone. Peter, the greatest of all apostles and "pillar" of the early church, is a reminder that you're in good company. We're not who we should be, yet by God's grace, we're in the process of becoming it.

BRIEF SUMMARY

We're all trying to prove our worth.

- *We build our identity based on what we are, what we do, or what we have.*
- *We desperately seek to be reassured and appreciated by others to feel worthy.*

The result of this search is threefold: we end up addicted to created things, enslaved to the opinion of others, and with empty hearts (nothing is enough to make us happy, whether we get what we so desperately wanted or not).
We all need to be awed—over and over again—by the fact that we have been justified in Christ.

- *We must base our identity on the gospel. The Holy Spirit wants to eradicate all fear by reminding me that Christ's sacrifice covers everything. We're now children of God!*
- *The key to developing a Christ-centered identity isn't thinking negatively about ourselves (feeling great guilt about our sin) or thinking highly of ourselves (feeling great complacency about our obedience), the key is to think little of ourselves and highly of what Christ has done for us.*

The outcome of living according to this identity is threefold: we are free from our addiction to created things (and we can enjoy creation without making an idol of it), we are free from the opinion of others (and we can either please or confront others as needed), and our heart is content because Christ is enough. He makes us worthy!

Why is it hard for me to live like this?

Since changing our identity is a ***process****, it takes time. It's accomplished as we increasingly enjoy being justified in Christ, and we no longer need to prove our worth (to God, to others, or even to ourselves). As God's views become increasingly more important in our hearts than the way men and women see us, we appropriate for ourselves the freedom that is ours through our "inheritance."*

FOR PERSONAL REFLECTION OR DISCUSSION IN SMALL GROUPS

1. *In what way has this chapter either changed or confirmed your understanding of how changes take place?*
2. *Sum up in one or two sentences the concepts that had the greatest impact on you in this chapter.*
3. *What things do you usually do or seek to feel important or worthy?*
4. *Do you feel addicted to anything? When you take a cold-hearted look at that addiction, what is it that draws you to it? How long does the pleasure of it last? How do you feel afterward? Is it worth it?*
5. *In what ways have you used your ministry or service in general as a means of feeling loved and accepted?*
6. *In your own words, how would you define what it means to have a Christian identity? What would someone have to do if they wanted to build their identity on Christ and not on their own merits?*

7. *What role does justification play in the process of the Christ-centered identity's formation?*

CHAPTER 9

A New Life Purpose

I love castles. The way I see it, medieval castles have unparalleled magnificence, beauty, and appeal. Few things give me more pleasure than leisurely and carefully studying their architecture. Their massive walls and towers and the contrast with the gorgeous country scenery that usually surrounds them strike me as an almost heavenly experience. When my family and I have the opportunity to visit one of these castles, we usually have a picnic just outside of it. We have a nice meal; my wife and I play with our kids; we all take lots of pictures. And all along, out of the corner of my eye, I keep sight of some spot on the castle. The way I see it, there's only one word that can define castles: they are simply "glorious."

Glorifying something or someone involves being able to <u>appreciate the qualities</u> of that object or person. To glorify something is to be able to admire the characteristics that make it stand out, that make it different, unique, appealing. In other words, ***to glorify is to be able to <u>see the beauty</u> in something.***

A few years ago, I was driving with my two young sons when Tomás, the eldest of them, asked me what it meant to glorify God. I asked him, "Buddy, who is the greatest soccer player in the whole world?"

Without hesitation, he replied, "Messi!" "What do people do when they go to the soccer stadium and see Messi play?" "They start chanting his name."

At that moment, all three of us started chanting together, "Messi! Messi! Messi!"

Then I asked him, "Buddy, why do they chant his name?" He replied, "Because he's the best. Because no one can do the things he does."

So, I told him, "That's what it means to glorify God. To glorify God is to be able to see that there's no one like him; that he's the best; that no one can do the things he does; that he's completely other and unique; that he's good and that his love is unparalleled."

Moments later, the three of us together began cheering, "Jesus! Jesus! Jesus!"

What Is the Glory of God?

In simple terms, ***the glory of God is the beauty of God.*** Everything that makes him unique, special, completely other, appealing, precious, magnificent, and virtuous. John Piper says it this way: "The glory of God is the beauty and excellence of His manifold perfections... It refers to his infinite and overflowing fullness of all that is good...The God's glory is the perfect harmony of all his attributes into one infinitely beautiful and personal being."[72] Tim Chester puts it like this: "The glory of God is the sum of all that he is: his love, goodness, beauty, purity, judgment, splendor, power, wisdom, and majesty."[73]

What, Then, Does It Mean to Glorify God?

To glorify God is <u>to be able to appreciate</u> his beauty. It is to appreciate, treasure, and value who God is. It is to find God worthy of our love and, therefore, love all of what he is. It has to do with finding tremendous pleasure in the reality of who God is and of all of what he has done for us (just as I find immense pleasure in castles and others find enormous pleasure, for example, in art). ***To glorify something is <u>to enjoy</u> it above all other things.*** To give glory to something is nothing other than to perceive that something as different and to say wholeheartedly to it, "You're not ordinary. You're extraordinary."

For instance, think of the best soccer players in world history or of the names of the most celebrated artists who have ever lived. What do we do when we talk about them? We exalt them! We praise them above all others. We see them as different. They stand out. They do extraordinary things. They're capable of doing tremendous and outstanding deeds no one else can do. Whether it is by painting or scoring a goal, for us, they stand out from the rest; in other words, we glorify them.

Before we go any further, let me clarify a critical concept for you. It's likely that as I try to describe the glory of medieval castles to you, you'll be thinking that a castle wouldn't have much appeal for you. As I briefly mentioned in chapter three, I feel the same kind of detachment or indifference towards paintings. I see the works of great artists such as Picasso, da Vinci, or van Gogh and I don't find them appealing. I'm not saying they're unsightly, but I don't appreciate them for their full worth. I see them, but I don't find them glorious!

A few weeks ago, I watched an interesting and funny video on the Internet where a Spanish soccer coach asked a Japanese player who is in the Spanish soccer league, "Are you considered handsome in your country?" In the video, you can see how the question makes both the Japanese player and his teammates who witness the scene start laughing.

Slightly embarrassed, the player finally replied, and the coach said something particularly striking, "I just don't know how to appreciate Japanese beauty. I lack the ability to discern whether you're handsome or not. I can't see you through the eyes of a Japanese girl."

This is our condition before God! We lack the ability to find him appealing unless the Holy Spirit opens our eyes and enables us to appreciate "the beauty and excellence of his manifold perfections." But please know this: to glorify something isn't just saying that Picasso's works are amazing. I can easily say that. To glorify something is to find Picasso's paintings amazing. It's to be mesmerized when you see them, to experience pleasure in admiring them, to talk about them with joy, to be willing to spend time and money just to see them. For instance, I live twenty minutes away from the Picasso Museum in Malaga and the only time I visited this famous museum was because there was no entrance fee and a friend who was staying with us wanted me to take him there. It's one thing to say that Picasso is amazing; it's quite another thing to appreciate him, experience him, and enjoy him.

Carefully think about the following questions. Can an unbeliever read the Bible and understand the truths it teaches? Can a non-Christian literature professor read a passage of the New Testament and gain an understanding of the meaning of the passage? Can a college student who doesn't believe in Jesus read John 3:16 and understand the gospel and the way to salvation? The answer to all three questions is the same: Of course they can! Any of them can ***understand*** the truth; what none of them can do is ***see the glory*** in it. They can't appreciate the value of what they've just read. They can't ***enjoy*** the truth, and so their lives remain unchanged. This is why the Psalmist prays, "*Open my eyes, that I may behold wonderful things from Your law*" (Psalm 119:18; emphasis added).

An unbeliever may understand the Bible perfectly well, but they don't regard it as amazing! Just as I can't appreciate the glory of Picasso's paintings, an unbeliever needs to have the Holy Spirit open their eyes to be able see the glory of Christ. Yet, if you think about it, you and I have the same problem. If the Holy Spirit isn't working in our hearts, we're in pretty much the same condition as they are (Ephesians 1:18-19). In some ways, our condition is more deceptive than that of an unbeliever! Why? Because we mistakenly think that understanding the truth (and even being able to communicate it to others) is synonymous with having found it glorious; we believe that accepting the gospel is the same as enjoying it.[a]

The first significant outcome of experiencing the gospel (for the first or the umpteenth time) is that I find Christ appealing all over again. Think about it for a moment. What is conversion? Conversion isn't merely believing; conversion is finding a treasure. But it isn't just finding any treasure. ***It's discovering the greatest treasure anyone could find, one for which it's worth losing everything else***. Matthew 13:44 says, "*The kingdom of heaven is like a treasure hidden in the field, which a man found and hid again; and from joy over it he goes and sells all that he has and buys that field.*" What happens when I undergo a deep change? The same thing (Philippians 3:8). I get a fresh, new view of something I already knew; that is, I can appreciate the glory of Christ. What does it mean to change? It means to find immensely appealing something that used to be of little value to me. It is to be able to appreciate God's beauty.

The Three Great Aspects of the Glory of God

I would like us to consider a concept that's absolutely crucial and yet, in turn, could cause a lot of confusion—at least it did for me for a long time.

> ***The glory of God is the means, the aim,***
> ***and the purpose of the Christian life.***

---

[a] We have to differentiate between spiritual understanding and spiritual experience. Defining the doctrine of sin isn't the same as being convicted of sin. Understanding God's omnipotence isn't the same as meekly leaning on his sovereignty. Explaining God's steadfast love isn't the same as enjoying it. Unfortunately, our hearts tend to believe that, because we understand a truth, we're living it. And not only that, but also that we're ready and qualified to teach others the truth we've just heard. (And we're typically quite happy to do so!) Ministering in the name of Christ isn't the same as enjoying him. As we have previously discussed, Matthew 7:22-23 warns us against this. "*Many will say to Me on that day, 'Lord, Lord, did we not prophesy in Your name, and in Your name cast out demons, and in Your name perform many miracles?' And then I will declare to them, 'I never knew you.'*"

What do I mean by this? I mean three things. First, that the glory of God ***changes us*** (2 Corinthians 3:18). In other words, appreciating the glory of God (all of what he is and has done in Christ) is the only means capable of producing deep changes in our hearts. Seeing Christ's unconditional love transforms us. Second, that we have been created, saved, sanctified, and will be glorified in order to appreciate the glory of God (Ephesians 1:3-14). The whole universe revolves around our being able to praise the abundant riches of "*the glory of his grace.*" As a result of this clear and decisive reality, ***our aim in life should be to treasure him more***, to enjoy him more, and to find ever greater delight in the person of God and in his work. In other words, in this second case, to live for his glory means to live to enjoy him. Third, that our life purpose must become for God to receive glory, either through us or through others (1 Corinthians 10:31). [b]

As we'll see in detail below, these three realities of the glory of God are an inseparable chain of consecutive outcomes. Only when the first thing happens does the second one take place, and only when the second thing happens does the third take place. That is to say, one is the outcome of the other, and it's **IMPOSSIBLE** to change the order. As I'll try and show you, I'll only be able to honor God when I am enjoying him; and I'll only be able to enjoy God after I've been able to see his glory. Let's look at these three ideas in detail.

*The glory of God is the **MEANS** by which we're changed*	*We change because we see his glory*	*Having an encounter with God through the gospel allows us to be amazed by God*
*The glory of God is what we **AIM** for in order to change*	*We change because we want to enjoy more of his glory*	*After we have this encounter, we remember that true life lies in living for him*
*The glory of God is our life **PURPOSE***	*We change because we want God to receive glory*	*When we truly enjoy God, we want him to be honored*

[b] As you can see, I'm making a distinction between "aim" and "purpose" to differentiate two aspects of a single goal. In other words, we live to glorify God, and this entails a dual goal: **to enjoy** and **honor** him. Both. I call the first our "aim in life" and the second our "life purpose." I make this distinction to simplify a somewhat confusing concept.

1. The Glory of God as a Means to Be Changed: Experiencing Our First Love All Over Again

Living for the glory of God is an outcome. Yes, I know that the Bible says that we must live "for" the glory of God and that the word "for" indicates purpose. Yet we'll never be able to do this unless we have first experienced the beauty of his glory. Think about it for a moment. I can't force you to find pleasure in castles. However, you can't force me to find pleasure, for instance, in eating grilled frogs. I hate frogs and toads with every ounce of my being! Although many people have told me that frogs are delicious (and they may be, I don't know), I have no intention of finding out. I find them utterly disgusting.

If someone says that they want to live for the glory of God, it's impossible for them to really do it if they aren't first, at that very moment, enjoying the virtues and excellencies of God. You can make the glory of God your goal, but you can't *live out* that goal unless you're first experiencing his glory. It would be as if someone were to tell me, "You must live to *enjoy* a barbecue of grilled frogs. They're glorious!"

My response to such a command would be, "Look. You can make me eat frog meat. You can persuade me that it's something good at which to aim my life. But until I FIRST begin enjoying frogs, *living* for eating them will only be an unattainable ideal, goal, or objective. Only when I find frogs tasty can I begin to enjoy or glorify frogs with all my heart."

Even though this illustration was a little disgusting (at least for my taste), can you see my point? ***Living for the glory of God is the outcome of enjoying the glory of God.***

Wonderful News

Allow to me puzzle you for a moment. ***The best news anyone could give you is that you can't live for the glory of God.*** Meditate on what you've just read. Neither you, nor I, nor anyone else, can live for the glory of God on their own. No one can please God. No one can put a smile on his face. No one is capable of bringing him any pleasure.

Please, don't be shocked or close this book. Far from being something negative and unbiblical, this is one of the most wonderful and liberating truths you can meditate on. Once you understand what I mean, you'll see it's true.

I remember that many years ago, when I was studying at a seminary in the United States, a professor said something that struck me so deeply that

I'll never forget it: "***God is only impressed with his Son***."[74] These words left a mark on my heart. I've given them a great deal of thought; however, I believe that I'm barely even starting to understand the extent of their implications. How can God ask me to glorify him if it's something I can't do? The answer is simple: What's impossible for me is possible for him.

In other words, the only way I can glorify God is if I'm living my life through his Son (John 15:5). Likewise, the only way I'll live my life through his Son is if I realize that I can't do it without him. So, what do I need? The gospel! A Savior who *forgives* me for not living for his glory and a Spirit who gives me the *power* to do so. What is the inevitable conclusion? ***I don't have to impress God; instead, I have to be impressed with him.***

The Christian life is about seeking the glory of Christ, with the gospel as a working filter, and about longing for him to be glorified as you are amazed by him. Can you see it? ***I can only honor him when I'm enjoying him.*** The key isn't to focus on what I have to do for him; instead, it's to be impressed by what he's done for me. When this happens, and only when it truly happens, will I be filled with the Spirit and have the power to do what I couldn't do before: glorify him.

You and I often mistakenly believe that we can glorify God. I'll go on missions. I'll share the gospel. I'll read the Bible more. I won't sin anymore. However, if you've learned a little more about your own heart through the first chapters of this book, you know that nothing we do for God is free from self-centered, selfish motivations. In fact, if you think about it for a moment, the very act of wanting to impress God is a selfish act! Many times, we live to try to get God to say, "Look what a good child he/she is." When, in reality, it's you and I who should be saying, "Look what a good Father he is!"

Several years ago, I was facilitating a church retreat with some leaders, and I was asked to share the famous passage in John 13:1-15, where Jesus washes the disciples' feet. In doing so, I briefly explained the first few verses and focused all my attention on what Jesus meant in verse 15 when he said, "*For I gave you an example that you also should do as I did to you.*" The core of the message could be summed up as follows: "Washing someone's feet means being willing to do for them what no one else would be willing to do." In other words, none of the disciples was willing to wash each other's feet, but Jesus was. As verse 15 says, our task is to imitate him. So, I spent forty minutes explaining this principle in detail and giving practical examples of how to live that principle, such as cleaning the restroom when no one else is willing to do it and things like that.

After the session, a pastor came to me, and, very respectfully, he said something like this: "I disagree with what you've shared. I don't think you've taught the core of the passage."

I was astonished because I genuinely believed that my exegesis was correct and that I'd interpreted the text correctly. Then he told me, "After listening to your talk, I leave this retreat without having looked beyond my own belly button, focusing on what I have to do; when the exact opposite should happen. ***I should leave this retreat looking at Christ, amazed by what he has done***, marveling at the fact that the God of the Universe became man, and that he's willing to wash my feet [i.e., the rottenest thing rotten thing in my heart] every day. When I enjoy this reality, I'll follow his example, and I'll do all of what you've said." He couldn't have been more right.

Your greatest effort shouldn't be directed at living for him, but rather at letting him live for you. Your primary focus shouldn't be on trying to bring him glory, but rather on seeking to enjoy his glory. Why? Because when you enjoy how wonderful and good he is, then you will be glorifying him! John Piper would say it this way: "God is most glorified in us when we are most satisfied in him."[75]

The Christian life is lived through his glory, for his glory. Although we usually focus on the second aspect, the most important one is the first. If I'm enjoying the glory of God, I'll make decisions and live my life *for* his glory. In fact, as Piper says, I already am! By enjoying the glory of God, I'm already living for his glory. Not only that, but also there's a feedback loop in this process. The more I enjoy God's glory, the more I long to live for it.

My professor was right, "God is only impressed with his Son." Three times in John 15, Jesus states that God's intention is for us to bear "much fruit" (John 15:2, 5, 8). Why does the fruit matter so much to God? The answer is in verse 8. Because when we produce "much" fruit, God receives "much" glory. This answer begs a new question: How is God glorified when we bear much fruit? The answer is in verse 5: God is glorified because it wasn't us who bore the fruit. It was Christ in us (John 15:5)! It's his glory because it's his fruit, not ours!

Understanding and living this principle is absolutely essential because *it involves everything we do:* praying, serving, preaching, evangelizing, discipling, counseling, eating, playing, working, going on vacation, and any other thing we could think of. If we truly desire to bear fruit and glorify the Father, EVERYTHING we do must be done through the Son. As John Piper so brilliantly illustrates it:

> In John 14:13, Jesus says, "*Whatever you ask in My name, I will do it, that the Father may be glorified in the Son.*" Suppose that you are totally paralyzed and can do nothing for yourself but talk. And suppose that a strong and reliable friend promised to live with you and do whatever you needed done. How could you glorify your friend if a stranger came to see you? You could say, "Friend, please come lift me up and put a pillow behind me so I can look at my guest. And would you please put my glasses on?" And so your visitor would learn from your requests that you are helpless and that your friend is strong and kind. You glorify your friend by needing him and asking him for help and counting on him.[76]

Piper's right. To give glory to the Father, we must live in dependence on the Son. To need the power of Another, one must look like a paralytic. To receive grace, we must be weak (2 Corinthians 12:9-10). That's why it isn't a matter of what we can do for Christ, but what he can do in and for us, so that every time he does it, he receives the glory. This is why the first step towards living *for* his glory is to live *through* his glory. Can you see it now? The chain can't be broken. Its sequence can't be altered. In order to give glory to God, I need to enjoy him first.

2. The Glory of God as My Goal in Life: Living to Enjoy Him

The glory of God is the means for change, and it's also our ultimate goal in life. Every time my wife and I plan our vacation, the first thing we do is find out if there are any castles in the vicinity of the city where we will be staying. We've had a taste of their glory, and we want to continue enjoying it. We all do this with that which we worship. Whether it be sex, sports, art, money, or castles, the fact of the matter is that, just like with drugs, you'll want to replay any pleasurable experiences you may have had.

Every time I visit a castle, the same thing happens: I just stare at it. If you think about it for a moment, the truth is that all castles are quite similar. There isn't much more to them than walls, towers, and wooden gates, but for some reason worth examining, I keep contemplating them! Do you think I'm crazy or obsessed? Think about sex. Doesn't something similar happen with it? For a guy who struggles with lust, is one look enough? Is one girl enough for him? However, aren't all models' bodies quite similar? What's the reason for this compulsive behavior?

And what about cars? Don't they all have an engine and four wheels? Is the kind of emblem on the hood or the car's particular shape and design really that impressive? What about clothes? Is it true that the difference between styles is so great? And shoes? Are dark blue shoes really so different from black shoes? (My wife says they are, but I honestly can't see it.)

All of us, absolutely all of us, become extremely meticulous and curious about the things we find valuable and attractive. Even when we're already familiar with them, we still analyze, study, and examine them. To test this, all you have to do is check your browser history and review your web searches. (There, you'll learn what you're actually interested in and what's truly valuable to you.) As we'll see in detail in Chapter 12, the most important job I have in life is to study, meditate, and contemplate the glory of God, so that as a result of admiring him, I can begin to enjoy him.

Tim Chester writes: "Let's sum up our motive for change: to enjoy the freedom from sin and delight in God that God gives to us through Jesus."[77] This quote makes me think of the sense of helplessness and despair that the friends and family of an addict feel (whether this person is addicted to alcohol or drugs). They want him to be free of his addiction so that he can really enjoy life to the fullest. This is what God feels for us (John 15:11)! But, Chester continues, "Our job is... to give up our ***<u>cheap imitations</u>*** and enjoy ***<u>the real thing</u>... Holiness means recognizing that the pleasures of sin are empty and temporary***, while God is inviting us to magnificent, true, full, and rich pleasures that last forever."[78] What's your drug of choice? What takes your breath away? What captures your imagination and makes you daydream? What do you regard as virtuous and worthy of praise? ***The secret to change lies in being certain that the glory of God is the true source of happiness.***

3. The Glory of God as My Life <u>Purpose</u>: Living to <u>Honor Him</u>

When I'm in Christ, the Holy Spirit changes my desires and shifts my goals. I *<u>can</u>* now do what I couldn't do before (glorify him); moreover, I *<u>desire</u>* to do it. To have the glory of God as my life purpose involves two things: honoring God and inviting others to honor him.

Two life purposes	*What am I chasing after?*	*What means are available to me?*
Honoring God	*For God to look good because of me*	*Singing worship songs, my lifestyle, and my service to God*
Inviting others to honor him	*For God to be known because of me*	*Getting involved in evangelism, discipleship, and missions*

To See Is to Desire to Worship

Have you ever wondered why people sing at soccer games or why audiences cheer after they see a wonderful artistic performance? The answer isn't complicated: every enjoyable thing brings about spontaneous adoration, compliments, and praise. C. S. Lewis said, "***I think we delight to praise what we enjoy because the praise not merely <u>expresses</u> but <u>completes</u> the enjoyment***."[79] In other words, praise is the consummation of our pleasurable experience. Like a young couple who are in love and constantly declare their love for one another. They already love each other, but verbalizing it enhances and completes the experience.

Singing to God is a wonderful way to bring him honor. Why? Because, from a biblical perspective, singing is the ***<u>outcome</u>*** of enjoying God. James 5:13b says, "*Is anyone cheerful? He is to sing praises.*" Can singing worship songs *<u>bring</u>* joy and be a *<u>source</u>* of joy? Yes, it can. But that shouldn't be the typical experience. Singing worship songs should be the *<u>outcome</u>* of being joyful, the result of it (just as cheering is the outcome of having watched a great show). The biblical ideal is for us to come to the worship time to sing praises. In other words, to honor God because I'm deeply in love with him, and I want to express that love.

Can God use worship songs to soften my hard heart and change me? Of course he can! But that's not his primary goal. Some time ago, my ten-year-old daughter and I were spending time together in God's presence, listening to worship music. She had been lying on a couch but, at some point, she began fiddling around with her legs and pretending to be riding an invisible bicycle. A while later, she began singing the song with reluctance as she slowly slid her back down the couch to the floor.

She's young, and I get it. It doesn't bother me at all that she plays or gets a little distracted, as long as she retains a certain degree of awareness of what we're doing. Eventually, I stopped the music, and I told her, "Sweetheart, what does it mean to worship someone?"

She replied, "To say nice things about them, to sing to them."

Then, in a deliberately exaggerated listless tone, I said to her, "What a nice shirt you're wearing."

She gave me a rather disapproving look. "I said something nice to you, didn't I?"

"Yes, but you weren't feeling it."

"That's right, sweetie. Worship isn't just singing or saying nice things about someone. ***Worship is feeling nice things for someone.***"

What I tried to explain to my daughter is what I'm trying to explain here. Saying something nice about someone should be the ***outcome*** of feeling something nice about them.

I'll admit it. I'm not a big fan of music. I know that our emotions (as opposed to our affections) can easily be manipulated by music. We often believe that we're praising God because a song moved us when, in reality, we're unaware that the only thing the song is doing is having an emotional effect on our hearts (much like a dramatic movie makes us cry, even though we know it's fictitious). However, I'll also be quick to admit how important and tremendously valuable worship music is. I've spent many of my most precious moments with God alone in my office, listening to worship songs and weeping like a child as I sang praises to him.

From a biblical perspective, music is extremely important! After all, the largest book in the entire Bible, the Psalms, is a songbook! I won't say much more than that, but to worship God, whether being present at church or alone in the privacy of our homes, is to join in anticipation of one of the most beautiful and satisfying experiences we'll have in heaven (Revelation 21:23-27). Not only that, but as I've pointed out a few times already, emotions are very important to God, and it's both necessary and healthy to express them (Matthew 22:37-38). As Psalm 47:7 (KJV) says, being able to sing "*with understanding*" (i.e., thoughtfully and consciously) what I truly feel for God is one of his most wonderful gifts.

Present Obedience, Present Glory, but Also Future Glory

To live for the glory of God is to live so that others may see God's character. The Bible is very clear when it declares that our lifestyle can bring honor to God. Matthew 5:16 says, "*Let your light shine before men in such a way that they may see your good works, and glorify your Father who is in heaven.*" In this sense, our lifestyle is so *other* that it stands out in such a way to our friends and neighbors who don't know God that they might say something like this: "I've never seen anyone love the way you do. It's very unusual. How can you live like this?"

When this happens, God is glorified. Living this kind of life isn't the duty of a few chosen ones. It's a command that we should all live out, not in church, but rather outside of it! At home, at work, and in all the smallest details of our daily lives. As Paul puts it in 1 Corinthians 10:31, "*Whether, then, you eat or drink or whatever you do, do all to the glory of God*" (emphasis added).

Some time ago, I asked a young man that I'd been discipling for several years what life experiences out of the many we'd shared had made the greatest impression on him. Just so you understand the context a little better; he'd lived at my home for a while; he went on mission trips with me; he heard me preach countless times; we evangelized together; we confessed our sins to each other; I gave him advice dozens of times, and much more. I was astonished by his reply. I thought he would tell me he'd been most impressed by a message or my wise counsel, but he didn't.

He said, "The thing that impressed me the most was that one time when we were at a gas station, and the attendant accidentally broke your windshield wiper, and you offered to pay for it. No one does that kind of thing when they're wronged."

Can you see it? Just a detail! Something "ordinary" but "completely other" and, at the same time, commonplace. I had honestly forgotten all about it until he brought it up. I wasn't even aware that he was paying attention. However, in a simple action, he saw the glory of God, and it made an impression on him.

As I mentioned earlier, "the power" to live this way isn't the outcome of working at it; rather, it's the natural outcome of enjoying the glory of God through the gospel. *When* this happens, and only when this happens *first*, we "automatically" begin ***to connect our joy to seeing God receive the glory***. What do I mean when I say this? Allow me to illustrate it with an example.

A few years ago, a close friend and I were discussing who was the best soccer player of all time. He said it was Cristiano Ronaldo, and I said it was Messi. (Obviously, anyone who knows anything about soccer will agree that I was right.) Why was I making such a strong case for Messi? Because, even though it may not be easy to see, I connect my joy and happiness to his victories. In other words, in a sense, when he wins, I win. When he scores a goal, I score a goal. When he receives glory, I rejoice! What a great paradox this is; I've never even seen Messi in real life! I don't know him personally. I've never shaken his hand. Nevertheless, ***for him to receive glory and recognition makes me happy! His glory is my joy!***

This is what God wants us to get to. Not to some compulsory, self-conscious effort to do things I don't want to do, but rather to an overflowing passion that I can't contain. This is exactly what happens to me when I talk about Messi. ***I have so much appreciation for him that I want others to appreciate him too!*** Do I have to force myself to talk about him? Of course not! They have to ask me to shut up about him! (Don't rush to label me a fanatic. The same thing happens to you with whatever it is that you happen to be passionate about.)

On the other hand, living for the glory of God not only brings honor to God today but, in a way, it "accumulates" glory for God for the great "*day of Christ*" in the future. Look at what Paul writes, "*And this I pray, that your love may abound still more and more in real knowledge and all discernment, so that you may approve the things that are excellent, in order to be sincere and blameless until the day of Christ; having been filled with the fruit of righteousness which comes through Jesus Christ, to the glory and praise of God*" (Philippians 1:9-11; emphasis added). Although this passage is very rich, and I'm tempted to elaborate on it at length, allow me to merely break down a key aspect that I want to highlight.

Paul says that when we learn to love better, we choose better and, therefore, we accumulate a "greater amount of fruit" for the day we stand before God. What is the outcome of this? God will receive glory! (Why God and not us? Because if you look closely at the same passage, you bore those fruits "*through Jesus Christ.*") I know what Paul is saying sounds a bit strange, but it's only strange until you update it with a more current example. If you take a moment to think about it, we all do this. We all do things *today* because we know they have a worthwhile effect *tomorrow*.

A good example, also used by Paul in 1 Corinthians, is that of athletes. 1 Corinthians 9:24-25 reads, "*Surely you know that many runners take part in a race, but only one of them wins the prize. Run, then, in such a way as to win the prize. Every athlete in training submits to strict discipline, in order to be crowned with a wreath that will not last; but we do it for one that will last forever*" (GNT). A 100-meter sprint is over in just ten seconds. A soccer game lasts ninety minutes. A marathon takes a few hours. Athletes spend most of their lives living "for future glory." They do things today to get something tomorrow. They spend most of their day exercising, practicing, taking care of their bodies, and working out. Why? For the glory that awaits them.

To live for the glory of God is to join in this great mission. It is to be passionate about that moment. It is to start thinking more often about the fact that very soon, when "the great day" comes, ***Someone I love with all my heart will be crowned.***[c] (If you're a parent, the feeling I'm describing is similar to the one you experience when your child excels at playing sports or when they finish a race. The anticipation of seeing them crowned encourages you to go to great lengths to help make it happen. Why? Because their glory is your joy.)

To See Is to Desire to Share

When my wife and I first got married and were still living in Argentina, one of the things we enjoyed the most was driving around Carilo, a well-known and very exclusive beach town on the Atlantic. We never went on vacation there; we couldn't afford it. Yet we weren't really dying to do that. What my wife and I liked doing was driving around, gazing at the fabulous houses in the area. Just as we do with castles today, we enjoyed admiring their architecture.

Picture this: I would draw a kind of mental grid of all the streets in Carilo, and every day we'd drive through a different part of this beautiful town. Sandy roads, huge pine trees of various sizes and colors, and an endless number of impressive houses owned by the "rich and famous." Neither my wife nor I really wanted to go on vacation to Carilo, much less live there. Just looking at the houses was enough for us. As we used to say, "We love to enjoy the riches of others." The point is, if you'd been in the car with us, you would have heard one word repeated over and over again every time we went on that drive. "Look! Look at that house! Look at this other one! Look at their yard! Look at the way they decorated it! Look how beautiful it is! Look! Look! Look!"

Every act of enjoyment brings about a desire to share. All of us talk about what we enjoy; we can't help it. We can't shut up about it. What happens when you come back from vacation, when you buy clothes, or when your favorite soccer team wins? You want to talk about it! In fact, you can't stop doing it! What do most people do when they take a picture someplace nice?

---

[c] The same principle is applicable to our service. When I serve God in Christ, I glorify Christ. "*Whoever speaks, is to do so as one who is speaking the utterances of God; whoever serves is to do so as one who is serving by the strength which God supplies; so that in all things God may be glorified through Jesus Christ, to whom belongs the glory and dominion forever and ever. Amen*" (1 Peter 4:11; emphasis added). The reason I'm not developing this idea yet is that we'll come back to it in detail in Chapter 11.

They share it on Facebook. We all want to share what is worthwhile and special to us.

To see is to desire to share. In our case, sharing how amazing God is to us is expressed in three practical ways: ***missions***, ***evangelism***, and ***discipleship***. I find the mission statement at *Bethlehem Baptist Church*, where John Piper is a pastor, fascinating. When they define the reason for their existence as a church, they do so with these very precious words, "***We exist to spread a passion for the supremacy of God in all things for the joy of all peoples.***"[80] What a great way to sum up why we're all here!

How is this accomplished in a practical and tangible way? By regularly getting involved in personal evangelism, discipleship of fellow believers, and supporting missions through prayer and charitable giving. ***No one*** who is a true Christian can stay away from these three areas. If I claim that God is my greatest treasure and have no passion for that treasure, there's something wrong! ***To experience the glory of God is to desire to share it with others. Conversely, if I have no desire to talk about God or for others to know him, it's only because I'm not enjoying him.*** It's because I fail to see and appreciate his worth and beauty.

What do I have to do if this is the case for me? Should I force myself to evangelize? Should I force myself to sing? Should I force myself to serve? I don't think so. As we'll see in the next chapter, that isn't the *first* step. What I need to do is go back to the million-dollar question: Why? Why am I not passionate about God? What is my goal in life today? What am I currently giving my heart to? What captivates me? What is competing for God's place? What do I find glorious that keeps me from seeing the glory of Christ?

Change begins when I make the correct diagnosis and administer the correct medication. After I can see what I'm trapped in, I'll be able to reach out to Christ for deliverance. As John Piper says,

> If you don't feel strong desires for the manifestation of the glory of God, it is not because you have drunk deeply and are satisfied. It is because you have nibbled so long at the table of the world. Your soul is stuffed with small things, and there is no room for the great.[81]

How Can I Tell If I'm Glorifying God?

I believe we can narrow down the answer to this question to a single word: contentment. How can I tell if I'm living for the glory of God right now? I think the best way to tell is if I can see that my heart is full, if I have joy, if his glory satisfies me and is enough for me. What is contentment? Contentment is a state of the heart where we are full, where our main desires are satisfied, and where our basic needs are met. According to the Bible, that state of inner satisfaction only comes when I drink the "water" that really satisfies (Isaiah 55:1-3; John 4:13-14).

Consider with me a passage that confirms this idea. Philippians 4:13 says: "I can do *all things through Him who strengthens me*" (emphasis added). In some circles, this verse is interpreted like this: "***Christ gives me the strength to do anything***." If this interpretation were right, which it isn't, what Paul is saying here is that Christ transforms me into some kind of superhero.

That means that, following this interpretation, Jesus can give me the physical strength to lift a car, stop a train, or to fly. The passage says "everything," so "everything" includes the strength to do anything. Although these are deliberately far-fetched examples, think about how mistaken this interpretation is. Have you ever met any Christian who has more physical strength than others and is kind of a superhero after praying or spending time with God? The obvious answer is: "No."

Well, a second and healthier interpretatio is that the passage refers to something spiritual rather than physical. In this case, what Philippians 4:13 is saying is: "***Christ gives me the spiritual power to endure anything***." If we look at the context for this passage, Paul is writing to the Philippians to thank them for an offering they had sent him. In verses 11 and 12, he says that he's learned to have no money for food and he's also learned to have money in abundance. In either situation, it's Christ who strengthens him.

That is, according to this interpretation, Jesus gives Paul the spiritual power to endure or deal with either a situation of scarcity or one of prosperity. He can do everything in him. (I admit that I used to interpret the passage in this way until just a few weeks ago when I returned to it and meditated on it deeply.) I believe that this way of approaching the passage is incomplete, to say the least.

In order to correctly understand the passage, we need to define certain key points. First, Paul is clearly talking about something spiritual and not something physical. Paul isn't talking about his stomach; Paul is drawing an analogy. He isn't saying, "A non-Christian can go without food for forty days at best. With Christ, that same person could fast for eighty." No, that's not the teaching here. Paul's talking about the heart, not the stomach!

Maybe, a more accurate paraphrase of the passage would be, "***Christ gives me the ability to be fully satisfied whatever my circumstances are***." I know that this interpretation looks quite like the previous one, but you'll realize that there's a big difference if you carefully think about it. Paul is saying more than just, "Christ gives me the strength to endure anything." Paul says that he's ***absolutely content, full, satisfied, and entirely happy*** in Christ! What Paul is saying is that he's discovered the secret that he has everything he needs in Christ.

If you think about it for a moment, Paul's repeating what he'd already said in Chapter 1 and Chapter 3. "*For to me, to live is Christ*" (Philippians 1:21) and "*I count all things to be loss in view of the surpassing value of knowing Christ Jesus my Lord, for whom I have suffered the loss of all things, and count them but rubbish so that I may gain Christ*" (Philippians 3:8). Can you see it? It's much more than just being able to effectively cope with abundance or hardship. I have some non-Christian friends who can do this just fine. Paul's talking about something far deeper and more comprehensive. Paul's talking about a radical change in my life purpose and my source of life.

Now, let me ask you something. How did Paul learn to live like this? The answer is in verse 12. Notice what that verse says, "*in any and every circumstance I have learned*" (emphasis added). This means that different circumstances in his life have shown him and taught him to live this way. That is, it's something we learn. It's not a natural thing! Good and bad circumstances have been teachers in his spiritual life that have allowed him to learn the secret that Christ is the only thing that can satisfy him.

But please notice that not only difficult circumstances or scarcity help him understand this, but also moments of great well-being have taught him that! To be honest, in my case, the moments of greatest abundance have been moments when I was least happy. Yes, you've read correctly. Let me give you a practical example.

A few years ago, we started a kind of family routine we call a "special time with Daddy." During "special Daddy time," my kids and I do something unique and fun together. Sometimes I take one child at a time; other times, I bring all three of them together. Soon after we started this routine, I decided to buy bikes for all of us so we could go out for a ride on Saturday mornings. I had originally intended to do this to spend quality time with the kids while giving my wife some kid-free, quiet time at home. Since I hadn't been on a bike for over two decades or more, it was quite novel for everyone.

The first day we did it was just amazing. It was almost as remarkable an experience for me as visiting a castle. I said to myself, "This is amazing!" Since we had only recently moved to Spain, and we lived by the sea, the landscape we saw while riding our bikes was as unfamiliar as it was inviting. The sun, the beach, the palm trees, the mountains... Riding our bikes together was priceless to me! Over and over, I would tell my kids, "This is heavenly!"

However, as the weeks went by, I started noticing my mood would shift every time we went out. The thing is that one of my kids would quickly get tired, and he didn't want to ride his bike for long. I remember constantly telling him, "A little bit more, Buddy. Just a little more. We just left the house." However, within a few minutes, he would insist. After starting to get internally upset by his persistence, I devised a strategy to shake the problem off. I told the three of them that I would buy them ice cream once we got to a place that wasn't far from our destination. Naturally, their attitude changed. But what happened when we had to go back? My son was tired again, which goes to show the obvious: bribery isn't a good driver for change.

After he complained some more, I snapped. I told him, "That's enough, son! You're going to keep quiet until we get home!"

Can you see what happened? What had begun out of a desire to show love for my wife and kids had turned into an unhealthy form of worship. My heart shifted. I traded what I desired. My being there was no longer an act of love towards my wife and kids; I was there to love myself. What was the result? I was no longer content in my heart, I spoke to my son in a hurtful way, and I ended that bike ride full of bitterness. Why? Because I traded worshiping God for worshiping created things.

What did this experience teach me? That nothing in creation has the power to fill the heart. Can you see it? ***Circumstances can be invaluable teachers that remind us that true life isn't in doing what we want, but it is hidden in Christ*** (Colossians 3:1-3). This is the great secret that Paul learned: to live for something that circumstances cannot touch. Not just to have the power to endure difficult circumstances, but ***for Christ to be my pearl of great price in everyday situations***. No one, and nothing, has the power to rob you of your joy if your joy is in the person of Jesus. When I have him, I have everything; without him, even if I have everything, I have nothing.

Freedom from Needing Circumstances to Change

Contentment is an outcome. Neither you nor I can force it. You can't force me to be happy; I either am, or I'm not. You can try to change the circumstances to make me happy, but you can't force me to be satisfied. If a car runs my son over, you can try to comfort me, hug me, walk with me in my time of grief, but you can't force me to be happy. As we said at the beginning of the book, if I don't like ballet, you can force me to go to a recital with you, but you can't force me to find pleasure in it and feel fully satisfied and happy in my heart.

The same goes for the glory of God. How can I tell if I'm glorifying God? The answer is very simple: If I examine my heart, and I find it free from other passions; that is, if appreciating the glory of God is enough for me, and it fills me. In short, if I'm content.

If this is not your case today, let me encourage you by elaborating on a teaching from Philippians 4. Paul says in verse 12 that: "*In any and [by means of] every circumstance I have learned*..." (emphasis added). What does this mean? That change is a process. Being content in Christ is something you learn. As mentioned earlier, God is using your current circumstances, even your struggles and your lack of joy and appreciation of God, as a means to change you deeply and fill you with himself.

One of the most vivid and clear examples in the Bible of how God uses our circumstances to draw us to himself is found in Hannah's life. In 1 Samuel 1:5, we learn that Hannah was barren. Few things back then were more shameful and dreadful for a woman than not being able to have babies. (It would be pretty much the same as going past a certain age without a boyfriend, a steady job, or a college degree in some circles today.) Hannah's heart was completely unsatisfied. If you read 1 Samuel 1:5-8, you'll notice that she was bitter, irritated, envious; she would cry, she didn't eat, and she was so empty that she was unable to enjoy her husband's genuine love.

However, Hannah does something that I would encourage you to do; she prays. She pours out her heart before God, expressing how desperate she was to have her wish fulfilled. "Give me a child, or I'll die!" (Hannah is the living image of how something we desire can be transformed into an idol.) What did God do? The opposite of what you would expect: he gave her what she longed for!

Why would God do that? It would seem as if he's doing the exact opposite of what we've seen in this chapter. It looks that way, but it isn't. God uses Hannah's unfulfilled desire to draw her to himself, to show her (and us) that we're living for the wrong thing.

In a very powerful way, Hannah's case is a perfect example of how the Spirit intercedes for us and "transforms" our prayers into something better.

> "*In the same way the Spirit also helps our weakness; for we do not know how to pray as we should, but the Spirit Himself intercedes for us with groanings too deep for words; and He who searches the hearts knows what the mind of the Spirit is, because He intercedes for the saints according to the will of God. [That is, he gives us what God wants to give us.] And we know that God causes all things to work together for good to those who love God, to those who are called according to His purpose*" (Romans 8:26-28; emphasis added).

Hannah prays for a baby, and while it's true that God gives her a child, God also gives her something better—something ***much*** better—***God gives her the gift of being satisfied in him***. 1 Samuel 1:18 says that, after praying, she "*went her way and ate, and her face was no longer sad*" [emphasis added]. When did she stop being sad? Was it when she got what she wanted? Of course not! She had no way of knowing if she was going to have a child or not. However, the following verses go: "*Then they arose early in the morning and worshiped before the Lord, and returned again to their house in Ramah. And Elkanah had relations with Hannah his wife, and the Lord remembered her. It came about in due time, after Hannah had conceived, that she gave birth to a son; and she named him Samuel, saying, 'Because I have asked him of the Lord*'" (emphasis added).

What is the great evidence that her heart really found contentment in God? The proof is that when it was time to give him up, she was able to let him go. In fact, if you pay attention to the passage, you'll notice that she didn't do it reluctantly, but with an *inexplicable* sense of joy and gladness. 1 Samuel 1:21-28 says:

> *Then the man Elkanah went up with all his household to offer to the Lord the yearly sacrifice and pay his vow. But Hannah did not go up, for she said to her husband, "I will not go up until the child is weaned; then I will bring him, that he may appear before the Lord and stay there forever." Elkanah her husband said to her, "Do what seems best to you. Remain until you have weaned him; only may the Lord confirm His word." So the woman remained and nursed her son until she weaned him. [Think about how short a time she had him with her!] Now when she had weaned him, she took him up with her, with a three-year-old bull and one ephah of flour and a jug of wine, and brought him to the house of the Lord in Shiloh, although the child was young. Then they slaughtered the bull, and brought the boy to Eli. She said, "Oh, my lord! As your soul lives, my lord, I am the woman who stood here beside you,*

> *praying to the Lord. For this boy I prayed, and the Lord has given me my petition which I asked of him. So I have also dedicated him to the Lord; as long as he lives he is dedicated to the Lord." And he worshiped the Lord there* [emphasis added].

Would you like to find out what 1 Samuel 2:1-10 (that is, the section right after one you just read) is all about? It's one of the most wonderful worship songs that any human being has ever written. But think about it! She wrote this song right after she left her only child, her little boy, at a stranger's house. Can you see it now? Where was her greatest joy? What filled her heart? Where did this woman get such contentment? (You already know the answer.)

However, if you think about it for a moment, there's a much more remarkable and striking question we could ask the passage. What happened to this depressed, self-centered, and bitter woman? Where did that empty, unsatisfied person go? The answer is simple: An encounter with God transformed her.

Don't be discouraged. There's hope just yet. God longs for you to appreciate his glory more than you long to appreciate it. More than that, he is using every situation in your life (even your unfulfilled desires) so that you can admire it.

Conclusion

All the glory this world can long for, feel, or offer (all the *Golden Globes*, the *Oscars*, the *Emmys*, all the promotions at work, all the increases on your paycheck, all the vacations, all the cars, all the houses, all the boyfriends or girlfriends, all the children, all the castles), ALL of it put together and much, much more is the kind of glory that God has and wants to share with you. This glory, which is available to you because of Christ, is the glory that God wants you to begin to experience and enjoy.

This is perhaps the best share of your inheritance. Why? Because God himself is his greatest gift to you. There's nothing and no one better than him. John Piper explains it in this way:

> Jesus *himself*—and all that God is for us in him—is our great reward, nothing less.... Salvation is not mainly the forgiveness of sins, but mainly the fellowship of Jesus (1 Corinthians 1:9). Forgiveness gets everything out of the way so this can happen. If this fellowship is not

> all-satisfying, there is no great salvation. If Christ is gloomy, or even calmly stoical, eternity will be a long, long sigh.[82]

God created you, saved you, and is sanctifying you to enjoy him. One day, that joy will be complete, but until then, keep Jesus' words in mind: "*These things I have spoken to you so that My joy may be in you, and that your joy may be made full*" (John 15:11; emphasis added). Who could place anything better before us?

To the only one who offers unparalleled pleasure, to the only one who satisfies us completely, to the only one who deserves our whole heart, "*to the only wise God, through Jesus Christ, be the glory forever. Amen*" (Romans 16:27)

BRIEF SUMMARY

What does it mean to glorify God? *It means to be able to appreciate his beauty; it means to love his virtues; it means to find increasing pleasure in all that he is and in all that he's done in Christ for you.*

What does it take to glorify God? *We can only live for the glory of God after we've first had a personal encounter with him (through the gospel) where we find him "appealing" all over again. To glorify something with our hearts, we must first enjoy it and appreciate its worth. My approach shouldn't be to try to impress God, but rather to live impressed by him.*

How do we go about bringing glory to God? *We can only honor God if we're living our lives filled with the Spirit of Christ. Anything else we do without him, no matter how good it is, will not bring him honor.*

How do I know if I'm giving glory to God? *First, if he's enough; if my heart finds his beauty increasingly satisfying. Second, if I'm willing to share my experience with others; in other words, if I'm spontaneously starting to evangelize and to disciple others and to get involved in missions.*

FOR PERSONAL REFLECTION OR DISCUSSION IN SMALL GROUPS

1. *In what way has this chapter either changed or confirmed your understanding of how changes take place?*
2. *Sum up in one or two sentences the concepts that have had the greatest impact on you in this chapter.*
3. *In your own words, how would you define the glory of God? What does it mean that the glory of God is the means, the goal, and the purpose of the Christian life?*
4. *Why can't someone glorify God on their own merits? In what areas of your life is it "natural" for you to try to do this? Why do you think you tend to go there?*
5. *What do you usually associate with pleasure? Why do you think this is so precious to you?*
6. *Do you currently feel passion for talking about Jesus to others? Why? Why not? What is the solution in order to start doing it? Do you have a non-Christian friend, family member, or co-worker in mind about whom you'd like to start praying for their salvation and for you to be on the alert for the opportunity to share the gospel with them?*
7. *Are you currently discipling someone? How would you define discipleship in light of what you've read in this chapter? Would you like to begin meeting once a week with someone to help them grow in their spiritual life? Perhaps you could read this or some other book together and discuss it every time you get together.*

CHAPTER 10

A New Ability to Obey

Undergoing deep change produces two major outcomes in the life of every believer. On the one hand, it gives me a ***new motivation*** to obey, and on the other hand, it gives me ***new power*** to do so. Let's look at each of these aspects carefully.

A New Motivation to Obey: To Remain in His Love

What is obedience? ***Obedience is an outcome.*** This is the most important truth you will learn in this chapter. This truth must be impressed upon your mind and engraved on your heart. Meditate on it because it's absolutely crucial that you fully understand it for any sort of real change to take place.

As we have emphasized throughout the book, ***what you do is the outcome of what you love***. You watch TV because *you enjoy it*; you go shopping because *it gives you pleasure*; you choose to date someone because *you like* them. Your actions are the outcome of what you find appealing, valuable, and worthy of your love. Therefore, ***true obedience is the outcome of enjoying Christ.***[a]

Jesus said, "*The kingdom of heaven is like a treasure hidden in the field, which a man found and hid again; and from joy over it he goes and sells all that he has and*

[a] In fact, if you think about it for a moment, ***disobedience*** is also an outcome. It's the ***outcome*** of your heart loving sin more than God and therefore choosing to disobey. Disobedience is the *fruit*, the *effect*, the *consequence* of what your heart loves. For example, if your heart loves prestige, ***as an outcome*** of it, you will disobey God by exaggerating, lying, highlighting your virtues, minimizing your defects, justifying yourself, making excuses, blaming others, etc.

buys that field" (Matthew 13:44; emphasis added). As we said in the previous chapter, true conversion isn't just believing; true conversion is finding that precious pearl. It's finding the greatest treasure for which everything else is worth giving up. In other words, to convert is *to begin* to treasure and love Jesus. To be sanctified is to *grow* in that love!

Take a closer look at the passage. Leaving everything and "selling all that he had" is the ***outcome*** of Christ becoming his pearl of great price. That is, first he must mean everything to you, he must be your greatest delight and your greatest love; and then, ***as an outcome*** of that, he changes your lifestyle, the decisions you make, and your priorities. This kind of appreciation for Jesus, which first takes place at the moment of our conversion, is the kind of experience we should long to re-live daily. That's the reason you spend time on your daily devotions each day.[b] That's why you go to church every Sunday. That's why you're part of a small group. The greatest goal you have in doing so is to be able to admire and to be amazed at Christ's love once again, just as you did on day one. The purpose of each of these activities, as Jesus would say, is to remember "*your first love*" or to increase it (Revelation 2:4; 1 Timothy 1:5).

Let me give you a clear, biblical example of how obedience works. Acts 1:15-16 says, "*At this time Peter stood up in the midst of the brethren (a gathering of about one hundred and twenty persons was there together), and said, 'Brethren, the Scripture had to be fulfilled, which the Holy Spirit foretold by the mouth of David concerning Judas, who became a guide to those who arrested Jesus*'" (emphasis added). In this passage, Peter says two absolutely precious things about the character of God. First, he says that God is faithful. In other words, when God says he'll do something, he always does it. If he predicts (through Scripture) that he'll do something, he consistently does it in every situation.

Think about yourself for a moment. What do you see when you look at your heart? I'll tell you what I see in mine. I see a heart that is divided, which is the opposite of faithfulness. I see an adulterous heart. I see someone who loves God one moment and, five minutes later, he loves himself. Now, what do you see when you look at God's heart? Unchanging love. Steadfastness. Faithfulness. Consistency. Peter says, "Brothers and sisters, when we consider God, there is no doubt about it. He is unlike us. He delivers." A faithful person is someone who has made a commitment to another person and (motivated

---

[b] Notice that, when we say the phrase "daily devotions," the very word "devotion" indicates that the act involves a deep passion. Devotion is a feeling of deep admiration inspired by the dignity, virtue or merits of a person, an institution, or a cause.

by their own character and not by the way the other person responds), never stops loving them and always delivers on their promises. Peter is clear. What God had promised "*had to*" be fulfilled.

Very well, so far, I haven't written anything particularly new or striking. However, keep looking at the passage. What did God plan for before the foundation of the world? What "*had to*" be fulfilled? For Judas to hand Christ over. This means that ***God designed the whole of human history in such a way that all the events in it led to one climax: his own death.*** In other words, everything that happened from Genesis 1 to Acts 1 was directed, controlled, and planned by God so that this portion of Scripture would be fulfilled.

Take a moment to think about what God did. All of us make plans. All of us plan a number of things. Personally, I like planning what my day will look like, what we're going to do as a family on the weekend, where we're going to go on vacation. You and I also make plans for work and for our ministries; we plan birthday parties; we make plans to go to the movies, and a thousand other things. We all make plans; we do it all the time. However, ***no one plans a way to suffer on behalf of others.*** Peter says that ***God arranged history in such a way that he'd be handed over by one of his friends***.

At that very moment (that is to say, after he remembers this precious truth about God's character), Peter says in Acts 1:21, "*Therefore it is necessary that [we choose one] of the men who have accompanied us all the time that the Lord Jesus went in and out among us.*" Notice the word "*therefore.*" What is Peter trying to indicate with this conjunction? I'll paraphrase it for you: "Because God has shown his love on the cross by planning his own life so that he'd be handed over, and because we read the Scriptures and we understand that he wants us to choose a substitute, *therefore (because of that, as a consequence, as an outcome of it)*, let us obey and choose a substitute for Judas."

How does Christian obedience work? Christian obedience works this way: God shows his amazing faithfulness and love and, THEREFORE (i.e., as an outcome of that), I find him worthy of all my love, trust, and devotion, and I obey him. What is obedience? ***Obedience is the outcome of having your eyes opened to what God has done, is doing, and will do. Obedience is the consequence of seeing his goodness.***[c]

---

[c] We see the same dynamic at work in the famous passage in Romans 12:1 (GNT): "*So then, my friends, because of God's great mercy to us I appeal to you: Offer yourselves as a living sacrifice to God,...*" The conjunction "so then," which in NASB is translated as "therefore," functions in the same way as the conjunction "*therefore*" in Acts 1:21. What does Paul say in this passage? The same thing I explained above. "Since" we've experienced God's mercy (the gospel), because we've tasted his mercy and since we've perceived his reality, ***THEN*** let's surrender our lives as a living sacrifice, holy and pleasing to God. Paul's clear. Surrender is the ***outcome***, the consequence,

Obedience Is the Outcome of Christ's Being Enough

If you conscientiously examine your behavior, you'll notice a meaningful truth: ***obedience is the outcome of being full, and disobedience is the outcome of being empty***. Think of a dad who's watching TV after a long day's work, and his two kids start arguing. What does he do? He yells at them in anger: "Stop fighting! I can't put up with you guys anymore! You're so inconsiderate!" What did this man just do? He just disobeyed God's law. The Bible clearly says that we shouldn't yell or speak in hurtful ways to others (Matthew 5:22; Ephesians 4:31). But why did this dad do what he did? I think you know the answer by now. However, let me put it differently for you. This dad snapped at his kids because he was ***empty***. What do I mean? I mean that, as far as he's concerned, this dad "needed" to rest, and he was trying to ***satisfy*** that need for rest by watching TV. Why did he respond with sin and disobedience to God? Because his kids interrupted him when he was "***recharging***" emotionally and spiritually.

What does someone do with their treasure? They hide it, guard it, and protect it. If it's money, they'll keep it in a safe deposit box in a bank. If it's a house, they'll install an alarm system and shut the door with a lock and key. If it's a car, they'll make sure to keep it in a garage. If it's their reputation, they'll make sure to suppress their impulses in public to avoid being ridiculed. If it's their break after work, they'll get angry and yell to protect that moment. Why do we go there? Because we love our treasures. Because we don't want to lose them. Because we don't want anyone to lay hands on them.

Picture the following situation. Let's say you inherit one hundred million dollars. What would you do with all that money? You'd place it in a CD account and go on to live the rest of your life off the interest it yields. Let's say that one evening you go out to dinner with your spouse and, after paying cash, the waiter gives you ten dollars in change. You immediately leave a five-dollar tip, and you put five dollars in the right pocket of your jacket. As you're leaving the restaurant, a guy rushes by and bumps into you. Without you even noticing, he slips his hand into your right pocket and picks it. A few moments later, you realize what's happened. What would your response be? Would you get worked up and call the police? Would you start screaming your head off? Would you get desperately anxious? Not likely. Why? Because even though

the fruit of having received God's mercy.

that guy has taken something valuable from you, he hasn't laid hands on your greatest treasure! Your one hundred million dollars are safe in a Swiss bank.

Congratulations! You didn't scream! You didn't get angry! You didn't get upset! Why? The answer is obvious. No one has laid hands on your treasure. No one has put a finger on what you really love. In other words, your non-sinful response is the outcome of still being a millionaire. You responded well because you are "satisfied" and "full" because you have everything you need and more. Your treasure is intact. But what would happen if you went home and, on accessing your bank account online, your balance was down to zero? What would your response be? Would you call the police? Would you start yelling? Would you be upset? Do I need to spell it out for you? Why? Because now they've taken away your most precious possession.

Every time we sin, we're saying that something other than Christ is our greatest treasure. If a dad yells at his kids because they interrupt his moment of rest, what this man is showing is that his children have laid their hands on his "treasure." At least at that moment, his reason for living and his greatest desire is to watch TV; his treasure is being able to unwind and rest. Did the dad in our story disobey God's law? Yes. Does this man have to stop yelling at his children? Yes. But, the most important question is, in <u>**WHAT**</u> way should he obey God? Is it by resorting to self-control? By turning off the TV when he returns home? By counting to ten before speaking?

The key to obedience is to realize that ***my response, good or bad, is an <u>outcome</u> of what "fills" me***, of what is my "greatest treasure" at that very moment, of what is my "pearl of great price." The key to obedience is to realize that I've exchanged Christ for the eight o'clock news. That he no longer is my source of life. As John Piper says, "***Sin is what you do when your heart is not satisfied with God.***"[83] Yes, your children have interrupted your moment of rest, but the key is to realize that the problem isn't your children or resting. The problem is that you've exchanged your treasure. If Christ were as valuable to you as those one hundred million dollars, if he *<u>truly</u>* had this *<u>precious</u>* place within your heart, your kids' interruption would be the equivalent to the five dollars that the guy in our story stole from you when you were leaving the restaurant. If something as insignificant as missing the news for two minutes triggers such a massive and disproportionate response, what have you just proved? That, at that moment, Christ wasn't what you loved most.

Sin is anything you do that shows that Christ isn't your treasure. As Romans 1:23 puts it, it's exchanging the glory of God for the glory of created things.

What is the solution? Should I bite my tongue when my kids interrupt me? No! ***The solution is to realize that I have to remember my first love!*** Can you see it? This man **WAS ALREADY EMPTY BEFORE** his children interrupted him. Always and in every situation, we're "empty" before we disobey. Why? Because disobedience is an attempt to "fill yourself." (Isn't that what the dad in our story was after by watching TV?)

As we learned in Chapter 4, we sin because sin offers a promise of happiness. Every temptation is an alternative, an offer of well-being, a wrong solution to your need (do you remember Jeremiah 2:13?). What should we do? We should return to our first love through the gospel. Only when you start enjoying Christ again as if he were as valuable as a hundred million dollars, will you be, without any major inconvenience, able to gladly allow five dollars to be stolen from you. Maybe you can now see it: obedience is the outcome of being full, and disobedience is the outcome of being empty.

Obeying Is the Outcome of Loving

John 14:15 reads, "*If you love Me, you will keep My commandments.*" For many years, I misinterpreted this passage. For me, loving Jesus was the same as obeying him. The way I would paraphrase it was: "Loving Jesus is keeping the commandments." However, read the passage carefully. That's not what Jesus is saying. Obeying Christ isn't the same as loving Christ. Jesus says that love comes first and that obedience follows. Someone can be perfectly obedient without loving. The Pharisees are the prime example! Obeying Jesus is the effect, the outcome, the consequence of loving Jesus. John Piper states it in this way:

> I reject the notion that love for Christ is identical to mental or physical acts done in obedience to his Word. When Jesus said, "*If you love me, you will keep my commandments*" (John 14:15), he was describing the ***effect*** of love, not the essence of love. ***First*** there is love, then there is the effect—obedience. The obedience is not identical with love.[84]

John 3:19 makes a noteworthy statement. The apostle writes, "*This is the judgment, that the Light has come into the world [that is to say, that Jesus came into the world], and men **loved** the darkness rather than the Light [i.e., rather than Jesus], for their deeds were evil.*" John is saying something very revealing. He's saying that God's "judgment," his way of assessing people, the standard he uses to measure the heart of humans is to determine ***what they love or hate***. Not their actions, but the thing their heart loves.

How do we know what a person loves? The passage also gives us the answer to that: through their actions. Their actions were evil ***because*** they loved the darkness! Their heart was in the wrong place, and so they rejected Jesus. What has to happen for someone to actually obey? What this person loves has to change. They have to stop loving the darkness (the misguided, unsatisfying things this world has to offer), and they have to start loving the light (Christ). What does it mean to change? It means to begin to love something I used to hate (the light/Christ) and to start hating something I used to love (my life outside of him). ***Sanctification is the process of finding more and more pleasure in the right place: Christ***.

A Change in Perspective

I'll never forget my first day as a student at Dallas Theological Seminary. I was in a foreign country, with people I didn't know, surrounded by hundreds of individuals from different parts of the world who, like me, had come to be trained and to learn more about the Bible. Everything was amazing for me. I couldn't have been happier. I was fulfilling my great dream of studying at one of the most prestigious seminaries in the world. Even as I write these words, I still feel a trace of the same emotions I experienced at that moment.

That day, the campus chapel was packed with teachers and students. I had my Bible open and a brand-new notebook ready to take notes and jot down anything they might say that I thought was relevant. When it was time for the message, the president of the seminary stood up and, taking the pulpit, he read from 1 Timothy 1:5. That was enough for me. After he read this verse, I just "zoned out." I was so struck by what Paul was saying in this passage that I couldn't pay attention anymore. I don't remember a single word this man said throughout his message.

1 Timothy 1:5 reads as follows, "*The goal of this instruction is love that flows from a pure heart, from a clear conscience, and from a sincere faith*" (ISV). Can you see what Paul is saying? Paul is giving the reason why a young man, like me at the time, attends a seminary (and it wasn't the reason I was there!). Paul is saying that ***the purpose of our instruction*** (in other words, the purpose of studying the Bible, of attending seminary school, of spending time in our devotions, of joining a Bible study group, going to church every Sunday, even the purpose in reading this book) ***is to learn to love better***.

I had come to this seminary to study the Bible, not to learn to love! (I was terribly mistaken.) However, pay attention again to what the rest of the passage says. The passage doesn't talk about three separate things. Paul *doesn't* say that the purpose of our instruction is love born of a pure heart, "*and to have*" a good conscience, "*and to have*" sincere faith—as if these were three different things. Read the verse carefully. Paul says, "*The goal of this instruction is love that **flows from** a pure heart, **from** a clear conscience, and **from** a sincere faith.*" "A pure heart," "a good conscience," and "a sincere faith" are modifying the word "love"!

In other words, the reason I seek instruction is to grow in those three aspects of love, so that my love will spring from these three internal and invisible realities (what we know as the unseen portion of the iceberg). That is to say, we receive instruction to learn to love (both God and others), with a heart that has increasingly pure motivations (a pure heart), that is free from evil thoughts (a good conscience), and that truly places its trust in the work of Another to do so (a sincere faith)! God's greatest objective is for me to change the way I love.[d]

When you and I think about change, we usually connect it to changing or modifying some type of behavior. I used to yell at my kids every night; now, I don't do it as often. I used to masturbate; now, I don't struggle with it as much. I used to cheat on my taxes; now, I tell the truth. However, from a biblical perspective, although change brings about changes in behavior, it's much more than that! Deep change, ***the change that God brings about, is to make the gospel wonderful***. It is to make Christ attractive; it's a kind of change where we're seduced by the beauty of all that God is for us in Christ.

What's the Great Commandment? How can we sum up everything the Bible teaches? Is it "*for you will obey* the Lord your God with all your heart, with all your soul, and with all your strength"? Of course not! The Great Commandment is to love him. It's for us to find him more precious than anything this world has to offer.

Think about it. What does it mean to magnify Jesus? What does it mean to exalt Him? I'll let Paul take this question: "*According to my earnest expectation and hope, that I will not be put to shame in anything, but that with all boldness,*

---

[d] If you look at Paul's letters, you'll notice that the apostle usually prays the exact same thing for the churches he writes to. "*May the Lord greatly increase your love for each other and for all people, just as we love you*" (1 Thessalonians 3:12 ISV). "*And this is my prayer, that your love will keep on growing more and more with full knowledge and insight, so that you may be able to choose what is best and be pure and blameless until the day when the Messiah returns, having been filled with the fruit of righteousness that comes through Jesus the Messiah so that God will be glorified and praised*" (Philippians 1:9-11 ISV).

Christ will even now, as always, be exalted in my body, whether by life or by death. For to me, to live is Christ and to die is gain" (Philippians 1:20-21; emphasis added). What does it mean to "exalt" Christ? What does it mean to "magnify" Christ? In Paul's words, it's for us to view all the other things this world has to offer as trash when compared to him. This includes castles, sex, money, rest, television, movies, art, your vacations, your boyfriend/girlfriend, your car, your family, and even your own life. (If you don't see it that way, check out Luke 14:26.)

Why does Paul say that "dying is gain"? Because you'll be face to face with Christ. Because you'll be able to see him without hindrance. Because you'll be able to enjoy him completely. Of course, you'll lose many things. You'll lose your family, your friends, your job, your home, your car, your vacations, sex, and countless other pleasures I couldn't begin to enumerate. However, it's gain because, even if you miss out on all of that, nothing compares to Jesus! In Piper's words, what does it mean to exalt Christ? For Christ to be ***"treasured more than all that life can give, and more than all that death can take***."[85]

A New Approach

Let me put it a different way. ***It's not about focusing on changing my behavior; it's about focusing on changing what my heart desires.*** This is an idea that should permeate your entire spiritual life. What God is after isn't just for me to stop watching pornography; what God is after is for me *to desire him more* than sex. What God is after isn't just for me to spend less money on clothes, but rather *for me to love him above* the opinion of others. What God is after isn't just for me to stop compulsively watching TV, but rather *for my heart to enjoy his presence* more than a movie. ***Sanctification is the process of change whereby God works in my heart through the Holy Spirit so that I may see Christ more and more beautiful and where, as an outcome of this, my values change. In other words, what changes is what I love, what I think, and what I do***.

God's purpose is for me to love him. When I love him, I no longer sin. As we saw with Jonah and as the Pharisees clearly show us, it's possible to not sin (in a traditional sense) and yet not treasure Jesus. If someone spends long hours watching television every day or following a strict diet to slim down, they've done nothing wrong. But what is it that their heart treasures? What is it that gives them pleasure? There's a definition of sin that I read several years ago that I really like. Sin is: "whatever weakens your reason, impairs the tenderness of your conscience, obscures your sense of God, or takes off your relish of spiritual things... that thing is sin to you, however innocent it may be in itself."[86]

Looking at Jonah's life or passages like Matthew 6:1 reminds us that ***we could obey God without loving him*** (we could give, pray, fast, evangelize and do a thousand "spiritual" things in self-love); yet at the same time, ***we can't love God without obeying him***. When I'm full of passion, captivated by his love for me, the outcome is that Christ works in me. This way, as John 15 says, we begin to produce "*much fruit*" (John 15:5). That is, we undergo tremendous changes, both on the inside and outside.

Obeying isn't doing the right thing; obeying is loving the right thing.
When I love what I should love, I do what I am supposed to do.
I can obey without loving, but I cannot love without obeying.

Distracted by Jesus

Let me share a personal experience with you that can help you better understand how this dynamic works in real life—in this case in particular, how it applies to a moment of trial. (I've deliberately changed several of the details in this story so as not to expose any of the people involved.) One of the things I struggle with the most is putting up with injustice. I usually have no problem asking for forgiveness if I've actually done the thing I'm being accused of, but if someone says something about me that isn't true, there's a volcano inside of me that starts boiling over.

Some time ago, I had to go through an experience like that when someone said some nasty things about me. This person didn't just privately make those allegations; on the contrary, they made very ugly and false accusations out in public in front of several people who witnessed the scene. This person then made sure to share those accusations with other people too.

When this person was done saying everything they had to say, a friend who had witnessed the event came up to me with tears in his eyes and said, "How can you stand by without saying a single word after all the lies and nonsense this person said about you?"

My response was, "Don't cry." (My friend was literally crying in frustration.) "I can honestly say that this has been one of the happiest moments of my life."

My friend gave me a puzzled look.

I continued, saying, "I'm enjoying Christ so much just right now that not only has what this person said about me not affected me, but I've also been extremely happy every last second of it! This is the first time in my life that I can say that I lived James 1:2, "*Consider it all joy, my brethren, when you encounter various trials.*""

For me, the experience I described above wasn't difficult; it was simply impossible! Can you see it? Yes, I obeyed the command in James 1:2, but it wasn't me who did it; it was Christ in me! (It was being distracted by him; it was being focused on him.) I do not respond well when confronted the wrong way. I do not keep quiet when I'm wrongly accused. I am not happy and full of joy in the thick of trial. There's no room for human merit here. It was God's supernatural work that made me capable of responding in ways ***I never could***!

The passage that always comes to mind when I recall this experience is Philippians 4:7 (NKJV): "and *the peace of God, which surpasses all understanding, will guard your hearts and minds through Christ Jesus*." That is what God did for me that day; he kept my heart and mind focused on Jesus Christ. What was the result? Great joy and peace!

Maybe you struggle with pornography; maybe you struggle with constantly being aware of what others think of you. Perhaps you feel you're a slave to your sin and that there's no hope. I totally get you. My struggle with putting up with injustice (along with many other things I would be ashamed to say) is as "impossible," equally "insurmountable," and just as "beyond my reach" as is yours. But I want you to have hope. It's not about striving to do something you can't do; it's about recognizing that it's impossible for you to obey. It's about acknowledging that you're loved despite your disobedience. It's about his incredible love seizing you and moving you.

A Secret Revealed

One of my favorite books is *Hudson Taylor's Spiritual Secret*. Taylor was the first missionary in history to penetrate the interior of China in the mid-19th century. He lived there for 51 years. He was rejected many times; he got sick and, on various occasions, he didn't even have any food. In one of his letters to a friend, he wrote, "It is pretty cold weather to be living in a house without any ceilings and with very few walls and windows. There is a deficiency in the wall of my own bedroom six feet by nine, closed in with a sheet, so that ventilation is decidedly free. But we heed these things very little."[87]

Hudson Taylor lost two of his children and his wife in the mission field (as I write this, just to think that something like that could happen makes the tears roll down). At the end of his life, someone asked him if it was worth it. If his devotion, his dedication, and his years of sacrifice had made up for all the difficulties he had faced. His answer was, "Sacrifice? ***I never made a sacrifice.***"[88] What makes a man claim such a thing? Let's look at a particular moment in Taylor's life that holds the key:

> "The Lord Jesus received is holiness begun; the Lord Jesus ***cherished*** is holiness advancing; the Lord Jesus counted upon as never absent would be holiness complete....
>
> "He is most holy who ***has most of Christ within***, and ***joys most fully*** in the finished work..."
>
> This last sentence, I think I now fully endorse. To let my loving Savior work in me His will, my sanctification, is ***what I would live for*** by His grace. Abiding, ***not striving*** nor struggling; ***looking off unto Him***; trusting Him for present power;... resting in the love of an almighty Savior, in the joy of a complete salvation, 'from *all* sin'—***this is not new, and yet 'tis new to me***. I feel as though the dawning of a glorious day had risen upon me. I hail it with trembling, yet with trust. I seem to have got to the edge only, but of a boundless sea; to have sipped only, but of ***that which fully satisfies***. Christ literally *all* seems to me, now, the power, the only power for service, ***the only ground for unchanging joy***."
>
> How then to have our faith increased? ***Only by thinking of all that Jesus is*** and all He is for us: His life, His death, His work, He Himself as revealed to us in the Word, ***to be the subject of our constant thoughts***. Not a striving to have faith... but a ***looking off*** to the Faithful One seems all we need; a resting in the Loved One entirely, for time and for eternity.
>
> [The authors of the book say,] We do not know just how the miracle was wrought; but 'As I read, I saw it all,' Mr. Taylor wrote. '***I looked to Jesus, and when I saw— oh, how joy flowed!***' ....
>
> It was ***the exchanged life*** that had come to him—the life that is indeed '***No longer I***.' Six months earlier he had written, 'I have continually to mourn that I follow at such a distance and learn so slowly to imitate my precious Master.' ***There was no thought of imitation now***! It was in blessed reality '***Christ liveth in me***.' And how great the difference!—instead of

bondage, liberty; instead of failure, quiet victories within; instead of fear and weakness, ***a restful sense of sufficiency in Another***."[89]

What was Hudson Taylor's spiritual secret? It was the same as Paul's in Philippians 4:13. His secret was to appropriate "the fathomless wealth of Christ" to satisfy every need, whether physical or spiritual.[90] This is what you and I need.

I'm Controlled by What I Love

Since love is a response, you and I are controlled by what we love most. If we love our reputation disproportionately, we'll be disproportionately controlled by the opinion of others. If we love our image, we'll be controlled by the current condition of our beauty. If we love our quiet time, we'll be controlled by what brings us satisfaction. If we love sexual pleasure, we'll be controlled by pornography. And the list could go on. ***The thing that controls us is our god, our master.***

If you're honest with yourself, you must have noticed that your heart can't say no to certain things. Don't think I'm any different. Sometimes I feel the best way to describe me is as a slave or an addict. I can't stop doing what I know I am not supposed to do. This feeling is completely normal (Romans 7:15). But why is it normal? Because, as we said in Chapter 3, love is a *response* to what we perceive to be our greatest good.

None of us lives without a master and free from being a slave to that master. You're either a slave to your own desires, which makes you an addict and leaves you thirsty and empty, or you're a slave to Christ, who is able to fill you with life and give you true freedom. Paul says in Romans 6:16 (NLT), "*Don't you realize that you become the slave of whatever you choose to obey? You can be a slave to sin, which leads to death, or you can choose to obey God, which leads to righteous living.*" Then he restates this idea at the end of the epistle by saying, "*For such men are slaves, not of our Lord Christ, but of their own appetites…*" (Romans 16:18). We all have a master. We're all controlled by what we love most. Therefore, ***the key to beginning to obey is to first change what I love***!

I Obey Because I Want More of His Love

Many people tend to ask the following question: Why should I obey God if he'll forgive me for absolutely anything I do? If you think about it for a moment, a person who asks this kind of question does nothing but expose the coldness of their own heart. Without even trying, they've just revealed that they're not a true believer or that they haven't really come to enjoy Jesus yet.

Asking that kind of question would be like inheriting one hundred million dollars and arguing, "Why should I follow the bank's rules and use an ATM for withdrawals? Why should I be forced to own a debit card? Why would they have me memorize a pin number? Those requirements don't sit well with me."

If someone said something like that, we'd surely tell them, "Why should you comply with the bank's requirements? So that you *enjoy* the money! With the money you withdraw from the ATM, you can go to the movies, to the theater, or on vacation; you can buy a car, a house, etc. Don't you understand the value of having one hundred million dollars?"

It sounds like a foolish argument, doesn't it? No one in their right mind would ask questions like these. However, the argument itself isn't all that foolish if you were to ask my youngest son. If you ask my four-year-old son whether he'd rather have ice cream or a debit card in his name with one hundred million dollars on it, what do you think he'll choose? (I don't have to tell you, do I?) What is my son's "problem"? The answer is simple: It's a matter of maturity, of ignorance, of blindness, of lack of "light." My son ***is incapable of appreciating the value of what he's being offered***. Do you get it now? We all have the same problem. The Bible says that sin increases our blindness (Ephesians 4:17-19; 2 Corinthians 4:3-4). It prevents us from appreciating Christ's value. It prevents us from enjoying him, which is why we ask these kinds of questions.

In Chapter 7, we mentioned that Christ left us the commands precisely ***to reverse this situation***. John 15:10 reads, "*If you keep My commandments, you will abide in My love, just as I have kept My Father's commandments and abide in His love.*" Do you remember what this passage teaches? Jesus doesn't say, "Live by my commandments, and I'll love you." Jesus says, "Live by my commandments, and you'll *experience* my love." In other words, keeping the commandments is ***the means*** for us to be able ***to appreciate*** and enjoy how much he loves us. That's why the next verse says, "*These things I have spoken to you so that My joy may be in you, and that your joy may be made full.*"

When we analyzed this passage at the beginning of the book, we said that Jesus' words in this verse are so amazing that they even sound heretical. ***The fruit, the outcome, the gift of living the way Jesus did will be experiencing as much joy as the happiest person who ever walked on this earth.*** This means that God wants us to enjoy as much happiness as his Son did! Where can we find this happiness? In one place only. Close to him. Why do we obey? Because we don't want to miss out on the appreciation that comes from his love. Because we want more of him. Because we have been loved, and we want to love the One who loves us.

It's Not about Loving Him Exclusively; It's about Loving Him First so that You Can Love All Other Things Well

I know I have put emphasis on the love of God, but I wouldn't want to be misunderstood. Enjoying Jesus doesn't just change our relationship with God. It also changes our relationship with the world. ***Enjoying Jesus allows us to also enjoy all the things God has given us, but without becoming a slave to them.***

Does the Bible say that you can't love soccer? Does the Word of God say that it's wrong to go on a diet? Does God condemn us for enjoying a nice vacation? Does the Bible say that we should love him ***alone***? The answer to each of these questions is the same. Of course not! Several times in the Bible, God himself tells us to enjoy all the things he has given us (1 Timothy 6:17-19).

As we have seen, the problem arises when we turn God's blessings into our reason for living (into idols) and love them excessively (i.e., more than him). Whenever this happens, the thing or person we love above God offers to give us life, but it ends up leaving us empty. However, when we enjoy Christ, we no longer seek to have these things fill the hole that only he can fill. In this way, for the first time, we can enjoy them without becoming addicted to them. We can now appreciate our family, friends, work, and possessions as gifts from a God who loves us. We can now enjoy God's creation because we're enjoying the Creator. ***We no longer go into the world to seek life; we go into the world being full of life***.

In fact, if you think about it for a moment, the same thing happens to a paralyzed person who is miraculously healed and can walk again. Their *whole* life changes! Not only can they walk again, but their *whole* life is affected. They can now do things free from pain, more quickly, and without depending on others. They can now easily run, jump, go to work, play tennis, basketball, or soccer, take a walk on the beach, hike in the mountains, or drive a car. Everything changes and their life is revolutionized because something has been healed.

The same thing happens when we enjoy Christ and he truly heals and fills our hearts. Now everything seems to have a different glow to it, and it's as if our "senses" have been enhanced. We enjoy our whole lives with greater intensity! Our relationship with our spouse deepens, we have energy and passion for serving our co-workers, we find ourselves to be extremely patient and compassionate as we listen to others, we even eat a delicious meal in a nice restaurant, and we're deeply grateful because we see who the Giver is behind these gifts. Being full allows life to overflow. This has always been Jesus' intention: that you would have an abundant life (John 10:10).

New Power to Obey

Several years ago, I was in the attic at home spending time with God and, after he spoke to me in a very real and powerful way, I ran down the stairs extremely happy and, unable to stop myself, I called out to my wife from the last landing, "God spoke to me! God spoke to me! God showed me something amazing!"

My wife looked at me with great anticipation and asked me, "What did he say to you?"

With great joy, I answered, "That I am a sinner!"

Only someone who has seriously tried to change, and failed miserably, knows that the best news anyone could possibly give you is that you can't change yourself. There's no better news than finding out that deep change depends on Someone else.

Please, do this for me. Think about this question for a moment. How would you describe a spiritual person? What comes to mind when you think about someone like that? Is it someone who's reading the Bible? Praying? Helping others? Evangelizing? Let me give you an answer that's more in tune with the Bible. ***A spiritual person isn't someone who does "spiritual things"; a spiritual person is someone who's filled with the Spirit.***

Being a spiritual person isn't (mainly) about what someone does, but it's about ***the way*** they do what they do. The *way* you obey is more important to God than your obedience in and of itself. God cares much more about whether you obey by your strength or his. Why? Because that is what he left his Spirit for! Paul says in Galatians 3:3: "*After starting your new lives in the Spirit, why are you now trying to become perfect by your own human effort?*" (NLT). Jonathan Edwards wrote, "Another reason why the saints and their virtues are called spiritual (which is the principal thing), is that the Spirit of God is dwelling as a vital principle in their souls."[91]

Keeping in mind that I'm a sinner, discovering my spiritual poverty, and recognizing that I don't have the strength within myself to change doesn't mean giving in to passivity. It doesn't mean that I should stop praying, that I should stop reading the Bible, that I shouldn't fast, and that I should wait for God to tap me with his magic wand and change me. ***Acknowledging that I don't have the strength to change demands that I seek strength elsewhere; it requires that I depend on the Person who can give me that strength.*** What is obedience? ***Obedience is the outcome of receiving a new power.*** It's the ability to do what you could never, ever do. It's the consequence of God's supernatural work inside your being.

Early Christians: Our Best Example

At the beginning of the book of Acts, we see a group of frightened, fearful, and disoriented people. If anyone has ever felt like a complete failure on a spiritual level, Peter and the rest of the disciples are at the top of the list. *All of them* fell asleep when the Lord needed them (Luke 22:45). *All of them* ran in fear when he was arrested (Matthew 26:56). *All of them* watched from a distance while he was being executed (Luke 23:49). However, by Acts 1, *all of them* do the only thing a human being can do to change: they go to the place where they can receive strength from Another; they wait for "what the Father had promised" (Acts 1:4).

I would like you to notice the major contradiction that Jesus' words seem to show in this episode. He says in Acts 1:4-5, "*Gathering them together, He commanded them not to leave Jerusalem, but to wait for what the Father had promised... the Holy Spirit.*" Now read what Jesus said to them **BEFORE** that "*And He said to them, 'So it is written, that the Christ would suffer and rise from the dead on the third day, and that repentance for forgiveness of sins would be proclaimed in His name to all the nations, beginning from Jerusalem. You are witnesses of these things.*'" (Luke 24:46-48 NASB).[e]

Can you see what just happened? Jesus told them, "I command you to go out into the world to be my witnesses, *but don't go out*!" "This is what I want you to do, *but don't do it!*" "*Don't do what I want you to do*!" What are the disciples supposed to learn from this? And how about Theophilus, the intended reader of both books? What is the lesson here for you and me? ***I can't do what God has sent me to do. I don't have the power to act the way God wants me to. I can't live as God expects me to live unless I'm experiencing the fullness of the Holy Spirit.***

[e] Now remember that the book of Acts is the second volume of Luke's gospel. They're both written by Luke and both addressed to the same person, Theophilus. That means that Acts 1 begins where Luke 24 ends.

My many attempts to break my cycles of sin, all my efforts to try to change, my desperate struggles to stop being a sinner are all completely useless—which is why seeing myself as a sinner all over again that day brought me so much joy. "Leaving Jerusalem" without the Spirit of God is a recipe for failure. ***No supernatural change is going to take place unless Someone supernatural is at work in your life.*** What do we get from this? ***The most important job we have in life is*** giving up our own attempts to change and ***being filled with the Spirit***.

Before moving away from Acts 1, I would like to show you one detail in this chapter that I think is just awesome. Acts 1:1-2 says, "*The first account I composed, Theophilus, about all that Jesus began to do and teach, until the day when He was taken up to heaven, after He had by the Holy Spirit given orders to the apostles whom He had chosen.*" Have you paid attention to the preposition there? According to Luke, it's "*by the Spirit*" that Jesus gives instructions to his disciples before he ascends into heaven.

In other words, it's the Spirit who tells Jesus: "Here's what I want you to tell them." In other words, it's as if the Holy Spirit were whispering in Jesus' ear, "Say this." (Think about it for a moment. What could be so important that the Spirit of God would go through the trouble of giving Jesus such specific instructions?) What does the Spirit say to Jesus? "Tell them not to go out! Tell them that it's better for You to go away so that I can come upon them! Tell them that, without my help, they can't do anything!"

Unless I'm mistaken, there's only one other time in the entire New Testament where the Holy Spirit is as clear and direct with Jesus as in this case. No doubt you know this event by heart; it's the time when he "*is led by the Holy Spirit*" into the wilderness to be tempted. I would like you to read the whole passage where Luke describes what happened "*Jesus, full of the Holy Spirit, returned from the Jordan and was led around by the Spirit in the wilderness*" (Luke 4:1; emphasis added).

Have you paid attention to the two underlined phrases? What is Luke saying? Just before the moment of trial, just before he was tempted, just before Jesus had to prove his obedience, Jesus needs one thing: to be filled with the Spirit! ***The very God of the universe become human needs to be filled with the Spirit to face temptation; what makes me think I can make it without having the Spirit myself?***

John 5:19 (NKJV) says, "*Then Jesus answered and said to them, 'Most assuredly, I say to you, the Son can do nothing of Himself, but what He sees the Father do; for whatever He does, the Son also does in like manner'*" [emphasis added]. Disciples can do nothing on their own. The Son of God can do nothing on his own. We can't do anything on our own either!

Many scholars who write about the Book of Acts claim that the book shouldn't be called the "Acts of the Apostles," but rather the "Acts of the Holy Spirit." The same should be said of your life and mine. They are his acts, not ours. As John 3:21 says, "*But he who practices the truth comes to the Light, so that his deeds may be manifested as having been wrought in God*" [emphasis added]. That is to say, by him.

The Fullness of the Spirit

Being filled with the Spirit implies desiring what the Spirit desires. What does the Spirit desire? I'll take a pass on answering this question and let Christ himself tell you: "*But when He, the Spirit of truth, comes, He will guide you into all the truth; for He will not speak on His own initiative, but whatever He hears, He will speak; and He will disclose to you what is to come. He will glorify Me, for He will take of Mine and will disclose it to you*" (John 16:13-14).

What is Jesus saying? That one day (and that day is precisely in Acts 2, the passage that follows right after the one we analyzed above), the Spirit is going to allow the apostles to see things that they hadn't seen before. What will they be able to see? That Jesus is absolutely glorious. That he is the most appealing being in the universe. That he is the pearl of great value and that nothing and no one compares to him.

What happened after the disciples saw that? The same eleven men, who were scared and full of fear, gained such courage that they were able to stand up to the same authorities who had previously tried to kill them (Acts 4:12; 19:20). What does it mean to be filled with the Spirit? ***To be filled with the Spirit is for the Spirit to show me the glory of Christ and for that glory to produce new desires and dreams in me.***

Why do we need to be filled with the Holy Spirit? The answer is very simple but extremely profound. ***We need the Spirit because we don't have the power to change what we desire.*** As you can clearly see from the figure, we have the power to do many things. We have the power to pray, read, serve, preach, and do a million other things, but we lack the power to change what we love. We lack the power to change what really gives us pleasure and motivates us. We lack the power to desire something different, or rather, Someone different. On our own, we lack the ability to realize that Jesus is better than sex, better than money, better than a vacation, better than a boyfriend, better than prestige, and better than anything else creation has to offer. We lack the capacity to perceive him to be appealing.

Therefore, what the Spirit does is open our eyes so that we can see what we could never see otherwise: the beauty and excellence of Jesus (Ephesians 1:18-19). The work of the Spirit is what John 16:14 says: to "glorify" him; to present Jesus to me as appealing; to allow me to see him for what he is: utterly amazing. When this happens, when I can see the character of Jesus (shown in its fullest form through the cross), then, and only then, do I obey in the full, biblical sense of the word.

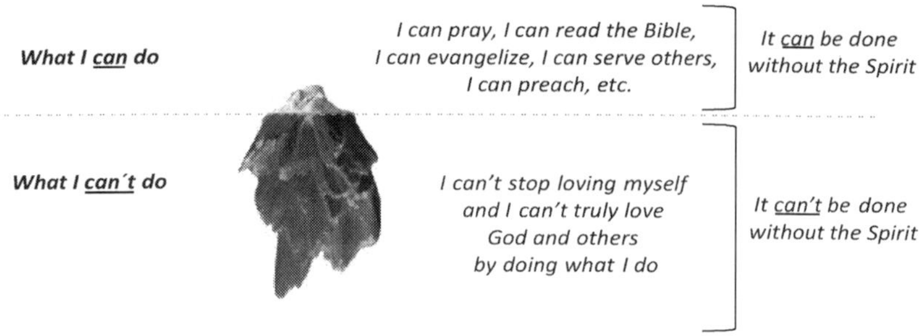

What does it mean, then, to be filled with the Spirit? Before I answer the question, let me puzzle you for a moment. I believe that the fullness of the Holy Spirit is often defined in the wrong way. We have a distorted view of what it really means. Being filled with the Spirit is often connected with different religious activities, such as praying, fasting, or reading the Bible, and also with various "acts of love" (such as yielding in the face of conflict, serving the poor, etc.). I think it's important for you to see that this isn't necessarily the case. Let me give you two examples from the Bible to prove it.

Imagine it's Saturday morning, and you're walking around downtown. It's a sunny day, all the restaurants are open, and lots of other people are walking around you. Imagine that you're standing in front of a large cathedral in the middle of a square packed with market stalls. Suddenly, you start hearing some people screaming and others rushing past, while an irate man seems to be destroying everything that stands in his path. What do you think? Is he a terrorist? Well, no. He isn't a terrorist; he's Someone filled with the Spirit. Matthew 21:12 says, "*And Jesus entered the temple and drove out all those who were buying and selling in the temple, and overturned the tables of the money changers and the seats of those who were selling doves.*"

When confronted with a scene like that, who would say that Jesus was filled with the Spirit? Who would connect that moment with being filled with God's love? Do you think maybe Jesus wasn't? There's no need for speculation; John 2:17 gives us the answer. The reason why Jesus destroyed everything in his path can be summed up in one sentence: "*Zeal for Your house has consumed me.*" In other words, he was "consumed," "full," "bursting" with passion for God and a desire for others to experience the same. That is why he overturned the tables.

Now let me show you the other side of the coin. It's nighttime. A group of soldiers is approaching Jesus. His best friends have been sleeping. He's been praying like never before in order to face the events ahead of him. Someone who had followed him for three years gives him a kiss. One of his disciples draws a sword and wounds the High Priest's servant cutting off his ear. "*Then Jesus said to him, "Put your sword back into its place... Or do you think that I cannot appeal to My Father, and He will at once put at My disposal more than twelve legions of angels?*" (Matthew 26:52-53). Later they will judge him. But he keeps quiet. They beat him, spit on him, take off his clothes, and once again, we see no reaction. The soldiers make fun of him. People sarcastically scream, "*If You are the Son of God, come down from the cross... He saved others; He cannot save Himself*" (Matthew 27:40-42). What does Jesus do when he is arrested? Nothing. What does Jesus do when they insult him? Nothing. What does Jesus do when they crucify him? Nothing. Being a witness to this scene, who would say that this man has power? Who would draw the conclusion that this man is filled with the Spirit? And yet, there never was and never will be a more Spirit-filled human being than this man is at this very moment.

On the outside, two polar opposites. On the inside, one and the same state of the heart. What does it mean to be filled with the Spirit?

> *It means that what I <u>love</u>, what I <u>think</u>, and what I <u>do</u> is influenced or controlled by the Holy Spirit in such a way that I <u>desire</u> for God to be glorified, I <u>seek</u> his kingdom, and I <u>act</u> by his power.*

Why does Jesus overturn the tables in the temple? Because the glory of God consumes him. Because that is what he *<u>loves</u>*, that is what he *<u>thinks of</u>*, and, therefore, that is why he *<u>does</u>* what he does. Why does Jesus give himself over to be crucified? For the same reason he does the exact opposite at the temple. I'll let him put it into words for me: "*And lifting up His eyes to heaven, He said, 'Father, the hour has come; glorify Your Son, that the Son may glorify You*'" (John 17:1). Jesus *loves* one thing only; he *thinks* of one thing only; for Jesus, only one thing determines why he *does* what he does: the glory of God. That's what being filled with the Spirit looks like.

The Bible compares being filled with the Spirit to being filled with alcohol; with being drunk. When someone is under the influence of alcohol, they dare to do and say things that they never would sober. They have "power," "courage," and "bravery." When someone is under the influence of alcohol, they are "free." To be filled with the Spirit involves something similar. It's to love what you'd never love (the glory of God and not your own). It's to think about what you'd never think about (the Kingdom of God and not your own kingdom). It's to do what you'd never do, for example, confronting others when you would remain quiet or not speaking up when you would typically confront them.

Being filled with the Spirit allows you to be someone you are not! It's starting to *feel*, *think*, and *act* in ways that are contrary to your nature. Why? Because you're being controlled and driven by Someone else. Let me say it in a way that's even closer to the Bible. What is it to be filled with the Holy Spirit? ***To be filled with the Holy Spirit is to love God with all my heart, with all my soul, and with all my strength and to love my neighbor as myself.***

To Obey Is to Find Pleasure

When most non-Christians think of obedience, they think of it in negative terms. The best image to illustrate this concept is a Nazi concentration camp. In a concentration camp, you follow every order you're given. When you're there, at all times, ruthless guards force you to do a number of things that you hate, such as taking off your clothes, living in confinement, walking in line, digging holes, or eating disgusting food. In other words, many people view obedience as a horrible and reprehensible act of self-denial. In other words, *to obey is to do what I don't want to do for someone I don't love.*

That's not what Christian obedience is. Christian obedience is something different. Christian obedience is a change of heart; it's a change of desires; it's a supernatural transformation of our deepest affections and longings. God isn't a guard at a Nazi concentration camp. You shouldn't think of God that way and respond to him from this perspective. God is the kindest being in the universe! God loves you with an infinite love! He has given his life for you!

To obey is to do what I desire (or am starting to desire) *for Someone I love* (or am starting to love). To obey is to see God's goodness and to appreciate the fact that life is in him! As 1 John 5:3 says, the more I'm filled with God's love (only when I'm filled with His love), "*his commandments are not burdensome*"! That is to say, they aren't "harsh," they aren't "heavy," they aren't "torturous." Jesus says it this way, "*For My yoke [in theory, something very heavy] is easy and My burden is light*" (Matthew 11:30).

How do we get to this paradox? How does something that used to be a burden now bring happiness? The answer is simple. As with Hudson Taylor, when you are *truly* in love, nothing you do feels like a sacrifice or takes any effort. Does it involve self-denial? Of course it does! Instead, you do everything with pleasure and with deep joy, and therefore you hardly think about it. Someone who is in love, who is *moved* by the love he feels for his beloved, finds *power* and *energy* to do all sorts of strange things that others would readily call crazy. What is obedience to Christ? To obey God is the ***outcome*** of being in love with him.

Do you think I'm wrong? Would it help you to know how Jesus obeyed? Let's have Jesus speak for himself. John 4:34 reads, "*Jesus said to them, My food is to do the will of Him who sent Me and to accomplish His work.*" What is Jesus saying? I'll translate it. Jesus doesn't obey out of *duty*; Jesus finds *delight* in doing God's will. For him, doing what God commands isn't a burden; it's something that he enjoys, that gives him pleasure, that fills him.

Do you remember the context around John 4? Jesus is hungry, and the disciples go into town to get food. While he's waiting, he talks to the Samaritan woman. Once they returned, the disciples "*urged Him, saying, 'Rabbi, eat'*" (John 4:31). Do you see what happened? Jesus enjoyed doing God's will so much that he wasn't hungry anymore! Doesn't the same thing happen to us when we're engrossed in something that captivates us—be it our job, a project, or something of the sort? We give ourselves in such a way that, without even realizing it, we lose our appetite!

No, Christian obedience isn't doing what I don't want to do. Christian obedience is changing what I love. When this happens, and only when this happens, will I do something that's entirely unthinkable for people: I'll say along with Christ, through his work, "*my food is to do the will of Him who sent me and to accomplish his work.*"

One Final Question: What Should I Do **When I Have No Desire** *to Obey?*

It's likely you're thinking: "I agree with what you write, but we live in a fallen world. What should I do when I have no desire to obey? How should I respond when I don't enjoy Jesus, and when the fullness of the Spirit feels like a very distant reality?" These are very legitimate questions because it's the reality that we *all* experience. I have written Appendix 1 to answer exactly this concern. Please read it now and think about its implications.

BRIEF SUMMARY

What is obedience? *Obedience is the* ***outcome*** *of enjoying God's love in Christ. Obeying, in a biblical sense, is something I can't do unless the Holy Spirit changes my motivations, and he gives me his power to do so.*

Why am I obedient? *Because I have been loved, because I want to remain in his love and because I want to love the one who loves me. Thus, biblical obedience involves three things:*

- *A motivation born of enjoying God's love.*
- *A kind of power born of being filled with the Spirit of God.*
- *A goal that is born of a desire to glorify God.*

Why am I disobedient? *Because I'm empty, and I'm looking for something that will fill my heart. Sin starts when I'm no longer satisfied with God.*

What's the key to obedience? *The key to obedience is to stop focusing on changing my behavior and to begin focusing on contemplating Christ. Change comes from appreciating him.*

What is the fullness of the Holy Spirit? *It's for the Spirit to have a genuine influence on what I love, what I think, and as the outcome of that, on what I do. In other words, for him to work in my heart so that I long for the glory of God, prioritize the kingdom of God, and use the power of God to live my daily life.*

FOR PERSONAL REFLECTION OR DISCUSSION IN SMALL GROUPS

1. *In what way has this chapter either changed or confirmed your understanding of how changes take place?*
2. *Sum up in one or two sentences the concepts that have had the greatest impact on you in this chapter.*
3. *Why do you think understanding obedience as an outcome is so relevant? What are the practical implications of seeing it this way?*
4. *Go back and look at the figure on page 9999 that shows the difference between what you can and cannot do. According to it, we can't change what we love, and that's why we need the work of the Spirit. What are the practical implications of this teaching for your day-to-day life?*
5. *In your own words, how would you define what it means to be filled by the Spirit? What do you do to be filled with him?*
6. *If you had to identify the area of your life today where you find it very difficult to obey God what would it be? (Bear in mind that today's struggle may be different from yesterday's or tomorrow's, and the idea here is to think about what I struggle the most with today.) Why do you think you find it so difficult to live in Christ in this situation?*
7. *Before answering this question, please read Appendix 1. What helps you the most to regain your passion for Christ when you feel far from him? Have you noticed any patterns that repeat before you drift away from God? That is to say, what usually causes you to withdraw emotionally from him?*

CHAPTER 11

A New Love to Serve

Serving Is an Outcome

If you've read the previous chapters, then you won't be surprised to read this statement: ***serving God is an outcome of enjoying God.*** The only way we can serve God (in the way he expects and desires from us) is by appreciating his unparalleled worth. Do you remember what love does? Love *responds* to what it regards as valuable and appealing.

If you're a musician (or if you've paid close attention to any musician), you know perfectly well what I'm talking about. Music is their "life." All musicians, even the most talented, devote countless hours to their music. They tirelessly practice, they repeat their scales over and over again, they meticulously train their voices, they carefully tune their instruments, and they make incredible efforts in "service" to their music. In short, musicians "devote their lives" to their music. Why would they do that? The answer is simple: They *enjoy* music! Because they find it beautiful, worthy, and appealing. In more religious terms, they "serve" music because they are fascinated by its "glory."

Can you see it? What do we need in order to "live for God"? What does it take for us to "give our lives" to him? What needs to happen for me to "devote my life" to his service? The answer here is also simple: *Before* I can serve God, I need to appreciate him. Before I give myself to him, I need to see his glory. In other words, serving God is the outcome of enjoying God.

> *The only way to serve God to his glory is*
> *to do it as the outcome of appreciating the glory of God.*

Let me illustrate this idea by asking a rather unusual question. ***How much money would you be willing to pay to serve someone else?*** Yes, you read correctly. Not how much money would you want to be paid to serve someone, but how much money would you be willing to pay to do so. "Me? Pay to serve? What kind of a question is that? Are you out of your mind? That's not how life works! You don't pay in order to serve; it works the other way around! When you do something for others, you get money in return." It's true. Whether you're a waiter, a pilot, a hairdresser, a taxi driver, an architect, a lawyer, or a company employee, in the real world, no one pays others to be allowed to do things for them. We actually get paid for their service!

I was reading a book by a well-known author that, frankly, the more I read, the less I enjoyed. I found the book tedious, repetitive, and irrelevant. When I told my wife about it, she asked, "Why do you keep reading it? Get another book. Read something else." However, since I don't like leaving things unfinished, I stubbornly continued to read. Then, just as I was about to give up and file it away forever, I read a line that prompted me to ask myself a question that shattered my heart. ***What price are you willing to pay to serve Jesus?*** As I thought about this question, I couldn't hold the tears back. Over and over, I kept asking myself, "What price am I willing to pay to serve? Nowadays, ***no one pays to serve***." On the contrary, even in Christian circles, everyone wants to be paid, or at least recognized when they serve others. (I feel tempted to write about the "gifts" certain pastors receive for preaching or certain singers for performing. Suffice it to say that I completely disagree with some of the figures they receive.) Meditate on this for a moment with me. Paying to serve? Paying money to serve on the worship team on Sunday? Paying to help with sound or to project the lyrics on screen? Paying to help set up the chairs? Paying to mop the church facilities? Paying to clean the restrooms? What kind of a crazy person would do that?

Do you know what I realized about my heart while meditating on this? ***I realized that I'm willing to pay for things that I consider "more" valuable and "more" important than serving Christ.*** I realized that "you don't pay for" these things, but for other things you do! I realized, for instance, that I'm happy to pay for the electric guitar that I want to buy for my son. I realized that I'm happy to pay for the mortgage on my house. I realized that I'm happy to pay the lease on my car. We're all happy to pay for any number of things we consider valuable! Clothes, shoes, internet service, a cell phone, digital TV, perfume, tickets to a show, and countless other things. Let me say it again. Paying to serve Jesus? Who does such a wild thing? As I continued meditating on this question, I was struck by a tremendously revealing truth. ***I'm only willing to pay for what I consider valuable.*** Then, as Luke would say about the prodigal son, "*coming to my senses,*" I reached the most painful conclusion. (Please read these words carefully.) As I meditated on the statement, ***<u>I realized that I don't value Jesus!</u>*** The sad truth is that I don't appreciate him, I don't consider him valuable, ***I don't love him (or at least I don't love him enough) for it to be worth paying to serve him. And how about you?***

> *You most <u>gladly</u> and <u>sacrificially</u> serve*
> *what you truly love and find appealing.*

<u>We all serve something</u>. But not just with our money, rather most essentially, with the surrender of our hearts! As we said in the previous chapter, you *<u>are a slave</u>* to that which is your greatest treasure and your greatest love. You *<u>answer to</u>* that master. Whether you want to or not, you serve it (Romans 6:16)! As Paul says in Romans 16:18, "*For such men are <u>slaves</u>, <u>not of our Lord Christ</u> but of <u>their own appetites</u>...*" What do you do if, like me, you have a passion for castles? You spend your money, time, and energy on them! You go on vacation to places with castles. You visit castle websites. You buy castle books. (I can testify to it. I have a fine collection myself.) That means that you *<u>serve</u>* that which is your greatest passion and which you consider "glorious."

What do you do if you're passionate about soccer? I'll quote exactly what a friend said to me a long time ago, "For me, my entire weekly schedule revolves around seeing my team play. If I have to do something during the week, I either do it before or after; but I never miss a game. I'm serious, Nico. During those two hours, count me out." What is my friend saying? What is going on in his heart and, as a consequence, in his day-to-day decision-making? *<u>He lives his whole life in service</u>* to his soccer team. His decisions, his schedule, and his availability are conditioned by making sure that nothing stands in the way of what he views as his greatest pleasure. Even if he can't see it or refuses to accept it, he is a slave! (Before you condemn my friend, ask yourself this question: What does your schedule revolve around?)

What does it mean to serve God with all your heart? ***Serving God is the outcome of loving him, of finding him appealing and special. Serving is the consequence of seeing God worthy of surrendering my whole being to him.*** (Just as a musician does with music, just as I do with castles, just as my friend does with his soccer team, and just as you serve your own passions.) Serving God is the outcome of appreciating the glory of God!

Before I give you a biblical example that supports this truth, carefully reflect on these questions. Who would like to be a complete failure in ministry? Who volunteers to serve God, knowing in advance that everything they do will be for nothing? Who could *eagerly and passionately* call out: "Me, Lord! I want to be the person you choose so that everything goes wrong"? Who ***wants*** that person? Who ***longs*** to be rejected, resisted, and persecuted by the very people they'll serve? Isaiah 6:8 reads, "*Then I heard the voice of the Lord, saying, "Whom shall I send, and who will go for Us?" Then I said, "Here am I. Send me!*" Why does Isaiah raise his hand like a child who wants to be chosen, calling out, "Me, me, me!"? Why does he volunteer to devote his whole life to the Lord, when the Lord himself tells him that the people he'll spend his life serving won't listen to his words (Isaiah 6:9-10)? Why does he "*respond*" the way he does? You can find the answer in earlier verses; because he has just seen the glory of God because he has just experienced the gospel again.

Isaiah 6:1-7 (ESV) says,

> "*I saw the Lord sitting upon a throne, high and lifted up... Above him stood the seraphim... And one called to another and said, 'Holy, holy, holy is the Lord of hosts; the whole earth is full of his glory!' ... And I said 'Woe is me! For I am lost; for I am a man of unclean lips, and I dwell in the midst of a people of unclean lips; for my eyes have seen the King, the Lord of hosts!' Then one of the seraphim flew to me, having in his hand a burning coal that he had taken with tongs from the altar. And he touched my mouth and said: 'Behold, this has touched your lips; your guilt is taken away, and your sin atoned for*'" (emphasis added).

What just happened? Isaiah has had an encounter with God. (Ideally, you and I should go through an encounter like that every day.) Two things happen when he stands before God. First, he witnesses the glory of God. Now, have you paused to consider a small detail? Isaiah isn't a new believer; the glory of God isn't something new to him. Yet, what makes this encounter special? He *appreciates the glory of God at a whole new level*. He has the privilege of appreciating God in a new way. If you don't mind my saying it old school, his "eyes are opened" so that he appreciates God above castles, music, soccer, clothes, a Mercedes Benz, or anything else this world has to offer. What happens right after that? Isaiah sees his own sin. But don't rush; revisit the observation we made earlier. Isaiah isn't an unbeliever. It isn't the first time he "sees" his sin. However, *it's the first time he's seen it this way!* As he stands before God, he "sees" his selfishness, his pride, his self-pity, the way he makes himself to be a victim, his uncleanliness, his lust, his passions, and how rotten his motives are in a way that he's never seen them before. Have you noticed this detail? This prophet's ministry is to *speak* on God's behalf. At this point, Isaiah had been "speaking" on behalf of God *for a long time*. However, what part of his body needs cleansing? His *lips*! Isaiah "speaks" on behalf of God, but even his "words" need to be cleansed. Not even his service is pure.

Can you see the paradox? There's nothing new in this encounter with God; there is, however, ***a new appreciation of something known already***. What happens next? Isaiah receives the miracle of forgiveness. All that's impure is removed. All his uncleanliness is removed. All his sin is forgiven. Then, and only then, after examining his heart and finding the forgiveness he receives to have made him worthy again, does he experience such uncontainable joy that he calls out, "Send me!" "I want to serve you!" "I don't care what needs to be done; *I want to* do it!" What is genuine service? Genuine service is the outcome of experiencing the gospel again. What is Christian love? ***Christian love is the overflow of joy that is shared with others.***

Serving is responding; serving is giving ourselves. Serving is being willing to make enormous sacrifices and, much like Hudson Taylor or Isaiah, not feel them as such. After all, think about it for a moment, who would get sad buying designer clothes at a third of their price? No one! However, would you have spent money by buying them? Of course you would have! Would it have cost you? No doubt about it! Then why wouldn't buying the clothes make you sad? In fact, why would it bring about the exact opposite emotion? Why would it bring you joy? Because you ***perceive*** that what you get in return (the clothes) exceeds the price (or "sacrifice") you paid. You look at the clothes and say, "It was worth it!"

Why would Isaiah do what he does? For the exact same reason that you spend your money on clothes, a cell phone, or anything else that gives you pleasure. Because he was able to "perceive," "appreciate," "see," "admire" the greatness of God and how amazing his much-needed forgiveness is. Because, when you *truly* enjoy the gospel, no sacrifice, no act of surrender, no service feels as such. In fact, the opposite is true; you experience it as one of the greatest privileges.

> "*It was by faith Moses, when he grew up, refused to be treated as the grandson of the king, but chose to share ill-treatment with God's people instead of enjoying the fleeting pleasures of sin. He thought that it was better to suffer for the promised Christ than to own all the treasures of Egypt, for he was looking forward to the great reward that God would give him. And it was because he trusted God that he left the land of Egypt and wasn't afraid of the king's anger. Moses kept right on going; it seemed as though he could see God right there with him. And it was because he believed God would save his people that he commanded them to kill a lamb as God had told them to...*" *(Hebrews 11:24-28, TLB; emphasis added).*

Serving Is a Miracle

Have you carefully read the subheading above? To serve God (to the glory of God) is a miracle! To serve God (while loving God) is a supernatural work! To serve God (enjoying God) is a work of God! From a biblical standpoint, service is an outcome of the work of his Spirit, not the consequence of human action. It's not your work; it's his!

Let me share with you a very simple illustration of what I mean. Imagine that you have a pear tree in your backyard. Let's say you don't like pears, so you want it to start bearing apples. What should you do to achieve your goal? Water the tree? Fertilize it? Prune the damaged branches? Of course not! If you did that, you'd continue to get the same fruit, pears! If you want for *that same tree* to start producing new fruit, ***something supernatural must happen to it on the inside***, at its roots—that is, in its "heart." What it needs is a miracle!

Likewise, unless there's an entirely supernatural change within us, you and I are going to produce "fruit" that is according to our own nature. What is our nature like? What is your natural tendency and my natural tendency? What do we do by default? I'll summarize it in one sentence: ***We use our service as a means to love ourselves***. You don't believe that to be the case? Think about this. Why do you make an effort to get to work early? Why do you follow your boss's orders? Why do you "serve" at work by putting in a huge amount of time and effort? Why, if needed, do you stay late? Is it because you are making "sacrifices"? Is it because you enjoy being pushed around? Is it because doing what your boss says gives you pleasure, and you love serving him? I doubt it. You do what you do because your work gives you something (money, status, prestige, etc.). You do what you do because you get something out of it. You do what you do because you love what your work gives you.

Neither you, nor I, nor anyone else can stop acting according to their own nature. Not even in service to God (Matthew 6:1; Philippians 1:15). Our selfish heart produces selfish fruit. Our proud heart produces prideful fruit. Our self-centered heart produces self-centered fruit. It takes a miracle, the work of God, to change this inertia!

Let me ask you something similar to what I asked at the beginning of this chapter. ***When was the last time you pleaded for someone to allow you to serve them?*** Yes, you read correctly. When was the last time you *begged* to be allowed to serve someone? "Begging to serve? Who does that?"

I know that my wife will try to talk me out of giving you this example as she's very uncomfortable when I set her as a good example; however, if you're reading these words, it's because, after much effort, I've managed to convince her. In the neighborhood we live in, there's also an elderly woman who walks her dog in front of our house every day. Ever since my wife, Annie, noticed her walk by, she felt a special burden for her. This woman lives by herself, she has a bad shoulder, and it's obvious that she finds it increasingly difficult to take care of herself.

Over time, Annie became friends with her until, a few weeks ago, she tenderly asked her, "May I come over clean your house?"

The woman replied, "I can't pay you, child."

With a sweet smile on her face, Annie replied, "Oh! That's not what I meant. I don't want you to pay me. I want to clean your house for free."

The woman gave her a puzzled look and said, "Now, why would you do that?"

"Because I love God, and I love you too," my wife replied.

Do you know what the woman's response was? "I hate God!".

Do you know what my wife replied? "It's fine. Even if you hate God, I still want to clean your house." And she did. (More than once, and with great pleasure!) Do you think my wife is special? Do you think she's someone out of the ordinary? Do you think she's extraordinarily good? She's not. Her "extraordinary" love is the outcome of an "extraordinary" thing.

Do you think her case is unique?

Let's keep asking the weird questions. ***Have you ever seen a millionaire plead with a person without financial means for the opportunity to serve them?*** No? Never? Well, read the book of Acts with me:

> "*A woman named Lydia, from the city of Thyatira, a seller of purple fabrics, a worshiper of God, was listening [to Paul]; and the Lord opened her heart to respond to the things spoken by Paul. And when she and her household had been baptized, she urged us, saying, 'If you have judged me to be faithful to the Lord, come into my house and stay.' And she prevailed upon us*" (Acts 16:14-15; emphasis added).

Lydia was a millionaire. At that time, purple fabrics were mainly used to make clothes for the royals. Selling this type of fabric was the modern-day equivalent of dressing up big Hollywood stars and owning a Christian Dior, Gucci, or Versace clothing store. Have you noticed the verbs Luke uses in telling the story? She "urged" them. She pleaded with them, "*Come into my house and stay.*" Apparently, Paul and his companions refused her generous invitation at first. However, this woman was so adamant that, according to Luke, they ended up being "*persuaded*" by her.

Her plea shows her passionate and sincere desire to serve. But beware! Don't be deceived by the conditional clause. In the original Greek, when Lydia says, "*If you have judged me to be faithful to the Lord…*" she's not contesting her own faith in the Lord. In fact, she's doing just the opposite, she's attesting to it! Commentators on the book of Acts agree that the best translation of her words would be. "*Since you all know that I am a true believer in the Lord...*"[92]. Or, "*given that I am* a true believer,"[a] allow me to serve you! *I want* to! I would love to help you!" Can you see what's happening? No one has to put a gun to Lydia's head for her to serve. On the contrary! People actually have to stop her from doing it! (I promise the same thing happens to me with my wife.

[a] If you think about it, we also use conditionals this way in English. A mother scolding her son may very well tell him, "*If you have ears*, listen carefully to what I'm going to tell you now..." In that case, the mother isn't questioning whether her child does or doesn't have ears; she's assuming he does. Her intention in using the conditional is to make use of rhetoric. We all do it all the time. The beauty of the Greek, which is different from English, is that it has a special grammatical structure to indicate this type of construction. Therefore, it doesn't leave room for doubt as to what the speaker's (in this case, Lydia's) original intention was. The same is true, for instance, in Philippians 2:1-2 when Paul says, "*Therefore, if there is any encouragement in Christ, if there is any consolation of love, if there is any fellowship of the Spirit, if any affection and compassion, make my joy complete by being of the same mind, maintaining the same love, united in spirit, intent on one purpose.*" Paul is not casting doubt on these things, he is asserting them! The "best" way to translate it would be, "*For there is* encouragement in Christ, *for there is* comfort," and so on.

I have to ask her to stop cleaning houses for people in need. That woman's house isn't the only one she cleans!)

What causes Lydia, my wife, or anyone else to have such desires? We find the answer in the passage itself. Luke tells us that this kind of service is unusual. It isn't natural for this woman (or my wife). This kind of service is the *outcome* of God's supernatural work in their lives. Verse 14 says that "*the Lord opened her heart to respond to the things Paul was speaking.*" Samuel Pérez Millos describes that "opening" in this way:

> The verb [opened] used here by Luke conveys the idea of opening something wide, ***the same way double doors are opened wide***. That woman's heart was opened by God so that through that opening not only the Gospel, but the Savior himself, could come in. It wasn't she who did that, nor was it Paul with his message, it was the Holy Spirit, so that the glory of salvation would belong only to the one who saves: God himself.[93]

What happened in Lydia's heart at the moment of her salvation is the same thing that happens inside our hearts every time we experience deep change. There was a divine intervention! Christian service is much more than "helping someone do the cleaning," "inviting someone into your home," "doing good deeds," or "devoting yourself to ministry," ***Christian service is an overflow of supernatural love in your heart.*** What happened in Lydia's heart is what Paul says happens in the heart of every true believer on the day of conversion, "*Because the love of God has been poured out within our hearts through the Holy Spirit who was given to us*" (Romans 5:5; emphasis added).

Can you see it? Christian service is the outcome of God giving you something you don't have: love! But not just any kind of love, divine love! A love that is like God's own love. Genuine, selfless, "other-centered" love. Christian service is the outcome of an "open-heart surgery." It's a change that God operates, through his Spirit, so that we're free from our natural inclination to love ourselves through everything we do.

If you take a close look at the passage in the book of Acts, you'll see it clearly. What God did in Lydia wasn't a change of *behavior*; what God did in her was change her *heart*. Please pay very close attention to these words. Lydia was already an obedient person! If you read the context for the passage, you'll realize that by the time Paul went to see her, she was already obeying

God. According to Acts 16:13, Lydia was praying, singing to the Lord, and keeping the Sabbath with other women, which means that Lydia, a non-Jewish woman, had converted to Judaism and was faithfully keeping Old Testament laws. Then, what kind of work did God do in her heart if it wasn't a change of behavior? The passage gives the answer: "*the Lord opened her heart to respond to the things spoken by Paul.*" In other words, God opened her eyes to "respond" to the gospel!

Now, let me tell you an important detail about the verb Luke, the author of the Book of Acts, uses here. "Respond" can be translated as "listened with intensity" (MSG), "to accept" (NLT), "to give oneself to," "to become fond of something," "to receive with pleasure." The idea the verb in the original Greek conveys is that of someone watching an engaging performance. It's the kind of attention you'd give to a *Cirque du Soleil* show.

Watching that sort of performance brings about a type of response, joyful surrender, and appreciation. It's impossible to *merely* "watch" the jugglers, the contortionists, and the tightrope walkers perform. When you see what they're capable of doing, you "watch intently," you "respond," you "give in," you "become a fan," you "receive their performance with pleasure." When you see a show like that, you can't help but say, "This is beautiful! This is amazing! This is wonderful!"

This is what Luke is doing by using this verb. ***God "opened" Lydia's heart so that she could "respond" to the gospel as the most precious thing in the universe.*** In other words, by the work of the Holy Spirit, Christ became her pearl of great price. What's the result? She has a passion for serving! (Just like Zacchaeus who can't stop giving! See Luke 19:1-10.)

Let me pause here for a moment and get into Lydia's mind. Let me paraphrase her thought process before she met Paul. Lydia's reasoning was something like this: "For God to accept me, I have to abide by the laws in the Old Testament. I have to pray, sing, obey and serve."

Now, let me paraphrase what Paul said to her, "God accepts you, not because you keep the laws; he accepts you even though he knows you can't keep them. The God you so greatly respect, Lydia, has died for you!"

When her heart was "opened" to this truth, the show Lydia experienced wasn't the trapeze act at *Cirque du Soleil*. The vision that Lydia caught, which is the same vision that Isaiah caught and that you and I must catch, is the glorious God of Heaven dying for us! The thing that Lydia understood is what 1 John 4:10 says, "*In this is love, not that we loved God, but that He loved us and sent His Son to be the propitiation for our sins*" (emphasis added).[b] Would you like to serve the way Lydia did? Your challenge and my challenge are the same; the key is to allow this reality to captivate us!

Can you see it? Lydia changed. But she didn't change her behavior; ***her appreciation of God changed!*** Lydia went from believing in God to having a beautiful God! Lydia went from serving God to discovering that God gave his life to serve her! Lydia went from obeying God to feeling God's love for her! This love, which we first experience in the moment of our conversion and which Paul says God pours into all of us through the Holy Spirit (Romans 5:5), is the same love that we must rediscover and treasure in order to serve others! Enjoying *this* love is what makes the greatest difference. ***I'm not talking about the love we should all have for God, but the love God has for us!***[c]

> Genuine service is born out of *enjoying the love* that Jesus *has* for us and is realized through the *love* and the *power* he himself provides (i.e., through his Spirit).

1 John 4:19 reads, "*We love, because He first* loved us" (emphasis added). In other words, we can't love, either God or others, unless we ***first*** experience God's love for us. That is, loving others is the ***outcome*** of enjoying God's unconditional love for us. Can you do acts of service without experiencing that kind of love? Of course you can! But if you take a close look at your heart, you'll realize that far from serving others, you're actually serving yourself; that far from offering others your love (even though on the outside you're

[b] Interestingly, in the Gospel of John, when Jesus assesses the heart of the Pharisees he doesn't say, "The problem with your heart is that you don't love Me." In John 5:42, Jesus says, "*But I know you [that is, I know your heart], that you do not have the love of God in yourselves*" (emphasis added). Can you see it? According to Jesus, their problem ***isn't that they don't love God***, their problem is that ***they haven't been able to appreciate the love God had for them***, which is why they reject Jesus and his cross (verse 40). What is the consequence of their rejection? They use their service to God as a means to gain renown. John 5:44 reads, "*How can you believe, when you receive glory from one another and you do not seek the glory that is from the one and only God?*" In other words, since they reject Christ's love (verse 38), they go about begging for love, desperately hoping that others will give them glory and bring them renown. They use their position to feel important and worthy. They use their ministry to make a name for themselves. According to Jesus, this is what extinguishes and invalidates their faith. "*How can you believe, when you receive glory from one another... ?*"

[c] Paul goes on to explain this same idea in 2 Corinthians 5:14-15 (GNT): "*We are ruled by the love of Christ, now that we recognize that one man died for everyone... so that those who live should no longer live for themselves, but only for him who died and was raised to life for their sake*" (emphasis added). Other versions of this passage read: We are "*ruled by*" (GNT) the love of Christ, it "*controls us*" (CEB), "*compels us*" (NKJV), "*urges us on*" (NRSV), "*compels us*" (NIV). The concept behind the Greek verb is that Jesus' love is what "moves" us, "drives" us, "motivates" us to stop living for ourselves and to start living for him. Do you get the picture? His love is the *force driving* us towards change. His love *ignites* in us the desire to live for him. His love *activates* our passion for service.

serving them), on the inside, you're extending your cup so that others will fill it and love you.

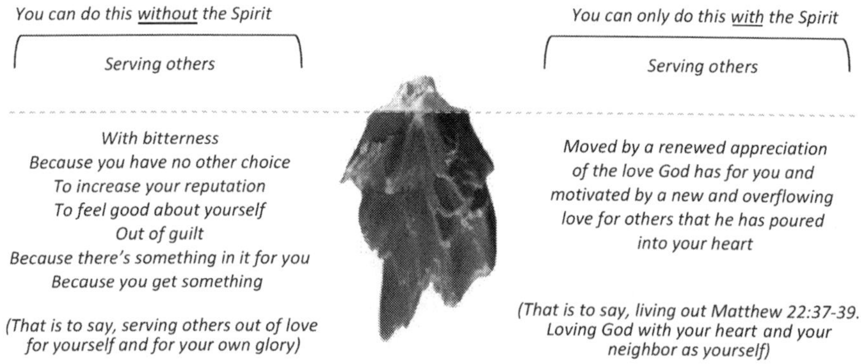

As the figure shows, the difference between these two types of service is huge. You can do the former, but neither you, nor I, nor anyone else can do the latter. Serving God in this way is the outcome of his work in you. It's a miracle. It's a supernatural thing. It's a change of the affections and of the deepest desires of your heart. It's a radical change. It's for a pear tree to be able to produce apples. Can you see it? ***No one experiences supernatural change unless Someone supernatural is at work in their life***. Yes, like the young missionary in Chapter 1, you can stop sleeping around on weekends, and you can go out into the world to share the gospel; however, unless God himself is at work in your heart, it's impossible for you to change what needs to be changed: the things your heart loves. No one really changes unless God changes them.

Right now, our three children are ten, eight, and four years old. My wife and I have found it extremely valuable for them to learn from an early age that they need to help at home. Ever since they learned how to walk, we've taught them to serve in different ways. Every day they make their own bed, clear the table, and help with different household chores. (Yes, they've broken a good number of dishes and glasses in the process, but it's been worth it.) Our three kids are obedient. They serve and help, yet little by little, the true condition of their hearts has begun to show.

"Dad, Tomás is taking too long to clear the table, and he's leaving the heavy stuff to me."

"Mom, Mica didn't do the cleaning she was supposed to do yesterday, so now it's her turn to do it."

"Why do I have to pick up Manuel's dish?"

"It isn't my turn to wipe the table today! Yay!"

My children serve, but do they find pleasure in service? Have they reached the point where they take pleasure in doing what they do? Is their service born out of an understanding of the love their mom and dad have for them? Do they love God by serving?

The Book of Deuteronomy says that my job as a father isn't to make my children obey and serve; my job as a father is to make them fall more and more in love with God. Deuteronomy 6:5-9 reads:

> *You shall love the Lord your God with all your heart and with all your soul and with all your might. These words, which I am commanding you today [to love God!], shall be on your heart [that is, they must first be a reality in my life; I have to love God]. You shall teach them diligently to your sons and shall talk of them when you sit in your house and when you walk by the way and when you lie down and when you rise up. You shall bind them as a sign on your hand and they shall be as frontals on your forehead. You shall write them on the doorposts of your house and on your gates [which means that it is my responsibility to make the love of God a daily reality].*

My burden as a parent isn't to have my kids pick up the table. My burden as a parent is that they may love God with all their heart, with all their soul, and with all their strength (I can make them do the former, but only God can make them experience the latter).

What I constantly ask myself isn't whether my kids will clear the table or not. What I constantly ask myself is this: How can I help my kids find God appealing? How can I help them be enticed by the cross? How do I become the means for them to fall more in love with him? What I long for is for them to love God, and not that they merely serve him!

Unfortunately, many people see Christian service the same way my kids see house chores; they see it as an obligation. However, in biblical terms, ***Christian service isn't about doing what I don't want to do. Christian service is the outcome of God changing what I love.*** Romans 14:7-8 reads, "*For not one of us lives for himself, and not one dies for himself; for if we live, we live for the Lord, or if we die, we die for the Lord; therefore whether we live or die, we are the*

Lord's." Christian service is much more than a change in behavior. ***Christian service*** ***is a change in what brings pleasure to our heart***.

Think back to the young missionary in Chapter 1. You remember him, don't you? Before he converted, he wanted to "be popular and successful" by sleeping with girls; however, after "converting" to Christ, he began to desire "to be popular and successful" by converting souls. What does it mean to serve God? Does it mean to share the gospel like this young missionary? Of course not! It's something much deeper than that. To serve Christ is for what my heart desires to undergo a change. As Paul says in the passage you just read, it is ***to stop living for myself and to start living for him***. Granted, the *outcome* of real change is a changed behavior. Naturally, I'll eventually start sharing the gospel. However, real change is a change in what I treasure. It's a transformation of what brings me pleasure. It's to cease to live for myself and to start to live for him. It's to join Paul in saying, "*For to me, to live is Christ* [and not the service or the ministry]" (Philippians 1:21).

In J.R.R. Tolkien's famous trilogy, "*The Lord of the Rings,*" there's a peculiar character called Gollum. Gollum is a horrible monster whose only goal in life is to own a beautiful gold ring. For him, nothing in the world is more valuable than this ring. He's so obsessed with this ring that he calls it "my precious" over and over again. This character, who was an ordinary man before finding the ring, progressively turns into a twisted creature due to his obsession with his "precious" ring. What Tolkien wants to show through Gollum is what happens in our heart when we obsessively give ourselves to our "treasures"—to our idols. When we do so, we turn into Gollum, someone with an unpleasant and horrible heart.

Do you see what I'm saying? Even service to God has the potential to turn you into a monster! Of course, on the outside, you'll seem very pious, respectable, and self-sacrificing, but on the inside, your selfish, proud, and self-centered heart will degenerate without your even being able to see it! Do you remember Matthew 7:22-23? "*Many will say to Me on that day, [notice how surprised these men are] 'Lord, Lord, did we not prophesy in Your name, and in Your name cast out demons, and in Your name perform many miracles?' [What are these men saying? 'Lord! We serve you!'] And then I will declare to them, 'I never knew you; depart from Me, you who practice lawlessness.'*" The most important question isn't: Am I serving God? The more important question is: ***Has what I find "precious" changed? Do I love Jesus more today than I did yesterday? Do I stop living for myself because I'm learning to enjoy the love God has for me?***

Am I content enough in Christ to find pleasure in serving others?
Is his love real to me?
Does his love for me bring about in me a new love for others?

When I was writing this chapter, I received an email from a non-Christian friend in Argentina who offered to help me rent out the house my wife and I inherited from my parents. My family and I have lived in Spain for almost eight years to the day. However, this was the first email I've ever received from my friend since we moved here. His email was very warm and pleasant. In fact, if you think about it for a moment, the reason my friend wrote to me is to "do something for me." He was offering to "serve me." He wanted to "help" me. However, the million-dollar question is always the same: Why? Does he love me? The answer is pretty obvious: No, he loves what he can get from me.

My friend is just like the young missionary in our story. Is he trying to serve? Yes. Is he trying to help? No doubt. But who is he serving? Who does he live for? What's "precious" to him? His money, not me. Don't get me wrong. Please, don't think I'm condemning him for it. This ***way of*** "loving," "serving," and "helping" is the way we ***<u>ALL</u> love, serve, and help.*** My friend *<u>uses</u>* our friendship to try to make money; I *<u>use</u>* my wife, my children, the ministry, and many other things to try to satisfy my own selfish ends. You don't believe me? Imagine for a moment that you're a young, single guy trying to find a girl to marry. Think about this: what kind of person would you be looking for? An ugly, scruffy, unattractive girl? A proud, stubborn, capricious woman? Someone who is selfish, unfaithful, and self-centered? I doubt it. I doubt that, on finding someone like that, you'd be moved to say, "In you...! In you who are such a selfish, unpleasant, and unattractive person, I'll pour out all my selfless and magnanimous love for the rest of my life!" No one would do a thing like that. We all get married out of selfishness; and we all love, serve, and help out of selfishness. Changing this inertia doesn't require an effort on our part; changing this tendency requires a miracle.

Let me make a confession. Do you know what I have tried to do in this chapter? Do you know what is my purpose in writing what I've written? My goal is to show you the most important truth that everyone must learn in order to serve God. ***Genuinely serving others isn't <u>hard</u>; it's <u>impossible</u>.*** Paul makes this clear in 2 Corinthians 4:7 when he says, "*But we have this treasure in <u>earthen vessels</u> [which is what Paul, you and I are], so that the surpassing* *greatness of the power will be of God and not from ourselves*." No one is able to serve God unless they realize they can't. Can you change what you love? No. Love is a response! Can you change others? No. If you can't change your own affections, much less will you be able to change the affections of others. The only two things that genuine service needs, true *love* and the *power* to change others, are things that *no one* has![d]

Serving Is Receiving

The introduction to this book begins with this statement: "Changing the Way You Change." This has been my goal throughout the book: To help you realize that you need to "change the way you change." Think about it for a moment. What is the first thing that comes to mind when someone thinks about serving others? The most common response is that "serving is synonymous with giving." Yes, that is true. Serving is giving, but from a biblical perspective, ***in order to give, we first need to receive.***

The apostle Peter says that "*whoever serves is to do so as one who is serving by the strength which God supplies*" (1 Peter 4:11; emphasis added). What is more important for Peter, to give or to receive?

The Apostle Paul says, "*But by the grace of God I am what I am, and His grace toward me did not prove vain; but I labored even more than all of them, yet not I, but the grace of God with me*" (Corinthians 15:10; emphasis added). How does Paul envision his ministry? Is it about giving or receiving?

In the Gospel of John, Jesus says; "*But he who practices the truth comes to the Light, so that his deeds may be manifested as having been wrought in God [that is, through God]*" (John 3:21). In John 15:5, Jesus says, "*apart from Me, you can do nothing.*"

These verses, and many others I could quote, clearly suggest that any act of service must be done through the energy and ability that God gives us. In other words, before we have something to give, we need to receive!

---

[d] It's important to point out that ***genuine service isn't a state, but a process.*** No one is "God-filled" all the time when they serve. It's true that the new birth produces a change within our heart and that it gives us a new nature; however, this new birth doesn't wipe out the old nature! That will happen when we are glorified. For this reason, we're trees that sometimes produce "pears" and sometimes produce "apples"—in fact, most of the time we produce a combination of them. In other words, we're full of mixed motivations. Until the day we're with Christ, there will be a tug of war within our heart. We must remind ourselves that we live in the "already but not yet." We're changing, but our complete and perfect change has yet to be consummated. This "in between time" leaves us living in a constant tension between what we can be in Christ and what we will one day be. What should we do when we don't experience the joy of Christ while serving Christ? The same thing we must do when we feel no desire to obey him. Do you remember Appendix 1? The same thing applies to obedience as it does to service. (If you haven't done it yet, please go ahead and read Appendix 1.)

Understanding this truth is absolutely essential for several reasons. Let's look at some of them together.

1. The Love of God in order to Serve God

Why do I first need to receive *before* I can give? Because, as we said several times before, no one can change what they love. While this truth is pretty obvious, I would like to challenge you to consider a truly relevant question. ***Is there ever a moment when love is no longer a response?*** Yes, there is. Love ceases to be a ***reaction***, and it becomes an ***action*** only *when the heart overflows with love*. In other words, only when we're completely full and fully satisfied.

Think about it for a moment. From a biblical perspective, there's only one person in the entire universe who's capable of loving like this: God! Because he's a triune God, he's the only self-sufficient being. He's the only one who has no needs. He's different from everyone else, and he doesn't need anyone—except for himself—to be completely full and fully satisfied. From eternity and for all eternity, he's been living in a relationship of perfect love where the Father loves the Son, the Son loves the Father, and the Spirit loves them both (Matthew 3:17; John 5:20; John 17:24; etc.). For this reason, he's the only one who can fully and genuinely love.

Only someone who doesn't need others can truly *love* others and *give* without seeking anything in return.

What, then, do we need in order to love? We need what 1 John 4:13 says; we *first* need to "receive," to "experience," to "feel" his love, so that we then have something to give. ***It's only after we appropriate his love for ourselves that we can begin to love as he loves***. Only when I'm filled with his love do I have the ability to cease to "react" and begin to "act." Only when I'm filled with him can I love and serve as he does.

> *The most important aspect of service isn't what I do,*
> *but why and how I do it.*
> *That is to say, what motivates me*
> *(whether I do it out of love for myself or God)*
> *and what empowers me (whether it's me or the Spirit).*

2. The Power of God in order to Serve God

Why do I first need to receive *before* I can give? Because I lack the power to change others. Jesus defines Christian ministry in a very particular way. For him, genuine service has to do with people being influenced in such a way by our lifestyle that our "unusual" way of life prompts them to look upwards. Matthew 5:16 says, "*Let your light shine before men in such a way that they may see your good works, and glorify your Father who is in heaven.*"

Let me ask you something. How do you get people to receive your love (through your service or any good work) in such a way that, instead of focusing on you, they get to "see" the Father in you? Let me push the issue even further. If you pay attention to the passage, it isn't just a matter of them "seeing" God, but of them finding him "glorious" because of what you do! It's about them finding him "magnificent," "appealing," "valuable," and "worthy of admiration." It's about your co-workers or fellow students seeing in you a lifestyle that can only be explained by saying, "This person's God is real and wonderful." Have you noticed Jesus' command? By the way I live, people must desire to love God! This isn't hard; it's impossible!

A few days ago, my wife and I were talking about a fairly well-known preacher whose messages tend to really minister to her. (I'll be honest, he doesn't quite grab my attention.) In discussing him, we started exchanging our views on his weaknesses and strengths. While we were sharing our thoughts, I realized that, although we were talking about somebody else, the underlying subject matter was me. Since it had become pretty obvious, I openly asked her, "Honey, what do you see when you see me preach?" So she tenderly said, "I see a great teacher." Now, don't be mistaken. She was paying me no compliments; she was criticizing me. What my wife was saying was, "I *only* see a great teacher." What she meant was, "You're a very good communicator, but you lack power!" Which is another way of saying, "I don't see the Holy Spirit at work, I see you." My response was, "You're probably right, thank you. It's very clear that I need more of him and less of me. Would you pray for me, please?" Did my wife's words hurt my ego? Yes, a little. But the truth is, she couldn't be more right. In order to minister to others, you don't need to be a great public speaker; you need to have an amazing God working through you.

In 1 Corinthians 2:1-5, Paul says,

> "*And when I came to you, brethren, I did not come with superiority of speech or of wisdom, proclaiming to you the testimony of God. For I determined to*

know nothing among you except Jesus Christ, and Him crucified. I was with you in weakness and in fear and in much trembling, and my message and my preaching were not in persuasive words of wisdom, but in demonstration of the Spirit and of power, so that your faith would not rest on the wisdom of men, but on the power of God" (emphasis added).(My wife often tells me that she prays these verses for me.)

Does this mean that we should be poor communicators and not prepare our messages in the best possible way? No. Paul also used rhetoric and modified his speech according to his audience (See Acts 17:16-34; 1 Corinthians 9:19-23). What he means is that unless God works through our words, our service, or our acts of love, none of our efforts will have the power to achieve the goal that, at least in theory, we are chasing after: for people to find God appealing! For them to glorify the Father who is in heaven! As Psalm 127:1 says, "*Unless the Lord builds the house, they labor in vain who build it; unless the Lord guards the city, the watchman keeps awake in vain.*"[e]

Where do I want to lead you with this? Back to your need for Jesus. We all minister by grace. We're all "earthen vessels." We all need what we don't have (2 Corinthians 4:7).

3. The Grace of God in order to Serve Him

Why do I first need to receive *before* I can give? Because contrary to what we'd think, serving God increases our debt to him. Have you carefully read that last statement? If it's true that, through his Spirit, God is working in us so that we can love and serve, then ***whenever we serve God we're not "giving God something back" or "paying him back" for what he's done for us, rather when we serve him (or do his will), we're receiving a bit more grace from him!***

Think about this: Who's changing us? Who's transforming our selfish heart into a heart that finds pleasure in loving others? Who gives us the power to obey him? Who answers our prayers when we need them? Who's both *with* and *in* us when we preach the gospel? Who gives us joy and spiritual fulfillment when we serve him? Who empowers us with supernatural gifts?

---

[e] After being used by God (to *heal* a lame man!), Peter said, "*Men of Israel, why are you amazed at this, or why do you gaze at us, as if by our own power or piety we had made him walk?*" (Acts 3:12). What is Peter saying? I'm nothing special. It's neither about my *power*, nor is it about my *obedience*; it's about *Jesus' influence* through what I do. God doesn't use me *because of* how capable I am or *because of* how obedient I am. God uses me *in spite of* my disobedience and by means of His gifts—that is to say, by grace! Yes, it's true that many times he uses my skills as a means for me to be used by him, but many other times he uses my lack of skill in order to do so.

Who gives us his Spirit? We must look at life through the right lens. Living our days in Christ *by His Spirit* makes us more and more indebted; far more than the day we converted! When we do something that we could never have done by our own strength, we further receive grace from Him!

Serving God isn't a way of giving back to God for what he's done; serving is a way of receiving more grace from him. No, ***the Christian life isn't about what we can do for God, but what he can do in and for us***. John Piper wrote, "Whatever returns we make to him for all his past goodness to us, we make by relying on his future grace. The only debt that grace creates is the 'debt' of relying on more grace for all that God calls us to be and do."[94] We have to acknowledge it. ***Justification produces a debt we cannot repay, sanctification enlarges it, and so does service!*** What's the result of this way of serving? The one who *does* the work and the one who *deserves* the glory receives it; that person isn't us, but him.[f] As Peter says, "*Whoever speaks, is to do so as one who is speaking the utterances of God; whoever serves is to do so as one who is serving by the strength which God supplies; so that in all things God may be glorified through Jesus Christ, to whom belongs the glory and dominion forever and ever. Amen*" (1 Peter 4:11).

Serving Produces Joy

I would like to point out something important. ***Serving others is the outcome of experiencing joy, but serving others also produces joy***. Jesus said, "*It is more blessed to give than to receive*" (Acts 20:35). This means that genuine service *is brought about by* the joy I already have in Christ; however, it also means that genuine service is a *driver* or source of joy. Both aspects are two sides of the same coin. There's no denying it. God has created us to serve. As Mother Teresa of Calcutta said, "Those who do not live to serve, are not fit to live." As Genesis 1:28-31 shows us, service and work aren't part of the fall; they're an essential part of God's original plan. This brings us to the last point I would like to consider before ending this chapter.

Serving God Isn't Something We Do; It's Part of Our Identity

If someone asks a Christian, "Where do you serve God?" do you know what the most typical response would be? "In church." This answer is as common as it is wrong. You *don't* serve God in the church; you serve God everywhere

[f] If you want to dig deeper into this idea that John Piper has called "the debtor's ethic," I encourage you to read Chapter 1 of a book he wrote titled *Future Grace*.

or else, from a biblical perspective, you aren't serving God; (without knowing it) you're serving yourself!

Colossians 3:23-24 says, "*Whatever you do, do your work heartily, as for the Lord rather than for men, knowing that from the Lord you will receive the reward of the inheritance. It is the Lord Christ whom you serve.*" This passage teaches us a very important lesson. The person who serves Christ visualizes *everything* they do as being for Christ. A person who serves Christ doesn't draw a distinction between the religious (what they do in church) and the secular (what they do outside church). A person who serves Christ does *everything* for Him. What determines whether the service is or isn't done for God isn't defined by the activity in and of itself; rather, it's determined by the *motivation* with which it's done. I may serve in church to my own glory and benefit, or I may serve outside the church to the glory of God and for his kingdom's sake. The place and the activity aren't in the least relevant!

I believe the Bible challenges us to make a paradigm shift. ***Serving isn't something I do; serving is part of who I am.*** The goal isn't to get to do things for others; the goal is to become someone I'm not: a servant. A person who enjoys serving! I have to change the way I see the service.

> ***Am I a servant? Or do I pretend to be one***
> *(when there's something in it for me)?*

The goal of a true believer isn't to serve in a ministry (although we all should); the goal of a true believer is much more ambitious. It's a much higher and more supernatural goal! The goal of a true believer is to come to a point where they serve others from a real love of wanting to bring benefit to them, from a sincere desire to seek their greatest good, from a sanctified ambition to desire their best interest and gain (Philippians 2:4). The goal is to become, unlike my friend in Argentina, a real estate agent for the glory of God and for the benefit of my neighbor, as opposed to doing it to make money. Contrary to the inertia in my heart, the goal is to become a husband who finds more pleasure in serving his wife than in being served by her. The goal is to become, counter to your own heart's passions, a person who uses their job (or their studies) to bring benefit into the world wherever God has placed them; and not for their own personal gain and well-being.

Do you remember Jesus' words in John 15:11? "*These things I have spoken to you so that My joy may be in you, and that your joy may be made full.*" How amazing! Experiencing as much joy as Jesus did! But where? When? Only for an hour and a half once a week when we go to church on Sundays? Of course not! The joy of Christ must be in us on Wednesday at ten o'clock in the morning in the middle of a business meeting. On Monday at three o'clock in the afternoon, while seeing patients at a hospital. On Friday at noon, while teaching fourth graders. At midnight on Saturday, while changing a diaper. If I don't have a heart full of joy to serve others in those situations (and, to add insult to injury, I think I'm serving God because I'm serving in some ministry at church); I'm living deceived into thinking I'm someone I'm not!

You can't limit your service to God to what you do at church. You can't separate what you do for God from what you do for yourself. Doing that would be divorcing your spiritual life from the forty or fifty hours a week that you are at work. If you do that, you'll be spending seventy percent of your time doing something other than glorifying God! ***Your workplace, your home, and out in the street are the places where you serve God and others (or where you fail to do so)***. Am I saying that you shouldn't serve in church? Of course not! What I'm saying is that if you only serve in church, it's because you're not a servant; you're just pretending to be one.

Think about it for a moment; what are the biblical requirements to serve as a leader in the church? To have first served at home! To have served my spouse, my children, around the neighborhood, at work! 1 Timothy 3:1-7 (ERV) says,

> *It is a true statement that anyone whose goal is to serve as an elder has his heart set on a good work. An elder must be such a good man that no one can rightly criticize him. He must be faithful to his wife. He must have self-control and be wise. He must be respected by others. He must be ready to help people by welcoming them into his home. He must be a good teacher. He must not drink too much, and he must not be someone who likes to fight. He must be gentle and peaceful. He must not be someone who loves money. He must be a good leader of his own family. This means that his children obey him with full respect. If a man does not know how to lead his own family, he will not be able to take care of God's church. An elder must not be a new believer. It might make him too proud of himself. Then he would be condemned for his pride the same as the devil was. An elder must also have the respect of people who are not part of the church. Then he will not be criticized by others and be caught in the devil's trap.*

Have you noticed how many of the above characteristics mentioned become evident in the church? I'll take that question for you. Only one: *being a good teacher*. All the other things are lived out in our day-to-day at home, at work, with our neighbors, and with our friends.

> *Everything you do is either an act of service to Christ or an act of service to yourself.*

Your heart is sold out for something, either Christ or your own selfish desires (Romans 16:18). It's your *heart* that's sold out, not your actions! Your actions may be very good, respectful, and helpful (like my friend who sent me that email), but what your heart really loves is what you truly serve. How do I know if I'm serving Christ or myself? When I don't divorce my behavior from my service. When my reasoning isn't "here I do this" and "here I don't do this" (here I come to "rest" or here I come to "work"). When service is less and less something I *do*, and it increasingly becomes something I *am*.

Let me offer practical advice that I'm currently finding to be immensely helpful in evaluating the way I live my own work life. How do most people feel when they return home after a long day's work? Drained. This is perfectly normal. Yet a deeper question is this: Is it OK to feel this tired? If what I feel is physical fatigue, then yes, most likely it is. But if what I feel is "emotional" exhaustion—although perhaps calling it "spiritual" exhaustion would be more accurate—most likely it isn't. Think about this. What is this fatigue saying about how I've lived my day? Have I lived my day in the flesh (using my strength to achieve my goals), or have I lived it in the Spirit (using his strength to achieve even higher goals)?

Think it through. If I have *really* gone through my day *in* Christ and I have lived it *for* him, why do I feel this way? If I need to "zone out," watching TV, reading a magazine, or doing something else that "gives me pleasure," ***what am I revealing about the "level of pleasure" that Christ gives me when I'm at work?***[g] Close to none at all! In other words, that I've lived my workday as an unbeliever. Anxious, burdened, worried, carrying on my shoulders the weight of responsibilities and pressures that all of us, believers and nonbelievers, face.

[g] Am I saying it's wrong to watch TV or read something when you come home from work? Of course not! I often do it myself. What I'm saying is something deeper. What I'm saying is that perhaps you shouldn't be experiencing such a high level of spiritual exhaustion if the Spirit of Christ has truly been your source of power and joy throughout the day.

That I've lived in a state of insecurity, of uncertainty, and where I need to be in control. That I'm a bitter person who's upset by their circumstances, and Christ has had no impact on the reality I had to face! He's been set aside. He hasn't interfered. He's been completely nullified.

Do you identify with this description? Great! It's OK to identify with it, but don't be condemned by it. The solution toward deep change isn't changing the way you act; the solution toward deep change is evaluating your motivations (identifying the "treasure" that drives you to live this way) and regaining the joy of Christ (remembering that he loves you and he wants to transform you).

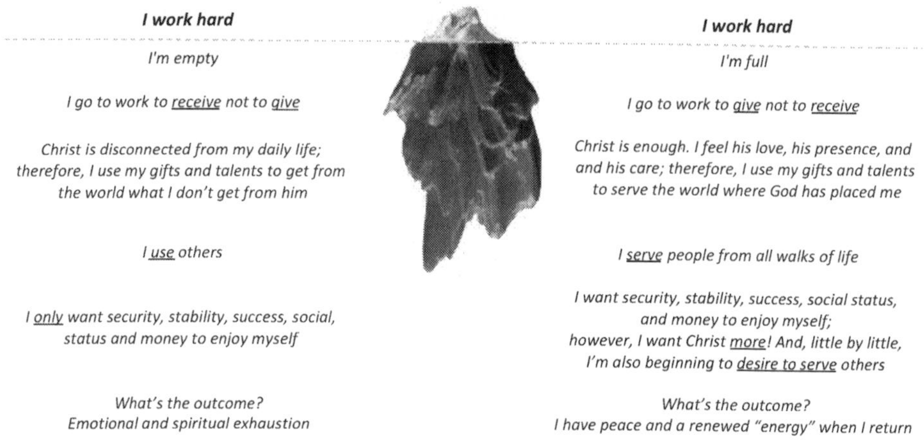

To live my day well is to enjoy
God's love so that it permeates everything I do.

Conclusion

Do you remember the way I started this chapter? Nobody's willing to *pay* in order to serve. However, that's not true. There's someone who was willing to do so. Mark 10:45 says that "*the Son of Man did not come to be served, but to serve, and to give His life a ransom for many.*" Christ came in order to serve and, in doing so, he didn't pay cash; he paid the highest price anyone could ever pay; he paid with his own life. If there were anyone unworthy of being served in this way, you and I would be top-shelf candidates. "*But God demonstrates His own love toward us, in that while we were yet sinners, [undeserving of such an act of service!] Christ died for us*" (Romans 5:8).

What does he expect from us? That we "return" the favor and pay him with our service? No. He expects us to be *amazed* at what he's done. But don't worry. When your heart shatters to pieces as you think of this truth, when you are broken from seeing his service, you too will serve as he did: with *joy!* "*Fixing our eyes on Jesus, the author and perfecter of faith, who for the joy set before Him endured the cross, despising the shame, and has sat down at the right hand of the throne of God.* For *consider Him who has endured such hostility by sinners against Himself, so that you will not grow weary and lose heart*" (Hebrews 12:2-3, emphasis added).

BRIEF SUMMARY

Serving is an outcome: *Only when I enjoy God can I serve with true joy.*

Serving is a miracle: *Only when I experience his extraordinary love do I begin to develop an extraordinary love for others. Christian service isn't just about performing acts of service to others. Christian service involves experiencing a change in what brings pleasure to the heart. It is to begin to experience the reality that "it is more blessed to give than to receive."*

Serving is Receiving: *Only when I am filled with the Spirit of God can I serve as he expects of me (in his power and for his glory). Service, far from repaying God for what he's done for me, increases my debt to him.*

Serving is an identity*: More than something I do, it's who I am.*

FOR PERSONAL REFLECTION OR DISCUSSION IN SMALL GROUPS

1. *Sum up in one or two sentences the concepts that have had the greatest impact on you in this chapter.*
2. *What does it mean that service is an outcome? Explain it in your own words.*
3. *How would you define genuine service? What would a non-genuine way of serving look like?*
4. *What should a person who longs to serve more do?*
5. *How would you explain the difference between "serving in the flesh" and "serving in the Spirit"? How does a person serve in the power of the Spirit?*

6. *Are you a servant in the workplace (or the classroom)? Do you serve at home? If your answer is no, why do you think it's so hard for you? What is your greatest desire or goal when you find yourself in these two environments?*

CHAPTER 12

A New Motivation to Seek God

Seeking God; an outcome or a goal? Both!

I love going to the movies. Enjoying a good movie with my wife is exciting to me, and I look forward to it with great anticipation. But let me ask you a question. Do I go to the movies *because* I have enjoyed a good film, or do I go to the movies *in order to* enjoy a good film? Don't rush to answer. If you think about it for a moment, you'll realize the answer is "both"!

What do I mean? I mean that the *reason* I go to the movies is that, at some point in life, I've had the chance to go to the movies, and I enjoyed the experience. In other words, the cause or driving force behind going to see a movie is that I've already had a taste of what it's like to watch a movie. However, on the other hand, I also go to the movies *in order to* enjoy the pleasure that theater has to offer. In other words, my *purpose* in going to the movies is to experience the same kind of pleasure I did in the past.

The same is true about God. ***Seeking God is an outcome of having found God, and it's also a means in order to find Him.*** As 1 Peter 2:2-3 (NLT) says, "*Like newborn babies, you must crave pure spiritual milk so that you will grow into a full experience of salvation. Cry out for this nourishment, now that you have had a taste of the Lord's kindness*" (emphasis added). Can you see the double dynamic? We desire to seek God (our purpose) as an outcome of having had a taste of his goodness (the reason).

Why is it important to discern and consider both realities? Because of the heart's highly subtle and unconscious tendency that Matthew 6:1 puts forward. Do you remember what we talked about in the first chapters? Even seeking God or practicing spiritual disciplines, such as fasting, praying, and giving, can be a means that I unconsciously use to love myself. ***<u>All of us</u>*** (yes, even you and I) ***are inclined to seek God in order to try to be accepted by him, to feel good about ourselves, or to prove our worth.*** Do you remember Dr. Martyn Lloyd-Jones' words about what sin is?

> In order to get an accurate idea of its essence and to really understand it, we must imagine a great saint, a man or a woman of extraordinary devotion and dedication to God, and we must look at them there on their knees, in the very presence of God. Even in this setting, the "self" is laying siege to the saint, and the temptation for sin lies in thinking well of oneself and in worship of oneself instead of worship of God. This, and not the other, is the true picture of sin…[95]

I'll never forget what a friend said to me many years ago. I asked him what he was learning in quiet time, and his answer was: "I'm learning to pray less." I was shocked at first by what he said. Learning to pray less? However, once I realized what he meant, I couldn't stop thinking about it for weeks on end. His statement was simply amazing. What did he mean by it?

Let me give you a personal example to illustrate it. I've been a missionary for over fifteen years. What is a missionary supposed to do when he gets up in the morning? Pray! However, what happens if I seek God, and I can't find him? What happens when I try to pray, and my prayers don't get through the roof? How do I feel? Exhilarated? Happy? Accepted? Loved with the infinite love the Father has for the Son (John 15:9)! No! I feel discouraged. I feel sad. I feel like a failure. Why? Because of the problem I just laid out before you. Because I approach God in order to *<u>earn</u>* his love, and not as the *<u>outcome</u>* of feeling loved by him. Because I approach God in order to *<u>give</u>*, and not to *<u>receive</u>*. Because I tend to approach God in order to *<u>fulfill</u>* a duty, feel good about myself, or appease the guilt that comes from failing to pray.

Approaching God as the consequence of a delight that I simply wish to prolong doesn't come naturally to me. Do you know what are some of the thoughts that run through my head? (Surely, they also run through yours, even if you're not a missionary.) What kind of Christian am I if I have such a hard time finding God every morning? How can God use me if, after so many years of being a believer, I'm unable to spend half an hour entirely focused on him? What kind of power do I hope to have to serve him today if I don't pray? How many biographies of great missionaries have I read who used to get up at four in the morning in order to pray? But me... me... me... Have you noticed? What's going on here? Where is the focus? Is it on the character of God or on mine? Is it on his love for me or my love for him? Yes, I'm drawing closer to God, but ***am I drawing closer to him as the outcome of being loved by God, or am I drawing near to God in order to be loved by him?***

My friend was right; I must learn to pray less. That's the first step in seeking God. I must learn the amazing truth that I don't need to "impress" God; that I don't need to "buy" his love; that I don't have to "bring my sacrifices" to persuade him of how good I am so that he'll bless my life or my ministry. What my friend told me a few years ago is the same thing that Jesus says in Matthew 6:7-8 (HCSB), "*When you pray, don't babble like the idolaters, since they imagine they'll be heard for their many words. Don't be like them, because your Father knows the things you need before you ask Him.*" Who is Jesus talking to? To believers! You (believers) shouldn't be like them (the gentiles or pagans) when you pray! Your reasoning should be different from non-believers' reasoning.

What my friend and Jesus mean is that there's a reasoning inside us (in *all* of us) that moves us to ***practice the spiritual disciplines as a means of "scoring points" before God.***

That reasoning goes like this: "I know I must pray. I don't really want to. But I feel guilty or lacking in spiritual depth if I don't spend enough time praying. What's the result? I use "vain repetitions." What does this mean? I'm praying more than I ought to. But the key to understanding this dynamic is to reflect on why I do it. Jesus gives us the answer. ***The reason we "pray too much" is that we don't know the heart of the Father.*** It's to have a pagan god. It's to believe that we must "buy" the God of the Bible. It's to think that we must "win" the heavenly Father over. It's to relate to God as if we have to "appease him." Pay really close attention to what Jesus is saying: God is nothing like we "*imagine*" he is! (The verb used here may be translated as to "think" wrongly, to "consider" erroneously, or to "assume" that God is a certain way that he is not).

Take a few moments to reflect on God's character as described by Jesus. He says, "*your Father knows.*" What does it mean that God "*knows*" what you need before you ask him? It means that he watches over *everything* that happens to you! That he's concerned with *everything* that happens to you!

That he cares about *everything* that happens to you! That he wants to step in and that his intervention (or lack thereof) is fully conditioned on what "*he knows*" is best for you. Can you see it? ***The fact that he's paying attention is a demonstration of his love.***

Have you noticed a detail here? It's very interesting that the passage doesn't say: The Father knows *what you are going to say* (although he does). The passage says, "*because the Father knows the things you need*." The emphasis is on God *knowing*, *understanding*, and *comprehending* our needs. Just like a parent with a young child.

My son Manuel, who's four years old at the moment, doesn't need to ask me to fix breakfast for him every morning. He doesn't have to ask me to put his seat belt on when we get in the car. He doesn't need to remind me to wrap him with a blanket in the winter. I already know these things! I know the things he needs. I'm invested in his life. I notice and supply these needs long before he asks me to do it! Almost every winter night, I wake up to tuck in "my three little cooties"—as I tenderly call them—because, every night by three o'clock in the morning, they'll typically have completely uncovered themselves. I look after my kids! I love them! I'm *always* seeking their wellbeing!

But no. The God of the Bible is different. He's a much better parent than you or I. As Jesus himself says, "*If you then, being evil, know how to give good gifts to your children, how much more will your Father who is in heaven give what is good to those who ask Him!*" (Matthew 7:11; emphasis added). My friend was right; I have to learn to pray less. Why? Is it because praying a lot is wrong? Of course not! The Bible praises persistence.[a] Learning to "pray less" doesn't mean spending less time with God; learning to "pray less" means that ***I have to learn to seek God not as a means to earn his love; but rather but as the outcome of having experienced his amazing steadfast love.***

Let me offer a practical indicator that can help you identify whether you are seeking God for the right reasons. Once you are done with your daily devotions, what makes you feel satisfied? Do you feel good because you've

[a] It's important not to confuse ***insisting*** (which is praised and encouraged in the Bible) with ***repeating words in vain***. The former shows a burden of the heart; that is, I repeat the same request because I really want it. The latter expresses a lack of connection of the heart. I "parrot" the same prayer, without thinking about it too much and without any actual engagement on my part. That is to say, I do it to fulfill a duty, as a means to feel good about having made an effort or to convince God that my "goodness" and "sacrifice" in prayer deserve a response from him. Ecclesiastes 5:1-2 reads, "*Guard your steps as you go to the house of God and draw near to listen rather than to offer the sacrifice of fools [i.e., of those who don't think or who disconnect their hearts from their prayers!]; for they do not know they are doing evil. Do not be hasty in word or impulsive in thought to bring up a matter in the presence of God. For God is in heaven and you are on the earth; therefore, let your words be few.*"

spent time with God or because you've been able to appreciate his love? In other words, do you feel good about having fulfilled a duty (which means the focus is on you), or do you feel good because, regardless of whether you "found" or "didn't find" him, he still loves you (which means the focus is on him)?

Are you happy when you seek God, or when you feel his love for you?

Henri Nouwen summed up this struggle well when he wrote the following prayer:

> Why, O Lord, is it so hard for me to keep my heart directed toward you? Why do the many little things I want to do, and the many people I know, keep crowding into my mind, even during the hours that I am totally free to be with you and you alone? Why does my mind wander off in so many directions, and why does my heart desire the things that lead me astray? Are you not enough for me? Do I keep doubting your love and care, your mercy and grace? Do I keep wondering, in the center of my being, whether you will give me all I need if I just keep my eyes on you?
>
> Please accept my distractions, my fatigue, my irritations, and my faithless wanderings. You know me more deeply and fully than I know myself. You love me with a greater love than I can love myself. You even offer me more than I can desire. Look at me, see me in all my misery and inner confusions, and let me sense your presence in the midst of my turmoil.... Yet, I am afraid to do so. I am afraid that you will reject me. But I know—with the knowledge of faith—that you desire to give me your love. ***The only thing you ask of me is not to hide from you, not to run away in despair, not to act as if you were a relentless despot***.[96]

The Means God Uses to Change Me

You and I have the same goal in life. ***We live to quench the thirst in our hearts***. Yes, some use castles, others use TV. Some use soccer; others use work. Some use a vacation; others use clothing or external beauty. Yet when we look underneath the surface, you, me, and every other human being, are looking for the same thing: We want our hearts to be full. John Piper poses the following question around this issue:

> How do you trust the statement "I AM YOUR SOUL'S SATISFACTION"? We must trust Christ for what he tells us to trust him for, namely, his gifts and promises. And what are they? ***The best gift purchased and promised by the Gospel is the gift of God himself***, revealed in Christ and offered to us for our enjoyment. What does it mean to trust a person who says: "*Whoever believes in me shall never thirst*" (John 6:35)? Or, to put it differently, what does it mean to trust a person who says: "My beauty and my glory are your soul's deepest satisfaction"? It means that trust must taste and embrace that satisfaction.[97]

Why do we seek God? Because he *is* life! Because *in* him is life! Because *seeing* him satisfies and transforms us (2 Corinthians 3:18)! As we'll see throughout the rest of this chapter, God has provided us various means to further our relationship with him and to appropriate this amazing reality for ourselves. These means, commonly known as spiritual disciplines, are means that God uses to reveal himself and change us.

Spiritual disciplines
1. *Meditation*
2. *Reading the Bible on a daily basis*
3. *Reading Christian books*
4. *Solitary prayer*
5. *Fasting*
6. *Listening to sermons*
7. *Confession*
8. *Evangelism*
9. *Retreat*
10. *Service*
11. *Worship*
12. *Simplicity*
13. *Bible memorization*
14. *Keeping a spiritual journal*
15. *Mutual edification among believers*

But before we zoom in on some of them, it's very important to understand a paradoxical reality around them. ***No one changes because of the spiritual***

disciplines, but no one changes without practicing them. What do I mean? The best way to explain it is through a tragicomic story you probably know. A man is shipwrecked in the middle of the ocean, and he finds himself floating with a life jacket. The man prays and asks God, "Lord, save me!" Then God sends a boat, but when they throw him a rope to pull him up, the man refuses to hold on to the rope. He prays once more, "Lord, save me!" So God sends a helicopter, and again the man refuses to be helped. This goes on a few more times until he dies. When he gets to heaven, the man is angry with God and confronts him for not going through the trouble to help him. The moral here is pretty obvious, isn't it? God makes use of different means!

In order to *save us*, God uses preaching: "*How will they hear without a preacher?*" (Romans 10:14). To *change us*, God uses spiritual disciplines. Can God perform the miracle of saving us without anyone preaching to us? Of course he can! Can God perform a miracle and change us if we don't have access to his Word or to any of the means he typically uses? Of course he can! But it's not the way he usually does it. God doesn't tap a magic wand in order to change us. God uses different means to do that. In fact, God engages us in the process of transformation. How? By holding us accountable for making use of those means.

You can't cry out, "Lord, change me!" and expect him to touch you with a magic wand and release you from your struggles. If I don't get up early to pray and read the Bible, if I hide and refuse to share my struggles with someone mature, if I stay home and watch TV when my small group meets, then I share the same childlike, self-deluded attitude the man in our story has. That means I don't really want to change; I want a wizard who'll swish their magic wand over me!

You are responsible for change!
Yes, you can't change what you love, but you can expose your heart to the One who can do it.

Given that throughout the book, I've emphasized time and again that you can't change yourself, and therefore it may seem as though I'm contradicting myself, let me use another example to illustrate how this dynamic works. Let's say that God gives you a rather strange commandment that goes like this: "Go and get soaked with rain." What do you have to do upon hearing this command? If you think about it, in a sense, there's *nothing you can do*—you can't make it rain! On the other hand, however, *there is something you can do*. If you're indoors, you can go outside! If you're in a desert, you can go somewhere where it usually rains. Can you make it rain? Of course not! But if you stay home, with a roof above your head, you'll never get wet!

Do you want to change? It's your responsibility to get out in the open! No, you can't change yourself. You can't change what you love. But you can use the means God has made available so that, as you lean on his sovereignty, he can use them to transform you. Can you see it now? No one changes because of the spiritual disciplines, neither does anyone change without practicing them.

> *The spiritual disciplines are the means God uses for us to regain, renew, and increase our joy in Christ and our appreciation of him.*

Let me change the analogy. Let's say you want to get a tan. What do you have to do? The answer is pretty obvious: you need to get exposed to the sun. Very well. Let's say you go outside and do that. Is that enough? Is that all it takes? What will happen to your tan if you only expose yourself to the sun for a day or two? It'll gradually fade away.

The same thing happens with your heart. A sermon a week isn't nearly enough to "warm" your fallen heart! What you need, if you *really* want to fall in love with Jesus, is to make a commitment to *constantly* expose your heart to him. Do you remember what Proverbs 4:23 says? "*Above all else, guard your heart, for everything you do flows from it*" (NIV).

Nothing in our lives should demand more time, energy, creativity, and effort from us than taking care of our own heart. Have you noticed the radical nature of the first clause? Taking care of your heart is more important than making money, going to work, or enjoying yourself; and it's more important than your own family! The passage literally says that you should make it a priority above "anything you hold dear," especially above any "treasure" or "any other thing you value." Why does the Bible make such a radical statement? Because **EVERYTHING** you do, be it your work, leisure, or caring for your family, is influenced by what your heart loves the most.

One of the things God has been teaching me this week is the way I *use* my family. Yesterday, my daughter asked me, "Dad, why do you spend so much time playing soccer with the boys when you spend so little time playing with me?" What do you think? Is it because I love them more than my daughter? Of course not! I do it because I love myself more than I love the three of them! The sad and painful reality is that I play with the boys more because I enjoy men's activities more than women's activities.

Can you see it? *Everything* we do, even the most mundane and "innocent" thing in life, is influenced by what captivates our heart (in my case, maximizing enjoyment while minimizing boredom). What does the Bible say we should do? We should guard our hearts. How do we do it? We do it in two ways. By exposing our heart to whatever can motivate us to renew our love for God (and others) and by protecting our heart from anything that might lure it into living for itself.

The most important duty I have is to ***protect*** *my heart from anything that might curb my appetite for God, and to* ***expose*** *my heart to anything that might heighten my hunger for him.*

Protecting the Heart

In Matthew 5:29-30, Jesus teaches an absolutely crucial principle for protecting our hearts. "*If your right eye makes you stumble, tear it out and throw it from you.... If your right hand makes you stumble, cut it off and throw it from you....*" I know you are familiar with the passage, but have you noticed a detail? Jesus isn't answering the question: what should I do *when* I'm tempted? That is, what should be my response ***while undergoing*** temptation? (The Bible says that, when I'm faced with temptation, I should ***flee***, just as Joseph did with Potiphar's wife in Genesis 39:12 or as Paul instructed Timothy to do in 2 Timothy 2:22: "*Now flee from youthful lusts...*") In the context of this passage, Jesus is answering the question: What should I do in order to ***prevent*** myself from falling? In other words, what should be my course of action ***before*** temptation arises? Jesus' command is very clear: ***I must eradicate anything that might lead me to fall.*** (Can you see it? Jesus is addressing a hypothetical situation, a future scenario.)

But pay attention to his words. According to him, there are two things I must do. On the one hand, I must "*tear out*" or "*cut off*" those good (yes, good!) activities, people, or habits that I'm presently participating in that entice me and tempt me to sin. What this means is that I have to identify them and stop practicing them. Television, social networks, cell phones, partying, a relationship that I know is a bad influence, a boyfriend, and so on are just a few examples; the list is endless. (The image that Jesus uses is very strong.

You have to "cut them off"! That is to say, the pain you feel when you leave them behind feels as if a part of your body has been torn from you! It hurts big time!) And, on the other hand, Jesus says that I must "*throw them from me*"; that is, I must keep them as far away from me as possible. In other words, I must take the necessary steps not to be near them again, and thus risk exposing my heart to fall again. [b]

I remember that when I was single and living in the United States, my church's entire college group participated in a huge country and western music venue. I asked a friend to come along, but he said, "I want to, but I know I shouldn't. If I go, when I get home, I'll spend all night thinking about things I shouldn't." His response was an incarnation of Matthew 5:29. Knowing the weakness of his own heart, my friend made a radical decision: He "cut off" the occasion to fall and "threw it away." Why didn't he go to the party? Was he trying to earn God's love? Of course not! My friend wasn't trying to earn God's love; my friend was trying *to protect* his love of God. My friend was doing what Proverbs 4:23 teaches; knowing how fragile his heart is, he was trying to guard it![c]

---

[b] If you look at the passage closely, you'll see that Jesus is definitely talking about good things, or at least neutral things. The eye is not evil! Neither are our hands! The problem is that they may provide ***occasion*** of sin. This means that they aren't sinful in and of themselves, but they may tempt me to fall into sin. Clearly "eyes" and "hands" stand for "anything" that may be an occasion for you to fall. Meticulously keeping track of your expenses may be an occasion for you to fall by taking control of your own life. Watching a TV series may be an occasion to fall by masturbating. Going out with your non-believing friends may be an occasion to fall by getting drunk. Is keeping track of your expenses, watching TV, or going out with your friends bad? Not necessarily. The point is to discern whether it's bad ***for me***! The question here is whether any of these things lead me to turn away from God and to sell my heart to something that's bad for my spiritual life. In 1 Corinthians 6:12, Paul says, "*All things are lawful for me, but not all things are profitable. All things are lawful for me, but I will not be mastered by anything.*" The key to discerning whether something is a stumbling block is to be honest with myself and ask two questions. First, is this beneficial to me? In other words, ***is it bringing me closer to God or is it driving me away from him?*** Second, ***is it overpowering me?*** One of the things we find most difficult is to admit that, even when we deny it, we are dominated by certain practices, habits or relationships that aren't bad in and of themselves, yet they control and overpower us. Be honest with yourself. It's not bad, but does it overpower you? As the wisest man to ever live on Earth asked, *"Can a man walk on hot coals and his feet not be scorched?"* (Proverbs 6:28). (In the next chapter we'll examine the difference between the *occasion* of sin and the *cause* of sin in detail. In doing so, you'll see that there's a great difference between the two, and several other concepts will become clearer.)

[c] An example similar to my friend's decision is the apps you can put on your mobile phone or tablet to block certain kinds of content. These apps can't ***change*** your heart, but they can ***protect*** it! If you think you've won your fight with pornography because you now have an app that can screen it out, you're ***wrong***. (Matthew 5:28 says that the battle ground is your heart, not your cell phone or tablet.) On the other hand, if you think you're strong enough not to need a filter, you're ***deceiving yourself***. ("*Therefore let him who thinks he stands take heed lest he fall.*" Corinthians 10:12, NKJV). You have a fallen heart and live in a fallen world; you need help! Why do we put up these kinds of "barriers"? Because we acknowledge our own frailty. Because we are aware of our own weakness. Because we accept how easy it is for us to give in to sin. And, ultimately, we do it because we've tasted of Christ's love and we don't want to "curb" the Spirit that enables us to appreciate and enjoy him.

An important caveat is to be made in this regard. ***We aren't all tempted by the same things, nor do we all need to put up "barriers" against the same things.*** Or, to put it another way, what may be an occasion for me to fall may not be an occasion for you to fall, and vice versa (1 Corinthians 6:12). Do you remember what we said in Chapter 10? Sin is "whatever weakens your reason, impairs the tenderness of your conscience, obscures your sense of God, or takes off your relish of spiritual things; that thing is sin to you, however innocent it may be in itself." What fits into this category? Anything! A TV series, video game consoles, dieting, a boyfriend/girlfriend, your passion for sports, buying something you really want, saving compulsively, and any number of other things. The point is to take Jesus' command to heart and consider, ***what is it that dulls my passion for God <u>today</u>, and therefore I must eradicate it from my life?***[d]

> *What activities, places, people, or habits **<u>curb</u>** my hunger for God and **<u>whet</u>** my appetite for the world?*
> *What would I need to do to "cut them off" and "throw them away"?*

The Way Life Works: The Law of Sowing and Reaping

I would like to briefly discuss one of the most misunderstood and poorly taught passages in the entire New Testament. Galatians 6:6-10 (NIV) reads:

> *Nevertheless, the one who receives instruction in the word should share all good things with their instructor. Do not be deceived: God cannot be mocked. A man reaps what he sows. Whoever sows to please their flesh, from the flesh*

---

[d] Is it possible that we might have to remove something or "cut it off" temporarily? Of course it is! It may be, for example, that at a certain point in your life it may not be convenient for you to have a boyfriend/girlfriend (maybe because you're trying to fill your heart with them, because you're in a rebound from another relationship, or because you need to mature spiritually, etc.). However, that doesn't mean you have to stay single forever. The same could be said about using Facebook, playing video games, watching TV at night, or any other thing. The key is to identify whether or not your heart is a slave to these things, and whether it's satisfied by the love of Christ enough in order to not be tempted to "sell out" to them again. The image that comes to my mind is the contrast between a china teacup and a plastic mug. How do I handle a china teacup? I cover it, protect it, and am especially careful when handling it. Why? Because I'm acutely aware of how valuable and fragile it is. If you knock or drop it, you could seriously damage it. How do I handle a plastic mug? I don't pay much attention to what I do with it. My kids can have it! Why? Because if you dropped it or they knock it down, the plastic cup is strong enough to easily withstand the impact. The same can be said about the heart. There are areas where I can move around without much care. The temptation to steal, for instance, would be an example in my case, because it isn't something I struggle with. However, there are many other areas where I need to treat my heart as if it were made of china. Once you know your own heart's weakness you realize that Jesus is right: there are battles I must win <u>BEFORE</u> I can face these things.

will reap destruction; whoever sows to please the Spirit, from the Spirit will reap eternal life. Let us not become weary in doing good, for at the proper time we will reap a harvest if we do not give up. Therefore, as we have opportunity, let us do good to all people, especially to those who belong to the family of believers.

If you pay attention, you'll realize that this passage begins and ends the same way: with a commandment. The way I would sum up this commandment is: "Be generous in sharing your goods or your money in order to do good to others." In verse 6, Paul declares that we should share "*all good things*" (i.e., our goods) with those who teach us, while in verse 10, he says we should do it with everyone (whether they're believers or not). In other words, the passage begins and ends in the same way: with an action on the outside. However, if we read verses 7 to 9, we'll realize that fulfilling this commandment is a *consequence* of something much deeper. It's the *outcome* of the work that is taking place inside the heart of the generous person.

Read quickly, this passage appears to say: "If you behave properly, you'll do well; however, if you behave poorly, you'll do very badly, and you'll end up in hell." (Or even worse: "The more money you give to others, the more money God will give to you. And the less money you give to others, the less money you'll receive.") No. This isn't what Paul is saying. This passage ***is talking about the consequences of living by and for the flesh and about the consequences of living by and for the Spirit***. In a nutshell, *the consequence of living for the flesh is to not desire to share* all the good things God has given me (i.e., being selfish and, as a consequence, miserable). At the same time, *the consequence of living for the Spirit is to be transformed into a person who enjoys giving both material things and themselves* (i.e., to become more generous and helpful and, as a consequence of that, to find true life).

Let me give you an example to clarify what I mean. Let's say it's your birthday and you want to throw an incredibly special party. This time you have decided to spare no expense and hire the best chef in the world to prepare a huge chocolate cake for all your guests. As you want to be on top of every detail, you decide to visit this famous chef and watch him prepare your cake. When you enter his kitchen, everything looks amazing. The furniture is luxurious, every appliance is in perfect condition, the ingredients are top quality, and everything seems to glow. As you watch the chef prepare the cake of your dreams, you begin to imagine what it will look like when he's done.

However, as he's mixing the final ingredients, you rush across the room and tell him, "Hold on a second." You then take a handful of olives, and you tell him, "Use this."

The chef grabs your hand to stop you, and, giving you a puzzled look, he asks, "What are you doing?"

You then rush one more time; you slice some ham and try to add it to the cake.

Once more, he stops you and tells you, "Are you out of your mind? What are you doing? You can't put that on a chocolate cake!"

So you tell him, "Wait a minute. Olives are delicious, aren't they? Ham is a delicacy, isn't it? You're a chef. You should know that."

To which he replies, "Yes, they are both very good, but you can't use them for this. It will ruin the whole chocolate cake."

So you tell him, "It's my birthday, and it's my chocolate cake. ***I can do whatever I want***." What's the outcome? Or rather, the consequence? A mess! You end up spoiling your own chocolate cake. You can't expect the outcome (the reaping) to be good if you insist on using (sowing) that kind of ingredient. What does the passage from Galatians teach? Exactly the same thing.

"Sowing to my own flesh" means using all the resources I have at my disposal to find life and satisfaction outside of Christ, mistakenly believing that this will bring me happiness. It's taking control of my life. It's doing whatever I want in order to be happy. It's making all my decisions and using all my resources (money, effort, creativity, time, fantasies, etc.) to attain something that promises to make me happy. It's spending hours on end watching TV, playing video games, working overtime, and doing any number of other activities (good or bad) that will curb my appetite for God.

What is the consequence of sowing to the flesh? What do you "reap" by living this way? The same thing as you would by adding ham or olives to a chocolate cake mix. It will ruin your heart! The consequence of sowing to flesh is that ***I become more and more disagreeable***. According to Paul's words, the consequence is "*corruption*" of the heart (see verse 8). The consequence is that I become increasingly selfish, proud, self-centered, insecure, wayward, needy, more and more concerned with my own "pain" and "needs"; conversely, I become increasingly less aware of the pain and needs of others.

In other words, I become the kind of person I am without God's presence in my life. As John Stott says:

> To 'sow to the flesh' is to pander to it, to cosset, cuddle and stroke it, instead of crucifying it. The seeds we sow are largely thoughts and deeds. Every time we allow our mind to harbour a grudge, nurse a grievance, entertain an impure fantasy, or wallow in self-pity, we are sowing to the flesh. Every time we linger in bad company whose insidious influence we know we cannot resist, every time we lie in bed when we ought to be up and praying, every time we read pornographic literature, every time we take a risk which strains our self-control, we are sowing, sowing, sowing to the flesh. Some Christians sow to the flesh every day and wonder why they do not reap holiness. Holiness is a *harvest*; whether we reap it or not depends almost entirely on what and where we sow.[98]

What does it mean to sow to the Spirit? The exact opposite. ***"Sowing to the Spirit" means taking advantage of and utilizing all the resources that God has provided so that you may receive his grace and be filled with him***. It's to use all my creativity, my effort, my money, my energy, and my thoughts in striving for Christ to become my greatest pleasure in life. It means exposing my heart to all the resources at my disposal to find life and fulfillment in the person of Jesus. In short, it means living a lifestyle where I'm constantly exposing my heart to things that can change it.[e]

> *"Sowing to the flesh" is saying "yes" to anything that curbs or diminishes my hunger for God.*
> *"Sowing to the Spirit" is to say "yes" to anything that strengthens or increases my hunger for God.*

The Inevitable Conclusion: I Need to Develop New Habits

After studying Galatians 6, what I'm about to write will make much more sense. There's hardly anything more important in your life than your habits.

[e] Should I seek God when I don't feel like it or when I don't desire to do it? Although the same principles that apply to obedience also apply to this question (see Appendix 1), let me keep my answer short and sweet. Of course you should! You shouldn't "force" yourself to seek God for fear of God; that is to say, for fear of losing his love or blessing over your life, but you should "force" yourself to seek God to regain the appreciation for him that you've lost. Motivation is the key here. It determines whether you're taking a legalistic approach and you're trying to "buy" God's love or favor, or whether you're desperate to overcome your amnesia and spiritual blindness and to "get wet" with the rain of his grace. As Paul says, there are times when I must "*strike a blow to my body and make it my slave*" (1 Corinthians 9:27, NIV). After all, how many times do we wake up without any desire to seek God and yet, upon doing it, we have a real encounter with him and regain our passion for him?

There's a famous saying that goes, "Sow a thought, and you will reap an action. Sow an action, and you will reap a habit. Sow a habit, and you will reap a character. Sow a character, and you will reap a destiny." (Can you see how similar this saying is to the passage in Galatians 6 that we've just discussed?) Would you like to know what kind of person you'll become in a few years? The answer is closely connected to the habits you have today. Do you *regularly* seek God? Do you lay under the sun *on a daily basis*? Is having an encounter with him *part of your daily routine*? There are many similarities between the physical and spiritual worlds. If I don't grow the habit of brushing my teeth, I'll eventually develop cavities, and my teeth will turn yellow. If I don't exercise regularly, I will accumulate fat, which will result in circulatory and cardiac problems. If my diet is built on hamburgers, Coke, and ice cream, I can't expect to be healthy! Good habits lead to good health; bad habits lead to poor health. It's easy to see the law of sowing and reaping in the physical world, isn't it? The key to change is to apply the same principle to your spiritual life.

Habits cannot change you,
but they do expose you to the One who can

John Piper describes the effects our habits and desires have on our spiritual life in a very interesting way:

> The greatest enemy of hunger for God is not poison but apple pie. It is not the banquet of the wicked that dulls our appetite for heaven, but endless nibbling at the table of the world. It is not the X-rated video, but the prime-time dribble of triviality we drink in every night. For all the ill that Satan can do, when God describes what keeps us from the banquet table of his love, it is a piece of land, a yoke of oxen, and a wife (Luke 14: 18-20) [things in our everyday life]. The greatest adversary of love to God is not his enemies but his gifts. And the most deadly appetites are not for the poison of evil, but for the simple pleasures of earth. For when these replace an appetite for God himself, the idolatry is scarcely recognizable, and almost incurable.
>
> Jesus said some people hear the word of God, and a desire for God is awakened in their hearts. But then, "*as they go on their way they are choked with worries and riches and pleasures of this life*" (Luke 8:14). In another place he said, "*The desires for other things enter in and choke the*

> *word, and it becomes unfruitful*" (Mark4:19). "The pleasures of this life" and "the desires for other things"—these are not evil in themselves These are not vices. These are gifts of God They are your basic meat and potatoes and coffee and gardening and reading and decorating and traveling and investing and TV-watching and Internet-surfing and shopping and exercising and collecting and talking. And all of them can become deadly substitutes for God.[99]

> *How do I <u>spoil</u> my appetite for God?*
> *By maintaining habits that drive me away from him.*
> *How do I <u>increase</u> my hunger for God?*
> *By developing habits that bring me closer to him.*

Exposing the Heart

In contrast to what I've tried to stress throughout this book, ***the spiritual disciplines aren't <u>dispositions</u> of the heart; they're <u>practices</u>!*** They're holy practices or habits whose purpose is to expose the heart to the One who can change it. They're ways of getting myself under the "rain." They're different things I can do to "get a tan."[f] Donald Whitney defines them as follows:

> [They] are the God-ordained means by which we bring ourselves before God, experience Him, and are changed into Christlikeness.... If the Lord might be compared to a pure, life-giving river, the spiritual disciplines would be those ways by which we come to the river to drink from, dive into, swim in, eat from, wash with, and irrigate with it.[100]

In 1 Timothy 4:7, Paul writes to Timothy: "*<u>Discipline</u>* yourself for the purpose of godliness." What the apostle wishes to communicate to his disciple

[f] Although you may find it shocking to read, spiritual disciplines are not a part of the fruit of the Holy Spirit. [The fruit of the Spirit is love, joy, peace, patience, etc. The fruit of the Spirit is not prayer, fasting, reading the Bible, etc.] By this I do not mean that they do not need to be **<u>driven</u>** by the Holy Spirit [I've stressed the need for this throughout the book]; what I mean is that the spiritual disciplines are the fruit of a personal decision. They are the outcome of "*disciplining my body and making it my slave*" (1 Corinthians 9:27). In other words, they are practices, and so the Bible's focus is on exercising self-control and disciplining myself to practice them. Should they be born out of an appreciation for God's love? Of course they should! [This is what I started this chapter with.] However, it is my responsibility to be diligent in putting them into practice. Someone once asked a renowned theologian, "Pastor, do you pray so that you will be able to get up early and seek God?" He replied, "No. I set the alarm and I get up."

is that, for him to be "pious" or "spiritual," he must be disciplined. I need to develop new habits. Why? Because my appreciation of God is at stake! As John Piper says,

> The question [in practicing the spiritual disciplines] is not of *earning* or *meriting* or *coercing* anything from God. [In other words, it's not about God blessing us because we've practiced them.] The question is: having tasted the goodness of God in the gospel, ***how can I maximize my enjoyment of him, when every moment of my life I'm tempted to make a god out of his good gifts?*** [That is, money, vacation, family, work, clothes, television, etc.] By what weapons shall I fight the fight of faith and guard my heart from alien affections and treasonous appetites?[101]

The answer to this question is: by means of the spiritual disciplines. They're the "weapons" that God has provided me to fight a battle that I can only win by relying on him. Let us briefly look at some of them.[g]

1. Meditation

I'll admit that I've deliberately done it! You're surely surprised that I haven't started with reading the Bible on a daily basis and that I haven't given priority to the Word of God. I've done this entirely on purpose. I don't intend to minimize the importance of the Word; my intention is to "shake you up" and to "make you uncomfortable" enough so that you'll think about and "wrestle" with why practicing this discipline might be so valuable. Paul Tripp says,

> "No one is more influential in your life than you are, because no one talks to you more than you do." Whether you realize it or not, you are in an unending conversation with yourself, and the things you say to you about you are formative of the way that you live. You are constantly talking to yourself about your identity, your spirituality, your

[g] But first, two disclaimers. First, in this chapter we won't examine all the spiritual disciplines. I think there's ample literature on the subject, so I'll merely highlight a few key elements that you may not read in other books. Second, there's no consensus among Christian writers as to which disciplines should be considered to be spiritual disciplines and which ones shouldn't. I've drawn a list of my own by merging the most accepted, traditional disciplines and integrating other, more contemporary disciplines I've applied to my own spiritual life, and I've found to be most edifying. As the Apostle Paul encourages us, "examine everything carefully and hold fast to that which is good." If you'd like to read more on the subject I recommend "Spiritual Disciplines for the Christian Life" by Donald Whitney and "Celebration of Discipline" by Richard Foster. (You may disagree with some elements in Foster's book, but, as I said earlier, use your best judgment to retain what's good.)

> functionality, your emotionality, your mentality, your personality, your relationships, etc. You are constantly preaching to yourself some kind of gospel. You preach to yourself an anti-gospel of your own righteousness, power, and wisdom, or you preach to yourself the true gospel of deep spiritual need and sufficient grace. You preach to yourself an anti-gospel of aloneness and inability, or you preach to yourself the true gospel of the presence, provisions, and power of an ever-present Christ.[102]

What is Christian meditation? It's engaging in an inner dialogue with the truths about God that you already know. It's to build the habit of using our imagination to think about God's greatness and about everything he's said to us. No. I'm not talking about emptying your mind and thinking about whatever pops into your head; I'm talking about ***meditating on the implications of truly believing what you claim to believe***; about having your *knowledge* of God turn into the *enjoyment* of God.

Let me give you an example to illustrate what I mean. If you were in a game show and the host said, "You've won a million dollars!" your heart would *immediately* start beating at a different pace, and your mind would start "fantasizing" or "daydreaming" about the myriad implications that this truth holds for your life. If your child needed to undergo surgery and you didn't have the money to finance it, you'd start crying tears of joy. If you wanted to go on vacation to the Caribbean, you'd start thinking about white sand and crystal-clear waters. If you wanted to retire, and you couldn't afford to do it, you'd picture the moment when you hug your wife, your children, and your grandchildren and tell them, with tears in your eyes, that you'll finally be able to do it.

When the heart believes a truth, when it *truly* believes it, it can't help but think about that truth and all its implications. If I tell you that God died for you (which he did! He was murdered for you!); that he wants to be your Father (the Creator of two billion galaxies and *everything* there is in them!); that he longs to be your Counselor (the only one who knows *all* the past, *all* the present, and *all* the future!); and these truths, as well as many others, don't elevate you to ***meditate on his power, nor to consider their amazing consequences, ramifications, and personal implications***, what do you think is happening? The answer is simple. I'm making true claims, but you don't really believe them. (It's as if I were to tell you right now that you've won a million dollars. It would have no effect on you because you wouldn't believe me!)

Contrary to what happens in a game show, what often happens within us is that the "intensity" or "level" to which God's truths are held in our hearts is very poor or practically non-existent. What is the root cause of this problem? Sin clouds our spiritual understanding (Ephesians 4:18). What is the solution to this problem? (A problem we *all* have!) The discipline of meditation. The goal of meditation isn't to introduce new information, but to enable us, through the help of the Spirit, to appropriate the information we already have in a deeper way. This is precisely the reason for Paul's prayer for the believers in Ephesus:

> *For this reason, I bow my knees before the Father… that He would grant you, according to the riches of His glory, to be strengthened with power through His Spirit in the inner man, so that Christ may dwell in your hearts through faith; and that you, being rooted and grounded in love, may be able to comprehend with all the saints what is the breadth and length and height and depth, and to know the love of Christ which surpasses knowledge, that you may be filled up to all the fullness of God (Ephesians 3:14–19; emphasis added).*

Can you see what Paul is praying for? That they would comprehend what they already comprehend. That they would know what they already know. Why? Because the Spirit is able to bring those truths we already know to a whole new level of fullness that we can't even imagine!

Believe it or not, you already know how to meditate. You've been doing it almost since the day you were born. Even though you don't think so, all of us meditate all the time! The problem is that we meditate on the wrong things. Who doesn't fantasize about sex? Who doesn't picture themselves changing a part of their body they don't find attractive? Who doesn't think about the kind of car they'd like to buy or the kind of vacation they'd like to enjoy? Who doesn't toss and turn weighing their options (or lack thereof) when it comes to buying a house or changing jobs? We all use our imagination! We all meditate! What needs to change is that upon which we meditate. That is the discipline!

A very simple exercise that has helped me put this discipline into practice is to use the two great truths of the gospel (I'm a great sinner and God is a great Savior) as a meditative filter to read through the circumstances of my day-to-day life. As I go through my day, I often ponder: How does this situation reveal that I'm living for the sake of my pleasures? (I find this question very helpful when things don't work out the way I want them to.) On the other hand, I think: How does this response remind me that God is different from me, that, in fact, he is the opposite of me, and that, far from condemning me, he wants to embrace me with his endless love? Can you see it? I try to meditate in the darkness of my own heart, and then I seek to be captivated all over again by the indescribable character of God.

> *The goal of meditation is to be amazed*
> *at the depth of my sins and the greatness of the grace of God*

Where should I meditate? When should I meditate? The psalmist says, "*How blessed is the man… [whose] delight is in the law of the Lord, and in His law he meditates day and night!*" (Psalm 1:1-2; emphasis added). What's the answer? All day long. That's why it's a *discipline*! It's a habit I have to develop. It's a practice that I must start including in every situation in life, even the simplest and most ordinary ones. Am I experiencing financial hardship? What are the implications of God knowing and wanting to take care of me? (Talk to your heart about it!) Am I going through an illness? Do I have a test? Do I fear something? What difference does it make that the creator of the universe claims to have every hair on my head numbered? (Preach to your soul about it!) Am I tempted to please others? Am I afraid of confrontation? Who said that he'll always love me, "*even if my father and mother abandon me*" (Psalm 27:10, HCSB)? (Remind yourself of the gospel!) Meditation transforms doctrine into *comfort*, theology into *emotion*, belief into *reality*. It's not about understanding God's truths; it's about God's truths being transformed, changing shape, becoming tasteful; it's about these truths looking "beautiful" for me and moving the affections of my heart.[h]

2. The daily reading of the Bible

Having discussed the importance of meditation, I would like to quickly make a claim that it's impossible to increase my appreciation of God unless I increase how much I'm exposed to his word. In doing so, we aren't seeking to increase our knowledge *of* God; we're seeking *God himself*. How do we

[h] If you want to read a classic on meditation, I recommend a book entitled "The Practice of God's Presence," written by Brother Lawrence.

deepen our appreciation of God? You already know the answer. We have to experience the gospel all over again.

As I tried to emphasize about meditation, the main goal in reading the Scriptures isn't to gain new information (even though gaining new information is very important); the main goal is for this information to have a transformative effect on the heart. Hebrews 4:12-13 (NLT) says, "*For the word of God is alive and powerful. It is sharper than the sharpest two-edged sword, cutting between soul and spirit, between joint and marrow. It exposes our innermost thoughts and desires. Nothing in all creation is hidden from God. Everything is naked and exposed before his eyes, and he is the one to whom we are accountable* (emphasis added)."

Have you noticed what the purpose of reading the Bible is? It's for me to see what God can already see! For the desires of the heart to be exposed! For my deepest desires to be made manifest! For me to discover my own motivations! Towards the end of the passage, it says there's nothing "*hidden from God.*" In other words, he already knows what I love. Who's the one who needs light shed on the problem? I am! So what do I need? I need to read his word so that it will "pierce" and "cut through" my heart! What does any cut do? It separates. In this case, it separates my "*innermost desires.*" It helps me to discern my impure motivations from the pure ones.

According to verse 12, the Bible strips my heart "*naked.*" In other words, it allows me to see what I love! (The same idea is conveyed in James 1:24, which tells us that the purpose of being exposed to the Word is to make you realize "*the kind of person you are.*") What happens after my heart is exposed? I realize once more how much I need God and his work; in other words, I appreciate the gospel all over again.

At this point, you may be thinking, "All right. You got me. I need to read the Bible every day. How should I do it? I read it, but I don't get much out of it." I have written ***Appendix 2*** to help you in this regard. What's so special about this appendix? It will give you practical tools to read the Scriptures with a double goal: to focus your attention on the heart and to do it in a Christ-centered way (to make the most of this appendix, I suggest that you read it quietly and without rushing).[i]

[i] IMPORTANT: If you're reading this book with another person or in a small group setting in church, I would recommend that you take an extra day to go over Appendix 2 in detail and, when you come together as a group, read different passages of the New Testament together so that you can put into practice the three principles discussed in the appendix.

3. Reading Christian books

To paraphrase the well-known saying: "Tell me what you read, and I'll tell you who you are." There are few things that influence our hearts more than the well-crafted thoughts contained in a good book. John Piper wrote: "I agree with Martyn Lloyd-Jones that the fight to find time to read is a fight for one's life."[103]

I know that most pastors will tell you to read the Bible, and of course, I agree with them, but I'm also aware that many people read the Bible without fully understanding it or, as I pointed out in Appendix 2, without the proper approach to hermeneutics (one that centers on the heart and the cross). To close this gap, I believe that reading Christ-centered books may help you develop a healthier worldview and, at the same time, it may allow you to enjoy God until you learn to make the most of the Scriptures by yourself. If what I'm saying sounds a little heretical, remember that the ultimate goal in seeking God isn't to read the Bible but to have a genuine encounter with Him. (In ***Appendix 3***, you'll find a ***list of recommended books***. You'll find high-quality resources to be nourished with healthy, uplifting literature.)[j]

4. Listen to Christ-centered sermons

I'm positive that Internet access has given us the possibility to enjoy one of the greatest blessings of the twenty-first century: to have access to listen to the messages of any preacher around the world. Honestly, few things have been more edifying to my spiritual life than developing the habit of listening to good preachers deliver their messages. I currently listen to one sermon a day.

How do I do it? I choose a pastor I like, typically someone from Appendix 3, and I listen to sixty or seventy of their messages so that I can get into their "mind" and start thinking the way they think and "understanding" God the way they understand him. Once I get bored, or I just feel like a change, I choose a new one, and I start over again. Where do I find the time to listen to so many messages? It's simple; I try to make the most of my "downtimes." In my case, I do it when I go out for a run or when I'm driving to church. Do

[j] Consider this. If you take up reading for fifteen or twenty minutes a day as a discipline, you'll be able to read a whole book each month. (This includes several days of "grace" where, for various reasons, you may be unable to do it). Think about it! Twelve books a year. If you do this in five years, you will have read sixty books! This implies that in just five years you will have had the chance to expose your heart to many of the greatest thinkers in the history of Christianity. What kind of impact do you think this practice could have on your spiritual life?

you have any idea how many sermons you could listen to on a half-hour daily commute to work? Without major effort, ***you could listen to over 500 sermons a year!*** (If you listen to a thirty-minute sermon each way, that's ten sermons a week. Multiply the ten sermons weekly by the 52 weeks of the calendar year, and there's your number.)

But imagine you do it half that time. On your way to work, you listen to a message, and on your way back from work, you listen to music (or, if you go to work using public transportation, you talk to a passenger about Christ or review all the verses you have memorized). Simply by using these "downtimes," you'll have heard five times more messages than you'd hear in a whole year at your church! Do you really think this routine wouldn't have a drastic effect on your spiritual life?

The key to practicing the disciplines is to integrate them into my schedule and daily routine

5. Prayer

Do you find it hard to pray? Welcome to the club; you're in good company. I identify with the words of Martyn Lloyd-Jones:

> I have often found it difficult to start praying in the morning.... I have found nothing more important than to learn how to get oneself into that frame and condition in which one can pray.... To read something which can be characterized in general as devotional is of great value. By devotional, I do not mean something sentimental, I mean something with a true element of worship in it.... Start by reading something that will warm your spirit.... You have to learn how to kindle a flame in your spirit.... You have to learn how to use a spiritual choke.[104]

Personally, I always read something before I pray (for instance, "New Morning Mercies" by Paul Tripp). I need to "warm" my heart up before I talk to God. I don't want to pray because I *have to*; I want to pray because I *long* to do it. Reading something inspiring helps me get there. [k] J.C. Ryle wrote:

[k] "I understand it was Soren Kierkegaard who said, '***Lord, make me a person who desires one thing only.***' That is what we seek through prayer. A heart whose ultimate goal is to find its source of life and joy in Christ. John Piper wrote: "James [4:3-4] pictures prayer as a petition to our heavenly husband. Then he ponders ***the***

> Praying and sinning will never live together in the same heart. Prayer will consume sin, or sin will choke prayer.... Diligence in prayer is the secret of eminent holiness. Without controversy there is a vast difference among true Christians.... I believe the difference in nineteen cases out of twenty arises from different habits about private prayer. I believe that those who are not eminently holy pray little, and those who are eminently holy pray much.[105]

6. Fasting

Think of a woman who is extremely quiet, sweet, and shy, who is easily embarrassed and an introvert. What would have to happen for this woman to become brave, daring, and uninhibited? If you think about it for a moment, it's not as complicated as one might think. All it would take for her to change in the blink of an eye would be for her to lose sight of her son in the middle of a big crowd or for someone to kidnap him. I'll tell you one thing. If she used to find it hard to speak up, she'd now talk to everyone and desperately ask if they've seen her little boy. If she used to be modest and shy about making conversation, she would now be bold, fearless, and straightforward. This woman would put aside all formalities, and, with utter desperation and earnest persistence, she'd do everything in her power to get her little one back.

Something similar happens with fasting. Psalm 63:1-5 (CEV) reads, "*You are my God.... In my heart, I long for you, as I would long for a stream in a scorching desert. I have seen your power and your glory... Your love means more than life to me.... I will sing joyful praises and be filled with excitement like a guest at a banquet.*" Through fasting, we make our hunger for God manifest. Unlike anything else, fasting cries out, "God, I'm desperate to find you again!"

What is fasting? In simple terms, fasting is abstaining from food in order to seek God with greater intensity. It's not simply abstaining from food (and checking out Facebook while you fast). Fasting entails setting aside time and dedicating that time to meet with God. It's limiting yourself from ingesting food in order to devote yourself to satisfy your spiritual needs.

---

possibility that we would actually ask our husband to pay for our visit to the prostitute. *'You ask and do not receive, because you ask with wrong motives, so that you may spend it on your pleasures. You adulteresses, do you not know that friendship with the world is hostility toward God?* The word 'adulteresses' is the key here. Why are we called 'adulteresses' in praying for something to spend on our pleasures? Because God is our husband and the 'world' is a prostitute *luring us to give affections to her that belong only to God*. This is how subtle the sin of worldliness can be. It can emerge not against prayer, but in prayer..." John Piper, *A Hunger for God*, 78.

Paradoxically, during fasting, you stop eating because you are hungry. It isn't hunger for food, but rather a hunger to experience God. In other words, fasting says "no" to our natural appetites in order to say "yes" to the deepest appetite of the heart: being satisfied with God.

> *Fasting is the manifestation of the unsatisfied heart.*
> *It's the silent cry of the spiritually hungry.*
> *It's the determination of someone*
> *who has tasted life and who wants to taste it again.*

What things should I fast from? From anything that enslaves you or tends to rob you of your hunger for God. You can fast from TV, social media, your hobbies, sports, eating in restaurants, you can even fast from speaking! (A professor and friend of mine who would typically raise his voice every time he attended the weekly teachers' meeting decided to fast from speaking, and he said nothing at these meetings for a year.) As Piper wrote, "We will do anything and go without anything if, by any means, we might protect ourselves from the deadening effects of innocent delights and preserve the sweet longings of our homesickness for God. Not just food, but anything."[106]

> *Fasting isn't about rejecting bad things;*
> *it's about rejecting good things in order to choose the best there is: God*

7. Confession

The two elders of our church and I have a weekly meeting every Wednesday afternoon to discuss different matters concerning the ministry in our congregation. Do you know what is the first thing we do every time we get together? We share the things we struggle with and our sins. Yes, all three of us open our hearts wide and, without trying to justify or cover up our defeat, we candidly express the most challenging battles we have had since the last time we met.

[1] Let me give you a bit of a practical advice. Purchase the book "*A Hunger for God*" by John Piper and, as you fast, read a chapter of this book followed by a time to seek God through prayer. Let me be even more specific. How about fasting any day of the week during your lunch break? (Yes. You can do it at the office, on the street, or in a workshop, why not?) The book is just seven chapters long, so you'll only need seven weeks to do it.

In doing so, we try to call our defeats by their name. What do I mean? We are very specific and clear about it, and we leave aside any generalizations. What things do we confess? Whatever needs to be confessed! Our sex life, the way we treat our family, our darkest thoughts (envy, pride, bitterness, anger, etc.). The rule is very simple. ***What should I share with someone else? The things I don't want to share with anyone!*** (All other things, you and God can work out together.) Why? Because precisely what I don't want to share is what has a hold on me, what enslaves me and prevents me from living in the light.

Galatians 6:2 says, "*Bear one another's burdens, and thereby fulfill the law of Christ.*" How will someone else carry my "*burden*" unless I share it with them? James 5:16 says, "*Therefore, confess your sins to one another, and pray for one another so that you may be healed. The effective prayer of a righteous man can accomplish much.*" What is effective prayer? ***It's the prayer I make for another person after that person has shared his sin with me!*** In other words, now that I know what your "burden" is because you have confessed, I can pray for you in an "*effective*" and informed way. (Naturally, the text makes it clear that this is a two-way street where I also share my struggle with you. There isn't a person who "ministers" and another person who is "ministered to" here. There are two people, and they both need to be restored and healed.)

How does confession help us? In many ways, but let me point out the two most important ways. ***First, it helps keep us from falling again***. You and I are well aware that there are sins and tendencies in our hearts that have become habits. We keep repeating them over and over again. We have prayed, fasted, tried to avoid falling, but nothing has happened; they're still there. Confession, as we saw in Appendix 1 is a *crutch* that can help us obey when we don't desire to do it. Who takes pleasure in "getting naked" in front of others and sharing their most secret failures? Knowing that you'll have to do it may be helpful in your moments of greatest weakness. Yes, I'm aware that it isn't the most Christ-centered motivator, but I'm also aware that the heart we have is still a fallen one. As I said in Appendix 1, crutches are temporary. We use them in times of weakness or when we have a particular area of struggle that is a "burden," and that we can't overcome without help (and this burden varies from person to person).

Why do we do it? So that God will forgive us? Of course not! We do this because we recognize that we have a weak heart, and we want to guard it so that we can present it to our true love and to him alone. As we read in

Matthew 5:29, we do this because we want to "throw from us" any temptation that might harm or impair the unique relationship we have with Jesus.

Second, confession helps us appreciate the gospel **once more**. As Richard Foster wrote: "God has given us our brothers and sisters to stand in Christ's stead and make God's presence and forgiveness real to us."[107] Is it just me, or do you also have moments when you need another fully fleshed human to remind you of the complete and full forgiveness of God? Confession gives you the gift of a "priest" in a friend to remind you that you're loved and accepted in God.[m] On the other hand, another great privilege of confession is that, by sharing your sin, you now have someone who knows the details of your struggle and can give you informed advice and a new perspective on why you're struggling with it and how to overcome it.[n]

8. Service

Since I've spent an entire chapter discussing service, at this point, I would only like you to reflect on a truth that's extremely relevant. Why do you think Jesus said, "*It is more blessed to give than to receive*" (Acts 20:35)? Why is someone *happier when they give* than when they receive? Take a moment to think about it before you read on. What is it about "giving" that "receiving" lacks? I would sum it up in three lines. Few things *liken you more to God* than serving others. Few things *make you experience God* more than serving. Few

---

[m] One of the strongholds of the Protestant Reformation was the "priesthood of all believers." In the process of rejecting the Catholic Church, we've lost the value of this precious truth. Mutual confession reminds us of it. As 1 Peter 2:9 claims, "*But you are a chosen race, a royal priesthood, a holy nation, a people for God's own possession, so that you may proclaim the excellencies of Him who has called you out of darkness into His marvelous light.*" We aren't just capable of ministering to "one another," but rather we're meant to do so.

[n] If you aren't in the habit of confessing the things you struggle with to another person, I know what you're thinking. "I have no one I can trust to do it with. Besides, what if I tell them about my innermost struggles, and then they just pass them around?" (There isn't a single country around the world where these two issues haven't come up when I discuss confession. Everyone thinks that their situation is unique and that there's nothing that can be done about it.) The truth of the matter is that we all have very "good reasons" for not sharing our struggles. What we need to ask ourselves is whether we care more about our reputation than our holiness. What do you love more, the opinion of others or your communion with God? Yes, there's a chance that someone might pass around what you share with them. In my own experience, I've only had it happen to me once. (And I believe I've shared my sins with over fifty people across various continents.) How about some practical advice? Try sharing something slightly deep with someone you trust and wait to see how they react. If their response is positive, you can gradually trust them with more and more of your "burdens." If you find that they don't know how to handle it, if they're shocked or if it simply doesn't help, find someone else. Restart the process until you find someone suitable for the job. As Ecclesiastes 4:9-10 says, "*Two are better than one because they have a good return for their labor. For if either of them falls, the one will lift up his companion. But woe to the one who falls when there is not another to lift him up*" (emphasis added). Now, let me clue you in on a secret. No one's going to approach you for a confession. You have to take the initiative! The key to taking up this discipline is for you to start practicing!

things *make you experience the joy of God* more than serving. Can you see the connection between these three statements?
Let me clarify this threefold connection by asking you a question. What would your idea of God be like without the incarnation of Jesus? Think about it for a few moments. What kind of God would you have if all you knew about who he is was what is written in the Old Testament? I believe this question is deeply profound, and it deserves multiple answers, but let me present you with an aspect of God we would never have known about if it weren't for Jesus. ***God has the heart of a slave***.

John 13:4-5 says, "*And taking a towel, He girded Himself. Then He poured water into the basin, and began to wash the disciples' feet and to wipe them with the towel with which He was girded.*" What does Jesus show us about God's heart? ***That God finds pleasure in serving***. Think about it. Who "*causes the sun to rise on the evil and the good, and sends rain on the righteous and the unrighteous*"? God does. What is he doing by doing that? He's serving us! What is prayer but a request for the King to serve us and grant us what we ask? What does he do when he answers our petitions? He serves us! Not only that, but he also displays the magnitude of his passion for serving us by *commanding* us to pray! In other words, he commands you to ask him to serve you! What kind of God does something like this?

I could go on with the list of ways God serves us selflessly, but I'm sure you get the idea. Now read Jesus' words again, "*These things I have spoken to you, so that My joy may be in you, and that your joy may be made full*" (John 15:11). Can you see the link between God's heart, his pleasure in serving, his command for us to be like him, and the outcome? "*It is more blessed to give than to receive*"? ***Giving likens you to God! Giving allows you to feel what he feels when he does it!***

God finds pleasure in serving

⇩

God wants me to serve

⇩

He who serves others becomes more like God:
he experiences the pleasure of giving

What is the inescapable conclusion of this threefold connection? You have to make a discipline out of serving. You have to choose an activity (I would say a weekly activity) where you can commit yourself to serve others. May I offer you some practical advice? I advise ***you to choose one activity within the church and one outside the church***, in your neighborhood, in your community, or at a community center. Why one inside and one outside? For various reasons, but I'll only give you two. God has called us to bless the world, not the church, to love our neighbor, not our brothers and sisters.

Do you remember the parable of the Good Samaritan? Who is my neighbor? The one who isn't a member of my community or close circle. In our case: non-believers. As Jesus said, "*For if you love those who love you, what reward do you have? Do not even the tax collectors do the same? If you greet only your brothers, what more are you doing than others? Do not even the Gentiles do the same?*" (Matthew 5:46-47; emphasis added). On the other hand, if we don't serve people outside the church, how will we show them the love God has for them? How will we talk to them about a God who left heaven to die for them if we don't leave behind our comfort zone in order to love them in practical ways and to talk to them about him?

9. Evangelism

I would like to end this chapter with a brief reflection on evangelism. My intention is that, as you have just done in regard to service, you may come to see the threefold connection between God's joy in evangelism, God's call to evangelize, and the experience of "divine joy" he invites us to share. In the well-known passage in Luke 15:1-32, Jesus shares three parables. The first one about a man who loses a sheep. Another one about a woman who loses a coin. And the last one, about a father who loses one of his sons.

Do you remember what the man does when he finds the sheep? He throws a party! He calls all his friends and neighbors and tells them, "***I want you to experience what I feel!***" "***Rejoice with me!***" Do you remember what the woman does when she finds her coin? She celebrates! She, too, calls all her friends and neighbors, and she literally uses the same words the man in the previous story did, "*Rejoice with me*!" In other words, "***Experience what I feel!***" Do you remember what the father does when he finds his son? He responds the same way. He throws a big party! "*Quickly bring out the best robe and put it on him, and put a ring on his hand and sandals on his feet; and bring the fattened calf, kill it, and let us eat and celebrate*" (Luke 15:22). Have you noticed that all these imperatives are a call for others to come and join them? The party isn't just for him and his son; the party includes all his relatives as well as his servants!

Can you see it? All three stories aim at communicating the same thing. When a person comes to Jesus, God's heart is so full of joy that the closest human experience is a party where not just one person rejoices, but *everyone* joins in the celebration. However, pay close attention! It's not just any kind of party! The idea here is similar to what happens when the national soccer team wins the World Cup, or when someone wins the lottery, and they invite everyone over for dinner, or when a member of your family who was diagnosed with terminal cancer beats the disease. Everyone gets together to celebrate because they all share in the joy! The joy of the shepherd, of the woman, and of the father is so great and special that they can't help but share it!

Now, what is it that sparks a great celebration in heaven? "*I tell you that in the same way, there will be more joy in heaven over one sinner who repents than over ninety-nine righteous persons who need no repentance*" (verse 7). Are you paying attention? God doesn't start the party when a hundred people (or a thousand) convert; no! God kicks off the party when *a single individual* comes to Jesus! Can you see how valuable a single conversion is to God? Can you see the overflow of joy that a single individual can bring about in God's heart? Is that the image you have of God? A God who recklessly goes about throwing parties as if he had won the World Cup?

Now, let me complete the picture. Go ahead and now think of a beggar. Imagine a person who has been homeless for years. Think of someone who hasn't had a shower in months, who hasn't brushed their teeth, whose hair is coarse, and whose stench is so strong that you can hardly go near them without pinching your nose. That was the state the prodigal son was in. Yet the passage says, "*But while he was still a long way off, his father saw him… and ran, embraced him [unclean though he was] and kissed him*" (verse 20). The verb in Greek indicates a continuous action. The idea here is, "And he kissed him, and he kissed him, and he kissed him some more! And he didn't stop kissing him!" Let me ask you one more time, is this the image that you have of God? A God who finds so much pleasure in embracing a repentant sinner that his emotions and his joy are so raw that he cannot refrain from kissing them! Do you get it now? The joy he experiences is the same joy he wants to share with you.

There's an aspect of God's happiness when someone comes to Jesus that you can only experience when you evangelize and bring someone to God's feet (Philemon 1:6). There's a nuance, a characteristic, a feature of God's heart that you can never experience unless you practice the discipline of evangelism (the same is true of discipleship). As someone once said, "You haven't fully lived your life until you've been used by God to save a life." Get into the habit of sharing the gospel with your friends and neighbors. Listen to the call of the One who tells you, "*Follow Me, and I will make you fishers of men... These things I have spoken to you so that My joy may be in you, and that your joy may be made full.*"

BRIEF SUMMARY

God's heart is different from what I make it to be. I don't need to "buy" God or try to "earn" his favor. God loves me like a father loves his son because he loves me on account of his Son. What do we get from this? I must learn to seek God by recalling how great his love for me is and not by trying to prove how great my love for him is.

The Bible calls me to protect my heart from anything that might curb my appetite for God, and it also invites me to expose my heart to anything that might whet my appetite for him.

No one's heart changes on account of their habits, but no one's heart changes if they don't have good habits. You can't manipulate or force God to do anything by means of your behavior, but you're responsible for exposing your heart to the means he typically uses to transform you. You decide where to "sow," but God is the one who produces the growth.

- *"Sowing to my own flesh" means using all the resources I have at my disposal to find life and satisfaction outside of Christ, mistakenly believing that this will bring me happiness.*
- *"Sowing to the Spirit" means taking advantage of and utilizing all the resources that God has provided in order that you may receive his grace and be filled with him.*

The spiritual disciplines are tools God uses to reveal himself and change me. Practicing these disciplines on a regular basis is absolutely crucial for spiritual growth.

FOR PERSONAL REFLECTION OR DISCUSSION IN SMALL GROUPS

1. *Sum up in one or two sentences the concepts that have had the greatest impact on you in this chapter.*
2. *Have you noticed that you struggle with approaching God as a way to "earn" his love or to "buy" his favor? Why do you think you're doing that?*
3. *You can't do anything to change yourself, but you can do things in order to change. How would you explain this dynamic where God is the one who changes us, but we are responsible for changing?*
4. *Is there any person, activity, or habit you should eradicate from your life in order to protect your heart? What would it take to leave this behind? Why do you think it's so hard for you to quit it (or leave them)?*
5. *What does it mean to sow to the flesh and to sow to the Spirit? In what ways do you usually do either?*
6. *How would you define the spiritual disciplines? Which one has been most beneficial to you? Why? Which of them do you think God is asking you to start practicing?*

CHAPTER 13

A New Attitude to Face Conflict

Conflict Helps Us Change

Among the many means God uses to change us, interpersonal conflict is at the top of the list. Few things can help us mature as much as disagreements; yet, at the same time, few things can "hurt" us more or "set us back" as much as an argument. Conflict can bring a new level of light into your life (by allowing you to see underlying passions that you couldn't see before), or it can increase your level of blindness (by persuading and deceiving your heart into thinking that the problem is outside yourself). Much like going through a time of tribulation, going through a time of conflict won't leave you unchanged. Either you'll grow to understand more deeply the disorderly affections of your heart and how to deal with them, or you'll be affirmed in your own blindness to a reality that, though unseen, has a grip on you and is the cause of your spiritual stagnation.

What Is Conflict?

Conflict is a difference of opinion between two or more people about a certain issue. For instance, I want to go to the movies, while my wife wants to go to the theater; I want to set the alarm at seven, but she wants to set it at six-thirty; I want to be more flexible with the kids, yet she thinks we have to be tougher. Conflict is a difference of opinion. As we relate to one another, this is perfectly normal, and having these kinds of differences isn't synonymous with having sinned. However, a difference of opinion about an issue has the potential to (and often does) escalate into something more serious and become sin. In this sense, it can be very useful to talk about two types of conflicts: disagreements and arguments.

A disagreement is a conflict that has been properly handled. You think "A," I think "B," and, after we discuss it, we arrive at a *mutually* acceptable solution. (Please note that it includes both parties and not just one.) An argument is a difference of opinion that involves some kind of sinful response. You think "A," I think "B," and because we can't see eye-to-eye, one or both of us (typically both of us) respond badly.

Disagreement	***Argument***
A healthy conflict	*An unhealthy conflict*
It's a properly handled difference of opinion	*It's a mishandled difference of opinion*
Both parties respond in a holy manner	*Both parties respond in a sinful manner*[a]

What are some of the characteristics that separate disagreement from an argument? When I disagree with someone, I can express my opinion without hurting them. When I argue with someone, I hurt them. In a disagreement, my goal is to bridge the gap between us. In an argument, my goal is to win. In disagreeing with someone, I'm controlled by the Holy Spirit, and the way I present my point of view isn't aggressive. In other words, I don't raise my voice; I don't use hurtful words; I don't use sarcasm to camouflage the "truths" I speak (Ephesians 4:13). In fact, in a disagreement, if the difference of opinion isn't resolved, I give the other person the gift of thinking differently from me, and I still love them. In other words, we agree to disagree. In an argument, the opposite of what you just read happens.

[a] When there's an argument, there are always two guilty parties. If one party doesn't *want to* argue, the other one *cannot* argue. There are always two parties involved. It may be possible that one party may have a greater share of responsibility than another. However, if a discussion escalates into an argument, both parties are responsible and both parties should focus on how each contributed to the conflict (even if their sin is "less serious" than the other party's sin). Naturally, though uncommon, there's also the possibility that one party responds in a holy manner, while the other doesn't. In such cases, the one who responds well will have disagreed with someone (something that's not sinful) and the one who responds poorly will have argued with them (something sinful). A clear biblical example is when church leaders confront an unrepentant church member (Matthew 18:15-20). There's a disagreement. The leaders don't sin, but the unrepentant person does.

Disagreement	***Argument***
I express my point of view without being hurtful	*I express my point of view by hurting the other party*
My goal is to reach a consensus	*My goal is to win*
I try to keep my arguments objective	*I tend to lie or exaggerate*
I typically ask questions to gain a better understanding	*I typically make categorical statements to prove a point*
I don't raise my voice	*I tend to raise my voice, yell, and/or use sarcasm*
I'm very careful not to say anything that might be hurtful	*I use hurtful words and even curse words*
I have the self-control needed to fully listen to the other person	*I don't let the person express themselves; I interrupt them*
I accept that I'm unable to know the other person's heart	*I think I know what motivates the other person, I judge them, and I assign emotions to their behavior*
I'm not condemnatory in showing the other person's problem	*I make the other person feel guilty; I condemn them*
I focus on the current problem	*I bring up old conflicts; I dig up the past*
The difference of opinion brings us closer spiritually	*The difference of opinion distances us spiritually*
If the difference of opinion isn't resolved, I still love the other person	*If the difference of opinion isn't resolved, I'm bitter*
I protect the other person's reputation, and I don't divulge our differences	*I'm eager to bring up the incident with others; I gossip*

David Powlison defines what an argument is in a tragicomic but accurate way:

> What is an argument? In an argument, you offend me by crossing my will. I respond by pointedly confessing *your* offenses to you! At the same time, I explain to you how all my failings are really your fault. If

> only you were different, I wouldn't be the way I am. You do the same to me, pointedly confessing my sins to me and excusing your own.[108]

What Gives Rise to Conflict?

Why do we fight? Why do we argue? The Bible gives us a clear, categorical answer. ***I argue when I don't get what I want.*** James 4:1-2 (NIV) says, "*What causes fights and quarrels among you? Don't they come from your desires that battle within you? You desire but do not have, so you kill. You covet but you cannot get what you want, so you quarrel and fight.*" I would like you to notice two important details in this passage.

First, James is writing to believers. When he says that they "kill" and "make war," he isn't literally saying that one member of the congregation picks up a knife and tries to stab another. Nor is he claiming that there are factions in church that are entrenched on both sides of the temple while firing machine guns at each other. James uses a hyperbole, an overstatement, to emphasize the fact that their argument with one another is as ruthless as if they were really at war.

Second, it's important to closely look at the Greek word that is translated as "passions" Greek is grammatically flexible enough to allow the speaker to combine two words to create a new one. In this case, James uses a word that would literally translate as "***over-desiring***." That is to say, "to desire beyond measure." An "over-desire" is an inordinate desire, an unbridled passion, a yearning that runs wild; it's like a horse that you can't stop. What James is saying is: ***An argument arises when my heart is controlled by a desire (good or bad) that I am unwilling to let go of.***

David Powlison describes our motivations for fighting in this way:

> So *why do* you fight? Notice that James does *not* say, "You are fighting because the other person is a blockhead; because your hormones are raging; because a demon of anger took up residence; because humans have an aggression gene hardwired in by our evolutionary history; because your father used to react in the same way because core needs are not being met; because you woke up on the wrong side of the bed and had a bad day at work." Instead, James says, you fight because of "your desires that battle within you." You want something but don't get it. The biblical analysis is straightforward and cuts to the core. ***You fight***

for one reason: because you aren't getting what you want... You fight because you want what pleases you, and what you expect and demand is being frustrated.[109]

I would like to take a moment to expose a popular reasoning we're so used to hearing that, maybe, without giving it much thought, we wrongly accept as true. Think about this. One of the most repeated phrases in a conflict situation is: "You're making me mad" (or, depending on where you come from, "You're getting on my nerves" or "You're aggravating me"). Think about these statements for a moment. What are they saying? I'll translate it. "You are the cause of my anger. You are the reason why I acted the way I did. If you hadn't done what you did, I wouldn't have gotten angry the way I did." Understanding James 4:1 is to ***understand that no one "makes me" react poorly; I react poorly because I am a sinner, and I choose to react that way***.

I'll never forget a TV interview given by two boys many years ago. I was a teenager living with my family in Argentina in those days. Around that time, the first shopping mall had just opened in the city where I lived. It was something entirely novel and exciting for everyone. In fact, early in the morning on opening day, thousands of people flocked to visit it. The TV interview took place a few weeks after the grand opening. In the midst of the buzz of this novel place packed with people and full of beautiful shelves filled with attractive special offers, two boys of about eight or nine years old had been caught stealing. Given their age, they couldn't do more than let them go with a warning. After the incident, a reporter interviewed the boys, and she asked them why they had done it. I'll never forget their response. The boys said, "Stealing was so easy that we couldn't help ourselves."

Think about what these boys just said. I'll translate it for you:

"It's not our fault; it's the mall's fault for being huge. It's so crowded that they can't catch us."

"It's the owner's fault for not installing cameras."

"It's our own bodies' fault for being so tiny that we were able to easily sneak out without anyone even noticing."

Wait a minute. No one forced them to steal. They decided to do it! What would your response be if a rapist said, "It wasn't my fault; she dressed provocatively"?

You'd say, "Wait a minute! No one forced you to do what you did. Maybe that girl was dressed provocatively (or not), but many people saw her dressed that way, and they didn't hurt her. You decided to give in to your passions!"

This is what James 4:1 says, "No one provokes me into reacting badly; faced with 'temptation,' I react badly because I'm a sinner."

At the beginning of our marriage, my wife and I used to argue about the same thing all the time; she didn't ask for forgiveness when she hurt me. The situation was extremely painful. I found it very unfair that whenever I hurt her, I would quickly ask her to forgive me, but when she hurt me, it was extremely hard for her to do the same. In fact, most of the time, she didn't do it at all.

At first, I accepted it. I patiently let her know that what she was doing wasn't right, but it soon became so painful that I began yelling at her. Every time this happened, it was incredibly painful. Afterward, I would end up getting angry with her (for "making me" scream), with myself (for screaming), and with God (for allowing this situation to continue happening). Things got so bad that I decided to ask for help from a Christian counselor that I deeply respect.

I remember telling him, with great pain and tears in my eyes, "All I want is for her to apologize to me when she hurts me. No more, no less. I don't mean for her to be perfect. I don't want her to stop sinning. I don't intend for her to never do anything wrong. I just want her to ask for forgiveness when she hurts me."

After I opened my heart to the counselor, I thought he was going to pat me on the back and say, "You poor thing. I hear you. What a good husband you are." However, that's not what he did. Instead, he told me, "We can't do anything about your wife. You've already told her that she hurts you, and she knows that that is a sin. Let's talk about your anger."

At that moment, I thought, "Talk about my anger? What is he talking about? Didn't he just hear what I said? My wife is the problem, not me!"

He then asked me a question that left me speechless and unable to respond, "How would Christ have reacted in a situation like this?"

I believe I hated this man for two weeks. It was impossible for me to accept that my wife was not to blame for my anger. After all, if she were to apologize to me, I would "have no problem" and "be the best husband in the world." It took me several years to come to terms with the fact that the one to blame for my own anger management issues wasn't my wife, but me. Yes, she needed to learn to apologize (none of us would argue that); however, I needed to learn not to yell. Can you see it? Nobody provokes my anger; I get angry only because I'm a sinner. ***I have to accept that I'm solely responsible for every irritable response I have.***

I know what you're thinking. Is it wrong for me to *desire* that my wife should apologize to me? Of course not! Not only is it not wrong, but it's also biblical for her to do so. ***The problem arises when I turn a desire (good though it may be) into a demand.*** Do you remember how the heart works? The heart loves. But what I'm loving when I get angry isn't Christ, but myself (and my desire for her to apologize to me) above Christ. As I wrote at the beginning of this chapter, I sin when my heart is controlled by a desire (good or bad) that I'm not willing to let go of.

I really like the example Paul Tripp uses to illustrate this idea. Grab a water bottle. Take the cap off. Shake it. What happens? The water starts coming out in all directions. Why? (Most people respond the same way.) Because you shook it! This answer is wrong. The water came out because there was water in the bottle. If the bottle had been empty or full of Coke, would water have come out of it? Of course not! Jesus said, "*For it is from within, out of a person's heart, that evil thoughts come—sexual immorality, theft, murder, adultery, greed, malice, deceit, lewdness, envy, slander, arrogance and folly. All these evils come from inside and defile a person*" (Mark 7:21-23 NIV; emphasis added).

Let me ask you a question. What would happen if you "shook" Christ? Grab him like a bottle and shake him. How does Jesus respond to being "shaken"? How does he respond to being insulted, attacked, and misunderstood? What is his response be to being spat on, abused, and nailed to a cross? His response, what comes from his heart is, "*Father, forgive them; for they do not know what they are doing*" (Luke 23:34). Can you see it? God used my wife's struggle as ***the means to show me that I am not like Jesus***. All it took was for me to be "shaken" just a little (Luke 22:31).[b]

[b] The Christian philosopher Cornelius Plantinga wrote, "***Nobody is more dangerous than a victim***." Cornelius Plantinga, Jr. *Not the Way It's Supposed to Be: A Breviary of Sin* (Grand Rapids: Challenge Books, 1995), 57. What does he mean by that? That wounded people tend to hurt others; that victims tend to feel justified in being aggressive, and that is extremely dangerous! If you think about it for a moment, that's exactly the argument terrorists put forward. A terrorist says, "We plant bombs because they have murdered our children." Can you see it? There's nothing more dangerous than a victim. What do abusers and molesters say? I abuse others because I was abused. I assault others because I was assaulted. However, that doesn't justify them! There are people who have been abused, yet they don't abuse others. There are people who have been assaulted, yet they don't assault others. Is what you've suffered wrong? Of course it is! Is your cause just? Quite possibly. But that doesn't give you a right to respond the way you do. The victim feels justified in attacking, and that's very dangerous. You're probably neither a serial killer nor a terrorist, but when you justify your aggressive behavior by saying you've been wounded, you're following the same pattern. The victim's mindset is, "I feel entitled to

To understand how to deal with conflict, it's absolutely essential that we understand the difference between the *occasion* for conflict and the *cause* of conflict. While the occasion is the external circumstances that tempt me to respond improperly, the cause behind my response is a decision to sin I make out of my own will. My daughter can't come back from school and tell me, "Dad, I didn't do well in math because the teacher forced us to take a test." Even though there might be some truth to it, the statement is incorrect. My daughter failed the test because she didn't study (that is the cause!). The exam is the occasion; it is the means that reveals that my daughter had failed to study. Surely there were other kids in my daughter's class who did study and who did do well on the same test. Can you see the difference?

Occasion	***Cause***
The external circumstances that give rise to a conflict	*My heart's sinful response to those circumstances*

Right now, as I'm writing this chapter in my home's attic, I've just overheard my daughter Micaela having an argument in her bedroom with Manuel, her youngest brother. (This is called divine sovereignty.) Ten minutes later, here I am writing again. What did I do? I went up to her, and I lovingly said,

"What happened, kiddo?"

"Manu and I had an argument."

"Why?"

"Because we were playing a board game, and he snatched the dice away from me."

"What did you do?"

"I pushed him."

"Why did you push him, honey?"

"I told you, Daddy, because he had taken the dice away from me, and I wanted them."

"What do you think has happened, honey?"

She paused for a thoughtful moment and then said, "I made a treasure out of the dice."

"Yes, kiddo. And who has to be your greatest treasure?"

She gave me a solemn look and pointed her index finger upwards.

hurt you because you've hurt me." So here is my question to you: How do you treat a person after they've hurt you? Remember. No one is more dangerous than a victim.

"Mica, what was your greatest treasure?"

"The dice, Dad."

"What do you have to do?"

"I have to apologize both to Manu and to Jesus."

"Yes, my love, and we must also ask for his help so that he may be your greatest treasure. Shall we pray?"

"Yes, Dad."

Can you see it? What sparked the quarrel wasn't the fact that her youngest brother had snatched the dice from her; that was the occasion. It was my daughter's sinful response that caused them to fight; that was the actual cause. My daughter knows full well (because we've told her many times) that, if someone does something to her that she doesn't appreciate, there are two proper channels to manage the conflict. First of all, she should talk to this person and tell them that she doesn't appreciate what they've done (in biblical terms, she can confront their sin). And, if the person fails to listen to her or continues to do the same thing, she can reach out to Mom or Dad and have them intervene (in biblical terms, she can appeal to the proper authority). However, if she yells at them, pushes them, or hurts them, then she's the one who has sinned and needs to be corrected.

Was what my youngest son did wrong? Of course it was! (In fact, I also had a word with him, and I disciplined him.) But the quarrel between the two took place because she made the dice her greatest treasure (and sinned by hurting her little brother to get it). My daughter can't blame my son Manuel for her shoving him; she has to take responsibility for her own actions. And so do we. Conflicts are realities with which we come face-to-face every hour of every day. Learning how to manage them in a healthy way (and helping others do the same) is one of the key challenges toward change.[c]

The word the Bible uses to identify the occasion is "trial." "*Beloved, do not be surprised at the fiery <u>trial</u> when it comes upon you to <u>test</u> you, as though something strange were happening to you*" (1 Peter 4:12, ESV; see also James 1:12). A trial is a difficult situation that God uses to reveal what is inside our hearts. Just like in the case of a math test, a trial is meant to bring to light

[c] If you think about it for a moment, we've already discussed the idea that we're currently analyzing in Chapter 3 using other words: "***I always do what I most desire to do.***" If you're playing soccer and you insult one of your teammates because he doesn't kick the ball your way, you can't justify yourself by saying, "I insulted him because I was open and he wouldn't kick the ball my way. I asked him like ten times." James would say to you, "No! You insulted him because you want the ball so desperately that you're willing to sin to get it. You did what you desired to do. Your (good) desire has become an 'over-desire.' That's why you insulted him." The problem with our unrestrained passions is that they often hide and find justification in our moments of trial.

what couldn't otherwise be seen. In the case of a student, it shows whether or not they've studied; in our case, it shows whether or not we will respond in a Christlike way or in a sinful way. The key difference between the two is that a teacher gives students a test so that *the teacher* can find out whether they have studied or not. God, on the contrary, makes us go through trials ***so that we can see the true state of our hearts***. He already knows! It's I who have no light on the matter.

How does temptation fit into this dynamic? ***Temptation is an idea***. It's a thought, a proposal, or an offer. Temptation is an invitation to respond in a way that is the opposite of what God expects of us in the moment of trial. What temptation does is offer me an alternative, a different path. At its core, temptation is a ***thought***. It's a sinful idea, a possibility, an abstract notion that our heart considers and contemplates carrying out.

Where do temptations come from? From Satan, from the world (i.e., from me considering following its way of thinking and behaving), and from our flesh (i.e., from our passions, James 1:14). These three sources give us wrong ideas or possible alternative responses. That is why the Bible claims that ***God tests us, but he never tempts us***. God uses challenging situations in our lives (trials), but God doesn't present us with sinful ideas of how to overcome those moments (he doesn't tempt us). In fact, he offers us a way out so that we can respond to the test in Christ (1 Corinthians 10:13)! That's why the Bible also says that we can rejoice in our trials (James 1:2); because if our response is in Christ, then our trials can bring about growth and deep changes! And that is God's ultimate goal in using trials.[d]

Occasion	*It's something on the outside*	*A hard trial or circumstance that "shakes" us*
Temptation	*It's something abstract*	*An idea different from what God wants*
Cause	*It's something on the inside*	*The sinful response of my heart*

What Is Anger?

Imagine you're walking around a shopping mall and, as you pass by a clothing store, you see a beautiful shirt at a 75% discount. You try it on, and it suits you

[d] If you understand what "deep change" is, you may be able to see that the goal of a trial isn't to make me stronger, the goal of a trial is to make me more dependent. It's that my trust in the grace of God increases and my trust in myself decreases.

perfectly. You walk over to the register to pay for it and, and without much thought, you hand your card to the assistant at the checkout counter. When you look at the receipt, not only did they not give you the discount they had promised, but they also charged you an extra 50%. Caught by surprise and unsettled, you ask the cashier what has happened, and the response you receive is: "The thing is, the discount only applies if you pay cash. If you pay by card, there's an overcharge of 50% on the tag price. I'm sorry. I forgot to mention that." Outraged, you tell them, "No, thanks. I don't want it." However, the shop assistant replies, "I've already charged you for it. There's no refund." What would be your response? The same as mine: you'd be angry!

What is anger? ***Anger is our heart's emotional response when we see something unfair happen.*** In Nehemiah 5, we find that the vast majority of the people of Israel were experiencing tremendous hardship. The situation was dire. As a result of a famine, many people had to sell their vineyards and houses to buy grain in order to provide for their families. Yet that wasn't the worst of it. The interest rates that nobles and officials were charging these people for this grain were so high that many had come so low as to sell their children into slavery to pay off their debt. (Put yourself in their shoes. Having to sell your own child so that your whole family won't die). When Nehemiah hears this, he says, "*Then I was very angry....*" (Nehemiah 5:6).

Can you see what just happened? Anger is the way we respond when we're faced with something that is wrong. One group of people is taking advantage of another group. Nobles and officials are collecting such overwhelmingly high interest that they're forcing the people to live in absolute ruin. Look at Nehemiah's words when he heard about the situation: "*I thought over this in my heart, and then I quarreled with the nobles and the prefects. I said to them, 'You yourselves are taking interest from your own brother!'*" (Nehemiah 5:7, LEB). Anger calls out, "I'm against that. I rebel against what you have done. What you are doing against the people is wrong." Anger results from seeing something and saying, "That thing matters... and it's not right." It's a reaction toward something you find offensive and wish to eradicate. It's an active displeasure toward something that's important enough to care about.

As David Powlison argues, there are two sides to anger.[110] ***In the first place, anger is always a moral issue***. When I get angry, I'm saying, "This is wrong. It needs to change." We'll see this further on in the same chapter in Nehemiah's own words, "*The thing that you are doing is not good*" (Nehemiah 5:9, LEB). It isn't good for my wife not to apologize to me. It's not good for me to yell at her. It's not good for the assistant at the store to refuse to take the shirt back. It's not good for the nobles and officials to collect overwhelmingly high interest from the people of Israel. Since anger involves a moral issue, ***every time I get angry, I place myself in the position of a judge***. Why? Because I'm passing judgment on someone else's actions. It will inevitably happen. Of course, it's not necessarily a bad thing, but it is an extremely dangerous one. As we will see further on, my heart needs to be filled with the Holy Spirit in order for me to be capable of holding this position with the right measure of love and truth (Galatians 6:1-2).

Second, anger always exposes my values. When I get angry, I'm saying, "This matters to me. It needs to change." Like Nehemiah, we "think over things in our hearts," and we can't keep quiet about it. What has happened is too important for me to remain silent. If you think about it for a moment, you'll soon realize that we don't all get angry about the same things. If, for instance, you make fun of me about my weight, I'll probably take it well and laugh with you. However, if you make fun of my wife or kids, I won't respond the same way. My weight isn't important to me (although it may hold great value for others), but my family is! ***Anger (when properly understood) reveals my values, what I love, and what is important to me***.

Have you noticed that I've placed the phrase "when properly understood" between parentheses? Many times, the reason for our anger seems to be one thing, but in reality, it's something else. For instance, I may get angry when my kids misbehave, but why do I get angry? Do I get angry because I'm watching TV and have to get up in order to discipline them? (That is to say, I get angry because I value my own comfort.) Do I get angry because my kids made a fuss when we were at the mall, and it reflected badly on me? (That is to say, I get angry because I value my image.) Do I get angry because they were noisy and wouldn't let me take a nap on a Sunday? (That is to say, I get angry because I value my own rest.) Or do I get angry because they aren't glorifying Christ, and I long for them to quickly rebuild their relationship with him? (That is to say, I get angry because I value them.) As we have seen from the beginning of the book, the key to discovering what drives my anger is to ask the question: Why? In doing it, you'll realize that your anger always reveals what you truly love. David Powlison describes this concept in this way:

> Every time you get angry, you make your values and point of view explicit. But anger isn't the only reaction that proclaims what you

> value.... Every time you open your mouth (or don't open your mouth) you are broadcasting your values to others.... Every word you say [or don't say]... tells something important about you.... Your emotional reactions and your choices always proclaim your values. [When you really care about something it moves you, as Nehemiah shows us; when you don't find it valuable it doesn't.] Every time you get angry (or don't get angry) you broadcast what matters to you [what your heart loves]....
>
> [We are endowed with an innate] evaluative capacity as hu-man beings. We evaluate everything—ourselves, others, weather, animals, ideas, dinner, God, prices, current events....Thumbs up or thumbs down. You can't escape working the way a human being works. Anger simply expresses with particular force and emotion our negative evaluations.[111]

The more important something is to us, the more we value it, the greater the level of disgust we feel. If a drunk driver crashes into my car, it'll surely produce anger within my heart. This is normal. Why? Because I care about my car. But if a drunk driver runs over one of my kids, I'll feel an infinitely greater level of anger. The appreciation I have for my kids doesn't compare to the appreciation I have for my car! This example illustrates two other essential aspects of the nature of anger that deserve attention.

Two Other Major Aspects

Anger always involves an emotional response. When I'm angry, my feelings are always involved. Or, to put it differently, without emotions, there's no anger. We clearly see this in Nehemiah's case (the passage says that he was "*very angry*"), and we can also see it in my daughter's case. Anger is an emotion. (Put yourself in Nehemiah's shoes. How could you help but feel "something" when a child is sold into slavery?) I believe that understanding this aspect of anger is critically necessary for most Christians. Why? Because, among Christians, anger is an emotion that produces tremendous confusion and guilt.

Our heart's tendency is to go wild between two equally wrong polar opposites. On the one hand, we suppress anger (covering up the emotions we feel), and on the other hand, we manifest anger in a sinful way (giving free rein to our emotions). Naturally, neither of these two responses is correct; yet trying to define Christian anger as a stoic, impassive reaction whereby emotions are completely disassociated is to distort the very nature of anger;

it is to fail to understand it. When you're angry, you feel pain; you feel *a great deal* of pain. That pain can either be correctly or incorrectly expressed, but it would be a huge mistake to deny its existence.

The key, in this regard, is to acknowledge that there may be valid and rightful feelings, while there are other feelings that are not. It's one thing for me to feel hurt; it's a different thing for me to feel like hurting someone else. It's one thing to feel I'm misunderstood; it's a different thing to desperately desire to be right. It's one thing to feel frustrated; it's quite a different thing to feel hatred towards another human being. It's one thing to long for someone to make amends for the pain they've caused (the way Nehemiah longed for it in Nehemiah 5:11); it's quite a different thing to refuse to forgive them until they do. It's one thing to desire justice; it's quite a different thing to desire to take revenge and to humiliate the person who hurt me. There are emotions that are appropriate and emotions that are not.

This leads us to another key aspect to think about. ***Anger*** **is not** ***intrinsically bad*** (Ephesians 4:26). Think back to Nehemiah's case, but this time, let me take a step back and briefly review the context. The nation of Israel is captive in Babylon. *All* of them are living in captivity in Babylon, nobles, officials, and the people themselves. At a certain point in time, they *all* leave Babylon together. They *all* take a very dangerous journey together, and, in theory, they *all* want to rebuild the walls of Jerusalem to the glory of God. (Notice the plural form in the passage when it says, "*Your servants who delight to revere Your name*" Nehemiah 1:11; emphasis added.) Moreover, they *all* have to fight together against their enemies as they build the wall; nobles, officers, and the people (Nehemiah 4:16-23).

However, one day, things change. After all they've been through together, one group among them (the wealthy!) takes advantage of the other group (the ones who barely had anything). Their level of selfishness and callousness reaches such a degree that they don't care in the least that their own brothers and sisters have to sell their children into slavery. (Can you imagine someone doing that to you after you have fought side by side? After you've risked your life to defend *their* sons and daughters?) Let me rephrase that; it would be wrong for Nehemiah not to be angry! It would be a sin for him not to feel pain and be disgusted at the things the nobles and officials were doing.

Can you see it? The end result of hating someone is not anger; it's indifference; it's not caring what happens to them. What drives Nehemiah's anger is the exact opposite. His anger is driven by his love for the people and by a deep, heartfelt hatred for what the nobles and officials are doing. Can you see it? ***Healthy anger can hate sin without hating the sinner***, which is what God does. Anger can (and should) feel rage towards a person's wrong, sinful behavior, but it also can and should continue to love the person in spite of their behavior. Rebecca Manley Pippert says,

> Think of how we feel when we see someone we love ravaged by unwise actions or relationships. Do we respond with benign tolerance as we might toward strangers? Far from it. We are dead against whatever is destroying the one we love.
>
> Loving people who are drug addicts is a good example. It is one of the most frustrating, infuriating experiences I have ever known.... [The author declares:] I also felt fury. Everything in me wanted to shake them, to say, "Can't you see? Don't you know what you're doing to yourself? You become less and less yourself every time I see you." I wasn't angry because I hated them. I was angry because I cared. If I hadn't loved them, I could have walked away. But love detests what destroys the beloved.... "The more a father loves his son, the more he hates *in him* the drunkard, the liar, the traitor."[112]

Do you know which Bible character gets angry above all other characters? God! Now you can see why. God gets angry because he loves us. God hates the sin *in* us and hates it because he wants what's best for us. God feels anger because sin destroys us, because it dehumanizes us, because it prevents us from approaching him, the source of all goodness (Isaiah 55:1-3; John 4:14). Anger isn't an emotion created by Satan; anger is an emotion created by God. He has the capacity to get angry, and he gave us that capacity, too.

Our great problem with anger, as with all other emotions, is that it has the potential to become sinful.

In order to explain how sinful anger works, I need to return to something I've tried to stress throughout the book. Our main problem isn't the desires themselves; it's the fact that we desire things in a disproportionate manner. Our problem is that we love things too much. We take something good (like my desire for my wife to ask for forgiveness) and love it more than we should. In doing so, we lose control of our emotions, and they too become disproportionate. In other words, ***loving something the wrong way produces the wrong kind of anger***. Loving something disproportionately (even if it is a good thing) produces disproportionate anger.

If I pull out a gun and shoot someone for driving past a red light and crashing my car, I'm expressing my anger the wrong way. Now think about it. Why is my anger inappropriate? Because I reacted disproportionately. But why did I respond disproportionately? That's the key question! The reason I reacted disproportionately is that I love my car disproportionately. ***When I love something disproportionately, I react disproportionately***. Naturally, this concept is quite easy to see in a hyperbolic scenario like in this example; the real challenge, however, is to see it in the little, ordinary situations of our daily lives. Why do we get angry in inappropriate ways? Because we love something more than we should. The underlying problem isn't anger in and of itself; ***the underlying problem is <u>my idolatry</u>***.

Now, what do I do to change if I struggle with anger? Should I count to ten? Should I try hard not to scream? No way! Deep change will only take place after I figure out that I am loving something more than I love Jesus, that I have "over-desires," even for good things (such as desiring that my wife should apologize to me). I need to get to a point where I can say with sorrow, "Lord, I haven't responded the way you would have. You weren't my greatest treasure. I have traded you for something I desired beyond measure. Yes, I've been hurt; but I've also been an adulterer. I've sold out to my passions. I need your forgiveness."

This conviction, when deeply felt, is what makes me need Christ's forgiveness again (and have new power to forgive others afterward). When I'm embraced by his unconditional love, I no longer need the things I so desired. Why? Because I'll have shifted what I treasure, and my heart will then be satisfied.

The Contrast Between Holy and Sinful Anger

The right kind of anger	*The wrong kind of anger*
<u>They feel hurt</u>. *They don't cover their emotions or hide them. They know they're weak, and they're honest about what they feel. If the wound is deep, instead of expressing their pain to the other person, they have the confidence to "hurl" their emotions in prayer before God.*[e]	***<u>They desire to cause pain</u>***. *They express their emotions by yelling or holding grudges. Even if they don't admit to it or can't see it, in the moment of anger, they hate the other person. They want revenge. They no longer think as much about what has been done to them as they do about how to inflict pain on the other person.*

(Continue)

[e] There are many instances when the wound we sustain is too great and emotions run high. In such cases, the Bible recommends two things. In the first place, you have complete freedom to openly voice your darkest

The right kind of anger	*The wrong kind of anger*
They are disgusted by the other person's sin. *They hurt for what the person has done, and they don't excuse them. They're not made of stone. However, they reject the sin and not the sinner. Even though they're hurting, they're able to continue to love the other person despite what they've done.*	***They're disgusted by the sinner.*** *Their pain is so intense that they're unable to continue to love the person who has hurt them. They hate sin and the sinner. They entertain thoughts and fantasies on how to hurt the other person.*
They have a just cause, but are able to avoid turning their desire into a demand. *They don't turn a blind eye to errors, sins, and failures; they confront them when necessary. However, they try to be objective and, if they notice that the other person is either blind or unresponsive, they wait.*	***Their cause (whether fair or unfair) becomes unfair because it turns their desire into a demand.*** *They feel they have a right to cause pain. Since they feel they're right or that they've been deeply hurt, they believe they're justified in their "tantrum" and aggressive behavior.*
They focus on enjoying God first, and, as an outcome of that, they're able to focus on their own interests and those of others in a healthy way. *It doesn't mean they don't think about themselves, but they think about themselves the right way. What does this mean? That they know that "life is not in doing what I want, but in God himself." This is why they place God above all else. Once all this falls into place in their heart, they can look after the interests of the kingdom, their own interests, and those of others in a well-balanced, biblical way.*	***They focus on their own interests alone.*** *They want something and, when they don't get it, they're incapable of seeing beyond themselves. For them, at least at that moment, their life boils down to the conflict ending the way they want it to. Self-centered anger says, "I am God! Things will be done my way. My desires are the divine law. If you transgress my sovereign will, you'll be punished. I have a plan for my own little kingdom, and nothing and no one will stand in my way."*
They express their pain in the right way. *They know that the way they communicate the truth is as important as the truth itself.*	***They vocalize their pain the wrong way.*** *They're torn between verbal aggression and emotional detachment (a form of punishment).*
Although they think they're right, they have an open, receptive attitude. *They aren't rigid, but they aren't a puppet either. They know they could be wrong, and there could be some truth to what the other person has to say that they can't see for themselves. They know that reality and their perception of reality don't always coincide. They accept their share without excuses.*	***They believe they're the owners of the truth, and they want to be right at all costs.*** *They don't think they can be wrong. When they speak, they're amazing "lawyers" (they have reasons and evidence for everything); when they keep quiet they're great "psychologists" (they think they understand the other person's reasons). When confronted, they're unable to acknowledge their share in the conflict.*

(Continue)

emotions and feelings to God. Don't be ashamed; he already knows what they are! Vocalizing them in prayer will help you. The Bible is packed with imprecatory psalms (I call them "psalms of anger") where the psalmist "hurls" it all out before God (and after doing so, he often either ends up asking God for forgiveness for his sin or worshiping God). For example, in Psalm 109:6 and following (CEV) David tells God, *"Cut his life [of the one who hurt him]… Make orphans of his children and a widow of his wife; make his children beg for food.… Let the people he owes take everything he owns.… Don't let anyone be kind to him or have pity on the children he leaves behind. Bring an end to his family."* Second, the Bible recommends that you you talk it through with a mature Christian. (I mean someone EXTREMELY mature. Not just a friend.) Ideally, you should talk to your counselor or pastor. The goal, in this case, isn't to vent your emotions, but to receive outside help and advice on how to manage the situation wisely (Galatians 6:1).

The right kind of anger	*The wrong kind of anger*
They focus on talking about the facts. *In trying to understand the motivation behind the other person's behavior, they encourage reflection, ask questions, and avoid making categorical statements.*	***They question motivations.*** *Although they don't see it or admit to it, they take on the role of the Holy Spirit. How? By pretending to know what motivates the other person and why. The Bible calls this the sin of presumption.*
They don't demand immediate changes. *They want to see the other person change, but they're aware that they can't demand such a thing and that change takes time.*	***They demand immediate change***. *Because they're so focused on what they want, they're incapable of keeping in mind that no one changes overnight.*
They talk about their anger with the right person. *They lovingly confront the person who hurt them and don't discuss the incident with others.*	***They talk about their anger with the wrong person.*** *Since they can't or won't confront others (either out of fear or pride), they talk to others (gossip).*
They are able to forgive. *Since no one can take their greatest treasure (Christ) away from them, anything anyone could do to them is infinitely smaller than what they still have. In turn, their heart is quickly stirred by the memory of the steady divine forgiveness they receive. Appropriating these two realities allows them to extend forgiveness to others.*	***They're unable to forgive***. *Since they've made an idol out of their desire (and the other person has "messed" with that idol), they lack the capacity to overlook the fault. They feel that something precious and priceless has been taken away from them. Even if they deny it, in reality, the thing that has been taken from them is more precious to them than Jesus himself.*
Being angry in a correct way doesn't require willpower; it requires superhuman strength; it requires being filled with the Spirit.	

Before we move on to the next item, I would like us to think through one last key point about misplaced anger. Sinful anger doesn't always manifest itself in the same way. In general, we tend to go wild between two equally wrong polar opposites. On the one hand, there are people who tend to erupt when they're angry; on the other hand, other people tend to remain silent in the same situation. The latter don't *appear* to be angry, when in fact, they're either hiding or denying their anger (even from themselves). If you think about it for a moment, in a boxing match, there are two ways to defend yourself against punches; by returning the punches (what people whose character is "strong" do) or by dodging the punches (what people whose character is "weak" do). Both (yes, both!) of them are sinful responses, and they work as wrong defense mechanisms. (Think about it. The person whose character is truly strong is the one who is strong enough to take those punches without *dodging* them or *punching back*; that person is like Jesus. Matthew 5:39.)

"Volcano" type people	*"Iceberg" type people*
They erupt[f]	*They hold back their anger*
They say everything that comes to mind without filters	*They don't usually speak their minds*
They tend to be very impulsive	*They tend to be quite shrewd*
They struggle with yelling	*They struggle with being bitter*
Anger is a momentary thing for them	*Their anger may last many days*
They tend to forgive others sooner	*They usually take longer to forgive others*
Although they can't see it, they're rarely judgmental	*Although they can't see it, they tend to be very judgmental*
They use words to punish others	*They use silence and distance to punish others*

All of us can respond in either way, of course, depending on the context we find ourselves in, the people involved in the conflict, etc., but in general, one of these two tendencies will dominate our wrong responses. ***How do you react when you don't get what you want?***

How to Respond in The Face of Conflict?

As previously discussed, "being strong" is to manage conflict the way Jesus would. (Without behaving either like a volcano or an iceberg.) It's neither denying my emotions and letting others walk all over me nor responding aggressively. "Being strong" is responding the right way. From a biblical perspective, there are three types of correct answers. Given that our responses may vary according to the circumstances, I would like to connect them to a traffic light. Green: when God moves us to confront the person's sin; yellow: when he signals us to wait; red: when it's in our best interest to overlook the fault and forgive the person rather than pointing out their mistake. Let's briefly discuss each of these.

[f] It's worth reflecting on how a person whose spouse regularly "erupts" may feel:
"I have to walk on eggshells [watch my steps or be careful]. I never know when the volcano will erupt He (or she) is so volatile, so intimidating It's scary, unfair, and oppressive. I feel beaten down, and if I'm not careful, I get beaten up. Yes, I do get angry in response. But my fear and hurt seem more front and center than my anger. I wouldn't ever dare express anger, or even the mildest disagreement. Sometimes I don't even know what I want anymore. Shall we have pizza or Chinese for dinner tonight? I don't dare even think about what my preference might be, let alone say something. I just pretend like don't care. I don't know what to do. I feel paralyzed, powerless, and overwhelmed by living in this atmosphere of hostility. Sometimes I even think it's all my fault, which is the very thing he accuses me of. If only I were different, then he wouldn't get so vile and violent. But in my saner moments, ***I realize that I am manipulated by his anger, and there's no excuse for how he treats me***." Quoted from David Powlison, *Good & Angry*, 31,32.

Forgiving	*It involves overlooking the fault*	*Proverbs 19:11*
Waiting	*It involves waiting for the right moment*	*James 1:19,20*
Confronting	*It involves pointing out the person's fault*	*Matthew 18:15*

1. Red Light: Ignoring the Offense

Although *in all three instances, I must forgive the person who hurt me*, there are times when I must forgive them without pointing out what they've done wrong. Proverbs 19:11 says, "*A man's discretion makes him slow to anger, and it is his glory to overlook a transgression.*"

What are some of the reasons God may ask this of me? ***First, it may be that the person who has sinned isn't in a position where they can be confronted.*** The Bible says that sometimes confronting someone who is blind only leads to further argument, and it makes the conflict worse. Proverbs 9:7,8 says, "*He who corrects a scoffer gets dishonor for himself, and he who reproves a wicked man gets insults for himself. Do not reprove a scoffer, or he will hate you, reprove a wise man and he will love you.*" [g] Does that mean I shouldn't confront someone because they'll respond badly? Of course not! In reality, only a handful of people respond well when confronted. If that were the case, we would never confront anyone! What this means is that I need discernment to recognize whether or not God is "giving me a red light" at this particular time with this particular person.

For instance, it may not be appropriate to confront a non-Christian co-worker who used abusive language when asking me to get something for them. I don't know about your non-believing friends, but mine tend to swear at each other all the time. However, if it were a Christian friend, it would be best to bring it to their attention. I remember a time when I was working with a Christian leader who routinely committed the same fault. Every time I pointed it out to him, he responded in an aggressive manner. At a certain point, since we didn't have to work together much longer, God was very clear in showing me that I should let it go and stop rebuking him. God's guidance is all about timing and not about rigid laws.

[g] Meditating on the second part of this verse is remarkably interesting: "*correct the wise*" (CEB). This means that a person can take the measure of feedback that is proportional to their level of maturity. The more mature I am, the more feedback I can take. Here's my question to you: Do you allow others to correct you? When was the last time someone did so? According to this verse, if it's been a while, it doesn't mean that you've matured—quite the contrary; it means that you're a scoffer who reacts poorly when someone dares to do it.

Second, I may not be in a position to confront the person. Proverbs 17:14 reads, "*To start a conflict is to release a flood; stop the dispute before it breaks out*" (HCSB).

Oftentimes I'm the one who's not in a good place to confront others, or I'm simply not the right person to do it. Maybe my emotional wounds are open; maybe I don't have the right motivation; maybe I'm looking for revenge through confronting them rather than helping them, etc. What can I do in a situation like this? Sometimes the best thing is to say nothing or, as we'll see below, at times, the best thing is to wait.

Finally, it's possible that God wants to work on my character and teach me to be more like him. As 1 Peter 2:20-25 says (read this passage if you're struggling with this), suffering *unjustly* is an aspect of our calling. Jesus remained silent and didn't open his mouth; sometimes (not always), we have to follow in his footsteps. If you think about it for a moment, ***forgiving others is the attitude that brings me closest to Godlikeness.*** (Please reflect on this idea. I think it's quite relevant.)

What does forgiving someone who's hurt me involve? ***First, it involves willingly and consciously enduring the weight of the offense***. Imagine you borrowed my car and you crashed it. Let's say that, for whatever reason, the insurance company doesn't cover the repair cost. What can I do? I have three options. I can have you cover the expenses for the entire repair. You and I can split the cost. Or I can relieve you of your debt and pay for the repair myself. With each of these alternatives, *someone must bear the cost of the damage*. Forgiveness means that I'm willing to absorb someone else's debt created by sin.

Naturally, we can't weigh all the kinds of damage people inflict on us in economic terms. Someone may damage your reputation or your self-esteem, affect your work, deprive you of your freedom, your opportunities, or your sleep, rob you of your joy, or cause you emotional or physical pain, etc. You can't put a price on these things; however, some form of damage has been inflicted, and that has a toll on the injured person. Forgiving is the opposite of condoning. *Condoning* is saying, "Nothing happened here." *Forgiving* is saying, "Something did happen, but I'm willing to endure it."

Second, forgiveness involves my wounded heart being able to heal by recalling the continuous forgiveness that I receive. What do I do in order to forgive? What do I do in order to bear the pain from my wound? By meditating on the cost Christ paid so that my sin could be forgiven (Matthew 18:23-33).

Only the gospel has the power to make me stop viewing myself as a victim of the sin of others and to begin viewing myself as someone who murdered the Son of God. When the equation is shifted (when I no longer see myself as a victim, and I begin to see myself as a perpetrator), my heart finds great comfort and healing, and so, once I'm healthy, I can forgive whoever has hurt me.

Finally, forgiveness involves renouncing keeping track of the offense or bringing it up in the future (1 Corinthians 13:5). When I forgive someone, I have no right to ever point out their sin to them again. To put aside an offense means that I deliberately choose not to talk about it, not to think about it, and not to let it grow into bitterness. If I can't dismiss the offense in this way, if it's too serious to ignore, or if it's part of a sinful pattern in the other person's life, it's best to talk to them in a loving, constructive way.

2. Yellow Light: Waiting for the Right Time

Suppose it's Friday night. A husband comes home shattered from work. His boss has just told him his wages had been reduced. The kids are running around the dining room, yelling. The in-laws have just arrived. The dog keeps barking for a walk. They all have to quickly get dressed and dash to a party. However, his wife is determined to tell him that he has failed to take out the trash, yet again, this morning when he left. Ecclesiastes says there's a time for everything; There's a time for confrontation, too. One of the greatest challenges when it comes to confrontation is having enough discernment (and being patient enough) to know if this is the right time to show a person their sin.

Yes, it's true that Jesus urges us to resolve the conflict quickly in Matthew 5:23,24.[h] It's also true that Paul says in Ephesians, "*do not let the sun go down on your anger.*" However, this doesn't mean that I should always and, in every situation, confront the person on the same day that they have committed the sin. What Paul means in Ephesians is that I shouldn't go to sleep with sinful

[h] As he does all through the Sermon on the Mount, Jesus makes a vast number of hyperbolic claims and uses overstatements to communicate the spiritual truths he wants to teach. For instance, when he says, "*Whoever hits you on the cheek, offer him the other also,*" Jesus isn't implying that only in a situation like this should you do it. What if someone steps on your toes, or punches you in the stomach or in the nose? He's obviously not speaking literally, but he is describing a mode of non-resistance. The same is true about Matthew 5:23-24 where he commands "*leave your offering there before the altar and go; first be reconciled to your brother, and then come and present your offering.*" I believe that the healthiest interpretation of this passage is to understand that Jesus is talking about an internal disposition and a desire to resolve the conflict as soon as possible, rather than saying that reconciliation should always take place on the same day as the dispute.

anger in my heart; that is to say, without having forgiven them! (As I said at the beginning, in all three cases, we must forgive the person.)

There are many situations where it's best to wait. An extreme case would be to try to confront someone who is under the influence of drugs or alcohol and who tends to be aggressive. Many times, the person who committed the sin isn't ready to be confronted at the moment they "burst," but they may be ready to be confronted at a later time when they've calmed down. It's also possible that the person is going through a very difficult time (such as a death of a loved one or being fired from work), in which case it's much wiser to wait before pointing out their error.

You have to remember a key fact. What are you seeking when you confront others? The goal of confrontation is twofold. On the one hand, it aims at showing the person their sin so that they don't do it again (the Bible calls this "*correction*"); and on the other hand, it aims at drawing them near to God and to the person they've hurt once more (the Bible calls this "*reconciliation*"). You should always ask yourself: if I speak up right now, will I accomplish these goals?

Finally, another reason why God may lead me to wait is on account of my own emotional and spiritual condition after having been hurt. Many times, I'm just not ready. James 1:20 claims, "*for the anger of man does not achieve the righteousness of God.*" A different version reads, "*If you are angry, you cannot do any of the good things that God wants done*" (CEV). Yet another says, "*An angry person doesn't do what God approves of*" (GW). What is James saying? That when you're angry in an unhealthy way (either by being a volcano or an iceberg), it's impossible for you to behave in a way that is fair. That is to say, it's impossible for you to resolve conflict the way God would.

In other words, anger crushes your ability to objectively look at reality and make wise, appropriate decisions when you're in that state. If you confront someone, you won't do it right! (How many times have you regretted saying things in anger?) What is the best thing to do? Wait. Forgive the person in your heart first, and then confront them (Proverbs 14:29).

3. Green Light: Confronting Someone

When a surgeon enters the operating room, he washes his hands; he sterilizes; he puts on gloves, a mask, and a garment, and he covers up his shoes. The room where the patient lies is carefully prepped. The nurses make sure the equipment is in proper working conditions, that the instruments are in the right place and that everything is tightly monitored for the critical moment when the operation will take place. When the doctor approaches the patient, he does so with great care, and he's extremely gentle when handling the patient's wound. Why? Because the patient is in an extremely vulnerable situation. Whenever I'm faced with a situation that requires confrontation, I have to bear in mind that I'm handling an open wound. My attitude and approach must be that of a surgeon.

When the Bible addresses the way we should confront a person, the word that could best sum up its entire teaching is empathy (Galatians 6:1). To empathize is to have the ability to put myself in the shoes of the person who's being confronted. That is to say, feeling that which they feel and thinking that which they think in the moment when I'm pointing out their mistake. While there's much that could be said about how to do it, I want to leave you with four practical tips.

- I must communicate my pain in the same way that I would like others to communicate theirs with me (Matthew 7:12).
- I must communicate my pain, remembering that I also cause pain to others (Romans 3:23).
- I must communicate my pain, knowing that I, too, can fall for the same thing (Galatians 6:1).
- I must communicate what hurt me, aware that I may be wrong (Jeremiah 17:9).

When should I confront someone? Although there may be more, let me give you two biblical reasons that may work as a guide.[i] The first reason is very clear: when you have truly and objectively witnessed another believer's sin. Matthew 18:15 says, "*If your brother sins, go and show him his fault in private; if he listens to you, you have won your brother.*" To remain silent when the Bible commands that I should confront is a sin. But how can I be confident that I should do so? The passage itself gives you the answer: when my motivation is

[i] The Holy Spirit is ultimately responsible for leading us to confront others. However, if confrontation is something new to you, let me offer a word of advice. By default, we all tend to have a certain way of dealing with disagreements. If you're a "volcano" you'll most likely confront others, while if you're an "iceberg," chances are you won't. There's a simple principle that can temporarily help you: "Speak up when you're tempted to remain silent. Remain silent when you're tempted to speak up." We could call this tip "fasting on words" (for the "volcano") and "fasting on silence" (for the "iceberg"). In time, and certainly through repeated trial and error, you'll manage to strike a healthy balance. I recommend the book "*The Peacemaker*" by Ken Sande for more details on how to solve conflicts and deal with disagreements.

to help them, to "win them over," to bring them back. If my motivation isn't to help them, then I should keep quiet.

The second reason to confront someone is when a "wall" has been built between you and that person. In Matthew 5:23-24, Christ says that if we know that someone has something against us, it's our duty to try to resolve it. What if the person doesn't respond well? What if they don't feel like making up? Paul gives us the answer in Romans 12:18, "*If possible, so far as it depends on you, be at peace with all men.*" The passage makes it clear that sometimes reconciliation isn't possible (even among believers).[j] However, in accepting this, we shouldn't miss the most important point that Paul is trying to make. I must seriously examine whether I've done *everything* in my power to make room for reconciliation to take place. If I can honestly say that I have, and if others who are familiar with the situation (ideally your pastor or leader) also agree that you have, then it's possible that you may have unresolved conflicts.

Finally, how should I apologize when I hurt someone? Let me first tell you what not to do. Don't say, "If I did something wrong or if you feel I offended you, please forgive me." Have you done something wrong or haven't you? How come you're asking? Could it be that, in apologizing in this way, I'm making the other party guilty of "feeling they've been offended"; that is, of "being overly sensitive"? I need to take responsibility for my own fault. To confess is to "homologate," which comes from the Greek word "to say the same as the other person." In more current language, "I agree with you; what I did was wrong." A humbler way to do it is simply to say, "Would you forgive me for...?"

The Key to Conflict Resolution

Responding well in the face of conflict isn't hard; responding well in the face of conflict is impossible. None of what I've written throughout this chapter has any value if you don't allow this truth to settle in your heart. Neither you nor I can live the way I've described so far. The whole theory is of no use if I'm not filled with the Spirit and if I don't enjoy Christ as my pearl of great price. The key to living this way is to realize that I can't do it—without supernatural help.

Arguments and disputes show one of the most clear and obvious truths that one can see both in the Bible and in life: ***Conflict is born in a heart that***

[j] As I've previously pointed out, even if the person doesn't want to make peace with me, I *can* and *must* forgive them for what they've done to me. Although reconciliation is something that involves both parties, forgiveness is something you can do by yourself with God.

isn't satisfied. Therefore, conflict is <u>ONLY</u> eradicated when the heart is full again. The key to eradicating conflict is contentment. It is that I should realize that I'm seeking to satisfy my heart with created things when, in fact, it can only be satisfied with the Creator.

You must go through the painful process I went through with my wife; you must stop looking outside yourself and start focusing on your own problem. Once you do, contrary to what your emotions cry out, you'll find your hidden idolatry; yet you'll also find a God who embraces you and loves you in spite of it. And, once you feel his arms around you, you won't feel the need to argue anymore because your heart will already be satisfied.

BRIEF SUMMARY

<u>What is conflict?</u> *Conflict is born out of a difference of opinion. Having a disagreement isn't wrong but turning a disagreement into an argument is.*

<u>Why do we argue</u>? *Although there are situations where we're tempted to sin, the reason why we fight is our own sinful response. We haven't obtained something that we love way too much, and we decided to sin in order to get it.*

<u>What is anger</u>? *It's the way we react when something that's important to us doesn't turn out the way it should. The most important thing when it comes to anger is to be honest with myself and to consider: Why do I get angry? What is it that really hurts me?*

<u>How should I respond in the face of conflict</u>? *Like a traffic light, I always have three choices:*

1. *To forgive the person by overlooking their fault.*
2. *To wait for the right moment to point out their fault.*
3. *To confront the person by pointing out their fault.*

FOR PERSONAL REFLECTION OR DISCUSSION IN SMALL GROUPS

1. *Sum up in one or two sentences the concepts that have had the greatest impact on you in this chapter.*

2. *Take another look at the list of characteristics that sets a disagreement apart from an argument. Which one(s) do you struggle with the most? Why do you think you tend to stumble over that?*
3. *What's the difference between the occasion and the cause for conflict? Do you find it difficult to take responsibility for your responses? What do you think God is trying to teach you through these difficulties?*
4. *In your own words, how would you define anger? In your opinion, what separates right anger from wrong anger?*
5. *Under what circumstances do you typically get angry? Who do you get angry with? If you take an honest look at your anger, why do you get angry? What is it that your heart treasures at that moment?*
6. *Handling conflict well has to do with learning to confront others in love. What do you find more difficult: confronting others or remaining silent? Why? What do you think God expects from you as you face new opportunities for confrontation? What's the key to responding the way he expects?*

CONCLUSION

Has Your Way of Changing Changed?

My goal in writing this book has been quite ambitious; I would even dare to say, humanly unachievable. My desire behind every word has been to achieve two impossible changes: changing your *heart* (the thing you love and desire the most) and changing your *worldview* (the way you read and interpret life). If I had to sum it up in one sentence, I would put it this way: My intention has been *to help you change the way you change*. Changing the way you change inevitably entails a change in your worldview.

What is your worldview? Your worldview is the set of beliefs through which ***you view, examine, and interpret EVERYTHING*** that happens to you. It's the lens you use to read ***EVERYTHING*** that happens to you. While it may seem redundant to state it this way, your worldview is the view you have of the world; it's your way of responding to the most basic and fundamental questions in life; for instance, what do I live for? What's wrong with the world? What's the real problem of the human being? What's the solution? In our case, what is real change? How does it happen? What can I do to change? How can I tell if I've actually experienced change?

The worldview that I have tried to share with you throughout this book may be summed up by the following chart. If you think about it for a moment, this chart applies to absolutely EVERYTHING: counseling, your way of reading the Bible, how to deal with trials, decision-making, parenting, discipleship, your struggles with sin, the way you preach, etc. The ultimate challenge for you is to figure out how these truths apply to your very own specific situation.

When you do, you'll notice something wonderful will happen: The way you change will begin to change. (If you want a practical example of how to do this, think about the chapter you just read. As you consider the three items in the chart, you'll notice that I've tried to apply this worldview to conflict resolution.)

The Problem	*The problem isn't so much what I **do** but what I **desire***	*The focus should be on the **heart** (Mark 7:21)*	*I can't change what I desire, which is why I keep doing the same thing I always do (**my idols drive my actions**)*
The solution	*In order to change, the solution is to notice once more **my desperate need for the gospel** (I'm still a spiritual adulterer)*	*The focus has to be on the work of **Christ**, who forgives me, and the work of the **Spirit**, who empowers me (2 Corinthians 3:18)*	*Only **a real encounter** with God can help me see my spiritual poverty and how valuable it is to be loved and accepted in spite of it*
The Outcome	*The result of having an encounter with God is that **it changes what I enjoy most** (Christ becomes my greatest treasure again)*	*The focus has to be on **whether I love** God and others **more than I did before**, not just on whether my behavior has changed (Matthew 22:37-39)*	*When my desires change, so does my lifestyle. I'm now filled with the Spirit, and I begin to **glorify God** in everything I do*

A Suggestion

Let me give you a bit of practical advice. Changing your worldview is a process that takes quite a bit of time. Many of the concepts we've looked at throughout this book need to settle in your mind and sink deep into your heart. This means that even though you may have understood and accepted them as true, a considerable amount of time will go by before you internalize them, and they become part of your worldview.

In a way, something similar to what happens when you make tea should happen. If you want the water to be completely infused with the contents of the teabag, you need to allow the bag to sit inside the cup for a considerable amount of time. You can't remove the bag right away and intend it to have a full flavor. The same is true about everything we've studied throughout this book. How can you "steep" the concepts we have seen and meditate more deeply on them? A practical thing you can do is reread the book with your church small group or with someone you're currently discipling. Doing so will allow you to rethink each of the ideas we've discussed and, by engaging in conversation about the book's content with another person or persons, you'll be "forced" to consider and decode the way these truths are part of your daily life. One of the things I've realized as a theology professor is that you really learn things (especially those that are complex) when you have to teach them to others. After all, you have no way out! Reading this book with others will be a blessing for your life, and it will also be edifying for them. Take advantage of the opportunity![a]

A Final Word

The day my wife and I got married was one of the happiest moments I've ever lived, yet it was also one of the most difficult and painful times I've ever had to go through. Just two weeks before our wedding, my older brother suddenly passed away due to an aneurysm. I'll never forget a conversation I had with my dad when I asked him if he thought we should go through with the wedding or if we should postpone it. Although he was utterly devastated, when I raised the question, he pulled himself together in the most impressive way, and using strong and resolute words, he said, "No way! You're not calling off your wedding. It will be the happiest day of your life!" I was stunned, especially by the level of confidence and conviction in his voice. Then he added, "Think about it, son, what would your big brother have wanted you to do?"

The wedding went ahead, and it was a unique, special day. As you can imagine, it was a very emotional time because of a combination of factors that are very difficult to put into words. However, out of the many of emotions and moments that unfolded that day, there's a single image that will forever be imprinted in my memory. I remember the exact moment my wife started walking down the aisle while I stood there waiting for her, completely dazzled. Just as if I were seeing her right now, I remember that, as she slowly made her way towards me with a tender and nervous smile on her face, I kept telling her over and over again, "You're beautiful.... You're beautiful.... You're beautiful...." For me, there was no one in that church but her. I was totally mesmerized by

[a] I suggest that as you study the book with others, you should all individually read one chapter a week at home, and then get together to discuss the questions at the end of each chapter. If you consider it necessary, you can add other questions to help clarify concepts or to open up the dialogue and help the interaction. The goal during the gathering would be twofold. On the one hand, to have a conversation about key concepts and to clarify any doubts. On the other hand, to share various practices on how to live and apply these truths in your daily life.

her presence. The whole world could have collapsed on itself, yet I would have remained enthralled with Annie.

Do you get the analogy? God is the bridegroom, and you're the one who's walking down the aisle (Ephesians 5:25-33; 2 Corinthians 11:2; Revelation 21:2). What a bridegroom feels for his bride is an imperfect, fuzzy, fallen shadow of what God feels for you as your wedding day approaches. It's a difficult image to take in, isn't it? How can God look at us like that? How can it be that he ***sees*** me as beautiful? Better yet, how can he ***call*** me beautiful? After all, that is the exact opposite of what I am! The only reason he looks at us and treats us that way is because of our older brother, Jesus Christ (Hebrews 2:11).

Although the analogy is imperfect, like my older brother, he made the wedding possible. He died in your place and, in doing so, has clothed you in white. He gave himself for you, and, in doing so, he gave you his beauty and holiness. He was rejected by the Father, and in doing so, he transferred the Father's complete acceptance onto you. That is precisely why everything that the Father feels, sees, and says about your older brother, he also feels, sees, and says about you. What does he say about Jesus, and therefore about us? "*You are My beloved Son; <u>I take delight in You</u>*" (Mark 1:11 HCSB). Or, as it says in the NLT, "*You are my <u>dearly loved</u> Son, and you <u>bring me great joy</u>.*"

Do you want to change? Let this truth penetrate your heart and transform you. You don't just have a random god; you have a heavenly groom, a God who is in love, a God who has made a commitment to you, and who is about to marry you (Revelation 21:2). Do you doubt it? Follow the advice my father gave me. Ask your older brother, "Jesus, how do you expect me to live in light of what you've done?" Do you know what his answer would be? "Live life feeling fully accepted by God. That's why I died for you...." (John 15:9). Enjoy his love. Embrace his acceptance. The big wedding is just around the corner.

APPENDICES

APPENDIX 1

What Should I Do When I Don't Desire to Obey?

What should I do when I don't enjoy Jesus? What should I do when I've tried to experience the gospel again, but it still feels like a distant reality? Should I, for instance, forgive someone even if I don't feel like it or read the Bible and pray even if I don't want to? In order to answer this question, we must remember one of the most important theological truths: ***We live in the "already but not yet."*** Yes, the Lord has *already* come, and he has brought his kingdom into this world and into those who believe in him. However, he *hasn't yet* restored all things, and our glorification (our complete and perfect change) is yet to be consummated. This "in-between time" leaves us living in ***a constant tension between what we could be in Christ and what we will be one day.*** This side of eternity, we shouldn't demand from ourselves realities that are reserved for a time when perfection has been achieved. Of course, we'll have moments of dejection, of lack of desire, and even of unexpected estrangement from God (what the mystics have called "the dark night of the soul"). We'll always have mixed motives and a measure of blindness in seeking to obey him. How should we, then, respond in a situation like that? I would like to give you five very practical tips.[113]

First, I must confess that my heart is cold. The Bible is very clear. According to Matthew 22:37-40, God is after our *whole* inner being. This also includes our feelings, our passions, and our desires. If God no longer captivates our heart, he deserves that we acknowledge what has happened. We can, and we should, go to him without reservation and tell him how we feel.

Second, I must ask God to give me the ability to see his "beauty" again. When you really want something, you "ask," you "seek," you "call" (Matthew 7:7-12). Jesus assures us that God is willing to answer these kinds of requests. More so if it has to do with enjoying him! Persistence, as the parable of the widow who asks for justice shows, is extremely valuable to God (Luke 18:1-8). Insisting in prayer is a way of showing that we really love God and miss him. Something similar happens with fasting. As John Piper says in his book *Hunger for God*, a book I recommend you read in times of lack of joy, "The birthplace of Christian fasting is the homesickness for God."[114]

> Our fasting is not because we are hungry for something we have not experienced [...] Its intensity comes not because we have never tasted the wine of Christ's presence, but because we have tasted it so wonderfully by his Spirit, and cannot now be satisfied until the consummation of joy arrives. The new fasting, the *Christian* fasting, is a hunger for all the fullness of God (Ephesians 3:19)...[115]

Allow me to encourage you and remind you of a major truth. Sensing the "absence of God" is evidence that you have found him. Being hungry for him is a sign that you've tasted him. Missing him is proof you were once close. This is what David expresses in Psalm 63:1-5 (NIV):

> *You, God, are my God, earnestly I seek you; I thirst for you, my whole being longs for you, in a dry and parched land where there is no water. [What is David saying? I'm not experiencing you, but I'm desperate to enjoy you again! I won't stop looking for you until I get to savor you again.] I have seen you in the sanctuary and beheld your power and your glory. [What is he saying? Although it isn't like that now, there was a time in the past when I was in the sanctuary, a time when you were close and when I really saw you and I perceived your beauty.] Because your love is better than life, my lips will glorify you [that is to say, I know that there's nothing that can fill the heart the way you do; I know that you're the best on earth]. I will praise you as long as I live, and in your name I will lift up my hands. [In other words, that's why I'll keep looking for you and I'll keep asking you to open my eyes.] I will be fully satisfied as with the richest of foods; with singing lips my mouth will praise you [That is to say, I trust that at some point I will experience you again].*

The "absence of God" is evidence that at some point you had found him. Being "thirsty" is a sign that he's at work. Keep at it. Your heart already knows it. If you have him, you have everything; however, if you have everything, but you don't have him, you have nothing. Don't stop looking for him, it's worth it.

Third, I must meditate on why I've lost my passion for God. Why is my heart cold? Why aren't I willing to forgive? Why have I lost my enthusiasm for Bible reading and praying? What gives me the most joy and happiness **TODAY**? What am I devoting my time, my thoughts, and my dreams to? Honestly, answering these questions will allow you to find out what has captivated your heart. In other words, it will allow you to ***identify what's drowning or extinguishing your desire for God***. We must remember that human beings ***ALWAYS love something***. Our hearts are always in search of a reason to live. This reason can change in a matter of seconds. At any given point in time, my reason for living may be watching sports; later, it may be winning an argument; and, a few minutes after that, it may be demonstrating that I'm a very spiritual person.

Since our heart is constantly deceiving us (Jeremiah 17:5), many times we can't tell what's holding back our spiritual growth. It's as if we have an invisible chain tied around our ankle, but we're still trying to walk. We're aware that we can't move forward, but we aren't able to see what's holding us back. Asking ourselves "why" helps us make this chain visible; it points to the root cause of the problem. It helps us realize that, for instance, the reason we can't forgive is that our reputation has been shattered and that we're bound by our bitterness (we make an idol of our image). It helps us see that maybe we don't feel like reading the Bible or praying because we go to bed late every night watching our favorite TV show (we make an idol of enjoyment). Asking "why" helps us to identify what we're giving our love to. Identifying our idols is the beginning of change. Why? Because it's only after I become aware of my condition that I seek the Doctor's help.

Fourth, I must continue to expose my heart to the gospel. If I'm pale and want to get a tan, what should I do? I should expose myself to the sun! Only then will I have the skin color I so desperately desire. The same goes for the heart. If it's cold, it needs to be exposed again to something that can warm it. One of the things I most enjoy doing in my free time is looking at our family photo albums. I could spend hours doing that. Why? Because seeing the kids when they had just been born, reminiscing about my honeymoon, or looking at a picture of my parents and siblings when we were little helps me remember and appreciate how much I've been blessed. Few things make my heart more tender than looking at these photos. They make me grateful; they move me; they touch me; they bring tears to my eyes. Being exposed to something helps you remember. The lack of joy in God is a matter of amnesia. It's a matter of forgetfulness. What do I need to fix it? I need the truth to stir something in me again. I need to appreciate the beauty of truth again.

In the famous passage from Romans 12:1-2, Paul says that the "renewing of the mind" is a constant endeavor. No one can survive on one sermon a week. So here's my question for you: What does God usually use to bring back your joy in him? Is it reading the Bible? A deep conversation with a friend? Listening to a good sermon on YouTube? Spending long periods of time alone as if on a spiritual retreat? Listening to Christian music? Reading Christian books? Talking to a counselor or a pastor? Few things are as helpful as verbalizing your struggles and sharing them openly with someone mature and willing to listen to you without judgment but who is also able to tell you the truth with love. If your heart is cold, it's your responsibility to expose it to whatever will make it pound. Use any of these or one of the many other outlets that can help you to treasure Christ again (we'll devote Chapter 12 to this idea).

Finally, I must do what I don't feel like doing, trusting that in time, God will rekindle the delight. Tim Keller illustrates this idea very vividly:

> Imagine that a baby bird falls from its nest in the sight lines of a fox. The bird cannot yet fly (hence the fall), but there is a small protective hole at the base of [the] tree that is within a scurry's reach. The fox pounces and sets out after the bird. What should the little bird do? Of course, it should scamper into the hole to get out of immediate danger. But if as time goes on all the bird ever does is scamper, it will never learn what it has been designed for: to fly. And eventually it will surely be eaten by the predators it is designed to escape.
>
> In the short run, we should simply obey God because it is his right and due. But in the long run, the ultimate way to shape our lives and escape the deadly influence of our besetting sins is by moving the heart with the gospel.[116]

God has called us to fly (Isaiah 40:31). In other words, he expects us to live a kind of life that can only be explained supernaturally. I don't mean to say that we'll always live like that, but what I'm saying is that, by his grace, we can progressively move in that direction, and that we shouldn't settle for a lifestyle that isn't born of sincere love for God. As C. S. Lewis said,

> Provided the thing is in itself right, the more one likes it and ***the less one has to "try to be good," the better.*** A perfect man would never act from sense of duty; he'd always ***want*** the right thing more than the wrong one. Duty is only ***a substitute for love*** (of God and of other people), like ***a crutch***, which is a substitute for a leg. Most of us need the crutch at times; but of course it's idiotic to use the crutch when our own legs (our own loves, tastes, habits, etc.) can do the journey on their own![117]

Yes, sometimes we must obey even when we don't desire to do so and when our passion for Christ seems to be a long way off. But, above all, we must appropriate the promises that Christ bought for us on the cross so that we live in the awareness that "*His divine power has granted to us everything*" *we need to live the way he intends for us* (2 Peter 1:3), and that the same power "*which He brought about in Christ, when He raised Him from the dead and seated Him at His right hand in the heavenly places*" (Ephesians 1:20; emphasis added) is at our disposal. *That* is our hope; it's his power, not ours. His steadfast love, not our loyalty. His love, not our effort. As John Owen said:

> The provisions of the law: fear of death, hell, punishment, and the fear of the Lord, should be treasured in the heart. But these are far more easily conquered; they will never stand alone against the assaults of temptation. They are conquered every day. A heart equipped with them will resist temptation for a while, but will soon give over. They should be coupled with an awareness of God's love.
>
> What should you treasure in your heart in order to overcome temptation? ***You need awareness of God's love in Christ, knowledge of the eternal design of his grace, delight in the blood of Christ and in his love in dying for us.*** Fill your heart with a delight in the privileges granted by Christ's death: our adoption, our justification, our acceptance, etc. Fill your heart with thoughts of the beauty of holiness, the gift purchased by Christ, the ultimate goal of His death ["*that we may be holy and blameless before Him in love*" (Ephesians 1:4)]. A heart equipped with such riches will have (in the ordinary course of walking with God) great peace and security from the distractions of temptation.[118]

What should I do <u>when I have no desire</u> to obey?
1. *I must confess that my heart is cold*
2. *I must insistently ask God to restore for me the privilege of seeing his glory*
3. *I must meditate on why I've lost my passion for God and what has replaced it*
4. *I must expose my heart to the gospel*
5. *I must do God's will even if I have no desire to do it*

A Great Predicament

The Bible clearly says that <u>believers sin</u>. "*If we say that we have no sin, we are deceiving ourselves and the truth is not in us*" (1 John 1:8). However, the Bible also says that <u>a person who sins isn't a true believer.</u> "*The one who says, 'I have come to know Him,' and does not keep His commandments, is a liar, and the truth is not in him*" (1 John 2:4). What's the answer to this paradox?[a] In other words, how can I tell if I'm a true Christian who disobeys from time to time or if I'm someone who *<u>believes</u>* they're a Christian when in reality they're not?

Although this question begs an extensive explanation, which I have no room to give here, and although each case is different in that what may help one person may not help another, I would like to share with you a very simple but rather imaginative illustration that I find very useful. Picture a piglet. What do piglets ***<u>enjoy</u>*** doing? Eating trash. Getting dirty. Let's say we sedate this little pig, we open up his chest, and we do a heart transplant on him; we give him a lamb's heart. What would happen when this little piggy wakes up? Little by little, he'll start ***<u>desiring</u>*** what lambs desire! He'll start eating grass; he'll enjoy being clean, etc. On the outside, he'll still be a pig, but on the inside, he'll have a new heart, a heart full of new desires. Yes, given that he's still a pig, from time to time, he'll get dirty and start eating trash again. And, if you were to look at him on the surface, you wouldn't find him very different from other pigs. However, on the inside, in his heart, there will be a big difference. Instead of joy, he'll feel ***<u>pain</u>***. Instead of happiness, he'll feel

[a] All of us have *<u>moments</u>* of disobedience and estrangement from God. All of us even have *<u>periods</u>* of disobedience and estrangement from him; this is perfectly normal. King David, for instance, spent almost a year away from God hiding his sin after having slept with with Bathsheba and having her husband murdered. However, 1 John 2:4 is talking about a *<u>lifestyle</u>* of disobedience and estrangement from God. That is to say, he's talking about someone whose lifestyle is contrary to the gospel. If you talk to this person, they'll say something like this: "Yes, I know that from time to time I sin. But it isn't so bad. Nobody's perfect. I *<u>don't really think</u>* I'm living too far from God." This kind of attitude is what John is referring to and what he calls blindness or self-deception (I John 1:8; 2:9; etc.). I say I know God, but I don't care if I sin and live apart from him.

emptiness. Instead of enjoying the experience, as he once did, he'll experience a deep sense of ***absence***. How do I know if my heart has changed? Because of the pain I feel as I drift away from Jesus, my pearl of great price.

Yes, sin still entices us. Yes, sin still ensnares us. Yes, sin is a reality that we still struggle with. In fact, sin still produces a great deal of pleasure, which is why we keep choosing it! However, the pleasure it offers feels and is perceived as *fleeting*, *incomplete*, and *unsatisfactory*. A true believer experiences an inner reality that makes a big difference. A true believer can honestly say to himself or herself, "***The level of pleasure that sin offers can't be compared to the level of pleasure I find when I'm around him***."

How do I know I belong to Christ? Because I have a genuine desire never to leave his side ever again. For a true believer, obedience produces joy; at the same time, disobedience doesn't bring them happiness. In fact, it has the opposite effect; it makes them feel isolated from the One who is their true source of life. For a true believer, nothing compares to being close to Christ. A true believer isn't someone who never sins; they are someone who sincerely desires never to sin again. As someone said, I still enjoy sin, but I hate the pleasure it gives me.

Some Signs

What are the most alarming signs that I may not be a true believer? Although there are more, I'll name the two most obvious. One is a lack of genuine repentance, and the other is spiritual blindness. What do I mean by the lack of genuine repentance? That I systematically refuse to take responsibility for my sin and, when I "accept" it, I often have completely self-centered motivations for doing so. You can go over Chapter 4 again, where we went over the difference between remorse and repentance. You can also look at Matthew 18:17 and see the description Jesus gives of someone who refuses to repent. Blindness, on the other hand, has to do with the misguided belief that comes from having convinced ourselves that "we're OK." ***No one is further from God than someone who thinks they're doing well.*** If you find this hard to accept, carefully think about the parable of the Pharisee and the tax collector in Luke 18:9-14.

Finally, what's the most obvious sign that you're a true believer? Although I would love to go deeper with this, I'll sum it up in one sentence. A true believer is someone who, little by little, with many ups and downs, with great failures on their track record, with their moments of doubt and lack of faith, even with cycles of sin they seem unable to break, is able to sincerely say, "***In spite of it all, <u>I am starting to feel</u> in my heart that God is my Father, my Redeemer, my Friend, my Healer, my Peace, my Comfort, my Provider, the One who sustains me, my King, my Lord, my Lover and my Everything.***"

APPENDIX 2

Practical Help for Reading Biblical Commandments

I'm aware that one of the main reasons many people don't read the Bible is simply that they don't understand it. Now, whenever you or I read Scripture, our primary task is to try to interpret it so that we find the author's ***intended meaning*** properly. (When we communicate, whether orally or in writing, we all want others to understand what we mean. No one appreciates it when they're misunderstood.) As Gordon Fee and Douglas Stuart point out in their book on hermeneutics, "A text cannot mean what it could never have meant for its original readers/hearers. Or to put it in a positive way, the true meaning of the biblical text for us is what God originally intended it to mean when it was first spoken or written."[119]

We're traditionally taught to study the Bible following a methodology that consists of three well-established stages. The first of these, *observation*, attempts to answer the question: ***What does the passage say?*** We go about reading the text like a detective who is studying a case. We try to collect as much data as we can. The second stage, *interpretation*, is aimed at clarifying the meaning of the text by answering the question: ***What does this passage mean?*** In other words, after collecting as much information as we can in the first step, we now try to consider what it means and what the author wanted to say to his original readers with what he wrote. Finally, at the third stage, *application*, one should raise the following question: ***What should I do according to this passage?*** In other words, how should I live in light of what I've read? Due to a lack of space, I won't elaborate on the first two steps. I believe there's a good deal of great literature that can help you in this respect if you are new to it.[a] However, when it comes to applying the Bible to our lives, I think the available resources that focus on helping us study the Scriptures so that we can experience real, deep change are rare. Even though much could be said about the application stage, I *will limit myself* in this appendix to helping you learn how to apply *any commandment* you may come across in the Bible in a Christ-centered way.

I think one key question we should ask is: ***How does the gospel (or the cross) affect my understanding of this commandment?***[120] If, on reaching the application stage, we ask the conventional question (what should we do based on this passage?), we'll explicitly, or at least implicitly, shift our focus back to human efforts. As I've stressed throughout the book, if they aren't connected to Christ through the Spirit, our efforts can never change us. Let's take lying as an example. If I read a passage that says I shouldn't lie and I conclude that the application for the verse is that "***I must stop lying***" (if that's what I'm doing) or that "***I must try hard not to lie***" (if the opportunity to lie presents itself), then I'm reading the passage as a non-Christian would. Why? Because I haven't factored Christ into the process of change! Do you need to have God in your heart to stop lying? Of course not! Many atheists don't lie. Many Jehovah's Witnesses are honest. Many Mormons don't do it either. If I don't include Christ in the application of the truth I've read, I won't be able to live that truth according to Christ's standards. (*Through* and *for* his glory. Keep Chapter 9 in mind.)

So, where can we go in order to learn a more appropriate approach to the passage?[b] The answer is simple. We must learn about the way Jesus reads the Bible. No one can teach us better than him. Where in the Scriptures does Jesus do it most clearly? In the Sermon on the Mount, more specifically in Matthew 5:21-58 (please read this passage if you aren't familiar with it). In this chapter, Jesus quotes six Old

[a] I recommend that you read Howard G. Hendrick's *Living by the Book: The Art and Science of Reading the Bible* Moody Publishers, Chicago, 2007.

[b] I would like to point out that the method I'm proposing here is by no means novel. You must be vigilant whenever anyone comes forward bearing a new revelation. Cults begin this way. Jesus is our teacher. The only novel thing about this method is that I try to present it in a simple and clear way so that it serves as a tool to better study Scripture.

Testament commandments (verses 21, 27, 31, 33, 38 and 43), and then he explains what each commandment means. What do we learn from his hermeneutics (i.e., from the way he reads Scripture)? How did Jesus look at, interpret, and apply the commandments? Before presenting you with a few insights on it, let me share with you a brief portion of a telephone interview I had with Dr. John Henderson that inspired me to write down what you'll read next.

> When Jesus preaches the Sermon on the Mount he isn't giving us new commandments, he's offering adequate hermeneutics [i.e., the proper way of interpreting the Bible]. Jesus is very clear in saying that what he's teaching isn't new commandments, but *the appropriate interpretation for old commandments*. In other words, what Jesus is saying is, "This is what God meant when he said we should not kill (verse 21). This is what God meant when he said we should not commit adultery (verse 27). This is what God meant when he said we should love our neighbor (verse 33). It goes much deeper than simply not killing someone. It goes much deeper than simply not sleeping with a woman who isn't your own. It goes much deeper than simply loving the one who loves me. ***God's purpose was to touch the heart and not merely to produce behavioral changes***. That was his intention *all along with Moses*; Jesus didn't reveal something new; he simply exposed it. This is the way they should have read the commandments all along. What Jesus showed us, from the standpoint of hermeneutics, is that ***the commandments should have worked as a scalpel capable of severing the heart in half and not as a staircase to try to get God's love or reach up to heaven***.[121]

In light of what we find in Jesus' hermeneutics, we may conclude that every time we read a commandment, we're confronted with three fundamental truths:

1. *It reminds us of the way we should live*
2. *It reminds us that we can't live this way*
3. *It reminds us that we need Christ in order to live this way*

First, and going back to the example of lying, when we read a passage that deals with deception, ***we're confronted with what we have to do.*** God's gracious and wonderful plan is for his children to always live in the truth.

However, as we give our heart a sincere look with the help of the Spirit of God, we realize that we still struggle with this sin to a great extent. We still struggle with being manipulative, with trying to present the best version of ourselves, with hiding certain details that could be to our own detriment, and so on. When we ask ourselves: "***What does lying really mean***?," we realize that doing all these things, and many more, are subtle ways of lying and that they're still very much a part of us.

Second, after carefully examining what is being asked of us, we're confronted with the reality that, no matter how hard we try, ***we can't live up to the expectation***. When we ask ourselves the question: "***Why do I lie in a situation like this?***" we realize what our true motivations are. These may revolve around being viewed as pious, not wanting to lose money in a certain situation, being perceived as not smart enough, etc. As we discover our true motivation, we unmask our hidden idol, and we realize that instead of loving Christ enough to have no desire to lie, we love ourselves so much that we were willing to do anything to get what we desire.

Finally, as we come face to face with the true motivations of our hearts, we're confronted with the reality that we ***need Christ's forgiveness and power to live out what is asked of us.*** We lie because, deep down, we don't love him. We lie because our hearts have somehow drifted away from him. We lie because we've stopped treasuring and cherishing Christ as our greatest reason for living, and we've traded him for whatever idol we presently have. As we acknowledge this reality and embrace our spiritual poverty, we need to be reminded that Jesus died because of this very attitude in us and that he still loves us with unwavering love. Once this happens, we enjoy our Savior again the way we did on the day of our conversion and, as on that day, the Spirit of God (who was grieving) regains a prominent place in our hearts, making Christ our reason for living again and empowering us so that we not only live the commandments by the *book* but also so that we do it in the *spirit* of the commandments. Therefore, the last question we'll make about the application for any biblical truth is: ***Can I enjoy Christ's love despite what I've done***? Can I see that I need to be filled with the Spirit in order to live anything that he asks of me?

In short, there are three main questions I should ask myself when I think of the application of any passage, in this case, as it pertains to lying.

	Three questions I should ask when I come across a commandment:	*What am I chasing after?*
1	*What does "lying" actually mean?*	*This allows me to get to the spirit behind the commandment*
2	*Why do I lie?*	*This allows me to identify what I'm idolizing*
3	*Can I appreciate Christ's love despite the fact that I lied?*	*This allows me to rediscover the gospel*

Let me give you an example. Just a heads up: when you first read it, it will sound really good, but if you carefully think about it, you'll see that there's more to it. (Again, it's not wrong; *there's simply more to it*.) In his book, *Problems of Christian Leadership*, John Stott (who I highly respect) shares two extremely valuable principles based on Colossians 3:17 and 3:23. The first of these goes like this: "*Whatever you do in word or deed, do all in the name of the Lord Jesus, giving thanks through Him to God the Father.*" The second one reads: "*Whatever you do, do your work heartily, as for the Lord rather than for men.*" Stott claims that, "according to the first verse, I'm to treat my neighbor as if ***I*** were Jesus Christ, but according to the second, I'm to treat my neighbor as if ***he*** were Jesus Christ."[122] Further on in his book, Stott restates this by saying that,

> [According to the first of these verses,] we behave toward people in the name of Christ.... We are his ambassadors on earth, we learn to think about people as he thought about them, and we learn to treat people as he treated them. We honor women as he honored them. We love little children as he did. We show compassion to those in need as he did, and we humble ourselves to wash feet as he did. The question in every situation is, What would Jesus do?[123]

Stott wraps up this idea by pointing out that, according to Colossians 3:23, the roles are reversed in that,

> "I'm to give him the respect and the courtesy which I would *give to* Jesus Christ....This is the principle that we can apply to everything we do. It is possible to clean a room as if we were expecting a visit from Jesus Christ. It's possible to cook a meal as if we were Martha and Jesus

> were going to eat with us. It's possible to serve the student as if he were Christ. It's possible to write a letter as if Christ were going to read it. It's possible to visit a home as if Jesus lived there.[124]

To understand our method of study is to understand that these insights from Stott are precious, yet also incomplete. From his interpretation and observation, we can draw two key questions. The first is: ***What would Jesus do in my place?*** The second question is: ***How do I do it <u>for</u> Jesus?*** However, there's a third question that we should always ask ourselves. This question is fundamental in order to live out these two principles! ***How do I do this <u>through</u> Jesus?*** We need to ask all three questions! If we only ask ourselves the first two, we'll only be shown <u>*what we have to do*</u>, but we'll miss out on being told <u>*in what way we need to do it through his Spirit*</u>.

Our hermeneutics must be such that it reminds us that it's impossible for us to live out ***either of the principles that Stott shares!*** Who can give others the honor and respect that <u>*Jesus himself would give them*</u>? Who can really behave toward others <u>*as if they were Jesus himself*</u>? Both these principles are beyond our reach. It isn't *hard* to live by both of these principles; it's *impossible* to live by them. This is why we need to engage in hermeneutics that will remind us that we need what we don't have: <u>***forgiveness***</u> and <u>***power***</u>. In other words, <u>***it's impossible to live the way Christ did without Christ***</u> (John 15:5).

Let's turn to a passage in the Book of James for another example of how to use these three questions when we come across a commandment. James 2:1 reads, "*My brethren, do not hold your faith in our glorious Lord Jesus Christ with an attitude of personal favoritism.*" The commandment in this verse is very clear. We are to make no distinctions in the way we treat people. However, if we remain on the surface of the commandment, on what it says, it may lead us to the wrong conclusion that we're indeed living this commandment to its fullest.

Let's then ask the first question we previously proposed: ***What does playing favorites <u>really</u> mean?*** Meditating on this concept should bring about a deep sense of conviction in us (just as it should every time we <u>*carefully*</u> examine the Word and seek to truly put it into practice. James 1:23-25). Playing favorites involves never interacting with a certain person or group of people. It's treating others better or worse according to their gender, skin color, hometown, social or economic status, spiritual maturity, denomination, or any other category that I may think of. It is to please someone I can benefit from in some way;

put in different terms, it's casting aside someone who has little or nothing to give me. It is to harbor resentment toward a certain person or group of people. It is the unhealthy habit of only trying to create community with those I like. It is placing people into my own little categories and treating them according to how they fit within those categories. Failing this way involves all of these actions and many more. Looking at the *spirit* of the commandment confronts us with the reality that we are much further from fulfilling it than we thought we were.

However, the analysis and application of the text shouldn't end there. If we only ask this question, we would have meditated exclusively on aspects related to our *behavior*, to our way of living out the commandment, yet we would have done nothing for our *hearts*, which is where the reasons, the motivations that lead us to live out the commandment, lie. This is why we must ask a second question: ***Why do I struggle with playing favorites?*** In answering this question, we'll be confronted with our spiritual darkness and poverty even more glaringly than before. What is it that is *driving* us to behave this way?

The hypothetical situation presented in James 2:2-3 makes it clear. Contrary to what one may think after a cursory reading of the passage, a careful reading of these verses will help us draw the conclusion that the problem doesn't lie in giving one person the best seat in church, while giving another the worst. After all, someone has to take each place! The root of the problem is ***why*** someone is given a particular seat, while a different person is given another. The implication being: "I give you this seat *because you're rich*, while I give you this other seat *because you're poor*." The problem is that there is a selfish, self-centered interest behind the action. It is possible, as some scholars have suggested,[125] that the man James is referring to is the synagogue usher who arranged for wealthy patrons to take the best seats in the synagogue so that they would feel welcome and honored and so their offerings would be higher. In any case, whether for this or any other reason, it's clear that there is a hidden agenda in this individual's heart that dictates the seating arrangement. His heart leads him to treat someone well **because** (consciously or unconsciously) it longs to get something in return from that someone. As we see in this example, playing favorites ***shows what our heart finds important*** (in this case, probably money).

It begs the question: Why do *we* play favorites? Of course, our answer may vary, but it will inevitably give away what our heart really loves, which has nothing to do with loving the person. We may very well play favorites for the sake of the honor we may enjoy in return for treating someone well and for associating with them; conversely, we may mistreat someone in order to "shake them off" because of the discredit it may bring to our name. We may play favorites for the sake of the power an influential person might give us; on the contrary, we may ignore someone because of the embarrassment the relationship might bring upon us. We may play favorites out of love for our ethnicity, our gender, our possessions, or for any number of other reasons.

The bottom line is to realize that ***the way we treat someone is more greatly influenced by what our heart loves and what rules it (our idol) than by who the person is***. If the love of money *currently* rules over our hearts, we'll treat the rich as special and ignore the poor. But *tomorrow*, if our heart is overcome by showing ourselves to be pious before our Christian community, we'll do the exact opposite! We'll now ignore the *same* person we treated kindly in the past (the rich), and we'll be kind toward the same person we ignored in the past (the poor). ***Why? Because what our heart loves or the thing that rules over our heart drives our behavior on the outside***. As David Powlison puts it, "Our cravings rule our lives; they directly compete with God Himself for lordship."[126]

Being confronted with this reality should bring about conviction of sin, and that conviction of sin a new awareness of how desperately we need Christ's *forgiveness* and *power* in order to be different from what we are. This gives rise to a third question: ***Am I able to see Jesus' love in forgiving such a blind sinner as I am?*** When I rediscover my need for Jesus, the Spirit of God will allow me to experience God's *steadfast* love, and he'll change my desires. He will first change what my heart really loves, making Christ my first love, and, as an outcome of finding my greatest pleasure in him, I'll no longer need the prestige, money, or power that I was seeking by making a distinction between people. This is the only way I can stop struggling with playing favorites. This is the only way to change not just my behavior, but my heart too.

In short, when we meditate on the application of any passage, either explicitly or implicitly, every passage tells us three things. On the one hand, it informs us what to do (with all the implications that living the commandment *actually* involves). On the other hand, it confronts us with the reality that we can't do it (by forcing us to reflect on why we do it, we're confronted with our true and dark motivations, with the thing our heart loves). And, finally, it motivates us to desperately run back to Christ to be forgiven and, by being empowered by his Spirit, to be able to live it out.

1	*What does it truly mean to keep this commandment?*	*What are the ways I tend to stumble on a daily basis?*
2	*Why do I fail to keep this commandment?*	*What is it that I currently value that drives me to disobey?*
3	*Can I appreciate God's forgiveness even though I have failed to keep this commandment?*	*I encourage you to pray that you'll be filled with the power of his Spirit so that you can live out what he has revealed to you.*

APPENDIX 3

Recommended Books

My goal in putting together this list of books and authors is to provide you with a biblical and Christ-centered set of resources to help you deepen your faith. The list can certainly be improved. There may also be different views on what other works and authors should be included. What's beyond discussion is that everything you find here will be sound doctrine and will deeply nourish your spiritual life. This list doesn't just reflect my own opinion; I have consulted pastors and leaders from different countries and different contexts as I put this list together. Read away and enjoy!

Nine Books Every Christian Should Read:

These ten books may or may not be the best ever written; yet they're the ten must-read books for a biblical and Christ-centered understanding of key aspects of the Christian life. So, if you haven't read any yet, start here!

1. Timothy Keller, *The Prodigal God*
2. Timothy Keller, *Counterfeit Gods*
3. Paul Tripp, *Sex and Money*
4. Paul Tripp, *War of Words*
5. Ken Sande, *The Peacemaker*
6. Jonathan Edwards, *The Religious Affections*
7. John Piper, *When I Don't Desire*
8. John Owen, *Of Temptation*

9. C. S. Lewis, *Mere Christianity*

BONUS: Tim Chester wrote a book called *You Can Change.* Chester and I speak the same language. In fact, I've quoted his book several times. If you want to continue to learn more about how to change, I recommend you read it.

Top Ten Christian Authors:

Although the list could be much longer, each of these authors is simply outstanding and highly recommended. Their books are biblical, with a sound theology, and very practical. Read as many of their books as you can find. You won't regret it.

1. Timothy Keller
2. Paul Tripp
3. John Piper
4. C. S. Lewis
5. Jonathan Edwards
6. John Owen
7. Philip Yancey
8. A. W. Tozer
9. John Stott
10. Martyn Lloyd Jones

BONUS: At some point in your life, you must read something written by Henri Nouwen. He is the Catholic author most widely read and quoted by countless evangelical writers. Although he has written one or two books containing questionable Catholic doctrine, most of his books are an amazing read. Follow the advice of the Apostle Paul: "Examine everything and hold fast what is good!"

Ten Books for You to Grow in Your Spiritual Life:

1. Donald S. Whitney, *Spiritual Disciplines for the Christian Life*
2. Richard Foster, *Celebration of Discipline*
3. A. W. Tozer, *The Pursuit of God*
4. C. S. Lewis, *The Screwtape Letters*
5. J. I. Packer, *Knowing God*
6. Brother Lawrence, *The Practice of the Presence of God*

7. David Platt, *Radical*
8. John Owen, *The Mortification of Sin*
9. Philip Yancey, *What's So Amazing About Grace?*
10. Timothy Keller, *The Freedom of Self-Forgetfulness*

BONUS: In 1678, John Bunyan wrote a book called *The Pilgrim's Progress*. If you haven't done it yet, read it; it's a classic book on the spiritual life. One more thing, Dallas Willard and Tim Chester have written several outstanding books on the spiritual life. If you're interested in the subject, check out their work.

Three Wonderful Books on ***Prayer****:*

1. Timothy Keller, *Prayer*
2. Philip Yancey, *Prayer: Does It Make Any Difference?*
3. Andrew Murray, *With Christ in the School of Prayer*

BONUS: John Piper wrote a fascinating book entitled *A Hunger for God*. This book will motivate you to pray and fast in ways that are unique. It will no doubt awaken a passionate, fresh desire to love God and have an encounter with him.

Two Essential Resources for ***Bible Study****:*

1. Max Anders, *30 Days to Understanding the Bible* (it's great for getting an overview of the entire Bible)
2. Howard, G. Hendricks, *Living by the Book* (it will give you self-study tools)

Five ***Inspiring*** *Biographies:*

1. Howard and Geraldine Taylor, *Hudson Taylor's Spiritual Secret*
2. Richard Wurmbrand, *Tortured for Christ*
3. Oswald Smith, *The Life of David Brainerd*
4. Halaran Popov, *Tortured for His Faith*
5. Basil Miller, *George Müller: Man of Faith and Miracles*

Four Highly Recommended Authors on ***Biblical Counseling****:*

1. Paul Tripp
2. David Powlison
3. Elyse Fitzpatrick

4. Edward T. Welch

BONUS: If you want to understand your heart from a biblical perspective, if you're interested in counseling others, or if you are or want to be a psychologist, read as many books as you can by these four authors. There's much confusion these days around counseling, self-help, and Christian and non-Christian psychology. These authors are trustworthy. I recommend that you start by reading Paul Tripp's *Instruments in the Redeemer's Hands*. Another book I highly recommend is Edward T. Welch's *When People Are Big and God Is Small.*

Top Six Books on Parenting:

1. Paul Tripp, *Parenting*
2. Elyse Fitzpatrick, *Give Them Grace*
3. Gary Thomas, *Sacred Parenting*
4. Tedd Tripp, *Shepherding a Child's Heart*
5. Tedd Tripp, *Instructing a Child's Heart*
6. Paul Tripp, *Age of Opportunity: A Biblical Guide to Parenting Teens*

BONUS: A must-have on parenting is a series of 6 recorded sessions by Henry Clay called Parenting by Heart. (Family Discipleship Training). It deals primarily with how to discipline your kids. The sessions are both very informative and practical. You can access this amazing resource at https://resources4discipleship.com/sermon-series/parenting-by-heart/ and listen to the sessions for free.

Top Six Books on <u>Marriage</u>:

1. Paul Tripp, *What Did You Expect?*
2. Gary Thomas, *Sacred Marriage*
3. Gary Chapman, *The 5 Love Languages*
4. John Piper, *This Momentary Marriage*
5. Timothy Keller, *The Meaning of Marriage: Facing the Complexities of Commitment with the Wisdom of God*
6. Dave Harvey, *When Sinners Say "I Do"*

Three Amazing Books on <u>Evangelism and Discipleship</u>:

1. Robert Coleman, *The Master Plan of Evangelism*

2. David Burt, *Manual de evangelización para el siglo XXI (Manual of Evangelization for the XXI Century)*
3. Colin Marshall and Tony Payne, *The Trellis and the Vine*

Five Books for Your Daily Devotions:

1. Paul Tripp, *New Morning Mercies*
2. Oswald Chambers, *My Utmost for His Highest*
3. Timothy Keller, *The Songs of Jesus*
4. Charles Spurgeon, *Morning by Morning*
5. Chris Shaw, *Lift up your eyes*

Two Books You Must Read If You Serve as a Leader:

1. Paul Tripp, *Dangerous Calling*
2. John Piper, *Brothers, We Are Not Professionals*

Two Key Resources for Any Church:

1. Mark Dever, along with other authors, has written a series of eleven books called *Nine Marks of a Healthy Church*. Each of these eleven books is excellent for church members to read and discuss in small groups. They cover topics such as discipleship, membership, discipline, etc.
2. Tim Chester, along with other authors, has written a series of books called *Gospel-Centered* (*Gospel-Centered Life*, *Gospel-Centered Marriage*, *Gospel-Centered Work*, etc.). This series, too, is an excellent series for small group settings.

Ten Authors You Can Use If You Want to Research Hard Questions and Apologetics:

1. Alister McGrath
2. Norman Geisler
3. Philip Yancey
4. Ramesh Richard
5. Kenneth Boa
6. C. S. Lewis
7. Lee Strobel
8. Josh McDowell
9. Os Guinness
10. Antonio Cruz

BONUS: Tim Keller wrote two outstanding books: *The Reason for God* and *Encounters with Jesus*. They're perfect for both reading and gifting to a non-Christian. (Wouldn't it be cool to do it and then ask them what struck them about these books or caught their attention?)

Five Authors to Study the Predicament of Suffering:

1. C. S. Lewis, *The Problem of Pain*
2. David Burt, *Llamados a sufrir (Called to suffer)*
3. Jerry Bridges, *Trusting God: Even When Life Hurts*
4. Donald Carson, *How Long, O Lord?*
5. James Dobson, *When God Doesn't Make Sense*

BONUS: Almost all of Philip Yancey's books deal with suffering; he also discusses intellectual uncertainties and the existence of God at length. Yancey is very open about his personal struggles; he's a great thinker who doesn't give overly simplistic answers. (You can also give his books as a gift to Christian and non-Christian friends in times of great suffering.)

Five Highly-Recommended Authors Who Have Written Several Bible Commentaries

1. All of John Stott's commentaries
2. All of David Burt's commentaries[a]
3. Thomas Constable's notes[b]
4. Martyn Lloyd Jones[c]
5. All of F. F. Bruce's commentaries

[a] His lectures and messages are available at http://www.sermonaudio.com/.
[b] His notes are available in PDF format at http://planobiblechapel.org/soniclight/
[c] Most of his books are expositions of a book of the Bible.

Five Authors for Theological Education:

1. John Stott
2. J. I. Packer
3. Wayne Grudem
4. R.C. Sproul
5. Edmund P. Clowney

NOTES

Chapter 1

[1] Adapted from Martyn Lloyd-Jones, *Studies in the Sermon on the Mount*, (William B. Eerdmans, 1984), 2:22-23.
[2] Paul Tripp, *Dangerous Calling*, (Wheaton: Crossway, 2012), 22.
[3] Timothy Keller, *King's Cross: Understanding the Life and Death of the Son of God*, (New York: Dutton, 2011), 79.
[4] Henri Nouwen, *Gracias! A Latin American Journal*, (New York: Orbis, 1999), 19.

Chapter 2

[5] Quoted from David Powlison's paraphrase of John Calvin in his essay essay, "I Am Motivated When I Feel Desire," *Seeing with New Eyes*, New Growth Press, 2011.
[6] Timothy Keller, quoted by Tim Chester, *You Can Change* (Wheaton: Crossway, 2010), chap 6.
[7] I have adapted these two questions from Robert Thun and Will Walker's *The Gospel-Centered Life* (Greensboro: New Growth Press, 2009), 57.

Chapter 3

[8] Adapted from Jonathan Edwards, *Religious Affections* (Christian Classics Ethereal Library) https://ccel.org/ccel/edwards/affections/affections
[9] Jonathan Edwards, quoted by John Piper, *God Is the Gospel* (Crossway Books, 2005), 64.
[10] Richard Wurmbrand, *Wurmbrand: Tortured for Christ*, (Colorado: David C Cook, 2018), 37.
[11] Thomas Chambers, "The Expulsive Power of a New Affection," in *The Protestant Pulpit*, ed. Andrew Watterson Clakwood (Grand Rapids: Baker Book House,

1947), 50.
[12] John Piper, *God Is the Gospel*, 15.

Chapter 4

[13] Paul Tripp, *Instruments in the Redeemer's Hands* (New Jersey: P&R Publishing, 2002), 92.
[14] Blais Pascal, quoted by John Piper, *The Dangerous Duty of Delight* (Colorado: Multnomah Books, 2011), iTunes, 25.
[15] C. S. Lewis, quoted by John Piper, *The Dangerous Duty of Delight,* 22.
[16] Thomas Watson, quoted by Elyse Fitzpatrick, *Idols of the heart* (Phillipsburg: P&R Publishing Company, 2001), 84.
[17] John Piper, *The Dangerous Duty of Delight*, 75.
[18] Timothy Keller, *The Meaning of Marriage*, (New York: Dutton, 2011), chap 2.
[19] John Piper, *When I Don't Desire God* (Wheaton: Crossway Books, 2013), 13.
[20] John Piper, *God Is the Gospel*, 106.
[21] John Piper, *The Dangerous Duty of Delight*, 17-20.
[22] Paul Tripp, *Instruments in the Redeemer's Hands*, 118.
[23] John Piper, *The Dangerous Duty of Delight*, 43.
[24] John Piper, *When I Don't Desire God*, 34-35.
[25] John Owen's views have greatly influenced the way I've written these words.
[26] Adapted from John Owen, *Triumph Over Temptation*, ed. James M. Houston (Colorado: Cook Communications Ministries, 2005), 75, Google Books.
[27] Richard Baxter, *A Christian Directory* (Morgan: Soli Deo Gloria Publications, 2012), 1:86, http://www.gutenberg.org/files/41633/41633-h/41633-h.htm
[28] Saint Augustine, The Confessions of St. Augustine, trans. E. B. Pusey, (Oak Harbor: Logos Research Systems, Inc.), 3.2.
[29] Paul Tripp, *Instruments in the Redeemer's Hands*, 231.
[30] Adapted from Donald Carson, *Christ and Culture Revisited* (Grand Rapids: Eerdmans Publishing, 2008), 46.
[31] Timothy Keller, *Counterfeit Gods* (New York: Dutton, 2009), xvii
[32] Adapted from John Piper, *Future Grace*, (Colorado: Multnomah Books, 2012), chap. 6.
[33] Tim Chester, *You Can Change*, chap. 6

Chapter 5

[34] Paul Tripp, *Sex & Money* (Wheaton: Crossway Books, 2013), 11.
[35] Richard Lovelace, quoted by Timothy Keller, *Gospel Christianity*, (New York: Redeemer Presbyterian Church, 2003), Leaders Guide, Course 1, 87.
[36] Translated from José de Segovia, *El asombro del perdón* "The Wonder of Forgiveness" (Barcelona: Publicaciones Andamio, 2010), 22.
[37] William Romaine, quoted by Tim Chester, *You Can Change,* chap. 3.
[38] Sinclair Ferguson, quoted by Tim Chester, *You Can Change*, chap 3.

[39] Adapted from Tim Chester, *You Can Change*, chap. 2
[40] *Ibid.*, chap. 7.
[41] Timothy Keller, *Center Church* Grand Rapids: Zondervan, 2012), 65, & 66-67.
[42] Paul Tripp, *Getting to the Heart of Parenting*, (CDR Communications, Inc. 2009), Session 3- Getting to the heart of behavior/Part1.
[43] José de Segovia, *El asombro del perdón "The Wonder of Forgiveness"*, 126-128.
[44] This illustration is adapted from Kyle Idleman, *Gods at War*, (Grand Rapids: Zondervan, 2001), 32.
[45] This illustration is my own. It's likely that Paul Washer was the first to use it.
[46] Paul Tripp, *Dangerous Calling* (Wheaton: Crossway, 2012), 215 & 216.
[47] John Piper, *When I Don't Desire God*, 14.
[48] John Newton quoted by Timothy Keller, *Counterfeit Gods.*

Chapter 6

[49] Adapted from John Owen, "Of Temptation," in *The Works of John Owen*, ed. by William H. Goold, (Edinburgh: Johnstone & Hunter, 1850-53), 6:132.
[50] Paul Tripp, *Instruments in the Redeemer's Hands*, 190.
[51] Adapted from Timothy S. Lane & Paul Tripp, *Relationships* (Greensboro: New Growth Press, 2008), 82.
[52] Paul Tripp, *War of Words* (Phillipsburg: P&R Publishing Company, 2000), 59.
[53] *Ibid.*, 59.
[54] Timothy Keller, *Gospel Christianity* (New York: Redeemer Presbyterian Church, 2003), Leaders Guide, Course 1, 80.
[55] Adapted from George Whitefield, *The Method of Grace*, Bible Bulletin Board, https://www.biblebb.com/files/whitefield/gw058.htm
[56] John Bunyan as quoted by John Piper, *When I Don't Desire God*, 70.

Chapter 7

[57] John Piper, *Seeing and Savoring Jesus Christ* (Wheaton: Crossway Books, 2004), 122.
[58] Adapted from Augustine, *The Confessions of St. Augustine* (Oak Harbor: Logos Research Systems, Inc.), 8.4.
[59] Adapted from Timothy Keller, *Center Church*, 46.
[60] John Newton, quoted by David B. Calhoun, Ph.D., "Amazing Grace" John Newton and His Great Hymn, *Knowing & Doing*, Winter 2013, (Springfield: C. S. Lewis, 2013), https://www.cslewisinstitute.org/Amazing_Grace_page5, 5
[61] Timothy Keller, *Counterfeit Gods*, chap. 2.
[62] Adapted from Jonathan Edwards, *Religious Affections.*

Chapter 8

[63] Timothy Keller, *Preaching* (New York: Viking, 2015), 66.

[64] Paul Tripp. *Sex and Money*, (Wheaton: Crossway Books, 2013), chap 1.
[65] Tim Keller, *Center Church*, 68-69.
[66] I believe it was Charles Surgeon who said these words of himself, but I'm not entirely sure. In any case, it's a question worth asking of ourselves as we dig deep in the condition of our hearts.
[67] Henri Nouwen, *The Essential Henri Nouwen*, (Boulder: Shambhala, 2009), 46 & 47.
[68] Timothy Keller, *The Freedom of Self Forgetfulness* (Chorley: 10Publishing, 2013), iTunes, 52. This short book provides tremendous help in meditating on how the gospel, if truly lived and enjoyed, can radically transform our identity.
[69] *Ibid.*, 52-53.
[70] Paul Tripp, *What Did You Expect,* (Wheaton: Crossway Books, 2010), chap. 5.
[71] I am unaware of who first wrote these words.

Chapter 9

[72] John Piper quoted by Sugel Michelén, *La gloria de Dios* (The Glory of God), July 2018, https://www.sermonaudio.com/saplayer/playpopup.asp?SID=811816384710
[73] Tim Chester, *You Can Change*, chap. 1
[74] John Hannah spoke these words in class in 2003; subject *HT101, The Church to the Modern Era*, Dallas Theological Seminary.
[75] John Piper, *Let the Nations be Glad! The supremacy of God in missions*, (Grand Rapids: Baker Books, 1993), 26.
[76] John Piper, Prayer: The Power of Christian Hedonism, October 23, 1983, Desiring God, https://www.desiringgod.org/messages/prayer-the-power-of-christian-hedonism.
[77] Tim Chester, *You Can Change*, chap. 2
[78] *Ibid.*, chap. 2.
[79] Quoted by John Piper, *God Is Most Glorified in Us When We Are Most Satisfied in Him*, July 1, 2015, Desiring God, YouTube, //www.youtube.com/watch?v=EoUkZC9ok-w.
[80] John Piper, *A Hunger for God*, (Wheaton: Crossway Books, 1997), 11.
[81] *Ibid.*, 23.
[82] John Piper, *Seeing and Savoring Jesus Christ*, 35

Chapter 10

[83] John Piper, *Future Grace*, (Colorado: Multnomah Books, 2012), Introduction.
[84] John Piper, *When I Don't Desire God*, 34.
[85] I've adapted a number of ideas throughout this paragraph from John Piper, God Is Most Glorified in Us When We Are Most Satisfied in Him, July 1, 2015, https://www.youtube.com/watch?v=eE-09ut2pzw
[86] These words aren't my own; however, I'm unaware of who the author is.
[87] Dr. and Mrs. Howard Taylor, *Spiritual Secret of Hudson Taylor*, (New Kensington: Whitaker House, 2011), 86
[88] *Ibid.*, 19.

[89] *Ibid.*, 103.
[90] *Ibid.*, 8.
[91] Jonathan Edwards, *Religious Affections*.

Chapter 11

[92] Translated from Samuel Pérez Millos, *Comentario Exegético al Texto Griego del Nuevo Testamento: Hechos (Exegetical Commentary on the Greek New Testament: Acts)* (Viladecavalls, Barcelona: Editorial CLIE, 2013), 1166.
[93] *Ibid.*, 1164.
[94] John Piper, *Future Grace*, (Colorado: Multnomah Books, 2012), chap. 2.

Chapter 12

[95] Adapted from Martyn Lloyd-Jones, *Studies in the Sermon on the Mount*, (William B. Eerdmans, 1984), 2:22-23.
[96] Henri Nouwen, *The Westminster Collection of Christian Prayers,* ed. Stewart, (Louisville: West John Knox Press, 2002), 307.
[97] John Piper, *God Is the Gospel*, 130.
[98] John Stott, *The Message of Galatians*, (Illinois: IVP, 1984), 169-170.
[99] John Piper, *A Hunger for God*, 15.
[100] Donald S. Whitney, quoted by Sugel Michelén "Las Disciplinas Espirituales y el Evangelio" (The Spiritual Disciplines and the Gospel) The Gospel Coalition, January 2012, https://www.coalicionporelevangelio.org/entradas/sugel-michelen/las-disciplinas-espirituales-y-el-evangelio/.
[101] John Piper, *A Hunger for God*, 62.
[102] Paul Tripp, *Dangerous Calling* (Wheaton: Crossway Books, 2012), chap 1.
[103] John Piper, *Brothers, We Are Not Professionals*. (Nashville: B&H Books, 2013), 79.
[104] Martyn Lloyd-Jones, quoted by John Piper in *Brothers, We are Not Professionals*, 82.
[105] J. C. Ryle, quoted by Tim Chester, *You Can Change*, chap 8.
[106] John Piper, *A Hunger for God*, 15.
[107] Richard Foster, *Celebration of Discipline*, (New York: HarperCollins Publishers Inc., 1998), 147.

Chapter 13

[108] David Powlison, *Good & Angry*, (Greensboro: New Growth Press, 2016), 130.
[109] *Ibid.,* 128.
[110] I have borrowed and adapted some of the ideas in this paragraph from David Powlison's *Good & Angry*, Chapter 4.
[111] *Ibid.*, 41 42.
[112] Rebecca Manley Pippert, *Hope Has Its Reasons*, (Dowers Grove: IVP, 2001), 100.

Appendix 1

[113] I have borrowed and adapted three of these tips from John Piper, *The Dangerous Duty of Delight*, 54.
[114] John Piper, *A Hunger for God*, 13.
[115] *Ibid.*, 42.
[116] Tim Keller, *Center Church*, 68-69.
[117] C. S. Lewis, quoted by John Piper, *When I Don't Desire God*, 18.
[118] Adapted from John Owen, "Of Temptation," in *The Works of John Owen*, 6:134.

Appendix 2

[119] Gordon D. Fee and Douglas Stuart, *How to Read the Bible for All Its Worth* (Grand Rapids: Zondervan, 2014), 23.
[120] I have adapted this question from David Helm, *Expositional Preaching: How We Speak God's Word Today* (Wheaton: Crossway, 2014), 71.
[121] Based on an interview with Dr. John Henderson on July 3, 2014, carried out by Nicolás Tranchini.
[122] John Stott, *Problems of Christian Leadership,* (Downers Grove: InterVarsity Press, 2014), 50.
[123] *Ibid.*, 50–51.
[124] *Ibid.*, 53.
[125] Adapted from John F. Walvoord and Roy B. Zuck, *The Bible Knowledge Commentary: New Testament Edition* (Colorado Springs: David C Cook, 1983), 124.
[126] David Powlison, *The Journal of Biblical Counseling*, Vol.16.1, Fall, 1997, 32.

Printed in Germany
by Amazon Distribution
GmbH, Leipzig

28580848R00197